PREGNANCY, BIRTH, and the EARLY MONTHS

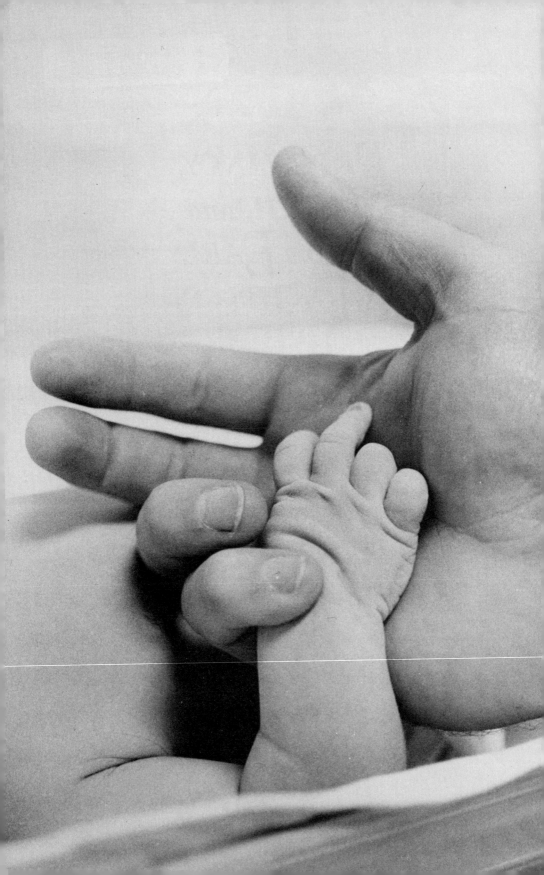

PREGNANCY, BIRTH, and the EARLY MONTHS

A COMPLETE GUIDE

REVISED

Richard I. Feinbloom, M.D.
Betty Yetta Forman, Ph.D.

A Merloyd Lawrence Book

ADDISON-WESLEY PUBLISHING COMPANY, INC.
Reading, Massachusetts   Menlo Park, California
Don Mills, Ontario   Wokingham, England   Amsterdam   Bonn
Sydney   Singapore   Tokyo   Madrid   Bogotá   Santiago   San Juan

Many of the designations used by manufacturers and sellers to distinguish their products are claimed as trademarks. Where these designations appear in the book and the authors are aware of a trademark claim, the designations have been printed with initial capital letters — for example, Milk of Magnesia or Robitussin.

Special thanks are extended to Newton-Wellesley Hospital and Lowell General Hospital for photographic assistance.

Library of Congress Cataloging-in-Publication Data

Feinbloom, Richard I., 1935–
    Pregnancy, birth, and the early months.

    "A Merloyd Lawrence book."
    Bibliography: p.
    Includes index.
    1. Pregnancy. 2. Childbirth. 3. Infants — Care. 4. Infants — Health and hygiene. 5. Postnatal care. I. Forman, Betty Yetta. II. Title. [DNLM: 1. Infant Care — popular works. 2. Labor — popular works. 3. Pregnancy — popular works. 4. Pregnancy Complications — popular works. 5. Prenatal Care — popular works. WQ 150 F299p]
    RG525.F44 1987   618.2   87–1758
    ISBN 0–201–10925–5 (pbk.)

Cover photograph by Dennis Hallinan / FPG
Cover design by Copenhaver Cumpston
Text design by Anna Post
Illustrations by Kathleen Gebhart
Photographs on pages ii, 28, 180, 220, 228, 270, and 336 by Ulrike Welsch
Photographs on pages xiv and 116 by Jim Harrison
Set in 10½-point Palatino by DEKR Corporation, Woburn, MA

ABCDEFGHIJ-DO-8987

First printing, August 1985

First paperback edition, January 1987

Contents

Richard I. Feinbloom, M.D., former medical director of the Family Health Care Program of Harvard Medical School, is the co-author, with the Boston Children's Medical Center, of the *Child Health Encyclopedia* and *Pregnancy, Birth and the Newborn Baby*. He is also the co-author of *Medical Choices, Medical Chances*, a guide to medical decision-making for doctors and patients. Dr. Feinbloom is Clinical Associate Professor of Family Medicine at the State University of New York Medical School at Stony Brook and medical director of the Community Health Plan of Suffolk, on Long Island. He is a consultant to the International Childbirth Education Association and was a founder of Physicians for Social Responsibility. He is the father of three children.

Betty Yetta Forman, Ph.D., is a writer and scholar who has taught at Harvard University and Wellesley College. Her special research interests are in women's studies, comparative literature, and the relationships among modern culture, technology, the family, and the individual. She holds the Ph.D. in Slavic Languages and Literatures from Harvard University and has done graduate work in social and developmental psychology at Yale University. Dr. Forman lives in Cambridge, Massachusetts.

Introduction:
Having a Baby Today

Having a baby has never been safer. Improvements in medical care, nutrition, and sanitation have removed most of the risks that accompanied pregnancy and childbirth in earlier centuries. However, our very success in improving safety has spawned a whole new set of issues related to the application of technology to pregnancy and birth as well as raised expectations for the problem-free birth of a perfect child. This book is designed to help families cope thoughtfully with the many decisions they need to make during pregnancy and childbirth. Because childbirth has become more complex through the technological progress that made it safer, expectant parents need reliable information.

Many issues in prenatal care and birth require decisions, and more than one approach to each can be justified. Choices to be made include where to give birth, genetic screening, position during labor and delivery, use of breathing techniques and other pain relief during labor, use of electronic fetal monitoring, routine use of ultrasound, and injection or oral administration of vitamin K to the newborn.

This book identifies these and other controversies in the course of discussing normal pregnancy and childbirth. We believe people need to be aware of the choices available to them so they can actively participate in decision-making. What is best for one family may not be attractive to another.

We have tried as much as possible to present these issues on three levels. First, what is the available evidence and how reliable is it? Second, what do advocates of various approaches say? Third, what do we, the authors, think? We hope that these clear distinctions will help readers make up their own minds and also stimulate them to join researchers in seeking better answers by participating in much needed studies of maternity care.

Our challenge to pregnant women and their partners to participate actively in making choices (and, as we discuss in Chapter 4, in acknowledging risks and responsibilities) reflects another of our beliefs, that having a baby is a normal process and should remain in the control of the parents. Health professionals should act as consultants to families, not managers. Doctors and midwives should "attend births," not "deliver babies," unless of course there is a medical problem. Childbirth itself is not a medical problem, but complicated childbirth is.

To dramatize these choices in prenatal care and birth, we tell the stories of two contrasting births. These two stories of birth represent the two extremes of current practice: one takes place in a *hospital setting*; the other, *in the home*. A third choice, *the family-centered birthing center* — either in a hospital or as a freestanding unit — synthesizes some of the best features of the other two.

Our stories illustrate not only points of divergence but also general principles that are widely accepted and that form the basis of our present knowledge of labor and delivery. They will provide you with a good idea of the options you may have for your own family.

The main questions raised in these stories are cross-referenced to complete discussions in Chapter 4 and elsewhere. The rest of the book proceeds chronologically, from care of the mother-to-be during pregnancy (Chapter 2), to care of the unborn baby (Chapter 3), choices in childbirth itself (Chapter 4), care of the parents in the days immediately after birth (Chapter 5), and then care of the newborn baby (Chapter 6). The more serious complications of both pregnancy and birth are presented in Chapter 7, in alphabetical order for easy reference. Finally, appendices on statistics for home, birthing center, and hospital birth and on organizations, support groups, and books on all aspects of pregnancy, birth, and childcare will enable interested readers to continue the education process that is an integral and never-ending part of becoming a parent.

While much of this book is designed to be referred to selectively, at the appropriate moment, we encourage all parents-to-be to read the sections in Chapter 3 on genetics (p. 117) and on protecting the fetus (p. 152) as early as possible in the pregnancy. We are fortunate in this generation to know so much more about protecting the health and safety of the unborn child.

We wish you, the reader, and your partner a joyous, healthy, and informed pregnancy.

ACKNOWLEDGMENTS

We especially want to acknowledge Stanley Sagov, M.D., Peggy Spindel, R.N., and Archie Brodsky for their help in formulating the critical and balanced approach to issues in pregnancy which we have used in this book.

We would also like to thank the other people who have contributed directly to this book. In addition to the many families who allowed us to participate in their care and to learn from them, we are deeply indebted to those people who instructed us, reviewed sections of the book, and provided technical and moral support: they include Roger Baim, M.D., David Baker, M.D., Carol Barham, Peter Bowers, M.D., Michael L. Brown, Ph.D., Audrey Entin, David Entin, Kitty Ernst, CNM, Janet Fischel, Ph.D., Jerry Friedman, Ph.D., Kathy Gebhart, Irene Giangregorio, Zbig Hopkins, M. Chauchat-Hopkins, James Macri, Ph.D., Kathryn McGowan, M.D., Alan Monheit, M.D.; Richard Pastor, Ph.D., Dale Pastor, and Will Pastor; Roberta Reeder, Ph.D., Barney Ritchen, Burton Rochelson, M.D., Melville Rosen, M.D., Anne Marie Shelness, Leo Sorger, M.D., Jack Stern, Ph.D., Martin Stone, M.D., Caroline Trunca, Ph.D., and Diony Young.

Finally, we express our thanks and appreciation to our loyal and talented editor, Merloyd Lawrence, and to the staff of Addison-Wesley, our publishers.

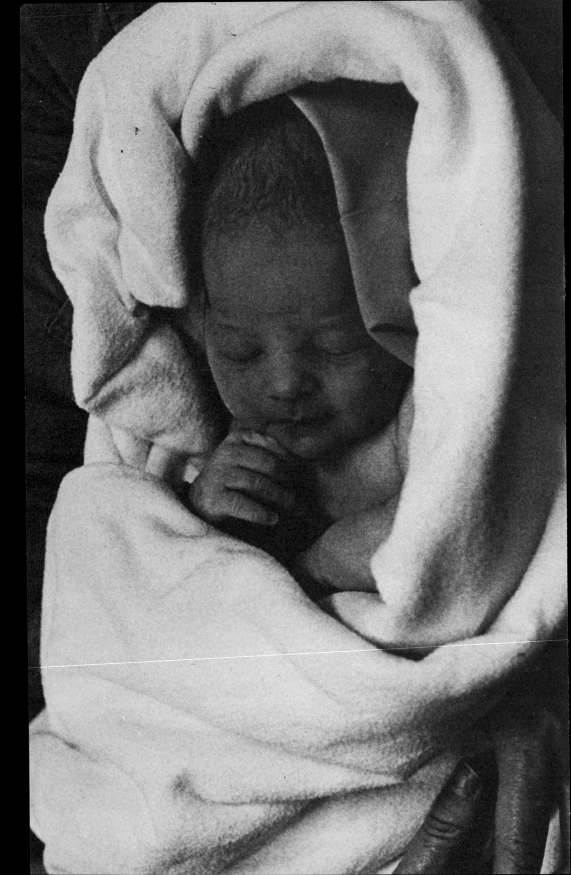

1

Two Births

Birth in the Hospital

On a warm spring night in a suburb thirty minutes from Sun City, Georgia, Joan and Sam Williams were sitting in their living room timing the contractions of Joan's first labor. They planned to have the baby in the local hospital.

The labor pains had begun irregularly in the early afternoon and had settled into a pattern by evening. When the contractions began to come at five-minute intervals, Joan knew it was time to start moving. A good friend, Melissa, had come over about an hour earlier to stay with Karen, Sam's three-year-old daughter by his first marriage. Karen was awakened and hugged by Joan and Sam. They told her that they were finally off to the hospital to get her a new brother or sister.

Joan and Sam lived in a ranch house in the moderately well-to-do suburb. It was not a place where you could easily get from one place to another by walking, and so the couple depended on their two cars for transportation. Although some people continued to go into Sun City for medical care, most used the local hospital.

The community hospital, affiliated with a large university center in downtown Sun City, provided rotations for its resident

1

physicians. It was well run and had a standard maternity floor. Although there had been talk of building an alternative birth center in the hospital, none was functioning at the time of our story. Home births, midwives, and out-of-hospital birthing centers were neither available nor very much discussed in this community. While their options were limited, the experience of Joan and Sam was similar in most respects to that of most American parents-to-be.

Joan and Sam were both college graduates. Joan was a real estate broker and Sam ran a retail clothing store well known in the area. Like most of their neighbors, they were politically conservative and socially conventional. They had been referred by friends to Dr. Philip Johnson who enjoyed a fine reputation in the community. A traditional obstetrician, he had recently become Chief of Obstetrics at the hospital.

Dr. Johnson was aware of the changes in maternity practice and supported building the proposed alternative birthing center, but his attitude grew more out of a desire to satisfy changing consumer tastes than out of any deep conviction that such a center would make a difference in the quality of the birth experience. He was unalterably opposed to birth at home and could not even imagine himself involved with such a "primitive" practice.

The late-night drive to the hospital over nearly deserted roads took twenty minutes. Joan waited in the lobby next to the Emergency Room while Sam parked the car. An orderly took Joan up to the labor and delivery area where she and Sam were ushered into a labor room in which one other woman was in labor. The room was not entirely strange to them, because they had toured the facility with other members of their hospital-sponsored prenatal class. Wilma, Joan's primary nurse during the rest of the eight-hour shift that had just begun, introduced herself to the couple at the door. She asked Joan about the progress of the labor so far — when she had last eaten or drunk, whether she had any allergies to medications — and recorded the answers on a medical record. She then asked Joan to undress and handed her a pale blue hospital gown. Once Joan's street clothes were put away, Wilma took her temperature, measured her pulse and blood pressure, and listened to the baby's heart with an ultrasound recorder. "All's well," she said. "Dr. Cooper will be here in a few minutes to check you."

Dr. Ellen Cooper, a house physician in training, entered the room about ten minutes later and introduced herself. She too reviewed the history of the pregnancy and labor, then checked the copy of the prenatal record which Dr. Johnson had sent to the hospital. She examined Joan's mouth, head, chest, breasts, heart, and abdomen. She then asked Joan to lie on her back with knees bent and legs apart to allow her to perform a vaginal examination. This part of the checkup was a bit uncomfortable. "It'll take just a second. Well, you're 4 to 5 centimeters dilated and 100 percent effaced." (See "Labor," p. 183.) She then pushed a little harder and Joan pulled back. "The head is well engaged and I think that the occiput, the point of the head, is directed toward your front and left. No doubt about your being in labor. You are off to a good start."

Wilma reappeared shortly after Dr. Cooper left and said, "Looks like you're staying. Mr. Williams, you can go down now to the Admitting Office to take care of the necessary forms. Then come right on back up." Meanwhile, Dr. Cooper awakened Dr. Johnson by phone to report on Joan's status. They agreed to draw the routine blood studies and to start an intravenous infusion. Dr. Johnson would come in when transition (p. 190) began; for the time being, Dr. Cooper agreed to keep him informed. Dr. Cooper returned to the couple, informed them of the call, and explained that she would now start the I.V. (intravenous injection) which they had been expecting. She placed a tourniquet around Joan's left forearm. When the veins over the top of Joan's hand popped up, Dr. Cooper washed the skin with an alcohol solution; she then injected a small amount of local anesthetic (Xylocaine) to numb the skin. She inserted a needle cover with a plastic catheter painlessly into the vein. When blood dripped from the needle, she released the tourniquet and withdrew the barrel of the needle, leaving the plastic catheter behind in the vein. Before hooking the I.V. into this catheter, Dr. Cooper withdrew about 5 cubic centimeters of blood, which was sent to the blood bank for typing and a cross-match with two units of blood that would be held in case of an emergency. After the I.V. was connected and flowing freely, a few twists of adhesive tape secured the catheter in place at the end of the tubing. With the flexible catheter in her vein, Joan knew that her fluid needs would be supplied intravenously, although she would be able to suck ice chips if she wished to. It was hospital policy to avoid putting anything into the stomach that, in the event of an emergency requiring general anesthesia, could be vomited up and aspirated into the lungs, with potentially disastrous consequences. (See "Fluids and Food," p. 196.)

Officially admitted, and certain that this was "the real thing" and not another of the several false labors that had occurred over the past few days, Joan and Sam were able to relax enough to notice the room. It was square, 20 feet on each side, included a bathroom, and had a single window which looked out over the hospital driveway and the flat, now dark, countryside beyond. The center of Sun City, with its cluster of modest high-rise buildings, could barely be seen off to the left. Dark green flower-print curtains hung beside the window and two familiar reproductions hung on the light green walls. The two single hospital beds could be enclosed by curtains mounted on ceiling tracks. Next to each was a fetal monitor the size of a large television set. Joan and Sam could hear the indistinct conversation of the nurses and attendants in the hall, punctuated by the distant ringing of phones and the rumble and squeak of passing beds, service carts, and incubators. Joan had been given disposable paper slippers to protect her feet from the chill of the tile-covered floor.

Wilma placed the external fetal monitor over Joan's abdomen and obtained a "strip" of the baby's heartbeat over a period of ten minutes and three contractions. (See "Principles of Fetal Monitoring," p. 134.) "Looks good. We can take this off for now." Joan got up and used the bathroom. The contractions had become perceptibly less frequent, and Joan proposed taking a walk down the corridor. Her roommate was in active labor and Joan found her restlessness distracting.

Joan shuffled along as Sam wheeled the I.V. pole and bottle beside her. After about ten minutes of walking, the contractions picked up and, for the first time in the labor, Joan hurt so much that she was forced to stop in her tracks. She wanted to get back to bed as soon as possible.

"Wow, does this hurt, Sam! I've never felt anything like it before." "Try your breathing now," said Wilma. Under her gentle but firm guidance, coupled with Sam's reassurance and back massage, Joan was able to regain her composure. But it was clear that

4

her labor was becoming active. It was time for another vaginal examination.

"Very good," said Dr. Cooper. "You're now 6 to 7 centimeters and definitely moving along. The nausea you described goes along with that, too. I'll call Dr. Johnson. I'm sure he's coming in soon. Meanwhile, it's time to attach the internal fetal monitor; but, before we do, we'll have to rupture your membranes. Also, if you'd like some anesthesia now, that too can be arranged. Let me know when you have your next contraction and we'll go ahead and rupture the membranes." (See "Labor," p. 183.)

To nick the amniotic sac, Dr. Cooper used a foot-long sterile, disposable, yellow plastic stick, which tapered into a hook at one end. Joan lay on her back with knees bent and legs apart. As the contraction built up, Dr. Cooper, who had inserted one gloved hand into the vagina, could feel the sac bulging tensely through the cervix. With the other hand she carefully guided the "Amni-Hook" to the sac and pricked it. Joan could feel the gush of the warm waters. Dr. Cooper kept her hand in the vagina to check for possible prolapse of the umbilical cord, a complication dangerous to the baby because of the vulnerability of the cord to compression by the head and interference with the baby's blood supply (See p. 325 for a discussion of prolapse of the umbilical cord.) Fortunately, in Joan's case, there was no evidence of this problem. Wilma checked the baby's heartbeat and reported that it was normal.

Dr. Cooper then prepared the fetal monitor wires for insertion. (See "Electronic Fetal Monitoring," p. 136.) She put the index and middle fingers of her left hand into Joan's vagina and rested her fingertips on the baby's head. With her right hand, she guided a hollow plastic tube containing the tiny wires over her fingers to the baby's scalp and twisted their corkscrew-like ends one full circle, tugging gently to verify that they had engaged with the head. She then pulled the plastic tube out of the vagina, leaving the wires behind. The other ends of the wires were plugged into the monitoring device. Red numbers on a screen on the front of the monitor console flashed the baby's changing heart rate in beats per minute as a speaker sounded each beat: "bum, bum, bum. . . ." The volume was adjusted to the level of a steady, soft background noise — a soft, lulling rhythm. Next, Wilma strapped a belt containing a pressure sensor around Joan's abdomen. Also linked to the monitor, it responded to tension in the uterus. A constantly moving strip of graph paper recorded two shifting lines, the upper representing the fetal heart rate and the lower, uterine tension. As the paper left the machine, it folded neatly upon itself on a shelf next to the monitor, accompanied by the faint whirring sound of the motor-driven roller.

Dr. Cooper showed Joan and Sam how to read the printout. With each contraction, the bottom line, which reflected uterine tension, inched upward, while the top line, which measured fetal heart rate, moved downward ever so slightly, the two lines coming closer together. As the contraction eased, the uterine tension line returned to its previous level and the fetal heart rate line simultaneously returned to its base. "That's what we call an early deceleration or slowing of the heartbeat along with the contraction. It is probably a normal effect of squeezing the head. Of course, we'll watch the pattern for any signs of stress in the baby." While Joan found these wires annoying, she and Sam felt secure that their baby's well-being was being monitored.

"I'll tell you," Joan said, "I'm really feeling these contractions now, breathing or no breathing, and Dr. Johnson said that I could have an epidural if I wanted one. I think I'm just about ready." Joan settled down in bed and the anesthesiologist was called.

As long as Joan was attached to the monitor it was impossible for her to walk around. The wires could be detached temporarily from the monitor to permit her to go to the bathroom, but walking along the corridors was not allowed. Sam sat on a chair next to the bed and held her hand. Together they listened to the heartbeat and watched the monitor. The contractions grew ever more intense. "I don't think I can stand this much longer. Even the breathing doesn't help now." Sam squeezed her hand, feeling more and more uneasy. Just then the anesthesiologist, Dr. Younis, entered the room. "I hear you'd like an epidural." He reviewed her record, repeating the questions asked earlier about allergies to medication, and about general health, and inquired specifically about any back problems. He then asked Sam to leave the room until the procedure was completed. Under the doctor's guidance Joan lay on her side and moved her back to the edge of the bed. Wilma faced her and arched her body over the bed, looping her arms around Joan's neck and behind her knees to keep her from falling over the edge and to position her for the procedure. Joan curled her legs up, curving her lower spine and tucking her head down toward her chest. Dr. Younis explained each move he would make and the sensation she would experience. Joan felt the cool antiseptic solution swabbed over her lower back and buttocks. Next, she felt the needle prick with the local anesthetic which numbed the skin. The long epidural needle, its hollow core filled with a precisely fitting wire-like metal stylet, was then inserted. The doctor guided it securely between the bones of the vertebral column and through the tough membrane that encased the epidural space. Joan could feel pressure but no pain. As the stylet was withdrawn from the needle, no spinal fluid returned, indicating that the needle, as intended, had not entered the spinal space. (See the section on "Pain Relief," p. 203, for more on epidural and spinal anesthetics.) A small amount of air was drawn into a syringe, which was then attached to the needle. The barrel of the syringe moved in very, very slightly, further confirming its correct position. The syringe was removed and the catheter threaded through the hollow needle. Joan reported a twinge of pain in one leg and was reassured that this was a common reaction to pressure by the catheter on a nerve root. The pain passed quickly as predicted. With its position now verified, the needle was withdrawn from the catheter, leaving the catheter behind in the epidural space. It was taped securely to Joan's back and she was then asked to roll over and center herself on her back on the bed. Anesthetic solution was now injected into the catheter, the end of which was capped and taped down.

Joan felt a numbness come progressively over her feet, legs, thighs, buttocks, and lower abdomen. She was still able to move her legs when asked, but not as well as before the anesthetic was administered. Most remarkably, her contractions were now barely perceptible. "What a relief," she said with a faint smile. Meanwhile, her roommate had dilated fully and was wheeled off to the delivery room. Joan herself was able to doze off for about twenty minutes. The room was dark, and the fetal monitor was turned down.

A half hour later, or about one hour from the time of placement of the epidural, Sam and Joan were happy to see that her doctor had arrived. On checking her, Dr. Johnson reported that she was still only 6 to 7 centimeters dilated, even during a contraction. He had kept his hand on her abdomen through the contraction and was, he said, impressed with the weakness of the muscle action and the long intervals between contractions that sometimes occur when epidural anesthetics are administered. "What I suggest at this point is that we add a little Pitocin to the I.V. to see if we can't move things along a little quicker. The baby is fine. There is no molding of the head and no swelling of the scalp to show that it is not fitting easily into the birth canal."

The idea of stimulating labor sounded good to Joan and Sam — both were growing impatient. Because Joan was beginning to feel the contractions again, more anesthetic was injected, with predictably good results. The Pitocin was added to a bottle connected to the I.V. The tube from this second bottle was connected to a regulator the size of a cigar box, which carefully controlled the number of drops of Pitocin to be delivered. The Pitocin did its job. Within thirty minutes, during which time gradually increasing doses of the hormone were given, labor picked up again with harder, more frequent contractions (barely perceptible to Joan) and with the opening of the cervix to a good 8 centimeters. Within another thirty minutes she was fully dilated and the perineum (the pelvic floor between pubic bone and rectum) was just beginning to bulge. Everyone concerned was pleased with this progress.

Dr. Johnson had intended that the anesthetic lighten up by the time Joan was fully dilated, so that she would be able to push, adding her force to that of the Pitocin-stimulated uterus, to bring about an earlier delivery. As sometimes happens, the timing was just a little off. The anesthetic effect was still present even though dilation was complete. Joan did not feel the urge to push that usually comes at this time. The baby's head was not moving down, even though the Pitocin was still running. In addition, the scalp tissues were beginning to swell, suggesting that the fit might be tight. Since a full bladder can obstruct the baby's descent, Dr. Johnson suggested that Joan try to void. But when Wilma placed a bedpan beneath her, Joan was able to produce only a small amount of urine.

The news from the monitor was disconcerting. There was some loss in "beat-to-beat variability" (see p. 135). This meant that the baby's heart rate was not changing very much from one moment to the next, a subtle point that gave Dr. Johnson some pause when he considered it along with all the other developments. "Basically, everything is still okay, but I'd feel better if we went into the delivery room now and put forceps on the baby's head to get him delivered. [See p. 213.] In the meantime, we'll turn off the Pitocin to give him a rest and have you lie on your side and shift the position of the uterus." Joan was wheeled in her bed to the delivery room. The monitor wires were temporarily disconnected. Sam was directed to the doctors' dressing room to change into a surgical scrub suit before entering the delivery room.

The delivery suite was a fully equipped operating room with a surgical operating table, a large adjustable ceiling light, and anesthesia equipment which included tanks, instruments, face masks, and many different dials. Off to the side of the room was a long table covered with surgical instruments; in one corner was a small open table and a radiant heater for the new baby. Wilma and Mary, the delivery room nurse, assisted Joan onto the delivery table. The fetal monitor was reconnected as Drs. Cooper and Johnson finished their surgical scrub. Dr. Younis reappeared and chatted amiably with Joan and Sam. The atmosphere was friendly. The door to the delivery room then swung open and Drs. Johnson and Cooper, dripping hands and arms immaculately scrubbed with antiseptic solution, backed their way into the room with arms raised to avoid touching anything. They, like everyone else in the room, wore surgical caps and face masks.

"Won't be long now," Dr. Johnson said reassuringly. "How's the anesthesia now?" "Not so good," replied Joan. "Okay, Dr. Younis, how about a little more of the epidural since we're going to need to do an episiotomy [see p. 214] and pull the baby out anyway." Dr. Younis promptly injected some more anesthetic solution through the epidural catheter. Sam watched as the two obstetricians carefully dried their hands and arms, dropping the wet towels to the floor. They put their arms into the sleeves of their sterile gowns, working them on with Mary's help, and put on their sterile gloves. They were now ready. During this preparation Mary placed Joan's legs into stirrup straps. Thus suspended under the knees, her legs felt like lead weights as the effect of the anesthesia returned and the pain of the contraction eased. Wilma then disconnected the monitor, unscrewed the tiny wires from the baby's scalp, and removed the strap from Joan's abdomen. She then cranked a lever near the middle of the table and

9

the half under Joan's legs folded down to the floor. "Now I'm going to wash you off," she said, and rubbed a wet gauze pad attached to a plastic handle over Joan's perineum and buttocks. Mary announced that she would pass a catheter through Joan's urethra into her bladder to empty it. This was accomplished with a return of clear yellow urine, which dripped into a basin Mary held in her other hand. Dr. Cooper now placed sterile green drapes beneath Joan's buttocks, over each leg, and over her lower abdomen. Mary turned on the overhead light and positioned it to illuminate Joan's perineum. "Now I'm going to do an episiotomy. You shouldn't feel it at all, but if you do, let me know." Dr. Johnson inserted the index and middle fingers of his left hand palm downward into Joan's vagina and tensed the perineum, now quite relaxed from the anesthesia, by pulling it toward him. With his right hand he inserted scissors between the fingers of his left hand, one blade on each side of the perineum, and made a two-inch cut, which Joan did not feel. The blades of the forceps were now inserted one at a time and positioned along the sides of the baby's head. Dr. Johnson brought the forceps' handles together and exerted an ever-increasing gentle traction. Soon, curly black hair appeared, followed by the head itself. Sam gasped with excitement. When the forceps were removed, Dr. Johnson gently pulled downward on the head, disengaging the baby's shoulder from beneath the pubic bone. The rest of the baby slipped out in a gush of amniotic fluid. "It's a boy!" The baby gave a lusty cry and immediately pinked up. Joan lay back in Sam's arms, overcome with relief and joy.

Dr. Johnson held newborn Jonathan on his lap, cut the cord, and handed him to Mary who received him in a warm cotton blanket. She brought him immediately to the head of the table for Joan and Sam to see. "He's beautiful," they exclaimed, almost in unison. "I'll be right back with him," Mary said as she carried the baby to the warming table where she dried him off and checked him over briefly. Next, she put a name-tag bracelet on his wrist and made prints of his feet for the identification records. She wiped off the feet, rewrapped him, and handed him to Sam, who had been waiting eagerly. "We'll put the silver nitrate drops in later when he stops at the nursery."

By this time the placenta had already separated and delivered, and Dr. Johnson was sewing up the episiotomy. He had already checked Joan's vagina and cervix for other tears and found none. He asked Dr. Younis to let the Pitocin I.V. run again in order to contract the uterus. The sterile drapes were now removed and the lower end of the table cranked back up. Sam had laid Jonathan in Joan's arms and both were gazing at him in blissful admiration. "You are finally here!" said Joan, as Sam touched the tiny ears and hands, gingerly, with one finger.

Birth at Home

Andrea Clayborn, thirty-three, was in active labor with her second child in the bedroom of her apartment in College Park, Massachusetts. She and her husband, Bob, had made a thorough study of the subject of birth at home and concluded that they could accept the risks involved, which they saw as slight. They had invited some close friends to join them in their home for the final hours of labor, along with their midwife and doctor. Andrea had wanted her parents to come, but they were so worried about the delivery that they decided to stay home and wait for a phone call. About fifteen people were now crowded into the bedroom for the last few contractions before the baby emerged. Their collective body heat helped warm the room on that cool New England autumn day.

This particular birth was taking place in a community that offered possibilities not available everywhere. A cosmopolitan center with two universities and over 100,000 people of diverse ethnic backgrounds, it attracted people like the Clayborns, who enjoyed its intellectuality and traditions of independent thought. Both Andrea and Bob were college graduates, and had done postgraduate work. Before the birth of her first child, Andrea worked in a day-care center, and Bob was a member of a management consulting firm. Both were politically active in the community. They had joined with eight other couples to purchase a large apartment building, which they converted into a cooperatively owned group of apartments with a shared backyard and basement-level meeting room. The idea for forming this cooperative resulted from a study project on alternatives in housing that they had undertaken through their church. Andrea and Bob were just the kind of activist people who might be attracted to having their baby at home.

They had attended a series of classes given by one of two organizations that prepared couples for birth at home, and they were well informed about the process of labor and delivery. They were convinced that the risk to them and to the unborn child was very small, especially because they had competent, experienced attendants and lived quite close to several hospitals. The compactness of College Park allowed them to be anywhere within a matter of minutes (traffic permitting), unlike many suburbs, where distances between home and hospital could be great.

In their community, critical reappraisal of medical practices, particularly those concerned with women's health, had taken root in the previous fifteen years. Consumer groups had brought pressure for a number of changes in hospital practice. The city was also a center of medical schools and teaching hospitals which were highly regarded across the country.

Most of the obstetricians in the city were opposed to home birth on grounds of safety and refused to participate in home deliveries. Therefore most of the home births in the area were attended by lay midwives, although one group of family doctors did offer home birth services. The Clayborns had chosen Dr. Bill Greenson, a partner in this group, to attend Andrea's birth.

These doctors had begun attending births in the home in response to requests from people like the Clayborns. Dr. Greenson had a long record of involvement with health-related groups, many with headquarters in College Park, that called for social reform of one kind or another, and was regarded as a social activist. He had been a physician long enough to know that practices that appeared radical once could soon come to be accepted, so that younger people simply would be unaware that things had ever been different. Breast-feeding was a good example. When he began to practice in the early 1960s, doctors, hospitals, and relatives offered little support for nursing newborn babies. But, by the time of Andrea's labor, the situation had changed so completely that there was perhaps too much pressure on women to breast-feed and too little tolerance for women who chose not to. In any event, Dr. Greenson's experience told him that it was important to listen to what the public was saying, and that change often came from outside the medical profession, whose prime role, he felt, was to act as a conservative but flexible arbiter that could resist changing fads while respecting real needs of patients.

Another unusual feature of Dr. Greenson's practice was his work with several lay midwives — women who had received their training in the supervised practice of birthing rather than in midwifery school. He would have been happy to work with formally trained and certified nurse midwives, but these were, by state law, permitted to work in hospitals only and forbidden to attend births at home. Midwifery itself had been legalized in the state only several years earlier.

Working as he did on the interface between the majority of his colleagues on the one hand and some vocal and assertive patients on the other, Dr. Greenson knew that his opponents in the medical profession would quickly note mistakes and seize on any problem, or even a mere rumor of a problem, to discredit home birth, even though the problem might just as easily have occurred in the hospital. Such a climate added a burden of stress and extra caution to the practice of home birth.

Andrea's labor had begun about eight hours earlier when vaginal leaking of thick, blood-tinged fluid followed loss of the mucous plug. She had called Lara, the midwife, and told her that labor had begun. Contractions followed soon after, occurring first at intervals of fifteen to twenty minutes. Andrea had busied herself with cooking, tidying up the apartment, and contacting friends and relatives to let them know that labor had begun. Her neighbor and close friend, Jean, agreed to be with her until the midwife arrived. Although the contractions now felt like sharp menstrual cramps, painful enough to make her pause, she did not yet feel the need to use any of the breathing and relaxation exercises she and Bob had so carefully rehearsed. She observed how remarkably calm she was this time in contrast to her first labor, when all seemed strange and unknown in spite of childbirth classes and extensive reading.

By early afternoon the contractions had become more frequent and regular, occurring every five minutes. Andrea called Lara and told her it was time. Lara arrived at the apartment within twenty minutes. Andrea also called Bob at work, and he made plans to return home immediately. After sitting through several contractions to get the feel of the labor, Lara did a vaginal examination with a sterile glove and reported that the cervix was 4 to 5 centimeters dilated, 100 percent effaced, and that the station was zero. (See p. 184.) Although not entirely sure, she felt that the baby's head was oriented so that the back of the head was pointing toward the front left side of Andrea's body. "No doubt that you're in labor and moving now into the second stage." Lara's words seemed to act as a spur to the contractions. The pains soon grew more intense and more frequent. Andrea moaned, "I think I need some help now." "Okay," replied Lara, "let's see what we can do. How about trying your breathing, light chest breathing with the next contraction." With the next pain, Andrea locked her eyes with Lara and the two of them breathed lightly together, Lara directing the action by shaping the depth and speed of Andrea's gentle panting. They continued for the next thirty minutes or so during contractions until it was clear to both that Andrea was pulling herself together again. As she did, the contractions seemed to space out somewhat, but they were no less uncomfortable.

"It looks like things are slowing down a bit. How about getting up and walking around for a while?" asked Lara. For the next forty-five minutes Andrea returned to working in the kitchen, but now she had to lean against the wall during the contractions. "They're getting stronger again. Maybe you should check me now." Two hours had passed since Lara had first checked Andrea, and she was surprised to find that there had been little change in the cervix. It had dilated barely half a centimeter, if at all. All that work and so little apparent progress . . . A look of disappointment came over Andrea's face. "I'm disappointed, and a little tired." "Now," suggested Lara, "is the time for a nice, warm tub bath. That'll perk you up!"

What appeared to be happening to Andrea was not uncommon, for labor often gets "hung up" in the latent period of the first stage. Andrea's labor might be regarded as "pokey." (See p. 193.)

The warm bath water felt soothing and made the contractions much more bearable. Andrea stayed in the tub for half an hour until the pains became more frequent and intense. She reported, for the first time, that she felt slightly nauseated. She had been nibbling food and drinking fluids avidly throughout the pregnancy, but at this point the thought of something to eat or drink made her sick to her stomach.

"Let's check you again. Dry off and come back onto the bed." Lara reported "7 to 8 centimeters dilation" and phoned Dr. Greenson. "Andrea's in transition and I think you should come now. She's 7 to 8 centimeters." When Lara put down the receiver, Andrea said, "Let's not call everyone in the house until I'm fully dilated. That'll still give them plenty of time to get up here." Jean, who had been designated "information officer" for the rest of the building, had a different idea. "Why don't I just let everyone know that you're getting near the end so they can put their spouses on alert?"

By the time Dr. Greenson, whom everyone called "Bill," arrived, about thirty minutes after being called, Andrea was fully dilated and reported feeling an urge to push. "Fine," said Bill. "You can begin pushing now." He waited until her contraction was over and then reviewed with her the philosophy of pushing that they had discussed before. "Remember, pushing is not anything you *have* to do. Do it only if it feels good to you. Your baby will be born regardless, and you don't have to rush the birth. Everything is okay and there is no hurry. Just follow your instincts. Let me suggest that you go to the bathroom so that you can sit on the toilet. The john is a great place to be at this point. Also, see if you can urinate. That will make things easier for both you and the baby."

From here on, Lara and the doctor checked the fetal heart rate after each contraction. This was difficult to do, because Andrea was sitting on the toilet and Lara had to get down on the floor to reach the lower part of Andrea's abdomen (under her "overhang") with the fetoscope and check her labia for the bulging that signals the further descent of the baby. As Andrea straddled the toilet with her legs spread wide apart, Lara inserted two fingers into the perineum and pushed down to expose the lower vagina to view with each contraction. Pushing felt so good to Andrea that she groaned her way through each contraction, unmistakable evidence of the imminence of the birth.

When Lara saw the first tuft of new, black hair appear just above her fingers pressing down on Andrea's vagina, she knew it was time to move Andrea back to bed. Soon Andrea was sitting naked on her bed, cradled from behind in Bob's arms. A plastic sheet covered the mattress to protect it from leaking amniotic fluid or blood, and disposable paper pads were tucked under

15

Andrea's buttocks. Midwife and doctor circled the bed, checking the baby's heart rate and descent. They wore street clothes but had removed their shoes. They did not wear masks. Emergency instruments for infant resuscitation were unobtrusively spread out on top of a nearby chest of drawers. Andrea's medical record and a labor chart on which essential information was periodically entered were also there. A ready-to-use tank of oxygen was tucked away behind the door, and a large black doctor's bag, partially open and off in a far corner of the room, bulged with emergency drugs, intravenous fluids, syringes, needles, tape, and similar supplies. Since Jean had called everyone to come up after Andrea had begun to push, a small crowd had assembled in the bedroom.

With each contraction Andrea moved her gaze about the room, pausing briefly to make contact with the others present. She had chosen to pant her way through each pain. The panting started slowly, increased in intensity and volume as the pain intensified, and then slowed down to culminate in a deep sigh. Her friends picked up the rhythm of her breathing and panted along with her. She seemed to draw strength from the collective energy in the room.

During the next contraction the baby's head parted the labia and a clump of black hair peeked through. Some stool also squeezed out of Andrea's rectum and Lara wiped it away. "Reach down and touch your baby, Andrea." Andrea put her hand to her vagina and touched the head just before it slipped back in with the end of the contraction. She smiled happily.

"Let's get a mirror down there," said Bill. "There's one in the closet," replied Bob. Dave, a neighbor, got the mirror and placed it at the foot of the bed so that Andrea and Bob could watch the perineum bulge with each contraction. This visual feedback, and Lara's and Bill's guidance, helped Andrea sense how hard to push to allow for the gradual stretching of her perineum.

"You'll see a lot better if you can get some light down there," said Lara. "Right," replied Bob. "There's a flashlight in the first drawer on the left in the cabinet in the entranceway. I just put new batteries in it." The flashlight markedly increased the visibility of the unfolding events.

Andrea had no choice but to push; she was driven by an irresistible urge. When her attendants judged it important to slow down the force of the labor, in order to allow a more gradual stretching of the perineum, they asked her to pant hard in order to stop herself from pushing. This was the only way she could overcome the urge. When she was panting, the only forces moving the baby along were those of the uterus itself and gravity, which came into play because Andrea was in a half-sitting position. All the while, Lara kept one gloved hand over a gauze pad applied to the perineum to guard against an unexpected forceful contraction. During a contraction she would release pressure only periodically in order to inspect the perineum for any sign of tearing. If the skin became white, it would mean a loss of circulation with the likelihood of a tear, and an episiotomy would be considered. (See p. 214.)

Just then, Bill lost the sounds of the fetal heart with the fetoscope. The most likely explanation was that the heart was simply out of range; but, without hearing it, there was no way to tell if its beating was normal. He put the fetoscope down and positioned the plastic sensor, attached by a cord to the hand-sized ultrasound monitor, over Andrea's lower abdomen, moving it about until the hoofbeat-like "bup, bup, bup . . ." was broadcast for all to hear. Smiles broke out throughout the room. Lara began applying hot, wet, well-wrung washcloths to Andrea's perineum. Jane and Tom, another couple from the cooperative, saw that hot water was always available to heat the cloths. Another neighbor, John, the official photographer, was clicking away. A tape recorder captured the sounds of the birth for posterity. Between contractions, Lara inserted the tips of her gloved index fingers between the perineum and the baby's head. She poured a little vitamin E oil into the opening created and massaged it into the rim of the bulging vagina, gradually stretching the tissue as she did so.

Several contractions later the baby's head crowned; that is, it remained visible at the perineum and did not recede with the end of a contraction. A look of ecstasy came over Andrea's face, and her breathing deepened — she later reported that at this moment she experienced a feeling akin to orgasm.

Lara asked Andrea to slide to the edge of the bed and hang her legs over. As she did, Andrea commented on the burning she felt in her vagina. Two of her neighbors, directed by Lara, sat on the floor next to Andrea and supported her legs. Bob and the pillows were still behind her so that she could comfortably maintain her sitting position at a 45-degree angle. When the baby's head crowned, Jean, by previous arrangement, went to wake up four-year-old Joseph who was asleep in another bedroom. Andrea noticed her leaving and smiled approvingly. Joseph, rubbing the sleep from his eyes as he was ushered into the crowded room, was in a state of amazement at the scene before him.

Two contractions later, the baby's head emerged completely as the labia folded back after it. "Here's your baby," exclaimed Lara. "Put your hands down to catch your baby."

Although the baby's eyes remained closed, its eyebrows twitched and its lips made continuous sucking movements. "Now hold on to the head and give a little push between contractions," said Lara, whose hand supported Andrea's perineum all the while. Andrea grunted, and the slippery baby slid out. "A girl. Oh, I'm so happy!" Lara and Andrea together firmly held the baby, who quickly let out a lusty, gurgling cry as they lifted her to Andrea's breasts and covered her with a cotton receiving blanket.

Andrea asked Joseph to climb into bed with them. He gently touched the newcomer's head. "Gently — that's right. Here's your new sister, Joseph," said Andrea as she gave him a hug and kiss. She reassured him that the blood he was staring at on the bed didn't mean that anything was wrong with her but was simply part of having a baby. (See p. 110 for more on preparing children for birth.) She then offered little Beth her first meal. The tension in the room suddenly yielded to cheering and applause.

When the umbilical cord stopped pulsing, Lara put a clamp on it about two inches from the baby's umbilicus. She then tied a sterilized white shoelace between the clamp and navel. Bob took sterile scissors and cut the cord between the lace and the metal clamp. Beth's sucking immediately stimulated Andrea's uterus to contract. Within minutes, heralded by a small gush of blood, the placenta was delivered. Both doctor and midwife breathed an inner sigh of relief at this point, because bleeding associated with a retained placenta was one of their biggest worries, particularly with a home birth. (See p. 219.)

Dr. Greenson asked Andrea once again to move to the edge of the bed so that he could inspect her vagina for tears. After blotting up the blood in the vagina with a sterile gauze pad, he spread the labia apart. With the field illuminated by the flashlight Lara held, he was able to identify two small, superficial tears near the urethra and one tear 1½ inches long, and ¼ inch deep right in the midline at the site of the episiotomy Andrea had had during her first delivery. In Dr. Greenson's view, sewing up the latter was optional, for healing would occur on its own. No one really knew whether the stitches usually taken would speed it up. Remembering the pain she had after the episiotomy and its repair, Andrea was delighted to leave well enough alone.

By now Beth had settled down and Lara encouraged Andrea to take a shower to freshen up and to allow her bedding to be changed. Before she got out of bed, Bill checked the baby over. "Except for being wet behind the ears, she's perfect!" Bill then applied some erythromycin ointment to Beth's eyes (see p. 264) and emptied the contents of two small glass vials of vitamin K solution into her mouth (see p. 258). Champagne corks began to pop and the food, which had been arriving steadily throughout the day, was brought out. Lara waited just outside the shower in case Andrea became dizzy. Soon the party began. . . .

Lara and Bill stayed for another hour or so, joining in the warmth of the occasion. They finished the necessary paperwork, put away their equipment, and waited to observe Andrea for any delayed bleeding or other problems. Lara would also check in on the first and third days following the birth, and both she and the doctor would be available for consultation by telephone. Both congratulated Andrea and Bob on what they said was a "truly superb job." After warm hugs, they took their leave.

Two Births Contrasted

The stories of Andrea and Bob and Joan and Sam represent two contrasting approaches toward birth. It would be impossible to capture, even in 100 stories, the wide variety of birth experiences. Between the two are all gradations of experience. For instance, many hospital births now take place in birthing rooms which are as close to one's own bedroom in appearance and feeling as possible. Not every home birth has a festive atmosphere, and not every hospital birth involves anesthesia and forceps. We deliberately chose our exemplary tales to highlight the most extreme differences in tone and approach.

Childbirth in America is in ferment. Pronounced shifts have occurred in the last twenty years. On the one hand, the technology available to deal with pregnancy, birth, and the newborn has expanded significantly. On the other hand, a major movement on the part of a vocal and critical public, spearheaded by organizations like the International Childbirth Education Association, seeks to reclaim family control over childbearing, a natural process which they perceive as having been almost completely ceded to physicians and hospitals since the beginning of this century.

The current scene is the product of the interwoven effects of these two currents. Alternative birthing rooms that make possible home-like hospital births have proliferated throughout the country. This concept is backed by hospitals for economic necessity as well as for ideological commitment. To compete in the childbirth marketplace, hospitals must adapt to patients' special wants and needs.

In most hospitals the alternative birthing centers (ABCs) are located in the main maternity wing. In others they are in separate facilities on hospital grounds in order to emphasize and develop their own identity. (The birthing center at the Beverly Hospital in Beverly, Massachusetts, is an example.) Separate birthing centers, not connected with hospitals, are located in many cities. (The best known of these is the Maternity Center Association in New York City, situated in a town house on the Upper East Side.) Finally, there are home births, which account for a very small but growing percentage of all births in the United States.

The experience of Joan and Sam is typical of hospital births in this country and probably represents at least 90 percent of all births in the industrialized world. It is the mainstream birth experience. The options of the ABC room, the birthing center, and home birth reflect only a minority experience, but one that appears to be influencing more and more hospitals, as well as the expectations of couples.

As we have seen, the two couples in our stories approached their births differently. Andrea and Bob were concerned with being in charge of their baby's birth. They wanted Dr. Greenson and Lara for support, guidance, and help with possible complications, but not for "delivering" their baby, not for making decisions they regarded as their own. Convinced that having a baby was a normal physiological process, Andrea came to view her body with trust — it was capable of conceiving, carrying, and bearing a child. Problems could arise, but she considered herself a healthy woman built to have babies, the daughter of a long line of women who had borne many children. She and Bob believed that they would, and could, carry out the birth with a minimum of medical intervention. However, they wanted the professional support of a doctor, in view of the possibility that a medical issue could arise.

People like the Clayborns are concerned that the medical profession has a financial stake in intervention: they are not paid as well to "do nothing" as they are to "do something." Patients with insurance don't protest. The Clayborns' is a cynical point of view, but one that others share. It is the concern of women like Andrea that provides so much of the energy underlying the reforms that are occurring in childbirth practices, such as the development of relatively noninterventive settings like ABC rooms and birthing centers.

The Clayborns also objected to many hospital rules, such as those about eating and drinking. Husbands might be able to come into the delivery room, but it couldn't be guaranteed. Being able to have an older child present is not guaranteed, either. Patients must usually stay in the recovery room for one hour. Bob and Andrea were wary of the attempt to control pain with drugs, because they regarded it as a "path of no return," the first step in an unending series of interventions. First, the epidural, next the fetal monitor, then physical immobilization, then Pitocin, then episiotomy, the forceps, the suturing of the episiotomy. . . . In their opinion, it all resulted in a managed delivery totally out of their control. Medication can slow down contractions, which then must be speeded up for the baby's sake. Complications can arise as the result of previous interventions. In their view, birth should be allowed to proceed as a natural process. The doctor and midwife should be present, always alert, ever on guard, but should not do anything *unless* events dictate. However, it can be hard, for people used to taking the active role, just to sit back, watch, and wait; not hurry things along, but simply suggest ways to ease the mother's progress. Andrea and Bob believed that the greatest gift of all is empowering another person to do for himself or herself, and this was exactly what they wanted from Bill and Lara.

Andrea and Bob saw their relationship with the doctor and midwife as a negotiated partnership, shared decision-making based on trust. Every decision they made, from having their baby at home to refusing analgesia, was a gamble in the face of uncertainty.

Throughout the pregnancy both Lara and Bill had informed the couple, as best they could, of the risks they were taking. A bad outcome, even death, can be related to delivery at home; although the odds are low, maybe one, or a fraction of one, in 1,000. Birth itself has irreducible risks, even under the best of circumstances and in the finest medical centers. There are special risks associated with the hospital, and risks associated with the home. The order of magnitude of the risks in either site is comparable although not identical. (See Appendix A.) If something *did* go wrong at home, and the couple had chosen to be there, they would have to live with the fact that they had picked the site. As Dr. Greenson had pointed out, although a chance of failure may be one in 1,000, if you happen to be the one, your risk is 100 percent.

While it is easy for a doctor and midwife to talk in these terms, just how well a young couple, whose only experience is one previous birth, can grasp the risk is another question. They had had little enough direct experience with normal birth, let alone its possible complications. Dr. Greenson, having been in practice some twenty years, often thought to himself that, if people really knew what they could be getting themselves into, they would likely never attempt anything.

Andrea and Bob wanted to be the stars of their delivery in a special way. For them it was a once-in-a-lifetime opportunity. Bill and Lara knew from previous experience that the power one could experience in oneself by rising to such an occasion could carry over into other aspects of life, setting into motion a cycle of growing self-confidence. They had seen this happen time and time again. Women gained increased self-esteem and a finer sense of their own capacities. Childbirth became, for many, a turning point toward power in a life marked by too little validation. For others, the birth was yet another building block in an already maturing sense of self.

The Clayborns also wanted to feel closeness as a family immediately after the birth. Although they knew that hospital nurses and doctors are certainly caring and responsible, they saw them as strangers. Children and friends are usually excluded from a hospital birth, or involved only as a rare exception. Andrea and Bob reasoned that, since relaxation is so important to dealing with pain, the relaxing feeling of being in one's own familiar surroundings could only help in a delivery. Being in an unfamiliar place with unfamiliar people, far away from those closest and dearest to you, was in itself a source of tension that could exaggerate the perception of pain and make it harder to deal with it by nontechnical means. Their twenty-minute tour of the hospital, helpful as it was, couldn't compare with the years they had spent together in their cozy apartment.

If a home birth is to work, a couple cannot be rigidly locked into a "natural childbirth," believing that hospitals are to be avoided at all cost. Such ideological attachment is dangerous, because it can cloud life-and-death decisions that must be made in haste. Dr. Greenson and Lara tried hard to undermine such rigidly held positions and refused to work with couples not willing to show flexibility.

The role of the midwife was important to Andrea. Lara had seen Andrea in the office and once at home and had formed a very close relationship with her even before labor and delivery. They were in frequent telephone contact during and after the pregnancy. Lara, a mother of two, had been attending births at home for the past three years. She believed that, as a woman who had experienced pregnancy herself, she brought to it a special sensitivity. She could offer an intuitive understanding of birth in a way that a man could not. Lara had become a midwife largely because she believed that women should reclaim charge of their bodies and because she wanted to assist families in bringing new babies into the world. Breast-feeding was an area of special interest. (See p. 245.) She was amazed at how easy it was for new mothers to have difficulty with breast-feeding, and how much a little support from an experienced woman could help. Like childbirth itself, breast-feeding had once been part of the traditional lore of women. But people had become distanced from the major events of life — birth, nursing, and death — and had turned to professionals for guidance.

Closely related to the issue of women attending women is the concern for rebuilding a sense of community. The loss of connection with normal life processes in a modern technological society parallels the breakup of the extended family where such connections were once established. Andrea attended classes organized by a local home birth group. These classes fostered a sense of community among the participants, who tended to form friendships that endured long after the births of their children.

During such prenatal gatherings (given also in hospital classes for birth education) the fear of failure, the ignorance of normal labor and birth, and the feelings of alienation from one's own body were discussed. Gradually the participants came to see their pregnancies as healthy processes for which their bodies are specifically designed. Their fears did not dissipate entirely, but receded into the background of their concerns to be viewed as simply part of the process of confronting pregnancy and birth as important life events. While these couples did not romanticize the past with its high infant and maternal mortality rates, they wanted to draw from the best qualities of the pretechnological and technological years, neither to treat every woman as if she were high risk, nor to ignore the potentially life-saving advantages that modern obstetrics can offer.

Joan and Sam Williams chose Dr. Johnson and the local hospital because they offered the security of experience and modern medical practice. The fact that the safety of their baby was the paramount concern was comforting to them. From Dr. Johnson's point of view, people like the Clayborns were misguided. He pointed out to his patients that never before had having a baby been so safe, and this safety came directly from the great strides obstetrics had made during the past fifty years: antisepsis, anesthesia, bloodbanks, improved surgical techniques, ultrasound, fetal monitoring, and so on. Advocates of home birth, he felt, took a grave risk in assuming that nothing could go wrong in a delivery.

In his career Dr. Johnson had seen too many things go wrong at the last moment, often suddenly and always unexpectedly, after all had seemed so perfect. He had sweated through these moments, but each had added a few gray hairs to his head. Emergency cesarean sections and other quick action could save mothers and babies if trouble arose. Dr. Johnson questioned whether any woman could be considered truly low risk, so quickly could her condition change. What doctor in his right mind would want to be in someone's house when such a complication arose? He was particularly upset on the several occasions at the hospital when he was asked to deal with a home-birth patient brought in as an emergency after a complication. He had laid eyes on neither the patient, nor her spouse, nor the lay midwife until that critical moment, and suddenly had to repair the situation.

Dr. Johnson could understand that some women wanted a "natural" childbirth and were willing to endure the pain involved. If so, they should use alternative birthing rooms like the one his hospital had on the drawing board. In such ABCs you can have the baby in bed and need not even go to the delivery room. He and his colleagues would be right next door to all of the equipment and other resources they might need.

Dr. Johnson felt that couples should ask themselves how they would feel if something *did* go wrong. The issue was not simply having a baby. It was having a baby "well," having a baby in as good condition as possible, one who would not only be born well but who would grow up free of neurological and other problems. Especially now, when women seemed to be having fewer babies and at later ages, there were real risks to consider. (See p. 304.) What if someone had a "great birth experience," but a damaged baby?

If having babies were a perfect process, doctors would not be needed at all. The medical profession moved in to fill the holes left by imperfect evolution and had done so with extraordinarily good results. Take a protracted labor, for instance. It hurts and can hurt badly. A safe, reliable method for dealing with the pain, like an epidural, has been a boon to countless thousands of women. True, all such measures have their problems. If the Williams's birth had proceeded without anesthesia, Pitocin or forceps might not have been necessary. But the result was still a more comfortable birth and a healthy baby.

Regarding the question of who should attend birth, Dr. Johnson felt that a midwife or family practitioner might be okay, but should work only under the supervision of a certified obstetrician. A family doctor could continue with the care of the baby after birth; but, once again, a pediatrician was likely to be even better qualified and trained.

When physicians like Dr. Johnson first began to practice, little was known about natural childbirth. The emphasis in medical school training and residency, indeed the thrill and challenge, was on complications. Residents did not tally the number of normal births they had attended, but, if you asked how many cesarean sections they had done, the number would be right on the tip of their tongue. Also, obstetricians did not concern themselves very much with the "doctor-patient relationship." Many women twenty or thirty years ago neither knew nor cared about the details of labor and delivery. They wanted to have their babies as quickly and as painlessly as possible. Few took classes or read books on the subject. But private practice was different from practice in a clinic, and nowadays the women are increasingly better educated, expect more attention, and are able to form a personal relationship with their doctor. An obstetrician like Dr. Johnson knew that the success of his practice could be largely attributed to a firm, yet gentle bedside manner. Experience had given him a reassuring authority. In four years of medical school, one year of internship, three years of obstetrical residency, and fifteen years of practice delivering hundreds of babies, he had gained this expertise. Joan and Sam Williams saw their doctor as more of an authority than themselves, even though they had taken a course in childbirth education and had read a few books. They felt he was certainly willing to hear their preferences, but they had no intention of crossing his hard-won professional opinion if the unexpected came up in labor. To Dr. Johnson and Joan and Sam, the hospital birthing system that had developed in this country, while not perfect, was without question the best.

In this chapter we have shown two reasonable, valid, and yet opposing points of view in regard to the way a delivery should be handled. Couples planning ahead should be aware of these alternatives and the reasoning behind them. Within these major decisions, about hospital/birthing rooms/home and obstetrician/family practitioner/midwife, are many other more limited but just as important decisions. In the following chapters we will take these choices up one by one.

CHAPTER

2

Making Wise Decisions during Pregnancy

Becoming Informed

Recent technological advances have created many new choices for pregnant women. Among them are whether to have an amniocentesis, whether to use the electronic fetal monitor, whether to have an epidural anesthetic, and whether to attempt to turn a breech before labor. Fortunately, increased sophistication in the nature of decision-making helps us cope more effectively with such complicated questions. This subject is discussed fully in a recent book, *Medical Choices, Medical Chances*, which Richard Feinbloom wrote with Harold Bursztajn, Robert Hamm, and Archie Brodsky. It includes a chapter on pregnancy and birth among its many topics.

The first principle of good decision-making is: be informed. Know what your choices are, their pros and cons. If you can, do your homework before discussing issues with your doctor. Be at least as informed about your health care as you would be about buying a new car. This book, many other books on pregnancy and birth, and the presentations in childbirth education classes are good sources of information. (See Appendix D for further reading.)

Whenever possible try to attach numbers to the odds of success or failure of a particular choice. This will give you a more concrete idea of your chances and will help you choose more wisely. For example, in choosing the type of delivery after a previous cesarean section, you need to decide whether to plan for a second cesarean or to take the chance of labor and vaginal delivery. Your choice will be better informed if you know that the risk of an old scar's tearing in labor is stated as less than 1 percent (or 1 in 100), in contrast to "very small." Figures are useful in weighing alternatives in medicine, just as they are in weather forecasts. If the chance of rain is 10 percent, you might plan an outdoor picnic, but if the odds are as high as 33 percent (or 1 in 3), you might shift indoors. Good data are not always available on a given question, however. Sometimes the best you can do is make an educated guess.

Even when statistics are available, judgment is required to see how they apply to an individual case. For example, although studies show that the odds for survival of very young premature babies vary according to the weight of the infant, some newly born premature babies appear to have a better chance than others of identical weight. From the beginning they are livelier and more vigorous and appear to respond to an all-out effort to bring them through their difficulties. Since statistics alone will not identify them, the judgment of experienced professionals must be taken into consideration.

Statistics are only as valid as the way in which they are collected. Data can be highly inadequate when not based on a randomized clinical trial. When you think of options in terms of odds, ask your doctor how secure the percentages are, or check the source of written statistics.

In addition to obtaining general statistical information, ask your doctor about his or her own track record. For example, what percentage of his or her patients required a cesarean section? How does this percentage compare with the national norm? and why? What complications has he or she personally encountered? Answers to questions like these will allow you to judge your doctor's philosophy of practice. If a diagnostic procedure such as amniocentesis (p. 130) is proposed, you should, in addition to learning about the risks of this procedure in general, find out the complications rate of the person who will do the procedure on you and how this rate compares with usual standards. What are the chances that the test will have to be repeated? What are the chances that an error will be made, leading to a mistaken diagnosis? If a drug is proposed during pregnancy or lactation, be sure to find out whether or not it has any potentially harmful effects on you or your baby. Except in emergencies, don't agree to any action unless you know what you are getting into, and don't be afraid to ask.

In the rapidly developing field of prenatal diagnosis, innovations are not always available in every part of the country, even though they have gone beyond the experimental stage. Screening for spina bifida (pp. 59 and 122) was, and to some extent still is, such an example. It has not become a routine part of prenatal care everywhere. Ask your doctor about prenatal screening in general, and read as much as you can to supplement his or her advice.

Participating in Decisions

Ideally, your doctor should urge you to participate actively in making decisions. But you may have to assert yourself to get the explanations you need, and asserting yourself in the face of authority may be difficult. To help yourself out, make a list of your questions and areas of concern ahead of time. Bring your partner or a friend with you if you need support. Some of the topics you will be discussing are complicated, and having someone else with you as a second listener and questioner can be a real asset. Since remembering exactly what was said can be a problem, you may want to bring a note pad or tape recorder and take notes as your doctor talks. If you run into resistance to your inquiries, or think that you are not being given enough time, share your reaction with your doctor. If you still make no headway, you may need to change doctors. If you do, let both your old doctor and your new doctor know your reasons. Doctors should have as great a stake in your active participation as you do. After all, they cannot be expected to know in all situations what is best for you. That is too much responsibility for anyone to have to assume.

Be aware that there is not always a single "right" answer that works for everyone. For example, for one woman the very likely risk of pain in labor may outweigh the very small risk of a complication from an anesthetic, but this may not be so for another woman. Decisions involve not only *probabilities* but *values* as well. So making a wise choice involves both knowing the odds and knowing how strongly you feel about each possible outcome. Clarifying your values is a serious time-consuming process that can be aided in many cases by discussion with others whom you trust — your doctor, partner, family, and friends. Your doctor may be an authority on probabilities, but only you can be the expert on yourself.

Many decisions can be reconsidered as circumstances change. For example, you may choose to keep an open mind about pain medication until you are actually in labor. Of course, this is not always possible, for there are emergency situations when there simply is no time for a full discussion of pros and cons. In circumstances like these, trusting your doctor is essential.

Sometimes it may seem that pregnancy has become as involved as a course in college, requiring dedication and study to keep up. But the reward, a good childbirth experience, is priceless.

A few words about uncertainty: Keep in mind that there is no absolute certainty, since certainty itself is an illusion. An element of chance is always present, even in the best of hands. Recognizing this uncertainty is the starting point, not only for gaining a degree of control over it, but also for maintaining peace of mind.

As a physician I (Richard Feinbloom) live constantly with the knowledge of uncertainty. When, for example, I say to a patient, "It looks like you have a viral infection. The odds favor it. I may be wrong, but I'd say that there is a 95 percent chance this is what it is. But if any of the following develop [here I list serious symptoms like higher fever, headaches, and so on] I need to be able to count on you to call me back, even at 2:00 A.M." I mean it just the way I said it. I need the active participation of the patient in order to do my job in the face of unavoidable uncertainty.

Some people say that by acknowledging uncertainty I undermine my patients' faith in me. On the contrary, I see that most people find it reassuring that I am "up front" about the uncertainty which we all know is there anyway. In a similar vein, most patients welcome my saying "I don't know" when I don't, and opening a book in their presence to check out a point. I also know from the studies my colleagues and I have done that acknowledgment of uncertainty is the only possible starting place for being a scientific practitioner in our time.

The challenging approach of informed choice that we propose is also one possible remedy to the malpractice problem so much in the news. When both doctor and patient are committed to facing the risks and benefits of a particular action before the fact, they are less likely to end up facing each other in court. A greater understanding of the blend of chance and skill, which always operates in medical outcomes, can lead to more realistic expectations. In an atmosphere of trust, of active participation on the part of the informed parents, and of openness on the part of the physician, childbirth can be a triumphant and heartwarming experience for all concerned.

Obstetricians, Family Physicians, and Midwives

One of the first and most important decisions is the choice of a professional who will attend the birth. This can be a family doctor, an obstetrician, or a midwife.

Sources of information include friends who have had babies, doctors who can refer colleagues, local affiliates of the International Childbirth Education Association (ICEA) or La Leche League (while ICEA or La Leche League will not as organizations refer you directly to a doctor or midwife, their members will be willing to speak with you as individuals), the National Association of Parents and Professionals for Safe Alternatives in Childbirth (NAPSAC), hospital departments of obstetrics (the Chief of Obstetrics may be able to match you to an appropriate doctor or midwife), and nurses who work on maternity services. Most hospitals provide tours of their labor and delivery areas; while there, ask the guide about the styles of the doctors and, if the hospital has them, midwives. The American College of Nurse Midwives (ACNM) will send you a listing of midwifery services in your area, and a listing of freestanding birth centers is available from the National Association of Childbearing Centers (NACC). The Midwives Alliance of North America, a new organization of lay and nurse midwives which promotes midwifery and provides referrals, will also send you information. (See Appendix B for addresses and other resources.)

At the first appointment with the doctor or midwife, state your own preferences to find out if he or she can satisfy them and if you would be comfortable working with each other. Use the visit as an opportunity to learn as well, taking advantage of the professional's experience and knowledge. Be open to having your point of view challenged. Having your partner or a friend join you on this first visit is a good idea, for they can support you, second your reactions, and help by asking additional important questions that might not immediately occur to you.

Make a detailed list of issues of concern to you. These may include policy on intravenous fluids, anesthesia, episiotomy, labor position, and so on. Find out at what point in labor you can count on the doctor or midwife being with you, and clarify coverage arrangements — what happens if he or she is away? In some large group practices the concept of "my doctor" is not even valid. While a woman may see the same person more or less regularly at each prenatal visit, she will be attended during labor and delivery by whoever is on call. This may or may not matter to you.

Obstetricians and *family practitioners* are the two types of physicians who attend births. Both are board-certified specialists. Obstetricians are certified by the American College of Obstetrics and Gynecology (ACOG); family practitioners are certified by the American Board of Family Practice. (Some communities still have general practitioners — general physicians who have not been certified by the American Board of Family Practice).

One advantage of an obstetrician is that he or she can deal with most complications of labor and delivery. For example, while obstetricians perform cesarean sections, family doctors in general do not, nor do they usually handle complicated births. Under these circumstances, family doctors usually have to call in an obstetrician to assist them. On the other hand, a family physician can continue to care for the family after the baby is born, a major advantage. The family doctor's relationship with the family is not limited to the pregnancy; it includes many other aspects of a family's medical needs. Thus, a family physician offers a family the opportunity for a more extensive and continuous doctor-patient relationship.

Childbirth not only leads to bonding between parents and baby but can produce warm feelings between family and physician or midwife as well. The person who attends a birth can have a permanent special place in a family's life. In comparison with midwives and obstetricians, family physicians have an advantage in being able to build more effectively upon this sound foundation simply because of more frequent subsequent contact, including care of the baby. Of course, much depends on the personalities of the individuals involved.

Not all family doctors provide prenatal care or attend births. Depending on where you live, you may have to search for one who does. The American Academy of Family Physicians is a source of information on family doctors in your area.

If a family doctor needs to call in an obstetrician for consultation, an extra fee may be generated, and most insurance companies will pay only one physician for attending a delivery. If the obstetrician in the end must perform a cesarean section, the insurance company will not also cover the family physician's or midwife's time, and a family may have to pay separate charges out-of-pocket. Families who wish to develop a relationship with a midwife or a family physician may find this financial risk worth taking. If a family uses an obstetrician, it will probably then retain a pediatrician for the infant.

When you interview an obstetrician, find out what percentage of his or her deliveries are cesarean sections. Any figure over 15 percent is high, *unless* the physician deals with a high-risk population. Otherwise, a high figure may suggest that his or her criteria for performing cesarean sections are too liberal and that he or she is "too quick to cut." (See p. 278 on cesarean sections.)

If you are planning an out-of-hospital birth, the issues to clarify are discussed in the first section of Chapter 4 (p. 181). If you find physicians willing to attend a home or birth-center childbirth, ask about the most serious problems they have encountered, relating to the site of birth, how they dealt with these problems, and whether they would deal with them differently today. A doctor's openness about his or her practice and willingness to acknowledge errors are qualities generally associated with the best practitioners.

Midwives form the third category of certified attendants. *Nurse midwives* are individuals who have both a nursing degree and midwifery training and who are licensed as such by the state. In most states they can now legally practice in hospitals, but their legal right to attend births at home is more restricted. The majority are women, and most belong to the American College of Nurse Midwives.

As a group, midwives are primarily prepared to deal with normal childbirth, specifically trained to deal with low-risk pregnancies, and apply nontechnological approaches to helping women with labor and delivery. Unlike many physicians, trained in the "disease model" of medicine, midwives do not view pregnancy as an illness or disease. By reputation and tradition and long experience they are highly attuned to the needs of laboring women. They are "women attending women," a concept central to the thinking of many critics of contemporary hospital childbirth practices.

Despite the outstanding track record of nurse midwives, until recently they have been blocked from full expression of their skills by opposition from obstetricians, in part because they represent serious competition. In general they have not been allowed to establish independent practices, as many would like, nor can they attend home births in many states. Their fees tend to be significantly less than those of physicians.

A large proportion of home births are attended by *lay midwives*, individuals who, for the most part, acquire their skills on the job rather than in formal training. Efforts are now being made to establish educational standards and licensure requirements for lay midwives.

Note: See Appendix B for information on midwives' associations and the section on "Birth at Home" in Chapter 1 for a description of a midwife's activities and relationship with an expectant couple.

Other Supports

Childbirth education classes are offered by most hospitals, by local affiliates of ICEA, and by various home birth organizations. Hospital classes generally support hospital policies and have an "in-house" quality about them appropriate for preparing families to have a baby in a particular institution. ICEA and home birth classes take a somewhat more independent stance in their discussion of childbirth practice. On the other hand, they are not free of doctrinaire positions. For example, home birth groups have an understandable bias toward the home as the best place to have a baby. Your reading and consultation with childbirth instructors and women who have attended different kinds of classes should help you choose an approach congenial to your personality and needs.

La Leche League provides support around breast-feeding and child care in general. Its members are available for individual consultation about problems with nursing by phone or in person (often in your own home). Participation in this group can begin before the baby is born.

All these groups provide opportunities for expectant couples and single parents to meet other couples, one of the most useful functions they serve. For many of today's isolated families, the creation of "community" is an essential step in building confidence for birth and child care. See Appendix B for the names and addresses of other support groups.

Your History

During your first visit to your doctor or midwife, a detailed history will be taken. The information you provide will be extremely important in deciding how both you and they will deal with your pregnancy.

Your general medical background will include a review of any drugs (prescribed or over-the-counter) you regularly take (see p. 153 on "Drugs during Pregnancy"), any chronic problems that might affect and be affected by the pregnancy, such as recurrent herpes infection (see p. 164), heart disease, phenylketonuria (see p. 265), hepatitis (see p. 163), or diabetes (see p. 167), and past surgical procedures, such as appendectomy, which would be important to know about in evaluating symptoms that may arise, such as abdominal pain (see p. 73).

Your health practices with regard to diet (see p. 82), exposure to cats (see p. 166), exercise (see p. 88), dental care (see p. 69), alcohol (see p. 171), caffeine (see p. 173), marijuana use (see p. 174), self-medication, and seat belt use (see p. 176) will all have a bearing on the pregnancy and should be reviewed.

Your menstrual history including menarche (age of first period), interval between periods, and date of last period or ovulation, if known, will be important in dating the pregnancy (see p. 48).

Your past pregnancies, including date of delivery, complications, type of delivery, use of episiotomy (see p. 214) and Pitocin (see p. 198), weight and condition of baby at birth and at present, abortions (see p. 305) (both spontaneous and induced), problems in conceiving, and perceptions of the quality of the birthing experience will all help to highlight aspects of the current pregnancy that require appropriate attention. For example, a past cesarean section (see p. 278) in and of itself will dictate a certain course of action as modified by the indications for which the section was performed.

It will be useful for your doctor or midwife to know whether you and your partner planned to have a baby at this time and what impact the timing of this pregnancy has on your lives. Do you need professional assistance in resolving ambivalence about the pregnancy or in making the decision to continue or terminate it? Do the answers to these questions relate to the quality of your relationship in any way? Would you benefit from marital counseling or further discussion with your spouse or partner?

Your family history takes on even greater significance in this era of rapidly improving quality of prenatal diagnosis and treatment. (See p. 117 on "Genetics" and p. 149 on "Treating the Fetus before Birth.") As we discuss in the section on genetics, clues to increased risk for a genetic disease in the fetus include your age, your racial and ethnic background, a history of having produced a genetically abnormal or retarded individual yourself (or a history of one in your or your spouse's family), recurrent abortions, and birth of a child with a major malformation or chronic illness.

It's a good idea to construct a family tree for each partner, beginning at the bottom of the tree with your and your siblings' offspring, if any, and tracing back through your generation, your parents' generation, your grandparents', and so forth. List under each person any chronic illnesses, including retardation, and any deaths, and their causes. You will probably have to consult your parents for information, and may find yourself making a few phone calls to relatives to fill in the details. Ideally, such information should be reviewed with a knowledgeable health professional even before you are pregnant — at a premarital examination, for example. But even your first prenatal visit is not too late.

Family histories will continue to be useful as we move toward testing all fetuses for genetic disorders. An added benefit of such family histories is that normal conditions that follow a hereditary pattern, like twins in the family (see p. 117), will also be identified and can then be watched for in the present pregnancy.

Finally, and of great importance, taking your history is also an opportunity for you to ask questions, to express concerns, and to get to know your doctor or midwife, and vice versa. It should be an educational experience for both you and the father-to-be.

Pregnancy Tests

A hormone indicating pregnancy can be detected in the blood of the pregnant woman as early as three days following fertilization, and in the urine within one week of the first missed menstrual period. This hormone, known as human chorionic gonadotropin (HCG), is produced by the placenta (or, more precisely, by the trophoblast, its earlier form). Presently available tests of HCG done in medical laboratories or physicians' offices are over 98 percent accurate. Over-the-counter urine pregnancy test kits (Daisy, Answer, and e.p.t. are readily available brands) are somewhat less accurate, giving correct readings 85 to 95 percent of the time.

These highly accurate and useful laboratory tests have taken much of the guesswork out of diagnosing pregnancy in its early stages. They are particularly helpful in confirming pregnancy when a woman has been waiting to conceive for a long time or has reason not to want the pregnancy. It is also useful in identifying possible causes for incompletely explained symptoms, such as those of an ectopic pregnancy (p. 293) or other rare conditions.

Pregnancy tests are not always necessary. Many women, particularly those who have been pregnant before, "know" when they are pregnant. They notice having missed a menstrual period, experience nipple tingling and breast firmness, and may be aware of an altered body state that is difficult to describe. The pregnancies of these women can be confirmed without testing by noting the physical changes in the uterus detectable on examination (p. 40) and the obvious signs of pregnancy present after several months.

The level of HCG rises rapidly during early pregnancy, doubling every two days. The level peaks at ten weeks of pregnancy, then gradually declines to about one-half of peak levels, where it tends to remain for the rest of the pregnancy. After an abortion, or miscarriage, the level falls off over the course of one week. But occasionally, if trophoblastic tissue has been left behind in the uterus, the hormone may be detectable for as long as several weeks.

In a very early pregnancy in which a miscarriage is suspected and ultrasound cannot yet provide an answer about the presence or viability of the embryo, measurement of HCG can be helpful, because pregnancies that are failing do not demonstrate the predicted rise in hormone level; it may plateau or actually decline.

Physical Examination

A CHANCE TO LEARN

The physical examination in pregnancy allows the doctor, nurse, or midwife to assess a woman's body for its readiness to carry a pregnancy and bear a child. It is also an opportunity for you to learn a great deal about the human body in general and the female body in particular. (see Figure 1.) If a woman chooses to include her partner, they both can learn about her body. The exam is also an opportunity for a woman and her doctor or midwife to build

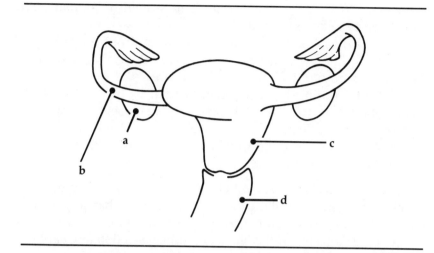

Figure 1. Female reproductive organs: (a) ovaries (b) Fallopian tubes (c) uterus (d) vagina

up trust between one another. The examination is clearly more than a simple checkup. You can add to the value of this experience in the following ways:

1. Read something about the female body and reproductive organs beforehand. Ask the doctor for any charts or other materials he or she can offer.

2. Ask questions whenever there is something you do not understand. Good open communication is essential throughout the childbirth experience. Speak up if you feel pain.

3. Try to relax and participate in the examination. So that the doctor or other attendant can feel the uterus and ovaries properly, the woman must relax. The examining hands, one in the vagina and the other on the lower abdomen, must move toward each other to feel the structures in between. If a woman's muscles are tense, she actually prevents herself from being examined. Thus, she has a stake in actively participating in the examination. A maneuver that helps relax the abdominal and vaginal muscles is breathing in and out twice deeply, "bearing down" as though to push out a baby, then "letting go" of the buildup of muscle

tension. Often these movements help women relax and allow themselves to be examined.

4. Ask for a mirror to see the cervix and other intravaginal structures. Many women have never seen the cervix, and this is an opportunity to understand its structure.

5. Bring your husband, partner, or a female friend who will be of support later. If you plan to have your husband or a friend present at the delivery, this is a chance to involve them from the start. Make clear to the doctor, nurse, or midwife that these are important members of the labor and delivery "team."

Learning to trust each other, to cooperate and communicate well during the prenatal physical examination, has implications that extend to labor and delivery when it will be vital to work together as a team. In the story of Andrea and Bob in Chapter 1, recall how effectively Andrea and the doctor and midwife communicated with each other as the baby's head was born. Such excellent teamwork during the "big show" grows out of numerous rehearsals in communication (both verbal and nonverbal) during prenatal visits.

THE PERINEAL MUSCLES

One part of the examination that requires collaboration between the examiner and the pregnant woman is the assessment of the perineal muscles. The perineum is the portion of the female body between the lower junction of the labia and the anus. (See Figure 2.) These muscles are used in childbirth, during intercourse, and in stopping the act of urination. Since many women are out of touch with these muscles, and relatively few exercise them regularly, their tone is apt to be weak. The examiner can assess them by placing the fingers of the gloved hand onto the perinuem just inside the entrance to the vagina and pressing down. The woman is then asked to tighten the muscles. The experienced examiner can determine whether tone is nonexistent, weak, average, or good. If your doctor or midwife does not check these muscles, you can do it yourself, using two fingers and pressing toward the spine. If your perineal tone is nonexistent, weak, or average, you should exercise these muscles. (Our suggestion is to tighten and

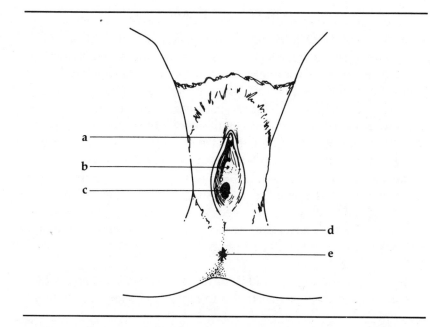

Figure 2. **External female genitals: (a) clitoris (b) urethra (c) vagina (d) perineum (e) rectum**

relax in units of five contractions, each lasting ten seconds, and to repeat the unit ten times a day whether or not you are pregnant.)

Toning these muscles can help prevent tearing during birth and minimizes the need for an episiotomy. Good perineal tone can also enhance the sexual satisfaction of both partners in intercourse: women can increase their chances for and control over orgasm, and many men appreciate the gripping sensation they experience when the perineal muscles are tensed. Strong perineal muscles also prevent "bladder sagging," as women age (particularly if they have had children), and stress incontinence, the involuntary passage of urine during sneezing, coughing, laughing, or lifting. These perineal exercises, also known as *Kegel exercises* (after Dr. Arnold Kegel, the physician who first described them), have traditionally been a part of female hygiene in many preindustrial societies, passed on from mother to daughter as part of folk knowledge. (See also p. 96 on prenatal exercise.)

THE PELVIC EXAM

While the initial examination during pregnancy should be complete "from head to toe," its focus is of course on the reproductive system. The pelvic examination includes inspection of the labia, determination of perineal muscle tone (as we have discussed), inspecting the vagina and the cervix (see p. 64 on physical changes in pregnancy), taking a culture of the cervix for gonorrhea (see p. 59), doing a Pap test of the cervix (see p. 59), feeling the uterus, ovaries, and rectum, and assessing the size of the pelvis.

The size of the uterus reflects the *gestational age* (length of time embryo or fetus is carried in the womb) and is recorded during early pregnancy in terms of weeks; for example, "six to eight weeks' size" (the uterus can first be felt to be enlarged at about six weeks' gestation). Later in pregnancy the uterus is measured with a tape (see p. 80).

The measurements used to determine how easily a baby could pass through the pelvis (as shown in Figure 3) include the following:

1. Estimation of the distance between the lower border of the *symphysis pubis* (where the pubic bones meet in front) and the *sacrum* (forward bend in the spinal column). This distance is judged by using the known measured distance between the tip of the examiner's extended middle finger and the thumbward side of the first knuckle of the index finger. In making this measurement, the examiner pushes deep into the vagina, reaching for the curve in the spine, a maneuver which may be slightly uncomfortable for the woman being examined. A distance of greater than 12.5 centimeters (just under 5 inches) is considered adequate for the head of an average baby. Often the curve in the sacrum cannot be reached by the examiner, indicating that the distance is at least as long as the examiner's hand measurement. The measured distance between pubis and sacrum is known as the *diagonal conjugate*. (See Figure 4.) Because of the angle of the pubis, the actual shortest distance between it and the sacrum (also known as the *obstetrical conjugate*) is about 2 centimeters less than the diagonal conjugate and measures, on the average, 10.6 centimeters (4.1 inches). These two measurements represent the smallest diameters of the inlet of the pelvis which the baby's head must navigate if it is to enter the birth canal.

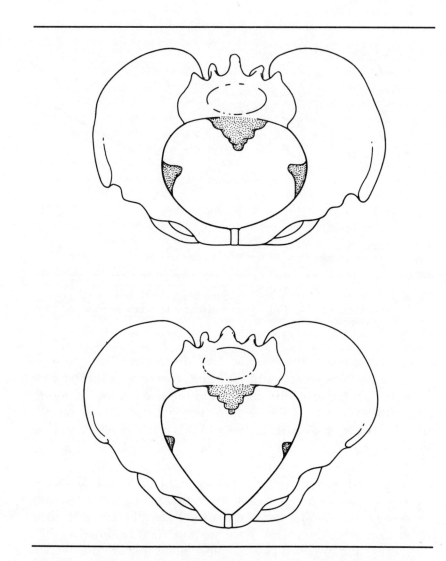

Figure 3. **Pelvis seen from above, showing sacrum and ischial spines.**
Female (top) Male (bottom)

2. Determination of the orientation of the sidewalls of the pelvis—whether straight, i.e., parallel; convergent, i.e., funneling toward the examiner; or divergent, i.e., funneling away from the examiner toward the woman's head. Either a parallel or a divergent orientation is considered favorable to passage of the baby; convergent orientation is less favorable.

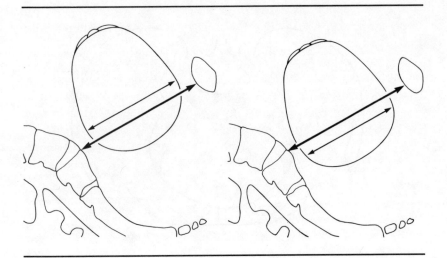

Figure 4. Descent of baby's head into the birth canal, known as "engagement." Bold line shows distance between sacrum and pubic bone.

3. Estimation of the *plane of least dimensions*. This plane is bounded by the lower edge of the pubis, two bony points (spines) of the ischial bones of the pelvis, and the junction of the fourth and fifth vertebrae of the sacrum (the last two just above the coccyx). The front-to-back diameter of this plane extends from the lower border of the pubis to the juncture of the fourth and fifth sacral vertebrae and measures on the average 12 centimeters.

Although a woman herself cannot see or feel her ischial spines, she can become aware of them if the examiner tells her when they are being touched. The spines can also be identified on a drawing or on a model of the pelvis. They are important landmarks of the birth canal and are used as a reference point to stage the descent of the baby. (See Figures 3 and 4.)

The examiner checks to see whether the ischial spines are flat or protruding into the birth canal. The distance between the spines is estimated. It should measure, at least, 10.5 centimeters. Another important measurement extends from the midpoint between these two spines to the junction of the fourth and fifth sacral vertebrae. This should measure 4.5 to 5.0 centimeters and is a measurement of the depth of the pelvis.

4. The relative convexity or concavity of the sacrum from front to back and vice versa. The more concave, the more room for the baby.

5. Estimation of the angle of the pubic bones, by following these bones downward from the pubis with the second and third fingers of the examining hand. The fingers should separate (pull apart) as downward movement progresses. The angle between the bones should be 90 degrees or greater.

6. Estimation of the size of the outlet to the pelvis is made by measuring the distance between the inner sides of the bones known as the ischial tuberosities, the bones in the middle of the buttocks which one "sits" on. This distance should be, at least, 11 centimeters (4.3 inches). A fist of average size should be able to fit comfortably between the inner borders of the tuberosities. This distance is also known as the transverse diameter of the outlet.

7. Determination of the position and the flexibility of the coccyx by feeling it directly through the rectum. Ideally, the coccyx should be flat; it should not protrude into the birth canal where it could obstruct labor. It should be movable and thus able to yield to pressure from the baby without cracking.

The "adequacy" of a pelvis for a particular baby is ultimately determined during labor itself, not by measurements made before (see p. 293 on "Disproportion"). However, knowledge of the architecture of the pelvis can be useful in making predictions about the probability of a successful vaginal delivery when labor progress is impaired. It is one of many factors taken into consideration in deciding how to proceed.

BLOOD PRESSURE

Blood pressure is measured at each visit. An inflatable cuff is secured over the upper arm just above the elbow. A stethoscope is placed on the artery that passes under the crease at the elbow. The cuff is inflated to stop the pulse below the cuff, and then is gradually deflated. The upper reading of the blood pressure, which is called the *systolic pressure* ("systole" refers to the contraction of the heart when blood is ejected with maximum force into the blood vessels), is determined by noticing the reading on the gauge when the pulse sounds first become audible. The lower reading, or *diastolic pressure* ("diastole" refers to the filling, non-contracted, phase of the heart cycle), is determined by noting the gauge reading when the pulse is no longer audible. The gauges are calibrated in millimeters of mercury. Thus, a pressure of 120 means that the pressure will balance or support a column of mercury 120 millimeters (about 5 inches) high in a thin tube. The systolic and diastolic readings are expressed as a fraction; the numerator is the systolic pressure and the denominator is the diastolic pressure. A reading of 140/90 is regarded as the upper limit of normal. If either figure is higher, blood pressure is too high (hypertension).

Blood pressure varies in a predictable way during pregnancy. There is a normal dip of about 5 millimeters in the systolic and diastolic pressures during the first and second trimesters.

Blood pressure determination is one of the most important serial measurements made in pregnancy. A blood pressure reading over 140/90 occurring with protein in the urine after the twentieth week defines *preeclampsia*, a relatively common disorder with important implications for pregnancy (p. 315).

Dating the Pregnancy

Many decisions about the growth of the fetus (see p. 301 on "Intrauterine Growth Disturbance") and the timing of delivery of a baby depend on accurate dating of the pregnancy (see p. 314, "Post-Term Pregnancies"). Every effort must be made to determine gestational age by twenty weeks, beyond which dating becomes progressively less accurate.

The *date of the last menstrual* period is the primary way of estimating when conception occurred (at roughly fourteen days before the next anticipated menstrual period). Even better is the last *date of ovulation*, as determined by basal body temperature. Another milestone, but not a very good one, is the *"quickening,"* the moment when a mother first feels her baby move, sometime between sixteen and twenty weeks. A mother's recognition of this sensation will vary, depending in part on whether she has had other pregnancies and is familiar with the sensation. Measurement of the size and the height of the uterus is an excellent dating method, particularly in the first trimester. (See Figure 5.) Between eighteen and thirty weeks of gestation, the height of the uterus measured in centimeters correlates fairly well with the number of weeks of gestation, especially in first pregnancies. The baby's heart can first be heard with a stethoscope between sixteen and nineteen weeks after conception, and by *doppler ultrasound* by twelve weeks (see p. 142).

With real-time ultrasound, fetal heart movements can be visualized by six to seven weeks. The gestational sac is visible as early as five to six weeks. Between eight and twelve weeks, the distance between the head and buttocks of the fetus, the "crown-rump" distance, dates the gestational age very precisely. Between sixteen and twenty-six weeks, measurement of the diameter of the baby's head can date the pregnancy to within 1.5 weeks of the gestational age with 95 percent confidence. Recently ultrasound researchers have found that the length of the femur (thigh bone) of the fetus,

Figure 5.   Growth of the uterus. Unbroken curve in middle is size of uterus at twenty-four weeks. Dotted line shows position of uterus after baby's head engages in the pelvis.

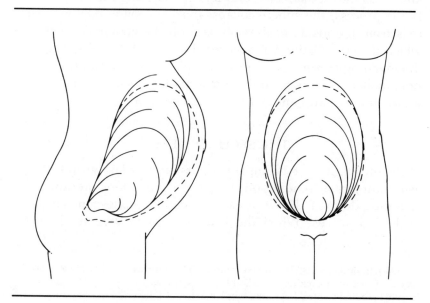

measured during the second trimester, is 95 percent accurate to within six days of the fetal age. Other physical measurements are being studied for their correlation with gestational age.

Growth of the Fetus

THE FIRST WEEK:
CELL DIVISION AND IMPLANTATION

Egg and sperm cells meet during fertilization to form one cell with forty-six chromosomes. From this one cell, through cell growth, division, and differentiation, the baby and placenta will develop.

After fertilization, rapid cell division produces a hollow sphere, the *blastocyst*. After passing through the Fallopian tube and reaching the womb, the blastocyst continues to enlarge. In another three or four days it attaches itself to the surface of the womb's lining. This is called *nidation*.

After seven days, the blastocyst, now composed of several hundred cells, invades the now prepared lining of the womb, known as the *decidua,* and gains a firm attachment to the mother. In the process, the sphere collapses, like a cooling popover. The cells from the inside of the sphere form the germinal disc from which the entire baby will develop. The rest of the cells compose the invading *trophoblast,* or primitive placenta. The trophoblast is unique, because it is the only human tissue, outside of malignant tissue, that invades another and is not rejected.

THE SECOND WEEK

Once the blastocyst is implanted, its trophoblast grows at an astounding rate, sending out finger-like projections into the surrounding decidua. These projections become honeycombed with walls and spaces. When the embryo is about two weeks old, maternal tissues are eroded to such an extent that the maternal blood vessels allow the mother's blood to rush into these trophoblastic spaces. Placental circulation is thus established, and the mother's blood begins to nourish the developing embryo.

The trophoblast also produces HCG (see p. 39), without which the entire lining of the womb, including the developing blastocyst, would be cast off. HCG in the mother's blood and urine is the hormone measured in tests used to detect pregnancy. (See p. 39.)

The embryonic disc, at this point, is a double-layered plate, resembling an empty sandwich. The upper outer layer is called the *ectoderm;* from it the skin, hair, nails, and the entire nervous system will develop. The lower layer is the *endoderm,* which gives rise to the digestive tract, the respiratory system, and many of their accessory glands.

Between these two layers a third layer, the *mesoderm,* soon develops. The muscles and tissues lining the abdominal and pleural cavities derive from it. Scattered between these three germinal layers are loose cells called the *mesenchyme,* which belongs to no one layer but acts as a sort of loose packing tissue between layers. The mesenchyme gives rise to the heart, blood vessels, bones, and cartilage.

THE THIRD WEEK

During the third week the oval germinal disc becomes pear-shaped and then takes on the form of the body of a violin. It also bends in the middle, losing its flat shape. Down the center of the ectodermal surface, which will become the baby's back, a couple of parallel ridges form. A groove or trench between them, known as the *neural groove,* will form the central nervous system. The heart and blood vessels also begin to develop during the third week of embryonic life.

THE FOURTH WEEK

Changes of great rapidity are taking place within the body of the embryo. Shortly after the laying of foundations for the nervous and circulatory system, the *gut,* or beginning digestive system, begins to form. By a process similar to the formation of the neural groove, the endoderm gives rise to the foregut in front and the hindgut in the tail region. A blind pouch in front pushes gradually forward, soon breaking through upon the undersurface of the head to form the mouth.

At four weeks and one-quarter inch long, the embryo does not yet look like a baby. It has a head and a tail, which can be distinguished readily. The neural groove has sealed over completely, and formation of the brain is progressing rapidly. In the head, the beginnings of the eye and ear can be seen. A growing area called the mandibular process is beginning to form the face. The heart is now a large bulge on the underside of the embryo, already beating rhythmically.

TWO MONTHS

By two months the fetus, over an inch long, has assumed a definite human form. It has eyes, ears, and a nose. The hands have fingers and the feet have toes. The head still looks too big for the body, which is potbellied because the liver is too large for the abdominal cavity. The sexual organs have begun to form. From now on the embryo will be called a fetus.

THREE MONTHS

In the third month of embryonic development many different organs of the body become more specialized. In the mouth, a series of ten tooth buds appear in both the upper and lower jaws.

The most dramatic changes of the third month are seen in the sexual organs, especially those of males. Differentiation is more rapid in males than in females, and by the end of the third month, close inspection of the fetus will reveal whether it is a boy or a girl.

FOUR AND FIVE MONTHS

The changes occurring during the rest of pregnancy are much more subtle. Development is largely a matter of simple enlargement and maturation of the various organs. The four-month-old fetus, though tiny, looks like a baby in every respect, although the head is still relatively large and the legs relatively short. The skin is thin, red, and wrinkled.

FROM SIX MONTHS TO BIRTH

By six months of age specialized structures in the baby's skin are formed. There is a fine growth of hair on the head and sometimes over the back and shoulders, whose color has little resemblance to the color of the hair the child eventually will have. Fingernails and toenails appear and grow slowly. At the time of birth they will project slightly at the tips of the fingers, and they will have to be trimmed in the first few days of life to keep the infant from scratching itself. Oil glands appear in the skin and manufacture a greasy, tenacious substance known as the *vernix caseosa*, which is like a salve or ointment.

By the end of the sixth month the fetus is fully developed. From now until term it needs only to grow in length, weight, and strength in order to face the demands of the world outside the womb.

THE PLACENTA

The *placenta*, or afterbirth, plays a central role in pregnancy. It is a flat, circular structure about 7 to 8 inches in diameter and an inch in thickness and weighs roughly one pound. It is composed of millions of finger-like projections, called *chorionic villi*, which are part of the fetal blood vessel system and connect up with the rest of the baby's blood vessels via the large umbilical veins and artery in the umbilical cord. In the body of the placenta, the villi are suspended in maternal blood. While there is no actual mixing of the circulations between the mother and the fetus, only a thin layer of cells covering the villi separates them. All the nutrients and oxygen pass into the baby's circulation across this layer. The baby also has an active metabolism of its own; the waste products from fetal metabolism, including carbon dioxide, pass into the mother's circulation.

Around the rim of the pie-shaped placenta membranes are attached. They are a thin, semi-transparent sheet of tissue which forms a bag-like round dome. Tethered at the end of the umbilical cord, the baby is suspended throughout pregnancy in the amniotic fluid within this rounded dome. Because of this fluid, it is practically impossible for the fetus to sustain injury from the outside.

The production of hormones is another important function of the placenta. Pregnancy places unique demands on the entire maternal organism; its special requirements must be met by adaptations that involve almost every organ system in the body. The uterus, breasts, and volume of blood in the body must increase tremendously. To some extent, the pelvic joints loosen. These and many other adaptations are largely brought about by the action of the placental hormones on the mother's body. The placental hormones are also thought to be important in maintaining pregnancy and, finally, in initiating labor.

Laboratory Tests

Several laboratory tests are routinely prescribed as part of the initial pregnancy assessment. Since most pregnant women will have contact with these tests, it is good that they have an idea of how the tests are taken and what their results are intended to reveal.

BLOOD TESTS

The *hematocrit* is a reading of the percentage of a thin column of centrifuged blood occupied by the red blood cells. The *hemoglobin* is a reading of the concentration in the blood of the oxygen-carrying pigment hemoglobin contained within the red blood cells. Each test can show whether or not anemia is present. One or both of these tests is usually repeated at thirty-six weeks' gestation.

URINE TEST

A test for protein and sugar (glucose) in the urine is done initially and at each subsequent visit. The presence of glucose in the urine is one way to identify women who are at increased risk for diabetes (see p. 167). Urinary glucose in and of itself does not indicate diabetes, a disorder which must be proven with blood glucose tests usually done following a standardized oral dose of glucose. Although as many as 70 percent of women will have glucose in their urine at some time in pregnancy, only 1 percent will also have an abnormal blood glucose pattern. A better way to test for diabetes is to *measure blood glucose* after a test meal of glucose. This is more and more done routinely at twenty-eight to thirty weeks, and earlier if a woman is at increased risk for diabetes.

It is not uncommon for protein to be present in the urine during pregnancy, and, within certain limits, *proteinuria* (protein in the urine) is regarded as normal. The amount of protein is graded from "zero" (none) to "four plus," as determined by a color change in the "dip stick" used for this measurement. During pregnancy a reading of "zero," "trace," or "one plus" is considered to be normal, while "two plus" or greater is considered abnormal, indicating kidney malfunction or preeclampsia (p. 315). An increase in the amount of protein by two gradations (from "zero" to "one plus," "trace" to "two plus," "one plus" to "three plus," or "two plus" to "four plus") is also significant in defining preeclampsia.

An elevated urine protein may be related to body position and does not necessarily indicate kidney malfunction. In the upright position, the pregnant uterus presses on the veins that drain blood from the kidneys, and protein can leak into the urine from the back pressure. This effect is reversed when a woman lies on her side, thereby rolling the uterus off of these veins. Thus, it is essential to collect urine for protein testing with the woman lying on her side to see whether the cause of the proteinuria was simply postural.

SYPHILIS TEST

The serological test for syphilis, or STS, identifies women with this disease so that they can be treated, thereby protecting their fetuses as well (see p. 166). Women who harbor syphilis often do not have symptoms. However, the microorganism that causes this disease can cross the placenta to infect the fetus. Treatment can prevent this dread complication.

BLOOD TYPE, RH FACTOR, AND
TESTS FOR ANTIBODIES
AGAINST RED BLOOD CELLS

Each of these tests identifies women at risk for producing antibodies against the red cells of their own fetus. Such maternal
antibodies can cross the placenta to attach to the fetus's cells,
causing them to be destroyed and removed from the circulation.
The effects on the infant include various degrees of jaundice
(p. 226), anemia, and heart failure.

This destruction of the red cells is most common in the case of
an Rh negative mother with an Rh positive fetus. Usually an Rh
negative mother beginning her first pregnancy is free of antibodies
to Rh positive cells. But during that last trimester of the pregnancy, and especially at the time of birth, small numbers of fetal
red blood cells can cross the placenta and enter the mother's
circulation. The mother's body recognizes the Rh positive cells as
foreign and makes antibodies to eliminate them. These antibodies
cross the placenta in the other direction to enter the fetal circulation, destroying the fetal Rh positive cells within the baby. During the first pregnancy with an Rh positive fetus the quantity of
anti-Rh antibody produced by the mother is too little and/or too
late to destroy enough of the fetus's red cells to cause harm. But,
should the mother carry another Rh postive fetus during a subsequent pregnancy, the additional exposure to Rh positive cells
will restimulate the mother's now sensitized immune system to
turn on antibody production to the Rh factor. The antibody produced can place the fetus in jeopardy. This is why the Rh problem
in a previously unsensitized woman is a problem for the second
or later pregnancies, not for the first one.

This once dreaded problem is now almost entirely preventable
through the use of a special gamma globulin called Rhogam,
which is rich in anti-Rh antibodies. Rhogam is given to the Rh
negative woman in time to attach to and eliminate Rh positive
fetal cells in the maternal circulation before they are able to sen-
sitize the mother. A first dose is usually given at twenty-eight
weeks' gestation and a second larger dose is given within seventy-
two hours of birth. This one–two punch prevents virtually all Rh
negative women from becoming sensitized, and has almost com-

pletely solved the Rh problem. (The twenty-eight-week dose is still under evaluation.)

The sequence of events described above requires that the blood type of the fetus be Rh positive. The fetus of an Rh negative woman can be Rh positive *only* if the father is Rh positive. (The gene for Rh positive is dominant.) If the father is Rh negative, the situation necessary for Rh sensitization cannot exist. If the father is Rh positive, the baby will have a 50 or 100 percent chance of being Rh positive, depending on whether the father is heterozygous or homozygous (p. 118), that is, whether he carries one or two genes for Rh positivity. At present, there is no way of knowing, short of amniocentesis and fetal blood sampling, whether the fetus is Rh positive or negative until birth, when the baby's blood (from the umbilical cord) can be tested directly. Therefore, Rhogam is given at twenty-eight weeks when the father is Rh positive (even though the baby might be Rh negative) and again at birth to mothers whose infants are proven to be Rh positive. For the same reasons Rhogam is given at the time of amniocentesis and abortion, or if the father's identity is uncertain.

If a woman already has antibodies to Rh positive cells, Rhogam will not reverse the process and is of no preventive value. Such women will already have antibodies from sensitization due to inadvertent transfusions of Rh positive blood, or from previous pregnancies with Rh positive fetuses in which Rhogam was not used. (These pregnancies may have involved not only Rh positive babies born at term, but also spontaneous or induced abortions (p. 305) of Rh positive fetuses, or amniocentesis (p. 130) involving an Rh positive fetus. In amniocentesis, the fetal blood vessels in the umbilical cord may be torn, resulting in a leakage of fetal blood into the amniotic fluid and thence into the mother's circulation. The fetus itself is usually not harmed during such accidents.) In all of these situations the potential exists for passage of fetal cells into the mother's circulation, with resulting sensitization.

The quantity as well as the presence of antibodies to fetal red cells can be determined. A rise in antibody titer indicates ongoing sensitization and identifies the fetus that is likely to be significantly affected. Based on this information, additional steps are called for to monitor the baby's well-being and to intervene when appropriate. (See "Treating the Fetus," p. 149.) Antibody levels are routinely checked at twenty-eight and thirty-six weeks and more often as indicated.

Individuals whose blood type is O have naturally occurring antibodies against blood types A and B. (These antibodies do not arise in pregnancy from sensitization of the mother through fetal-maternal transfusion, as is true for an Rh negative mother with an Rh positive fetus.) Nonetheless, anti-A, and, to a lesser degree, anti-B antibodies can also cross the placenta, leading to destruction of fetal red blood cells, which manifests after birth as jaundice and/or anemia. Since the anti-A and anti-B antibodies already existed in the mother prior to pregnancy, there is no way to prevent their formation during pregnancy. The resulting jaundice and/or anemia in the newborn, known as ABO disease, is dealt with as necessary (see p. 266). If ABO disease has occurred in one infant, there is an almost 90 percent chance of recurrence in siblings with the same blood type.

Some women have rare blood types which can be the basis of antibody production against the incompatible cells of their fetuses. Gamma globulin comparable to Rhogam is not available to prevent such sensitization. In this circumstance the best one can do is monitor the antibodies and intervene as indicated (similar to the procedure in the case of an already sensitized Rh negative mother). The antibody screening done routinely at the initial pre-natal visit identifies women with so-called "atypical antibodies" that reflect the rarer blood types.

RUBELLA

The rubella antibody titer identifies the adequacy of the mother's immunity to rubella (German measles), a virus which can cross the placenta to infect the fetus with varying degrees of harm, including deafness, cataracts, mental retardation, and heart defects. (See p. 166 for a discussion of congenital rubella syndrome.) Because of this threat, public health policy in this country aims to immunize all girls prior to their childbearing years. The suspected exposure of a nonimmune woman to someone with probable rubella during pregnancy calls for monitoring the mother's antibody level to see if it rises. A rising level indicates infection in the mother and possibly in the fetus. Infection in the mother raises the question of aborting the pregnancy, since there is at present no treatment for rubella in either the mother or the fetus.

Women who are not immune to rubella are encouraged to receive rubella vaccine following the pregnancy to avoid this problem in future pregnancies. They should receive the vaccine only when using effective birth control, in order to prevent the vaccine virus from infecting the fetus of an unsuspected pregnancy.

URINE CULTURE

The urine culture identifies women with urinary tract infections, whether or not they are causing symptoms (most do not). According to available studies, urinary tract infections are associated with increased risk for the mother and fetus, especially for premature labor and low birth weight. It appears that treatment with antibiotics can prevent these problems. Some women are justifiably critical of the use of antibiotics for the treatment of asymptomatic infection, out of a concern for the possibly harmful effects of these drugs on their fetuses. In point of fact, however, no harmful effects have been reported with the drugs commonly used (see p. 71).

PAP TEST

The Papanicolaou test (Pap test) of the cervix is used to screen for cancer of the cervix. Pregnant women are not more vulnerable to this disorder; testing in pregnancy simply takes advantage of the fact that a pelvic examination is being performed as part of the initial prenatal evaluation. The Pap test is done again during the postpartum examination.

GONORRHEA CULTURE

The gonorrhea culture of the cervix is performed along with the Pap test. Women who harbor this germ, which can infect the baby at birth, should be treated with antibiotics (see also p. 161).

AFP TEST

The alpha fetoprotein (AFP) test is now being offered to more and more women during the second trimester as a way of detecting open neural tube defects and other severe problems. If it is not offered at your hospital, ask where it is done near you. These abnormalities of the baby's brain and spinal cord include *anencephaly* (failure of formation of the brain) and *meningomyelocele*, a defect of the spinal cord and vertebral column (spina bifida). These anomalies can occur in as many as one in 500 pregnancies. Alpha fetoprotein is normally made by the fetus in amounts which increase with gestational age. It is normally secreted into the amniotic fluid and crosses the placenta into the mother's circulation. Fetuses with open neural tube defects secrete increased amounts of AFP into the amniotic fluid. The amount absorbed into the maternal blood also tends to be greater. An elevated level of AFP in the mother's blood can lead to the identification of 90 percent of those fetuses that have open neural tube defects. Ten percent of the affected fetuses are not detected by this test, because the AFP levels in their mothers fall within the normal range and further studies are therefore not done.

The AFP test is performed on a sample of the mother's blood drawn at between fifteen and eighteen weeks' gestation. If levels of AFP are high relative to gestational age, further tests are done.

First, the blood test is repeated after two weeks. If AFP is not elevated this time (as commonly happens), the fetus is considered normal. If the second test is also elevated, an ultrasound (p. 142) examination is performed to date the pregnancy more accurately, to determine the number of fetuses present, to inspect the fetal spine and head for defect, and to determine the normalcy of the placenta. If an error in dating the pregnancy is found (this would account for the increased maternal AFP level on the basis of advanced gestational age), if twins are present (twins produce more AFP than does a single fetus), or if cystic areas are found in the placenta (these could account for direct transfer of AFP), usually no further studies are done, because the elevated maternal AFP can be explained.

If ultrasound testing reveals no explanation for an elevated maternal AFP level (or if a spinal defect is suspected), an amniocentesis is performed to measure the level of AFP in the amniotic fluid. By the standards for AFP measurement now in use, about 98 percent of fetuses with open neural tube defects will be detected through high amniotic fluid AFP level. There is also the risk that about one-half of one percent of normal fetuses will be mistaken for abnormal and aborted, although this can now be prevented (see below).

A normal amniotic fluid AFP in the presence of an elevated maternal blood AFP can mean that the fetus is normal, or that it falls into a "mixed" group of fetuses that do not have neural tube defects but that, on follow-up, demonstrate other problems that bear close watching. These include various congenital abnormalities, intrauterine growth disturbance (p. 301), likelihood of premature birth (p. 318), and miscarriage (p. 305). Thus, the yield of the AFP test goes beyond the important goal of identifying the fetus with an open neural tube defect.

To summarize, a consistently elevated AFP level in the blood of a pregnant woman does not necessarily mean an affected fetus, but does identify those who are *at increased risk* for neural tube and other defects. A normal maternal AFP, it should also be stressed, is no guarantee against having a neural tube defect, since 10 percent of affected fetuses are missed. In this respect, the AFP screening test, valuable as it is, is imperfect. Amniocentesis is much more accurate, but, of course, more risky and costly as well.

A recent refinement in testing the amniotic fluid of fetuses suspected of neural tube defects is the measurement of *acetylcholinesterase*, an enzyme normally produced in nerve tissue. It appears to be more specific than AFP for discriminating between fetuses with neural tube defects and normal fetuses. Thus, using this test almost precludes mistaking a normal baby for one with a defect, and vice versa. Ask about the availability of this test in the screening program used by your health service. There is now some preliminary evidence that a low AFP level can predict chromosomal abnormalities such as those seen in Down syndrome. AFP may prove very valuable in identifying the at-risk fetus in women whose pregnancies are otherwise at low risk, based on maternal age (under 35) and on family history.

It is important to be sure that the AFP test is done at a reliable laboratory. The 1983 approval by the U.S. Food and Drug Administration of commercially manufactured AFP testing kits may lead to the performance of this test by laboratories inexperienced in AFP testing and not tied into a coordinated patient care service. The chances for error would thus be increased.

Check with your doctor about the quality of the lab that will test your blood. Another good source of information on lab quality is the genetics counseling program at a university medical center in your area.

Whether AFP screening is the best way to identify fetuses at risk for neural tube defects is controversial. Advocates of routine ultrasonographic examination make the point that fewer cases of neural tube defects will be overlooked with this latter approach.

OTHER TESTS

Other nonroutine tests are done in pregnancy when particular risks are suspected. As examples, all discussed elsewhere in this book, we mention the testing of couples of Ashkenazic Jewish background for Tay-Sachs disease (p. 120), the checking of high-risk women for hepatitis carrier state (p. 163), and the culturing of women for Group B streptococcus (this last test may become routine). We can look forward to new developments in the years ahead as laboratory science increasingly identifies actual or potential problems in pregnancy. (See "Protecting the Fetus," p. 152.)

Physical Changes

WEIGHT GAIN AND GROWTH OF UTERUS

The most dramatic and obvious physical changes in pregnancy are those related to the woman's weight and shape. A woman with an "average" pregnancy, who is carrying one baby, has an overall pregnancy-related weight gain of twenty-five to thirty pounds. The fetus accounts for 7.5 pounds, the placenta and membranes 1.4 pounds, the amniotic fluid 1.8 pounds, increase in size of the uterus 2.1 pounds, increase in maternal blood 2.8 pounds, breast size .9 pounds, fluid in the skin and other tissues 3.7 pounds, and maternal reserves 7.4 pounds. (See p. 82 for discussion of optimum weight gain.)

During pregnancy the capacity of the uterus increases 500 to 1,000-fold. (See Figure 5, p. 49.) Its existing muscle cells stretch and thicken, and the elastic and fibrous tissue increase markedly, adding to the strength of the uterine wall. Its blood supply also increases.

For the first few weeks of pregnancy, the normal pear shape of the uterus is maintained. As the embryo grows, the uterus becomes more globe-like and, by the third month, spherical. Then it elongates more than it widens to assume an ovoid shape. After the third month the uterus is too large to be confined in the pelvis, so it rises into the abdomen. As it grows further, it comes in contact with the front wall of the abdomen, pushing the intestines to the side, and eventually reaches almost to the level of the liver.

Weight gain in pregnancy begins slowly, only to pick up steadily later on. It is obviously correlated with the size of the uterus. About two pounds are gained during the first third of a pregnancy; the other twenty-five or so pounds are gained during the second and third trimesters with some leveling off during the last few weeks.

The growth in size of the uterus can be represented on a graph in the form of a straight line which is directly proportional to the gestational age. This relationship is true primarily in first pregnancies and less so in late ones. Between the eighteenth and thirtieth weeks of gestation this relationship is particularly good, especially in first pregnancies. A commonly used rule of thumb is that the number of weeks is the same as the number of centimeters of uterine height. The measurement of uterine size is a good indicator of fetal growth.

Any abnormalities in the growth of the uterus need to be explained. As determined over several months, smaller than predicted uterine growth suggests *intrauterine growth disturbance* (p. 301) and/or *oligohydramnios* (p. 300), the relatively uncommon condition of insufficient amniotic fluid, and should prompt further evaluation. Excessive uterine growth also requires an explanation. Its causes include errors in dates (that is, believing the fetus to be younger than it actually is); *hydramnios* (p. 300), the condition of too much amniotic fluid; multiple pregnancies (twins or more); *hydatidiform mole* (p. 299); or simply the presence of a large baby, whether or not this reflects maternal diabetes.

From the beginning of the second trimester the uterus contracts irregularly. Toward the end of the pregnancy, women are able to perceive these contractions and report that they feel like menstrual cramps. They are named for Braxton Hicks, the physician who first described them. During the last two weeks of pregnancy Braxton Hicks contractions can occur as often as every ten to twenty minutes. They may be quite uncomfortable and account for "false labor," uterine contractions that are not accompanied by progressive dilation of the cervix.

At times a distinct bulge can be seen and felt in the midline of the abdomen between the two rectus muscles which run from the lower rib cage to the pubic bone. This bulge results from a spreading apart of these muscles, which deprives the mid-abdominal wall of one of its major supports. The gap between the muscles is now bridged primarily by skin and *fascia*, which stretch relatively easily in response to the enlarging uterus. Treatment of this separation of the recti (also called a *diastasis recti*) is discussed in the section on prenatal exercise (p. 88).

CERVIX AND VAGINA

During pregnancy the cervix softens, enlarges, and turns a purplish-red color. Its mucous glands, along with those of the vagina, markedly increase in number and in the production of secretions. These glandular secretions account for the thick white vaginal discharge so commonly seen. Soon after conception the cervical canal is filled with a clump of thick mucus — the *mucous plug* — which is expelled either during or shortly before labor.

The vaginal wall characteristically becomes duskier, softer, thicker, moister, and more elastic, all in preparation for the stretching it will undergo during delivery. The labia enlarge and turn a dusky blue.

ABDOMEN AND SKIN

In about 50 percent of women, reddish, slightly depressed skin markings, called *striae gravidarum* (the "lines of pregnancy"), are present by the third trimester on the skin of the abdomen and sometimes on the breasts and thighs. After delivery these markings gradually change to silvery colored lines which shrink down as the contracting abdominal and breast skin firm up. They are permanent "scars" or *stretch marks* of the pregnancy. Their cause is unknown. There is no way to either prevent or eliminate them, and creams and ointments sold for this purpose simply do not work.

In many women (primarily those with dark hair and complexion), the skin of the midline of the abdomen becomes pigmented from the pubic bone below it to close to the tip of the breast bone. The dark line curves around the umbilicus. Neither the cause nor the significance of this line is known, and it rapidly disappears after delivery.

It is quite common in pregnancy for brown patches to appear on the face and neck. They are known as *chloasma* or the "mask of pregnancy." They usually disappear after birth.

In Caucasians in particular, tiny red spots commonly appear on the face, the neck, the upper chest, and arms. On inspection with a hand magnifying lens, each red dot is seen to consist of several tiny blood vessels branching from a central feeder. If pressure is gently applied to the center with, for example, the point of a pencil, the entire network is deprived of its blood supply and blanches. These *"spider hemangiomas,"* as they are sometimes called, are believed to be related to increased estrogen levels during pregnancy. Why some women have these spots and others do not is not understood, and their significance is not known. They disappear after birth. Another transient skin change is *redness of the palms*. Like the "spiders," this redness is believed to be related to estrogen levels. Its significance is unknown and the phenomenon disappears after delivery.

BREASTS AND PREPARATION FOR BREAST-FEEDING

Women commonly experience tenderness and tingling of the breasts as one of the earliest signs of pregnancy. The breasts increase in size, often dramatically, and become lumpier as the milk-producing glands enlarge. Delicate blue veins appear beneath the skin and reflect the increased blood flow. The nipples enlarge and darken and are more erectile. Scattered through the *areola* (the dark circle around the nipple) are small bumps which are enlarged sebaceous (oil) glands (also known as the Glands of

Montgomery). After the first few months, if the nipple is squeezed, *colostrum,* the thick yellow fluid which comes in before the milk, will come out.

A woman who plans to breast-feed should buy a nursing brassiere large enough to support her breasts both during the last few months of pregnancy and during nursing. The brassiere can be worn day and night if the breasts are heavy, or if she feels uncomfortable. An easy way to prepare the nipples for the baby's sucking is to leave the flaps on the nursing brassiere open as much as possible, allowing the nipples to rub against the clothing and gradually toughen.

Although not absolutely necessary, some women (especially those with *inverted nipples*) find it useful to toughen the nipples by grasping them gently and firmly between the index finger and thumb and rolling them back and forth while tugging slightly (Figure 6). Rotate the position of the fingers one quarter turn at a time until all areas of the nipple are covered. This exercise can be done two to three times daily during the last trimester. Briskly rubbing the nipple with a terrycloth towel will accomplish similar results. Expressing colostrum during the weeks preceding birth is not necessary and may be harmful in terms of increasing the chances of nipple infection.

In general, it is not necessary to use any ointment on the nipple, although you may want to use some kind of soothing oil. Since soap is drying and best avoided, water alone suffices for cleaning.

An inverted nipple can be identified by pressing the areola between the thumb and the forefinger. A normal nipple, or one that is simply flat, will protrude, while a truly inverted nipple will retract. Inverted nipples are uncommon, since most nipples that appear to be inverted are merely flat and will pose no difficulty for breast-feeding. Inverted nipples are best treated with a nipple shield, which fits over the breast and encourages the nipple to protrude (Figure 7). The rubber tip of the shield should be removed, leaving only the circular plastic base with a hole in the center to be applied over the areola inside a well-fitting brassiere. The constant pressure of the shield will cause the nipple to evert (protrude) through the hole. Since rubber shields pull on the skin and retain moisture, avoid them and use only plastic or glass ones.

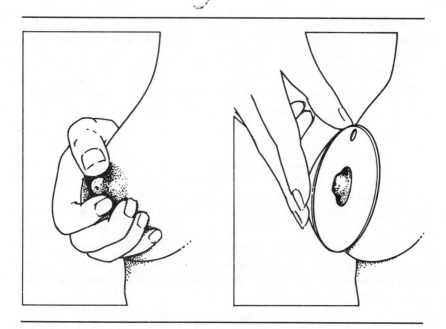

Figure 6. Toughening the nipples   Figure 7. Nipple shield

CIRCULATORY SYSTEM

In pregnancy blood volume increases about 45 percent. The contribution to this increase is not the same for the two major components of the blood — the red cells and the plasma. The red
cells increase about 25 percent, while the plasma expands by 40
percent. The result of this disproportionate increase is that the
hematocrit (the percentage of the blood made up of red blood cells)
actually falls, since there are fewer red cells per unit volume of
blood during pregnancy than when a woman is not pregnant.
Thus, the standards for defining anemia based on the hematocrit
are different in pregnancy from those in the nonpregnant woman.
The predictable fall of the hematocrit begins between the sixth
and eighth week of gestation.

During pregnancy the resting pulse rate increases an average
of ten to fifteen beats per minute. The volume of blood pumped
by the heart increases significantly during the first trimester and

even slightly more during the second and third trimesters. *Heart murmurs,* which reflect increased blood flow within the heart, are common in pregnancy. These "flow" murmurs must be distinguished from those related to heart valve disorders, for which antibiotics against infection of the valves may be indicated during labor.

RESPIRATORY SYSTEM

Most pregnant women are aware of an increased desire to breathe during pregnancy. This breathlessness results from a decrease in the space available for the lungs as the growing uterus presses up on the chest cavity from below. Women report breathing late in pregnancy to be easier when and if the baby sinks into the birth canal before the onset of labor (see discussion on "Lightening," p. 77).

URINARY SYSTEM

During pregnancy more blood flows through the kidneys. Normally, a small amount of protein is passed from the blood to the urine and can be detected in the urine. As the amount of blood filtered increases, the amount of protein passed in the urine also increases, accounting for the common occurrence of measurable protein in the urine of the pregnant woman (see p. 54).

The urine collecting system undergoes dilation during pregnancy. The ureters, the muscular tubes that transport urine from the kidneys to the bladder, are relatively lax and dilated, in part a result of hormonal influences and in part a result of partial blockage of the lower ends of the ureters by pressure from the expanding uterus. The right ureter is subjected to further compression by the enlarging veins from the right ovary (which lie directly over the lower end of the right ureter) and by the weight of the uterus which is usually rotated to the right. The dilation of the ureters and relative stagnation of urine flow through them is believed to be a factor in the increased susceptibility of pregnant women to urinary tract infection (see p. 71).

GUMS AND TEETH

Gums soften and thicken during pregnancy, probably in response to increased blood flow. Even with the mild irritation of tooth-brushing, they may bleed very easily. A lump of thickened gum tissue (called a *pregnancy epulis*) may bleed vigorously when touched. Both the normal swelling of the gums and the pregnancy epulis disappear after delivery.

The increase in the size of the gums predisposes pregnant women to *gingivitis*, a gum inflammation which can weaken the supports of the teeth. For this reason, daily brushing, flossing, and regular dental cleanings and checkups are more important in pregnancy than ever before. Contrary to folk traditions you may have heard, pregnancy creates no more long-term dental problems than those encountered in nonpregnant women, assuming, of course, that you pay careful attention to diet and dental hygiene.

Psychological Issues

For some couples the change in body size and shape raises certain anxieties. For one, it is a public announcement of their sexual relationship, the only one our society has for an essentially private act. Indeed, some couples may have feelings of embarrassment about "publicizing" what they have been "up to."

The major issue, however, has to do with a woman's self-image as it is affected by society's standards of beauty. Our mass media decry obesity and overvalue extreme slimness as the only real kind of beauty. Being pregnant is often confused in the popular mind, and in the minds of the pregnant woman and her partner, with being fat or unattractive. Because of the intense concern of women in our culture with their weight and figure, growing abdominal girth touches a sensitive nerve. A woman may be concerned that she is no longer attractive to her partner, while a man may worry about whether he can still see his partner as beautiful.

Weight gain and increase in size are not the only issues in the sense of decreased attractiveness. Other body changes, such as

large sagging breasts, puffiness of the skin, stretch marks, swelling of the vulva, increased vaginal secretions (p. 64), and tan
spots on the face (p. 64) may also contribute to the sense of loss
of physical appeal.

Birth itself involves "distortions" of the female anatomy (bulging of the vulva, bleeding, stretching of tissues, and so on), which
can be seen as inconsistent with views of woman as a sexually
attractive being. "How could a man ever again want to sleep with
a woman he's seen giving birth?" — a question frequently asked
by men and women alike — reflects this concern. Couples can
use such fears and reservations about pregnancy as opportunities
to acknowledge their concerns to each other, drawing closer
through considering them together.

For all of us, a reconsideration of our arbitrary standards of
beauty and generally fearful views of pregnancy is in order. To
be pregnant is to be beautiful, powerful, and creative, to make a
direct contribution to the continuance of human life on earth.
While we modern urban people may have lost our direct connection with the beauty of pregnancy and birth, we have access to
the ritual, poetry, and art of our own and other cultures to guide
us. (See Appendix D for some suggested readings that can help
re-endow childbirth with awe and respect.) In addition, many of
the suggestions given in the section "Children and Birth" (p. 107)
can help hesitant or fearful grown-ups welcome pregnancy and
birth with the joyful acceptance they deserve.

Common Problems

MORNING SICKNESS

The very common queasiness experienced by women during early
pregnancy may extend beyond the morning hours. The cause of
this loss of appetite, nausea, and sometimes vomiting during the
first trimester is not fully understood. Hormonal influences are

"Common Problems" is adapted from Sagov, Stanley E.; Feinbloom, Richard I.;
Spindel, Peggy; and Brodsky, Archie. *Home Birth: A Practitioner's Guide to Birth Outside
the Hospital.* Rockville, Md.: Aspen Systems Corporation, 1984.

believed to play a major role, although proof for this hypothesis is lacking. There is no evidence to indicate that the decreased food intake associated with morning sickness is harmful to the fetus, a fact that should be reassuring. Measures that have been proven helpful in relieving the symptom, more by experience than by research, are eating small, frequent meals, e.g., six per day; separating the taking of liquids and solids by one-half hour; taking a dry unsalted cracker or biscuit before getting out of bed in the morning; and using the vitamin pyridoxine (B_6), in 40 to 100 mg. doses daily. The drug Bendectin, despite FDA approval and lack of conclusive evidence so far that it was a source of birth defects, was voluntarily withdrawn by the manufacturer because of controversy (including litigation) over fetal damage. Ask your doctor about safe remedies rather than attempting to dose yourself.

Severe nausea and vomiting in early pregnancy suggest hydatidiform mole (see p. 299). Causes unrelated to pregnancy also need to be considered. After eliminating known causes of severe vomiting, the diagnosis of *hyperemesis gravidarum* can be entertained. This serious but fortunately uncommon disorder usually requires hospital care to prevent sometimes life-threatening maternal illness. The cause is unknown, although psychological factors have been suggested and hypnosis as a treatment has been effective in some cases.

FREQUENCY OF URINATION

Among several causes of increased urination in pregnancy, the most important is decreased bladder capacity resulting from compression of the bladder by the growing uterus. Another factor which contributes to increased output of urine is the consumption of extra fluids, whether they are intended to relieve constipation or assist in treating urinary tract infections. Frequency of urination may in itself reflect a urinary tract infection and should be watched. When in doubt, a urine culture should be obtained (see p. 59).

URINARY TRACT INFECTION

Urinary tract infection can be frequent and bothersome during pregnancy. The relative slowing of urine flow from the kidneys to the bladder during pregnancy is a factor that both predisposes a woman to urinary infection and interferes with its treatment. Since urinary infections can lead to premature labor and delivery, they should be recognized and treated promptly.

Infection can involve the lower urinary tract (bladder and urethra), the upper tract (ureters and kidneys), or both. Upper tract involvement is suggested by symptoms like fever, chills, nausea, vomiting, and abdominal or flank pain. The signs of lower tract infection (*cystitis*) are urgency and frequency of urination along with pain or burning (*dysuria*).

A woman can often feel the pain on urination as localized "inside" the bladder or "outside" on the genitalia. Pain "outside" suggests vulvar irritation related to vaginitis in which the inflamed labia burn on contact with urine. In this situation an examination of the vagina should be performed and any vaginal or cervical secretions examined under the microscope. Cultures for *Monilia* (see p. 165), gonorrhea (see p. 161), or herpes virus (see p. 164) may be appropriate, and treatment is specific to the identified cause.

Symptoms and signs of upper urinary tract infection present a more serious problem. Since treatment with antibiotics by mouth customarily recommended for those with lower tract infection may not be adequate, the woman may need to enter the hospital for intravenous treatment.

The evaluation of urinary complaints also requires a urinalysis and urine culture. The presence of the typical symptoms described above and the presence of white blood cells along with bacteria in the urine argue for the diagnosis of urinary tract infection and the initiation of treatment.

The cornerstone of treatment for urinary tract infection is antibiotics. In addition to completing a full course of antibiotics (that is, not stopping treatment at the first sign of improvement), a woman should

1. increase fluid intake to at least six to eight glasses per day
2. acidify the urine with cranberry juice and/or two grams of vitamin C per day
3. urinate every two hours if possible, never holding in urine
4. urinate after sexual intercourse

5. after a bowel movement, clean herself with toilet paper, moving from front to back only
6. return for urine cultures three days (usually) after beginning treatment and again seven days (usually) after finishing the course of medication.

Note that neither increased fluid intake nor acidification alone has been proven to have made a difference in treating urinary tract infections, so it is better to follow the doctor's prescription and not rely on these measures alone for relief.

Single-dose antibiotic therapy for urinary infections is becoming increasingly popular for nonpregnant women but has not been tested during pregnancy for effectiveness or possible ill effects on the fetus.

PAIN IN THE LOWER ABDOMEN AND THIGHS

Pain in the lower corners of the abdomen, especially on the right, is common in pregnancy and is believed to result from stretching the uterine supports, especially the round ligaments. This pain, sometimes known as "round ligament syndrome," usually occurs at about twenty weeks and must be distinguished from pain arising from appendicitis, cholecystitis (inflammation of the gall-bladder), kidney stones, urinary tract infection, hernia, and other disorders. Pain that arises in the supporting structures of the uterus is related to position. It usually improves when a woman lies down, especially when she is turned to the painful side. It is not normally associated with fever, loss of appetite, nausea, vomiting, diarrhea, or urinary symptoms. On physical examination, there are no signs of tenderness from pressure over the painful area, a response that is more common in the other conditions mentioned. Most women are able to accept stretching pain as long as they know it does not represent a threat to themselves or their babies.

Numbness or pain in the upper front thigh is believed to result from pressure of the uterus on the nerve that loops toward the thigh over the brim of the pelvic bone. The resulting discomfort is similar to that experienced in the arm as a "funny bone" (also related to pressure on a nerve, in this case the ulnar nerve, which can be subjected to pressure as it crosses the inner part of the elbow). Numbness in the thigh can often be relieved by lying on the back or side, especially on the numb or painful side. This symptom does not usually persist after delivery.

Recognizing *appendicitis in pregnancy* can be tricky. First, loss of appetite, nausea, and vomiting are common in pregnancy, as they are in appendicitis. Second, the enlarging uterus displaces the appendix upward out of its usual position in the right lower part of the abdomen, confusing diagnosis. Third, some degree of white blood cell elevation is common in pregnancy, as it is in appendicitis. A high index of suspicion is required if this diagnosis is to be made early, prior to rupture of the appendix. The safest approach is to err on the side of early operation if appendicitis is suspected. (See also p. 299, "Gallstones.")

Pain in the pelvic girdle late in pregnancy and the feeling of "coming apart" is related to the loosening of the ligaments (sinews), which allows the pelvis to "give" during passage of the baby through the birth canal. It is a counterpart to the molding of the baby's head, made possible by its open cranial sutures (see p. 188). There is no specific treatment other than avoiding activities that can intensify the strain. Very rarely, the pubic bones actually do separate and require strapping.

PAIN IN THE UPPER ABDOMEN

Pain in the upper abdomen deserves a call to the doctor. There are several causes that need to be sorted out, including gallstones (see p. 299), heartburn (see p. 77), and preeclampsia (see p. 315).

FIBROIDS

Fibroids are benign (non-cancerous) tumors of the uterus that become more common as a woman gets older. If present, fibroids commonly increase in size during pregnancy. Although they usually cause no symptoms at all, they can occasionally be mildly annoying or become sources of confusion. For example, a fibroid may suddenly increase in size and cause pain, usually because of bleeding inside the tumor. This difficulty resolves with time alone.

Fibroids may give the false impression that the uterus is larger than it is, thereby leading to a mistake in estimating gestational age. A fibroid that impinges on the cavity of the uterus may be a factor in causing miscarriage (see p. 305). Fibroids that are strategically situated in the lower portion of the uterus may obstruct labor, but this is very rare. Generally, fibroids shrink markedly after delivery. During pregnancy they can be visualized with ultrasound (see p. 142) and differentiated from other masses in the pelvis.

HAIR LOSS

Hair loss, which results from premature cessation of growth in the hair follicles, is one of the more distressing developments of pregnancy and the postpartum period. Fortunately, even though it may persist up to one year, it is temporary. This conversion of the follicles from the growing (anagen) to the resting (telogen) state resembles normal hair follicle behavior at the end of a normal growth cycle. Birth is one of the causes of a widespread premature conversion of hair follicles from the growing to resting state. Diffuse hair shedding during combing may occur within three months of delivery. Should there be any question of this diagnosis, the shedding phenomenon can be duplicated by stroking the hair with a gentle tugging action. The hairs removed can be examined under a microscope, and, in the usual case, all of the follicles will be seen to be in a resting stage.

CONSTIPATION

Less frequent, harder stools that are difficult to pass are common in pregnancy. Factors that contribute to constipation include slowed intestinal muscle action (peristalsis), which results in increased resorption of water and drying of the stool, and pressure on the rectum by the baby. Hemorrhoids may intensify and in turn be intensified by constipation. Constipation may be corrected through increased fluid intake, increased fiber intake (raw fruit and vegetables, bran, psyllium seeds, and so on), and exercise. A gentle laxative like Milk of Magnesia may be used as necessary. Stool softeners like *dioctyl sodium sulfosuccinate* are also useful.

VARICOSE VEINS AND HEMORRHOIDS

Varicose veins of the legs, rectum (hemorrhoids), and vulva are common in pregnancy, particularly in women whose relatives also have or had them, suggesting a familial susceptibility. The pressure of the pregnant uterus on the large vein (vena cava), which drains blood back from the pelvis and legs, is a major factor in varicose veins in pregnancy.

Although some women complain of aching, the significance of *varicosities of the legs* is primarily cosmetic. They can be relieved by elevating the legs (getting off one's feet and keeping the legs outstretched in a horizontal position) and using elastic ("support") stockings.

Hemorrhoids can bleed and form painful fissures. They are aided by measures to prevent constipation (see above), sitz baths in warm water, lubricating creams, suppositories (witch hazel, Anusol), and avoidance of straining to eliminate (having what the English call an "unhurried motion"). Thrombosis (clotting) of an external hemorrhoid can be very painful. The clot can be removed under local anesthesia. If bleeding persists, or if the hemorrhoids cannot be pushed back into the rectum or become infected, hemorrhoidectomy (removal of the hemorrhoid) may be required, although this is very unusual in pregnancy. Tying off the hemorrhoids or injecting them with fluids that dissolve them are measures that are preferred over surgery.

Varicosities of the vulva may be contained and relieved with counter-pressure by a foam rubber pad held in place by a belt.

While women can look forward to relief from varicosities of all kinds following delivery, hemorrhoids may be more pronounced in labor and the immediate postpartum period. Because of the improvement normally expected after delivery, surgical correction of varicosities should be delayed if at all possible until the necessity for it becomes clear.

DIZZINESS ("LIGHT-HEADEDNESS")

Light-headedness, especially when one quickly stands up after lying down for a while, is common during pregnancy. It is in part related to delay in the return of blood to the heart because of the pressure the uterus exerts on the veins of the abdomen. When insufficient blood is pumped through and out of the heart, dizziness results. Getting up slowly will prevent it.

LEG CRAMPS

The calf cramps many pregnant women have are thought to be related to excessive phosphate intake or excessive milk consumption. A nutritional treatment (which has never been critically evaluated by a controlled study) suggests changing the source of calcium by decreasing milk consumption; instead, taking one gram of calcium lactate per day or increasing the intake of green vegetables, egg whites, or other sources of dietary calcium. Physical measures to relieve a cramp include massage and stretching maneuvers to bend the foot upward at the ankle. When lying in bed, avoid pointing toes straight down or under.

LIGHTENING

"Lightening" is the sensation women experience as the baby drops during the latter weeks of pregnancy. It is not the same as engagement, which refers to the passage of the head (or buttocks in a breech) to the level of the ischial spines (see Figure 3, p. 45). Lightening is accompanied by less shortness of breath, decreased pressure in the stomach, the feeling that the baby has "dropped," increased pressure in the pelvis, increased backache, more frequent urination and constipation, the initial appearance or aggravation of hemorrhoids and varicose veins of the legs, swelling of the legs and feet, and possibly more difficulty in walking. Nothing much can be done about lightening except to recognize what it represents and to bear with its associated discomforts.

HEARTBURN

Heartburn is a common problem in pregnancy and represents the backing up (reflux) of the acid contents of the stomach into the esophagus (food tube). Factors that contribute to heartburn are compression of the abdominal organs, including the stomach, by the enlarging uterus; the elevation of the stomach above the uterus; alterations in the action of the "valve" between the esophagus and the stomach; and loss of muscle tone in the esophagus and stomach.

Heartburn can be largely prevented by eating smaller quantities at a time and by avoiding lying down immediately after eating and, if these measures fail, by using antacids at the end of each meal. If the symptoms come on when a woman lies down, the head of the bed can be raised 6 to 8 inches by blocks beneath the bedposts to allow gravity to work against reflux.

EDEMA

Edema, or fluid accumulation in the tissues, is indicated by visible swelling and is normal in pregnancy. Edema of the feet and legs is very common in the third trimester and is related to increased venous pressure in the lower extremities due to pressure of the uterus on the large collecting vein in the abdomen (vena cava). In this respect, it is similar to the swelling of the forearm and hand that occurs when a tourniquet is tightly wound around the upper arm. When the uterus, in effect, acts as a tourniquet on the large veins that drain blood from the legs, backup of blood and the passage of protein-rich fluid from the vessels into the skin result. When one sits or stands in an upright position, the force of gravity also contributes to this phenomenon. Many women report that late in the day their rings are tight and their faces are puffy, showing fluid retention in the upper part of the body. In traditional medical teaching, generalized edema (affecting other than the legs or feet) was considered an indication of increased risk for *preeclampsia* (see p. 315), and salt restriction and diuretics were prescribed. Recent research has shown that neither edema nor weight gain alone during the third trimester are predictive of increased fetal problems.

If edema is annoying, raising the legs will help. The best treatment is to lie down for one hour, one to two times per day, on the left (to tip the uterus off the vena cava). Elastic hose will help reduce the swelling, but some women find these stockings too uncomfortable to be worth the bother.

VAGINITIS

Vaginal infection is common in pregnancy, and *Monilia* (a yeast) is the major culprit. Symptoms of infection are itching, burning, and a vaginal discharge. When the vagina is examined with a speculum, the yeast infection resembles white cottage cheese. Microscopic study of a sample reveals the characteristic branching structure of the budding yeast. Several effective anti-fungal creams are used for treatment.

Monilia in the vagina can be picked up by the baby during birth and infect its mouth, producing the condition known as *thrush* (p. 165). One reason given for performing a vaginal examination late in pregnancy is to detect a monilia infection which may not have bothered the woman enough for her to seek help.

FATIGUE

Even in the most physically fit women, fatigue is a very common feature of pregnancy. While psychological factors may play a role, it is likely that weariness has a still unexplained physical basis. Pregnant women tire easily and need to rest and sleep. There is no "treatment" for this problem other than rest, especially rest that is not associated with guilt over being tired or shirking responsibilities. For most women, fatigue is more common during some periods of the pregnancy than others. While some women are tired throughout the pregnancy, others actually report having more energy than ever and experience no fatigue at all.

EMOTIONAL SENSITIVITY

In pregnancy, most women report wide mood swings and unusual sensitivity to the surrounding emotional climate. For no apparent reason, or with only the slightest provocation, an otherwise well-composed woman will burst into tears. This heightened reactivity is no reason to avoid stress or to ask to be treated "with kid gloves." Knowing that emotionality is a normal feature of pregnancy should promote understanding by the woman and those around her that outbursts and withdrawals are normal and need not be taken too seriously.

Later Prenatal Visits

Later in pregnancy the prenatal visits continue the themes established earlier — taking the initial history and performing the first physical examination and laboratory tests. These later visits offer expectant couples an opportunity to take a more active role. Women can weigh themselves, for example, and can check their own urine for protein and glucose. Couples can learn to listen to the fetal heart with the fetoscope and feel the various parts of the baby through the abdominal wall. They can keep their own records, plotting the growth of the uterus and the increase in weight over the course of the pregnancy. A woman can pay particular attention to the first feeling of fetal movement, recording the time and date (p. 132), and she can note changes, especially decreases, in fetal movement toward the end of pregnancy. Decreases should be reported promptly to the nurse or doctor. Couples can come to the prenatal visits together, and can even include their children (see p. 107 on preparing children for childbirth). They can share their observations, fears, and pleasures with the doctor or midwife. And they can insist on fully understanding what is happening and what choices they have throughout the pregnancy.

It is just as possible for couples to lay claim to their own prenatal care as to labor and delivery. The doctor, or midwife, then becomes a ready resource and a support, not a director of the birth. Obviously you need to decide if you want this kind of relationship and will accept the responsibilities it implies. Indeed, many people elect a less active role for themselves.

In uncomplicated pregnancies, visits after the initial examination are traditionally scheduled every four weeks until the thirty-second week, then at thirty-four and thirty-six weeks, and weekly thereafter until birth.

The content of the visits depends on the age of the pregnancy. Weighing in (p. 82), checking the urine for protein and glucose (p. 54), and measuring blood pressure (p. 47) are standard procedures. Maneuvers having to do with the uterus and baby obviously depend upon the size of the uterus, which by the second trimester (twelfth week) has risen out of the pelvis into the abdomen. The height of the uterus is determined by stretching the measuring tape from the pubic bone up and over the uterus to its top (see Figure 5, p. 49).

By sixteen to twenty weeks it is possible to hear the baby's heartbeat with a stethoscope. Since the fetal heart sound transmits best through the baby's back, the location of the loudest sounds suggests the position of the back. In normal head-down (vertex) presentations, the heart tones are generally heard below the mother's umbilicus, while in breech presentations they are heard best above it. Hearing the tones best in front of the abdomen suggests that the back is pointing forward. When the baby's back is pointed toward the mother's back (also called posterior position), the heart tones are apt to be loudest in the mother's flanks.

It is possible for a woman's partner (or another interested observer) to hear the heartbeat by placing an ear directly on the abdomen. An extra long tubing attached to the stethoscope will allow the woman herself to listen. An inexpensive conical wooden listening device, shaped like a megaphone, may also be used. With an ear against its tip, the examiner places its base directly on the abdomen. These devices are available through the International Childbirth Educational Association and its affiliates (see Appendix B) and often from doctors or midwives themselves.

By normal adult standards, the normal heartbeat of the fetus is very fast, ranging from 120 to 150 beats per minute. It is sometimes faint and hard to hear, but this does not mean there is anything wrong. Since the sounds have to travel a variable distance through amniotic fluid, the wall of the uterus, and the fat, muscle, and skin of the mother's abdominal wall, it is easy for them to be muted.

With doppler ultrasound (p. 142), the fetal heartbeat can be detected as early as the twelfth week. The sounds heard through the ultrasound monitor are not those of the heartbeat itself but are machine-made sounds triggered by the movements of the heart, as sensed by the machine from echoes of sound waves pulsed to the heart. The visual detection of fetal heart movement by ultrasound imaging can occur as early as the sixth or seventh week of fetal life.

During the last trimester an examiner can feel the baby itself through the abdominal and uterine walls. The firm pressure required to outline the baby will not harm it. The woman can assist the examiner by letting her abdominal muscles relax completely; blowing air out and holding that position helps relax the abdomen. By feeling the location of the baby's head and buttocks, the examiner can tell whether the fetus is head-down (vertex), breech, or transverse (lying horizontally) (see p. 184). Each of these positions has implications for subsequent care in pregnancy. Palpation is also a reasonably good guide to the number of fetuses present, whether one or more (see p. 331 on twins). The baby's size can be estimated as average, large, or small, a judgment useful in predicting the fit of the baby to the birth canal.

It is also possible to tell whether or not the head has descended into the pelvis. The examiner does this by feeling whether his or her fingers can get around the bottom of the head and come toward each other. If the fingers surround the head, it is still high in the abdomen; if not, it has descended into the pelvis. By differentiating between the lumpy hands and feet and the smooth back, and by the location of the heartbeat, the examiner can conclude whether the back is facing left, right, front, or back. Good abdominal relaxation makes this examination easier. Here too the pregnant woman can contribute to a successful examination.

Although it need not be done routinely, there are several reasons for repeating the vaginal speculum examination during the last two to three weeks of pregnancy. These reasons include rechecking the measurements of the pelvis (p. 44), determining the "ripeness" of the cervix (its position, dilation, and effacement) (p. 184), and detecting monilial or other vaginal infection (p. 159).

Nutrition and Weight Gain

A good diet is a cornerstone of a healthy pregnancy, necessary to create a healthy baby and to sustain the mother through pregnancy, delivery, and nursing. Nutritional needs of women increase during pregnancy and nursing because the woman is really "eating for two." The best available advice on diet can be summarized as follows:

1. Follow the Daily Food Guide on pp. 84–86, using the foods on the Checklist of Recommended Foods on p. 83. Vegetarians can refer to the Vegetarian Diet Guide on p. 87.

Table 1. Checklist of Recommended Foods

Foods	Daily Amount
Milk*	1 qt.
Eggs	1–2
Meat	2 servings (liver often)
Cheese*	1–2 servings, additional snacks
Grains (whole, enriched)*	4–5 slices or servings
Legumes, nuts	1–2 servings a week
Green and yellow fruits, vegetables	1–2 servings
Citrus fruit	2
Additional vitamin C foods	Frequently, as desired
Other vegetables and fruits	1–2 servings
Butter, fortified margarine	2 tbsp. (or as needed)
Other foods: grains, fruits, vegetables, other proteins	As needed for energy and added vitamins and minerals

*During lactation, add 1 additional serving daily of dairy products and 1 additional serving of grains. Drink 2 to 3 qts. of fluid daily and continue the 30–60 milligram daily supplement of elemental iron. (See also p. 258 for a discussion of vitamins during breast-feeding.)

Source: Reprinted from the *Handbook of Maternal and Infant Nutrition* by Sue Rodwell Williams, copyright © 1976 by SRW Productions, Inc., Berkeley, California.

2. Gain a minimum of twenty-five pounds, unless you are overweight to start.
3. Gain weight gradually and steadily.
4. Supplement your diet each day with iron (30–60 milligrams elemental iron) and folic acid (400–800 micrograms).
5. Do not attempt to lose weight during pregnancy.
6. Do not restrict your intake of salt (sodium); use iodized salt.
7. Do not take diuretics (fluid pills).

Optimal weight gain during pregnancy has long been a subject of debate, still not fully resolved. Limiting weight gain through restricting food and salt and using diuretics, as recommended by many doctors in the 1950s and 1960s, has been proven conclusively as harmful to both mothers and babies. These practices have been discarded, giving way to a much more liberal attitude toward diet in pregnancy.

Gaining less than fifteen pounds in thirty-six weeks correlates with lighter and shorter babies who are at increased risk for

Table 2. Daily Food Guide for Pregnancy

Foods	Daily Amount	Suggested Uses
I Protein-rich foods		
A. *Primary protein*		
1. Dairy products; milk, cheese	1 qt. milk or 4 oz. brick cheese or 4 cups cottage cheese	Beverage; in cooking; or milk-based desserts such as ice milk custards, puddings, cream soups; cheese in cooked dishes; salads; or snacks throughout the day
2. Eggs	2	Breakfast use; chopped or sliced hard eggs, in salads; custards; whole boiled eggs; deviled eggs, plain or in sandwiches
3. Meat	2 servings (total of 6–8 oz.); liver frequently, 1–2 times a week	
B. *Supplementary protein*		
1. *Grains*		
Enriched or whole grains, breads, cereals, crackers	4 to 5 slices or servings whole grain or enriched	Bread, plain or toast; sandwiches; with meals, snacks, cereal (breakfast or snack); cooked grain as meal accompaniment (corn, rice, pasta, grits, hominy, hot breads; corn bread, biscuits, etc.)
2. *Legumes, seeds* Nuts Dried beans and peas Lentils	Occasional servings as meat or grain substitute, or in combination with meat or grains	Cooked and served alone or in combination with grains, cheese, or meat; soups; salads; nuts as snacks or in salads; peanut butter sandwich

Table 2. *Continued*

Foods	Daily Amount	Suggested Uses
II Mineral-rich foods		
A. *Calcium-rich*		
1. Dairy products	1 qt. milk (as above)	As above
2. Grains, whole or enriched	4–5 slices or servings (as above)	As above
3. Green leafy vegetables	1 serving	Cooked or raw in salads
B. *Iron-rich*		
1. Organ meats, especially liver	1–2 servings per week (as above)	
2. Grains, enriched	4–5 slices or servings (as above)	Breakfast cereals; main dish; combination with meats, cheese, egg, cooked grain foods, enriched breads
3. Egg yolk	2	As above
4. Green, leafy vegetables (as above) or dried fruits	1–2 servings	Cooked or stewed; raw in salads; snacks
C. *Iodine-rich*		
1. Iodized salt (sea salt does not contain iodine)	Daily in cooking and on foods	On salads; in cooked food dishes; according to taste
2. Seafood	1–2 servings a week	Main dish; salad; sandwiches
III Vitamin-rich foods*		
A. *Vitamin A*		
1. Animal sources		
Butter fat (whole milk, cream, butter)	2 tbsp. butter	In cooking or on foods
Liver	1–2 servings (as above)	Main dish
Egg yolk	2 (as above)	As above

*B vitamins are well represented in grains, as is vitamin E. Milk is vitamin D enriched.

Table 2. Daily Food Guide for Pregnancy, *continued*

Foods	Daily Uses	Suggested Uses
2. Plant sources		
Dark green or deep yellow vegetables or fruits	1–2 servings (as above)	Cooked dishes; salads; snacks
Fortified margarine	2 tbsp.	In cooking and on foods
B. *Vitamin C*		
1. Fruits		
Citrus	1 or 2 servings	Snacks; salads; juices
Other fruits: papayas, strawberries, melons	Occasional serving to substitute for 1 citrus portion	Salads; snacks
2. Vegetables		
Broccoli, potatoes, tomato, cabbage, green or chili peppers	1 serving as a substitute for 1 citrus occasionally	Cooked snacks; salads; juices
C. *Folic acid*		
Liver, dark green vegetables, dried beans, lentils, nuts (peanuts, walnuts, filberts)	1 serving	Cooked as main dish or soups; snacks; in salads

Source: Reprinted from the *Handbook of Maternal and Infant Nutrition* by Sue Rodwell Williams, copyright © 1976 by SRW Productions, Inc., Berkeley, California.

survival and well-being. The more underweight a woman is at the start of her pregnancy, the greater the negative effect. Thus, how much weight to gain depends in part on how much a woman weighs initially.

For the average woman, the recommended goal is twenty-five to thirty-five pounds. Practically speaking, this means eating to the point of satisfaction from a well-balanced diet without too many high-calorie foods. If a woman is underweight, she should make every effort to achieve this goal. If a woman is of average weight, or especially if she is overweight, her target should be twenty-five or even twenty pounds.

Table 3. Vegetarian Diet Guide

1. Follow Daily Food Guide for Pregnancy.
2. If neither milk nor eggs are included, take a supplement of 4 micrograms vitamin B_{12} daily. The need for partial supplementation must be determined if goat and soy milk are consumed.
3. Select a variety of plant foods to obtain "complete" proteins. Examples of complementary food combinations which satisfy the body's protein requirements are: rice and beans; rice, wheat, and soy; rice and sesame seeds; rice and milk (rice pudding); wheat and milk (lasagne, macaroni and cheese); wheat and beans (baked beans and brown bread); cornmeal and beans (chili and tacos); and peanuts and milk (peanut butter sandwich and milk).
4. If milk is not included, supplement diet with 1200 mg. calcium and 400 IU vitamin D daily. Partial supplementation will be necessary if less than four servings of milk and milk products are consumed.
5. Use iodized salt.

When considering the possible consequences of gaining more than twenty-five pounds, an increasingly frequent occurrence, the evidence is not clear. For one thing, babies of such women tend to be larger, and may be more difficult to deliver vaginally. A study from Australia, where many inductions of labor were performed (possibly affecting some of the results), showed that pregnant women who weighed over 200 pounds had an increased incidence of hypertension and increased blood sugar and were more than twice as likely to have large infants weighing more than nine pounds. Their labors were likely to be longer, their babies were more likely to have depressed respiration and circulation at birth, and they were more likely to bleed and develop fever following delivery.

Diabetes is more likely to accompany obesity. Some authorities recommend that women who are shorter than 5 feet 5 inches and weigh more than 150 pounds, or taller than 5 feet 5 inches and weigh over 180 pounds, should have a glucose tolerance test to detect diabetes (see p. 167).

Most complications associated with large weight gain are effectively dealt with in modern obstetrical units. However, even if an obese pregnant woman does well during a delivery, she still has to deal with the problem of being overweight after her baby is born, a situation best avoided. On the other hand, being obese and newly pregnant is not the time for losing weight, or even for maintaining the same weight. Even obese women should gain weight, being careful to stay on the low side of the guidelines discussed. How weight gain is distributed through pregnancy is discussed on p. 62.

The question of fluoride supplementation of the pregnant woman's diet is currently receiving attention. There is some evidence that in utero exposure of the fetus to fluoride may reduce the occurrence of cavities in the baby after birth. More studies are needed.

The nutrition guidelines in Tables 1–3 are for the average well-nourished woman who has completed her own physical growth. Adaptations of these guidelines are required for adolescents or for women with special nutritional needs. If you find it difficult to include all the recommended foods, discuss this with your physician. Vitamin supplements are commonly recommended. See also books on nutrition listed in Appendix D.

Exercise and Relaxation

The purpose of prenatal exercise is to improve muscle strength and stretch tight muscles, since muscles can become tensed and shortened as well as weak. Many common discomforts of pregnancy — backache, varicose veins, cramps, constipation, breathlessness, heartburn, postural discomfort — can be prevented or alleviated through a balanced program of exercise and relaxation. Also, a woman in good physical condition can withstand the rigors of a long or hard labor, as well as the exertion needed to care for the new baby, better than a woman who is "out of shape." But conditioning takes time to develop, and the sooner a pregnant woman begins exercising, the better.

"Exercise and Relaxation" was written with the help of Elizabeth Noble, R.P.T., Director of the Maternal and Child Health Center, Cambridge, Mass. It is adapted from Sagov, Stanley E.; Feinbloom, Richard I.; Spindel, Peggy; and Brodsky, Archie. *Home Birth: A Practitioner's Guide to Birth Outside the Hospital.* Rockville, Md.: Aspen Systems Corporation, 1984.

Prenatal exercise has, in addition to strengthening and stretching muscles, several benefits that enhance the birth experience. Women who exercise regularly throughout pregnancy gain heightened body awareness, confidence in their physiological functions, and knowledge of how these functions are affected by the changes brought on by pregnancy. A woman who learns to "bond with her body" can better trust her uterus and can "let go" during labor. After delivery the physical fitness skills learned during pregnancy should be continued as an integral part of a healthy lifestyle.

CHOOSING AN EXERCISE CLASS

Although there is an increasing number of registered physical therapists in the obstetrics and gynecology section of the American Physical Therapy Association who are trained to support women in achieving good musculo-skeletal care during the childbearing years, in many communities there are none at all. Often, there are no exercise classes available, either. While health spas, fitness centers, yoga classes, and dance schools may offer prenatal or postpartum exercises, they vary greatly in quality. Unfortunately, many of these programs neglect the muscles of the pelvic floor and reflect little understanding of physiological changes in pregnancy. However, as long as a woman "listens" to her body and does nothing that causes strain or pain, she can usually reap the benefits and avoid the hazards of any reasonably good exercise program. With increasing consumer demand, more quality exercise classes should become available, so women should make their preferences known. If no classes are available, the exercises that follow should be of help.

Exercise classes for pregnant women and their partners may be held separately, or together with general childbirth education classes. In either case, they provide contact with other childbearing couples. In addition to gaining group support, couples in these classes can learn about other resources early in their pregnancies, when they may still be open to making choices and changes in their birth arrangements.

The ideal exercise class has a small number of participants who can be individually evaluated and supervised, rather than trained as a group to "follow the leader." The instructor explains the rationale for each position and movement, along with the role of the muscles in pregnancy, birth, and afterward. The best classes present the exercises in a broad context, coordinated with breathing, relaxation, and psychological preparation for birth.

GENERAL PRINCIPLES

A suggested exercise session lasts for one and one-half hours and consists of roughly equal proportions of calisthenics, stretching, and relaxation, and then some aerobic dance or free movement. The exercises need be done only a few times each to be beneficial, but they must be performed slowly and properly. Jerking and straining should be avoided. The goal is increased body awareness and comfort, not training for the Olympics. Quivering muscles, or sudden jerky movements designed to bypass a weak muscle group, indicate that the exercise is too difficult and should be modified. Once an exercise is mastered and is no longer taxing, it is preferable to make it more challenging, to change the position of the body instead of merely doing it more times.

Breathing must be coordinated at all times with exercise movement. A good rule of thumb is "exhale during exertion." Straining while holding the breath in the throat has an undesirable effect on the circulation in pregnant women. It prevents blood from returning to the heart; hence, less blood is pumped from the heart to the lungs to receive oxygen and then into the body. Since less oxygenated blood can reach the mother's tissues, including the placenta, less oxygen is available to the fetus. Exhaling during exertion not only prevents such negative cardiovascular effects but also avoids strain on the pelvic floor and abdominal muscles. In fact, exhaling during exertion actually improves the return of blood to the heart, as positive pressure is maintained in the abdomen relative to that in the chest. This principle is even more important during the pushing stage of labor.

A woman should become conscious of the natural expansion of the chest and abdomen during inspiration and their contraction during exhalation. Strange as it may seem, not everyone breathes in the most physiological way. Some people contract their diaphragms during expiration, rather than the reverse, and need this pointed out to them. Tightening the abdominal muscles on exhalation is a good preliminary exercise that demonstrates the role of these muscles in forced exhalation.

While exercise programs can be expanded beyond the basic principles and movements discussed here, it is important that the muscles most stressed in childbearing — the abdominals and the pelvic floor — are emphasized. In the average woman, both are weak. While more visible, the abdominal muscles are rarely exercised in our society. People mostly sit or stand and rarely squat. During pregnancy, these muscles must meet the demands of increased weight gain, changes in the center of gravity, support for the enlarging uterus, and the stresses of labor.

ABDOMINAL AND BACK MUSCLE EXERCISE

The abdominal wall muscles provide much of the support for the spine and thus play an important role in the health of the back. Together with the *gluteus maximus* muscles — the major muscles of the buttocks — the abdominals control the angle of the pelvis in relation to the spine, an angle that affects stability and stress of the lower back. The common view is that backache is due to weakness of the back muscles, but, if anything, back muscles are usually too tight rather than too weak. Thus, it is the abdominals that need emphasis in back-strengthening programs.

The abdominal muscles run from the lower edge of the ribs in front and on the sides to the rim of the pelvis. You can feel them if you lie on your back, knees bent, and raise your head and shoulders. Move your hand around over your abdomen from your ribs to your pelvis and feel the firmness over the entire area. The abdominals actually consist of several sets of muscles:

- The *recti,* which run straight down the center of the abdomen and consist of two bundles about 3 inches in width, one on each side of the midline, separated by about an inch and a half of tough fibrous tissue.
- The *obliques,* two layers of muscles which run diagonally, one on each side of the body, from the ribs to the pelvis, crisscrossing in opposite directions.
- The *transversus,* which is wrapped around horizontally.

During pregnancy the growing uterus stretches the abdominals from a straight line between the pelvis and ribs to an expanding curve between upper and lower attachments. Therefore, it makes sense to begin abdominal strengthening exercises as early as possible.

The *curl-up* is the basic exercise for the abdominal muscles. A curl-up is a modified sit-up done to a maximum of 45 degrees off the surface, with knees bent and the back of the waist flat on the surface used. To exercise all of the abdominal muscles adequately, curl-ups should be done in both straight and diagonal directions.

For a diagonal curl-up, twist one shoulder toward the opposite knee, alternating shoulders on successive curl-ups. Then lie flat after each curl-up. Repeat the exercise up to fifty times, but stop if it starts to hurt.

The work of the abdominals can be progressively increased by changing the position of the arms, as follows:

1. In the initial position, the arms reach toward the knees, assisting the movement (60 percent abdominal muscle effort).
2. The next progression involves a neutral position with arms folded across the chest (80 percent effort).
3. Finally, the arms are clasped behind the head to increase the leverage (100 percent effort).

Each woman begins at the appropriate level and progresses at her own pace. The physical changes that occur in later pregnancy make the more advanced curl-ups (nos. 2 and 3) too difficult.

It is important to check continuously throughout pregnancy for any separation of the rectus muscles. Such a separation is called a *diastasis recti.* This condition is usually observed after the fifth month but may be seen earlier in women who have it left over from a previous pregnancy. Many women notice the bulging in the midline of the abdominal wall as they get up off the floor after exercising or as they get out of bed or bath. Although diastasis recti is quite painless, it may lead to postural backache because of abdominal wall weakness.

To check for diastasis, lie on your back with knees bent. Raise your head (which activates the recti muscles), allowing your hands to reach toward your knees. You or your exercise coach can then check the width of the soft area between the tense rectus muscle bundles. If three or more fingers can be placed between the contracted recti muscles, diastasis recti is present. With this degree of separation, the bulging can usually be seen as well as felt.

A woman with a diastasis should avoid strenuous work with the abdominal muscles, as in double leg-raising exercises on the back (described below) and heavy lifting or straining. She should also be careful, when arising from the floor or bed, first to roll on one side and then push herself into a sitting position with her arms. It is usually not possible to "close the gap" of a diastasis during pregnancy because of the progressive and continuous stretching of the abdominal wall by the enlarging uterus. However, couples can be reassured that it is possible to bring these muscles parallel again with exercises after the birth. The presence of the diastasis recti requires that a woman's exercise program be modified only with regard to curl-ups; the other essential exercises are still suitable. If the recti muscles cannot stay parallel when the head only is raised, it makes no sense to increase the load by bringing the shoulders off the floor as well. Furthermore, the oblique abdominal muscles contract when the shoulders curl forward. Because they attach to the sheath covering the recti muscles, their action will lead to further strain and muscle imbalance, which can increase the diastasis.

To perform the modified curl-up, the woman with a diastasis recti lies on her back with knees bent, hands crossed at the area of the gap to support the muscles. She performs head raises only, taking care that the abdominal wall is pulled *in* as the breath is exhaled, in order not to increase the bulging. She should do the exercises frequently for a short time, following the same program postpartum. After a few days postpartum, the woman can evaluate the gap while performing a modified curl-up without hand support. If the diastasis persists, she should continue the modified curl-ups. If the muscles are parallel at the midline, she can slowly increase the curling up by bringing the shoulders off the floor, but only little by little. Too rapid progression can lead to reseparation.

Note the difference between curl-ups and the kind of sit-ups that unfortunately remain popular in many fitness classes. These involve lying flat on the floor with legs extended and straight and literally sitting up. With curl-ups, the knees are bent to stabilize the lower back (lumbar spine). The movement is limited to the abdominals and is never more than about 45 degrees forward flexion off the surface. A sit-up, which involves a 90-degree movement, is performed primarily by the iliopsoas muscles which run from the front of the upper thighbones to the lower spine and pelvis. When these muscles contract they pull the spine and the thighs closer together and hollow the spine, just the effect one wants to avoid. The abdominal muscles, on the other hand, roll the body forward as the ribs approach the pelvis without straining the lower spine. The abdominals do most of the work in the early part of a sit-up. The second half of a sit-up hardly exercises the abdominals at all and may actually conceal weak abdominal muscles, as is typically seen in a person who jerks quickly through the first phase of the movement. Keeping the legs straight and, as is sometimes done in sit-ups, fixing the feet with external force (as, for example, by tucking them under a horizontal bar) further encourages use of the iliopsoas muscles and thus increases lumbar strain. *Avoid these sit-ups at all times.* Conversely, bending the knees minimizes use of the iliopsoas and brings the abdominals into full play.

PELVIC TILTING AND BRIDGING

Pelvic tilting movements focus on the lower part of the abdominal wall and can be done in many positions. The action is to decrease the curve of the lower spine (the small of the back) by squeezing the buttocks tightly together and pulling in the abdominal muscles, thus rotating the pelvis to the back (posteriorly). Like curl-ups, pelvic tilting exercises can be done progressively in three different positions while lying on the back:

1. The knees are bent, the feet flat on the floor.
2. With heels sliding along the floor, the legs are extended as far as possible while the pelvic tilt is maintained. With practice and increasing muscle strength and control, the tilt will be possible with the legs fully extended.
3. Finally, with the tilt maintained, the legs and thighs are raised to a vertical position with the knees bent. Then the thighs and legs are simultaneously and gradually lowered and extended to the point where the pelvic tilt is maximally stressed yet

maintained. Usually this point occurs before the thighs are lowered 45 degrees. Many women will be able to lower the legs as far as 45 degrees only after considerable practice.

There is a difference between leg lowering as described and double-leg raising with which it is often confused. In double-leg raising, the woman lies on her back with her legs outstretched and perfectly straight. She then lifts the stiffened legs together from the surface upward. The problem with double-leg raising is that, during the most difficult initial part of the movement the pelvic tilt is out of control because the iliopsoas muscles, not the abdominals, do the work. As with a seesaw, the short lever of the pelvis rises before the longer lever of the outstretched legs. This exercise has caused much discomfort and aggravation of back pain. The point is not simply to raise or lower the legs. You must be able to maintain the pelvic tilt and protect the lumbar spine while the muscles that do so are stressed and thereby strengthened. *Double-leg raising should be eliminated from any exercise program, especially one designed for pregnant women.*

Basic pelvic tilting can also be done in sitting, standing, kneeling, side-lying, and the "hands and knees" positions. In the "hands and knees" position, the work of maintaining the pelvic tilt can be increased by extending first one arm, then one leg, then opposite arms and legs together. In this exercise, the abdominal and gluteal muscles hold the pelvis in line with the spine against gravity and the leverage of the different arm and leg positions. This position is a good one for the woman with a diastasis who cannot do curl-ups. The "hands and knees" position also relieves backache and pressure from the uterus, and the progressive exercises mentioned improve balance and strengthen the arms and shoulders.

Bridging is the act of raising the buttocks off the floor. It helps improve the pelvic tilt by strengthening the gluteal muscles, which pull the pelvis down in conjunction with the upward movement of the abdominals. Bridging is done lying on the back, preferably with the legs straight at the knees and heels resting on a low table or footstool. The buttocks are lifted from the floor to form a bridge with the body. If this exercise is done with the knees bent, the woman must be taught to feel the difference between gluteal contractions and the leverage exerted by the hamstrings which run from below the knee to the "sitting bones" of the pelvis. The closer the heels are to the buttocks, the more substitution occurs with the hamstrings, which can extend the hips when the knees are bent. The value of the exercise is thus reduced. Bridging should be done with the pelvis tilted back and buttocks held as firm as possible.

PELVIC FLOOR EXERCISES

The importance of the muscular and fascial layers that comprise the pelvic floor cannot be overemphasized. The pubococcygeus muscle, which connects the coccyx ("tail bone" or tip of spine) and the pubic bone at its center, is of particular importance. In our culture, the muscles of the pelvic floor are typically not exercised, and many women are actually unaware of them. The three main functions of the pelvic floor are

1. to support the pelvic abdominal organs and the increasing weight of the uterus in pregnancy
2. to provide sphincter control of the anus and urethra
3. to enhance sexual response, since healthy muscles grip and massage the penis during intercourse, and vigorously contract during orgasm to provide increased satisfaction to the woman and her partner.

Structural changes in the pelvic floor — such as laxity and various degrees of sagging of the uterus, bladder, or rectum — are common in Western society, particularly in women who have borne children. Functional changes, such as urinary stress incontinence (the leakage of urine with coughing, sneezing, or straining), lack of sexual satisfaction for either partner, and incomplete emptying of bowels or bladder are also very common. Most women believe that stress incontinence and "falling-out feelings" are normal side effects of pregnancy, since many of their friends suffer the same symptoms. Smoking, obesity, and chronic chest conditions, which all cause increases in intra-abdominal pressure, all aggravate pelvic floor dysfunction. Although softening of tissues related to hormonal and blood supply changes and some descent of the pelvic floor are normal during pregnancy, adequate urinary control can and should be maintained throughout.

Healthy pelvic floor muscles can help facilitate the safe progress of the baby during the second stage of labor. Well-exercised muscles with enhanced blood supply can better withstand stretching before their fibers become underoxygenated or stretched to the point of tearing. Dr. Arnold Kegel, a pioneer in studying the pelvic floor, has shown that during the crowning of the baby's head a strong pubococcygeus muscle remains protected by the pubic bones, while a thin, fibrous unexercised muscle is dragged down with the fetal head and is more likely to be injured.

There are problems in learning to contract the pubococcygeus, because the action is internal and out of sight, and no bones are involved in the movement. Without some sort of feedback, women may not be able to judge their efforts and may become discouraged. Many are unaware of the pubococcygeus and cannot contract it in isolation from other muscle groups. Typically, they tighten other muscles, such as the buttocks or inner thighs, when asked to tighten this muscle. Since vaginal examinations are not performed during exercise or childbirth classes, it is essential for the woman, perhaps with the aid of illustrations, to locate this muscle herself.

A woman can become aware of this muscle while urinating. Simply stop in midstream several times, paying attention to the muscles you use to accomplish this action. If you cannot do this, you will need to reeducate this muscle. The muscle can also be identified and evaluated during the initial prenatal physical examination (see p. 42). Stretching the vagina with one finger, toward the rectum, while at the same time trying to squeeze, is another way for a woman to identify this muscle.

Once a woman has identified the correct muscle, she tightens the anal and vaginal sphincters, thereby also raising the perineum (the region between the lower end of the vagina and the anus). Useful analogies to this action are the rising of an elevator and the drawing up of a hammer. The muscular contractions must be done slowly enough to recruit as many muscle fibers as possible. Contract/relax exercises (also known as "Kegeling") can be done at any time. In particular, the pelvic floor should be braced during such exertions as sneezing, coughing, or lifting.

Research has shown that the pelvic floor readily fatigues with exercise and that the average woman cannot make more than a few contractions of consistent strength. Similarly, holding a contraction for more than ten seconds is beyond the ability of most unconditioned women. The exercise should be done "little and often," just three or four contractions in a series followed by a rest interval. A total of about fifty should be done daily before, during, and after pregnancy. Sexual intercourse is another opportunity for the practice and improvement of pelvic floor control and has the advantage of feedback from one's partner. Pelvic floor exercises can be done anywhere, anytime. They should become as routine as brushing the teeth. In societies where squatting is common, the pelvic floor is always strong, because it must support all the internal organs in this position.

STRETCHING EXERCISES

For health and well-being, flexibility is as important as strength. The muscle groups that are tight are typically the hamstrings, calf muscles, inner thighs, hip flexors (muscles that bend the thigh toward the abdomen), and back extensors (muscles that straighten out the back as in a position of "attention"). Yoga exercises are particularly suited to enhance flexibility. (See Appendix D.)

The hamstrings can be stretched by standing with one leg elevated on a chair or table, by "long sitting" (knees straight, legs outstretched), and by lying on the back and lifting *one* straight leg at a time. (Avoid double-leg raising, as described previously.) In pregnancy these positions are preferable to bending forward, which usually involves rounding of the back and excessive pressure on the spinal discs (the structures that act as shock absorbers between the individual vertebrae). In stretching the hamstrings it is important to bend at the hips rather than bend the spine.

Calf-stretching can be done kneeling on one knee ("half-kneeling") with the foot of the forward leg firmly applied to the floor as weight is shifted progressively forward, or by standing with one foot in front of the other; the knee of the rear leg is kept straight with its foot planted squarely on the floor as the forward knee is bent. The hip flexors can also be stretched in the half-kneeling position, one foot in front of the other, with the weight transferred on to the forward foot until a pull is felt in the opposite groin. The back can be stretched in a "tailor-sitting" position (knees bent, ankles crossed, and legs allowed to fall apart). The trunk is then bent forward to bring the head toward the floor. A modified back stretch can also be done in a "half-tailor-sitting" position (one leg outstretched and one leg bent) with trunk bent to either side. Sitting with the legs extended ("long sit") and holding the back at a 90-degree angle (without leaning on the arms) is an excellent stretch and postural exercise. The back can also be buttressed against a wall and the exercise made more difficult by raising the arms while keeping contact with the wall. Squatting with the heels flat is another recommended sitting position. It is also useful for the second stage of labor.

The adductor muscles (which pull the thighs inward toward each other, and which contract when something is held between the knees) can be stretched in a sitting position with the soles of the feet together, allowing the force of gravity to let the thighs fall apart. The "pelvic clock" exercise of Moshe Feldenkrais can also be done in this position and increases pelvic awareness. This maneuver involves sitting on the floor with the soles of the feet together and rotating the pelvis, first clockwise, then counterclockwise.

AEROBIC EXERCISE

Aerobic exercise refers to activities that increase the pumping of blood by the heart and the movement of air in and out of the lungs. They include any combination of walking, skipping, jumping, jogging, and dancing, using backward, forward, and sideways directions for variety. Other aerobic activities include running, cross-country skiing, brisk walking, and non-weight-bearing activities, such as swimming and cycling. "Warming up" and "cooling down," including stretching before and after the aerobic exercise, is particularly important and too often overlooked. Women should continue with their favorite sports, listening to their bodies for signs about what to do and how much, as the pregnancy progresses.

Many expectant mothers take yoga classes or belly dancing, both of which, if done in moderation and with commonsense precautions, can be helpful in physical preparation and body awareness. Dance and free movement help pregnant women to feel graceful and creative and to express their changing feelings during the course of pregnancy.

POSSIBLE RISKS OF STRENUOUS EXERCISE

Although regular exercise and peak physical fitness are almost a cult in contemporary American life, evidence is accumulating that seems to suggest pregnancy may not be the best time to train for the Boston Marathon. For example, researchers at the University of Vermont, who studied a small sample of pregnant women, reported in 1982 that endurance exercise of moderate intensity (jogging) appeared to influence pregnancy outcomes adversely if continued beyond twenty-eight weeks. The jogging women surveyed experienced an increased incidence of premature labor and premature rupture of the membranes. (See "Labor," p. 183.) Their babies were, on an average, one and one-quarter pounds underweight. Interestingly, only a few of the women who jogged regularly at the beginning of pregnancy continued to jog to term. Most stopped or cut down on their own because of tiring, musculo-skeletal pain, or other causes.

The immediate effects of jogging on the fetus were studied at Lackland Air Force Base in Texas in 1982. A significant rise in the fetal heart rate was shown during maternal jogging over a distance of one and one-half miles. (Similar effects have been observed when a mother's body temperature increases from fever or a hot tub.) The heart rate returned to its pre-jogging baseline after an average of twenty two minutes after jogging. Nonstress tests (see p. 141) performed before and immediately after jogging were normal, and no harmful effects were observed on the babies after birth. No matter how inconclusive, this study tends to highlight the fact that exercise does have an effect on the fetus in ways we do not fully understand. We cannot assume that these effects are positive, and it should sound a note of caution to exercise enthusiasts. Pending further studies, our advice is to avoid highly strenuous exercise during pregnancy and to stick to the exercises recommended above.

RELAXATION

An ability to relax is a great asset during birth when a couple learns that actively "being" is as important as "doing." For one thing, relaxation during labor allows the mother to conserve energy. Giving birth involves using the forces that push the baby down the birth canal as well as reducing the forces that oppose this descent. "Tightening up" increases resistance; "opening up" decreases it. In a sense a pregnant woman "allows" her baby to be born simply by yielding to the forces pushing the baby out. As in sexual intercourse a woman must allow birth, like orgasm, to happen. "Letting go" through increased body awareness is a skill that can be learned and practiced.

Sheila Kitzinger, noted British childbirth educator, has described the "puppet-string" approach to relaxation. In a comfortable lying position, with plenty of pillows, one imagines various parts of the body attached to strings operated by a puppeteer who can pull the strings straight up or at various angles. The strings can be pulled in any combination: for example, the right shoulder and the right index finger can move together, or the right shoulder can move with the left knee, and so forth. A woman can "activate" the strings herself. Or she can ask her partner to do so and to let her know which ones are being "pulled." After a string has been pulled, so to speak, allow the muscle to relax and the body part involved to sink back into a resting state.

The method of relaxation based on Stanislavsky acting techniques uses imagined activities. In a relaxed sitting or lying position, with eyes closed, get in touch with various parts of your body by imagining them engaged in activities such as chewing sticky taffy, walking barefoot on sharp pebbles at the beach, kneading dough, following an airplane overhead to the distant horizon, tasting a sour lemon, and so forth. Do not actually make these movements. Do them only in your mind. With each imagined action, notice which muscles become tense then relax them. Notice the difference between the muscles when they are tense and when they are relaxed.

In point of fact, relaxation cannot be taught. People learn how to relax *indirectly*. Although childbirth classes often include training for "conscious release," this is not physiologically possible because the receptors that control muscle tension do not reach a conscious level in the brain. Thus, the most effective "body work" approach to relaxing a muscle is to tighten the muscle that has the opposite action. Examples of this approach include "dragging down" the shoulders for tense and elevated shoulder muscles, "fingers long" to extend overactive finger flexors, and "dragging down" the jaw for tension in the face. As you do these exercises, note which muscles are tense and which are relaxed. In actively dropping your jaw you can become aware of relaxation in the muscles of your cheeks. Further details of this approach, which works key areas of tension in the body, can be found listed in Appendix D under "Exercise and Comfort."

Mental relaxation must be encouraged along with physical release. These skills form the basis of yoga and meditation programs. Focusing on the natural rhythms of breathing will quiet the mind and facilitate general body relaxation. Controlling the breath, on the other hand, requires effort, diminishes body awareness, and impairs relaxation. Couples can experience these phenomena for themselves by alternating control of the breath with simple observation of it. (See next section.)

The passive state of mental relaxation can also be obtained by repeating the number "one" or any other word silently to oneself, or by using a mantra as in meditation. The procedure, adapted from Herbert Benson's *Relaxation Response*, is as follows:

1. In a quiet environment, on an empty stomach, sit in a comfortable position and close your eyes.
2. Deeply relax all your muscles from your feet to your face — feet, calves, thighs, lower torso, chest, shoulders, neck, head. If this is hard, try tensing each part and then relaxing it.
3. Breathe normally through your nose. Pay attention to your breathing, and to the air moving through your nose. Do not over-breathe. As you breathe out, say "one" or another word silently to yourself.
4. When other thoughts and feelings come into your mind, just let them be. Do not push them away; but do not pay attention to them either. Be indifferent; adopt an "oh, well" attitude.
5. Continue this practice for ten to twenty minutes. Open your eyes to check the time, but do not use an alarm. Then sit quietly for several minutes, at first with your eyes closed and later with eyes open. Repeat once or twice a day.

The relaxation exercises described above do not work well after a heavy meal.

Breathing Techniques

As part of a changing emphasis in childbirth education, many practitioners are reevaluating traditional psychoprophylactic breathing techniques, such as the Lamaze and Bradley methods. This rethinking recognizes that each woman's labor is different and that women, left to themselves, and encouraged to experiment, are capable of finding the laboring position and breathing patterns that work best for them.

Increasingly, controlled patterns of breathing are coming to be considered excessively rigid. This view in no way minimizes their historical importance as a reaction to the totally anesthetized childbirth advocated in the earlier part of this century, nor does it deny the continuing appeal of these methods to women who would consciously "control" pain in childbirth. All too often, however, there is a preoccupation with fixed patterns of breathing that do not respond to the needs of the body. Breathing normally, and in response to internal cues, may be more beneficial. The purposeful alteration of breathing, with the goal of pain control through distraction, consumes energy and limits feeling and awareness. Women who have had a normal childbirth often report that it is lack of energy, rather than unbearable pain, that is their most common difficulty during labor. This lack of energy may result from anxiety and tension and may be exacerbated rather than helped by the distraction techniques and breathing interventions taught by childbirth educators and in books.

On the one hand, shallow chest breathing does not permit sufficient fresh air to enter or sufficient stale air to leave the lungs for adequate gas exchange to occur in the tiny air sacs. On the other, if this type of breathing becomes rapid, dizziness and light-headedness (symptoms of hyperventilation) may occur as the woman accelerates her breathing to "stay on top" of her intensifying contractions. Hyperventilation also leads to chemical changes in the blood that decrease its oxygen-carrying capacity and change its acidity. Both effects are transmitted to the fetus, impairing its well-being.

Although women are commonly taught to achieve an inverse relationship between the speed and depth of respiration (the slower, the deeper; the faster, the more shallow), research has shown that, as the breathing rate increases, women in labor do not naturally decrease the amount of air they breathe in and out with each breath. The rate of breathing is the only practical guide for couples. It should not exceed twenty breaths per minute, and ideally should be much less — to stay within optimum limits.

Traditionally women have been told after full cervical dilatation to "breathe in, hold your breath, and push!" — an effort that results in a forced expulsive effort against a closed glottis. This approach is now being reconsidered. The closed pressure system formed after even five seconds of forced breath retention leads to increased pressure inside the chest, reduced return of blood to the heart and lungs, and a reduction of the amount of blood pumped by the heart to the body, including the placenta. Thus, blood flow to the fetus can be impaired. This breath-holding also results in reflex tensing of the pelvic floor, which increases resistance to the baby's descent, just the opposite of what is desired.

A more beneficial approach, according to our recent thinking, is to push with lips pursed to let air out gently during bearing down; in effect, "breathing the baby out."

The birthing center at Pithiviers, France, directed by world-famous obstetrician Dr. Michel Odent, works on the assumption that women know how to give birth if left alone. No formal prenatal instruction is given. Instead, women come to the center about a week before their due date and learn what they need from other women who have just given birth. They spend much time singing around a piano, and, when they go into labor, they are free to assume any comfortable position, sometimes even laboring in a warm pool. The reported results are excellent.

It is the personal opinion of the authors that childbirth education, including breathing techniques, should be kept simple, with emphasis on natural events and normal physiology. If childbirth can be seen as an involuntary process, one that need only be allowed to unfold rather than controlled, the laboring woman will be better able to direct her energy within instead of dissipating it by attempting to put her mind outside her body. Each woman should strive to find her own way, fully realizing that women already know how to have babies if left to themselves.

Sex during Pregnancy

Sexual feelings fluctuate widely during pregnancy and may at times disappear altogether. For example, in early pregnancy a woman with morning sickness is likely to be little interested in intercourse with her partner. Several studies indicate a drop-off in desire in the third trimester as well. At other times, some women report a strongly increased desire for sex.

The dramatic changes in a woman's body, which are part of a normal pregnancy, run counter to some of our society's most cherished ideals of beauty. This may affect her own attitude and her partner's. In our culture, which tends not to acknowledge and respect the sexuality of the pregnant woman, these changes are thought of as anything but sexual "turn-ons." Couples would do well to concentrate on their own positive feelings toward each other, deemphasizing any stereotyped negative feelings toward sexuality, pregnancy, and sex and pregnancy.

Intercourse is perfectly permissible during pregnancy, although adjustments in position and penetration will have to be made to accommodate the woman's expanding abdomen. The man-on-top ("missionary") position is too uncomfortable for late pregnancy; a side-by-side or sitting position is preferable. After the baby has "dropped," rear-entry positions are particularly comfortable, with the woman kneeling, crouching, or lying. Lots of pillows can be used for support, to keep weight off the abdomen. Pillows and more pillows are to intercourse during pregnancy what a rocking chair is to breast-feeding.

Sheila Kitzinger has pointed out that, in advanced pregnancy, it may be better for the man to ejaculate just before a woman comes to orgasm. An erect penis in a heavily pregnant woman may prevent her from making the kind of pelvic movements that will bring on orgasm. In pregnancy, as at other times, the man should be aware that the clitoris can be overstimulated. A good general rule is that, once the clitoris has become swollen, the man should ask the woman when she wants penetration.

During pregnancy, many couples prefer forms other than intercourse to express sexual feeling: cuddling, showering together, massage, caresses that lead to orgasm. The sensitivity of a woman's breasts and nipples often markedly increases in pregnancy.

They can become the focus of erotic arousal but need to be handled gently.

Pregnancy offers couples the opportunity to explore what for them may be new forms of expression, which can be continued after the birth. The topic of lovemaking during pregnancy has inspired much recent interest and a number of books (see Appendix D).

Labor and delivery can be a profoundly sexual experience. Childbirth educator Niles Newton has identified eleven points of comparison between undisturbed childbirth and sexual excitement:

1. Change in breathing.
2. Tendency to make vocal noises.
3. Facial expression reminiscent of an athlete under great strain.
4. Rhythmic contraction of the upper segment of the uterus.
5. Loosening of the mucous plug from the opening of the cervix.
6. Periodic abdominal muscle contraction.
7. Use of a position in which the woman's legs are drawn up and spread apart.
8. A tendency to become uninhibited.
9. Unusual muscular strength.
10. A tendency to be unaware of the world, and a sudden return to alert awareness after climax (orgasm) or birth.
11. A feeling of joy and well-being following the orgasm or birth.

Obviously the degree to which a couple can experience labor and delivery in such sexual terms will depend on the setting in which birth takes place and how it is conducted. Relaxation and a sense of security are important factors.

Common fears related to intercourse and orgasm during pregnancy relate to the precipitation of an abortion (miscarriage), the initiation of premature labor, and harming the baby in some way. In point of fact, there is no evidence that intercourse causes miscarriages, although it may be the "last straw" in a pregnancy that was going to abort anyway (see p. 305). While there is some evidence that intercourse and orgasm may trigger the onset of labor, research findings are divided on this question. The general consensus is that intercourse is not considered to be a factor in premature labor, and there is no evidence that intercourse harms babies.

In a few situations intercourse during late pregnancy is best avoided. These include:

1. after the breaking of the amniotic sac which allows communication between the uterus and vagina, increasing the chances of infection of both the uterus and fetus (see p. 320 on "Premature Rupture of the Membranes")
2. premature labor controlled with drugs (see p. 319)
3. placenta praevia (p. 312)
4. impaired well-being of the fetus, as, for example, in the infant suspected of having intrauterine growth disturbance (see p. 301).

Even in such situations there is no conclusive evidence that intercourse is harmful, even though the connection seems logical. There is, however, no evidence that it is safe. If the outcome for the baby is poor and the couple has had intercourse, they may wrongly blame themselves for adding to the problem.

It is possible for all expectant couples to achieve better sexual response. Many women who were unable to or could only occasionally reach orgasm before pregnancy report becoming orgasmic thereafter or for the first time achieving multiple orgasms. Such women also report that they feel more pride in their bodies, have more confidence in themselves as sexual beings, and are more sensual and sensitive; that sex is more relaxed, less pressured, more playful; and that trust and intimacy with their partners have increased.

Pregnancy presents a couple with the opportunity for close, honest communication about sex and other issues. Every "problem" mentioned is also an opportunity for enhanced growth and understanding in the magnificent context of creating a new life.

Children and Birth

As more people now strive to make birth a family-centered experience — whether in the hospital, birthing room, or home —

"Children and Birth" is adapted from *Children at Birth* with the kind permission of Jenifer M. Fleming.

they are becoming more concerned with preparing the older child for the birth and arrival of the new sibling. Since many couples find this complex and difficult, we have gathered some specific advice from parents who have successfully done so. Some of them chose to include an older child during labor and delivery; many did not. In any case, thoughtful preparation of the child is always important.

Most parents we consulted emphasized three points:

1. The key to success in preparation is the attitude of the parents — if the child is to be unafraid, enthusiastic, and excited about the birth, the parents must be that way, too.
2. The bonding that takes place after birth should occur not only between the parents and the newborn but between the older child and the new sibling as well.
3. Children participate to the degree that they are comfortable. They should not be forced or pressured to do more than they want to do; and they should be permitted as much, or as little, involvement as they can deal with comfortably.

CONVEYING THE UNFOLDING OF PREGNANCY AND THE TIME OF BIRTH

Tell your child about the expected baby as soon as you are sure you are pregnant. Many parents say their child needed the nine months as much as they did. Even though time is a difficult concept for small children, they seem able to grasp it if it is linked to their own experiences. Some parents used the signs of the seasons to convey the passage of time. If, for example, the baby is due in June, a parent may say something like this: "First there will be fall when the leaves turn pretty colors, then winter when the trees are bare and it is cold and snow is on the ground, then Christmas when we have a tree and presents and Santa Claus comes, then spring when the crocuses peep above the ground and the willows turn yellow. Then the forsythia, then the lilacs, . . . and . . . then 'our baby' will be born when the roses bloom." Of course, when you try to convey time this way, the age of the child will be a factor; but several parents found this pattern understandable to children who, some as young as two and one-half years, quickly memorized the sequence.

One mother said she used pictures showing the month-by-month changes in the uterus and fetus to make up a "time-line" for the wall of her daughter's room. Many physicians and midwives give out illustrated booklets that lend themselves to this use; you can buy special sets of posters, or copy the illustrations in available picture books on pregnancy (see Appendix D). Each month the child adds the appropriate picture to the time-line. This way the child gets a clear sense of the progression of the pregnancy, not only from the pictures, but from her mother's increasing girth as well. Another idea for a time-line is a series of photographs of the mother, taken throughout the pregnancy, showing her changing body configuration. These can be taken by the child.

Inspired by Advent calendars used at Christmastime, several parents successfully used this idea to prepare their children for the birth of a sibling, particularly children from two to eight years old. (We suggest making the calendar run at least two weeks beyond the due date in case the baby arrives late.) Simply make a calendar of those days around the due date with little movable doors or windows for each day. Behind each window put a surprise, preferably one related to new life — a baby animal toy, a robin's egg, or seeds.

FAMILY CELEBRATIONS AND ACTIVITIES

Family celebrations — holidays, birthdays, festivals — can be used to convey passage of time before the birth of the baby. For some families Christmas with its focus on baby Jesus is the time to celebrate babies in general, first anticipating their coming, then marveling at their birth, and finally rejoicing in their arrival. Repeating Christmas traditions that center around the birth of a baby (like the calendar above, candles around the house, familiar music) helps young children get into the spirit of the event and makes it real for them. The same can be achieved with birthday customs already followed in the home — cake and candles, presents, singing, and retelling family members' past birthdays. Children of all ages, and adults too, love to hear the story of their birth. Retelling and rehearing their own beginnings helps them prepare for another birth in the family.

109

Many parents found that focusing attention on a pet helps a child understand that another being needs care and space of its own, that it has a will of its own, and that its needs must be respected. Try to visit younger animals in pet shops or in children's zoos or in the homes of friends, to provide children experience with new lives. With pets children can learn, over a period of time, that care is an ongoing, never-ending circle of love and attention. Of course, contact with human babies is even more to the point.

The idea of a nickname may come from the child when he or she refers to the baby during the pregnancy. If not, parents can suggest one, realizing it may not catch on. One eighteen-month-old had a beloved doll she called "Wolly." When she saw her mother's belly growing, she transferred the name to the baby inside. She would talk to "Wolly" and would pat her mother's stomach. The nickname, thank goodness, did not persist after little sister Katy's birth, but it did help the toddler relate to her new sibling during the pregnancy.

Often it helps to talk about the baby as a special gift to the whole family, to be cared for by everyone, just as the older child was a special gift to the parents. The older child may then more easily appreciate the idea of preparing gifts for the baby when it is born (receiving blankets, quilts, decorated T-shirts, mobiles, special songs). Children can participate in making these gifts. Families who enjoy music together can make up or choose a particular song to welcome the new baby. They can rehearse it together before the baby comes so that it becomes a kind of theme song in the home for many days, or even years, after the birth.

PREPARING THE CHILD
FOR THE PHYSICAL ASPECTS OF PREGNANCY,
LABOR, AND BIRTH

Include older children in visits to the midwife or doctor. Explain that these people will be at the birth to help you have the baby. As the pregnancy advances, children usually enjoy listening to the heartbeat and feeling the baby kick and move around. Whether or not you have your child present at examinations and any other special procedures depends on your inclination, the preferences of the caregiver, and the age and developmental level of the child. If at all possible include the child in visits to the hospital to meet the doctor or look through the nursery window. If you plan a home birth, explain to an older child that you might have to go to the hospital for help.

You may wish to bring your child to certain birth classes. Classes that use slides and pictures of births are particularly useful, depending on the interests and age of the child. Birth movies can give a child who will be attending a home birth a real sense of the sights and sounds of birth. Let children meet the midwife, nurse, or labor coach. Ask class leaders and check libraries and bookstores for well-illustrated, informative books on birth and the arrival of a new baby (see Appendix D).

Visit friends who have new babies, especially those whose pregnancies you and the child may have followed. Contact with babies gives children a better idea of what newborns are like — how tiny and helpless they are, and how gentle and loving one must be with them. Children ofter enjoy watching and imitating the exercises a woman does in preparation for birth, including relaxation and breathing techniques.

Depending on the age and temperament of the child, you may want to discuss any fears he or she has about the birth; for example, what happens if the baby does not breathe right away. Be alert to the child's questions and observations and aware of the deeper meanings they convey. You will be amazed at the distorted ideas children at any age can have, and will have a good chance to correct them then.

INCLUDING THE CHILD AT THE ACTUAL BIRTH

If you plan to have children present at the actual birth, you need extra preparation. Talk about the hard work of pushing the baby out, and the concentration and patience it takes to have a baby. Show them the different positions you might assume, and let them hear the kinds of sounds you might make. One family played a tape of their first labor to their older child, to accustom him to the sounds. These were, of course, the sounds of his own birth.

Don't forget to talk about blood — the "good blood" — and its purpose and value when the baby is born. Talk about how a baby

looks when it first comes out of the mother and about the importance of the placenta to the baby.

Give the child a task. Four- and five-year-olds can be a great
help giving you ice chips and orange juice, for example. Older
children can help time contractions, wipe your face with a washcloth, hold your hand, breathe along with you, hold a flashlight,
and so forth. Although most children want to feel useful at a
birth, expect that they may also need to be out of the room for a
while. Make them as aware as possible before the birth that they
can choose to be there or not, and that whatever they choose is
all right with you.

Identify a caretaker for the child. Unless children are well into
their teens, most will need someone at the birth who is there
solely for them. Explain to the child that, while Mommy is having
the baby, she won't be able to give him or her the same kind of
attention and care that she normally does. For this reason, this
other familiar and loved person will be there. The person you
choose for the caretaker role should be comfortable with birth in
the setting you have chosen. Consider having this person join
you at several childbirth classes, and show him or her the books
about pregnancy and birth that you particularly like. Also, this
"birth-sitter" should understand that, if the child does not want
to be present at the birth, that is fine and his or her job is to stay
with the child.

Define the father's role at the birth. Will he be the caretaker for
the child and leave others to support the mother, or does he want
to be primarily involved with her? The child should know in
advance what role the father will play.

A surprise bag of goodies, suitable to the age of the child, will
keep most children interested and peaceful during what might be
a long labor. For young children, these small treats are often the
most exciting part. Their interest will alternate between the items
in the bag with aspects of the labor and delivery.

Parents who have included their older children in a birth say
that it does not eliminate sibling rivalry. But, as one parent reported, "there seems to be a deep reservoir of trust and love from
the older to the younger," because, as her three-year-old said to
the baby, "I saw you born."

If given the chance, children have a wonderful capacity to
respond to an experience in ways that adults find difficult to

imagine. One four-year-old was overheard describing to a friend of the same age the recent birth at which she was present: "Mommy cried, the baby cried, and there was blood, but it was good blood."

AFTER THE BIRTH

After the birth when you first see your older child — at the hospital or at home — reassure him or her that you are fine, physically tired, perhaps, but in no way hurt or unrecognizable. You are still the same person, still the child's mother. Birth is such a dramatic happening that a young child may feel that the world has turned upside down. The child, especially one under six, should see you behave "normally" again — walking, talking, and laughing. This is especially important if the child had been present at birth and had seen you assuming strange positions and making extraordinary, possibly frightening, noises.

Make time during the days following birth for some quiet cuddling and attention to the child alone, perhaps when the father or a friend is with the baby. Depending on age and temperament, your child may ask for a lot of this kind of physical reassurance immediately, or the child may act reserved and appear to reject you. Sometimes this diffidence comes from a feeling of awe toward you and the new baby, and sometimes from feelings of anger and the fear of rejection. Don't be alarmed; such withdrawal is a common reaction, particularly in children aged five to eight.

Children need time to integrate the experience of birth, just as you do. If you continue to show that you love and care for them as well as for the new baby, they can begin to share affection and positive feelings toward you and the baby at their own pace. Older children as well as parents need time to bond with the newborn. Give them as much freedom as you can, within the limits of safety for the infant, to explore, touch, kiss, and handle the new sibling. With a younger child, you may have to make it very clear from the beginning that you are not going to allow the baby to be hurt or even pressed too firmly. Demonstrate touch to your child by encouraging him or her to gently hug the baby, touch the baby's hair, hands, and feet, even hold the baby. Each day set aside special play time for the newborn and sibling.

A festive birthday party soon after birth can be a long-remembered highlight for the sibling. Include children in the preparations, such as making and decorating the cake. The party is the time for the special song or version of "Happy Birthday." If you are celebrating with champagne, offer children their own small glass with juice or soda, so they can join in the toasts. Children love to receive and give gifts, and gift-giving can express love within the family. Gifts to the older child from the parents, the new baby, and others, and gifts from the older child to the new brother or sister, all are appropriate. For preschool children, well-chosen books are particularly fitting. If a child like dolls, nothing makes a more appropriate gift. Consider setting up an area somewhere especially for the older child, where he or she can care for the doll with replicas of the equipment you use for caring for the real baby — changing table, diapers, bottles. Over the succeeding days additions can be made to keep up interest.

To head off difficulties with the older child during nursing times, keep a big jar filled with packets of nutritious snacks (raisins, nuts, sesame sticks) especially for the older sibling. (This is an old La Leche League suggestion.) The child can then have a snack at nursing time and sit with mother and baby. The child might enjoy decorating the jar and putting his or her name on it. Select a jar the child can open and keep it within reach.

Bath time can be a delightful time to include the older child. Newborns love water, and it seems to have a soothing and pleasurable effect on children of all ages, whether they need to be scrubbed or not. With adult supervision, the older child can support the baby in the water and feel very useful and trusted. Time spent touching and caressing during the bath and immediately after can teach lessons in gentleness and care. After the bath, a little warm oil can be massaged into the skin.

Make a picture sign to teach a small child about the importance of not disturbing a sleeping infant. Such a sign can depict each member of the family engaged in quiet activity while the baby is sleeping. At times when the baby needs to sleep, have the older child hang the sign on the baby's door. The child will quickly learn about a baby's need to be on its own and to sleep without being disturbed.

Older children will probably experience jealousy toward the baby and long for "the good old days" when they had their mother all to themselves. It is important that children understand and eventually accept that the baby is here to stay, but it is equally important that both parents take time to do things individually or together with older children. If you have more than one older child, make sure that whoever had been "the baby" does not get dropped by the older siblings in favor of the new arrival. You may need to talk about this with the older children before the birth. Even if the father is the primary caretaker for the older child during the few weeks following birth, it is important that the mother spend time with him or her as well. After those first few weeks, even if a woman is busy nursing the baby full time, there will always be some brief periods when the sleeping baby can be left with the father or a friend while the mother takes the older child on one of those favorite trips to the library, park, or ice cream parlor. There should be "special" time each day at home for the older child to read, talk, cuddle, and play with the mother while baby sleeps.

3

Caring for the Unborn Baby

Genetics

NEW OPTIONS FROM GENETIC SCIENCE

There are many exciting aspects of the rapidly developing field of genetics that offer the possibility of actually correcting gene abnormalities. This discussion, however, focuses on only those advances in genetics that already have applications in family planning. To understand these advances you need to know the meaning of several technical words and understand one or two elementary concepts. You should find the small effort amply rewarding, for genetics is a subject that will affect us more and more in the years ahead.

Mendel, the founder of modern genetic science, showed that the first generation of a crossing of two distinct varieties of any organism received a *dominant* hereditary unit from one parent and a *recessive* unit from the other. We now call these hereditary units *genes* and know that they occur in pairs, each parent contributing one gene. Genes are found in the nucleus of each cell, carried on rod-like structures called *chromosomes*. When the offspring has obtained a combination of a dominant gene from one side and a recessive gene from the other, the dominant gene always prevails. Individuals with this combination of a dominant and a recessive gene are said to be *heterozygous*, having two unlike genes for a particular characteristic. If they receive the same type of gene from both parents they are said to be *homozygous*, whether the gene is dominant or recessive. For a recessive gene to be physically expressed, the offspring must be homozygous, having received that one recessive gene from each parent.

Mendel's theories are usually expressed in symbols. Dominant genes are shown in capital letters (XX). Recessive genes are designated by the corresponding lowercase letters, (xx). A pure dominant strain of yellow-seeded peas, for instance, is symbolized as YY. This genetic formula is known as the *genotype*. A pure recessive strain (for instance, of peas with green seeds) is shown by the genotype yy. When these two strains are crossed (YY by yy), all progeny will have the same genotype Yy. You will see how this works if you think of the four possible combinations: the first Y combining with the first y to produce on Yy, and then with the second y to produce a second Yy; then the second Y combines with the first y to produce the third Yy, and with the second y for the fourth Yy. These are known as *heterozygous hybrids*, and all have the same demonstrable characteristic known as the *phenotype*, which is in this case yellow seeds, since yellow (Y) is dominant over green (y). (Note that the letter Y is used as an abbreviation for the phenotype "yellow." Later in the discussion Y will be used in a traditional way to refer to the male sex chromosome.)

GENES THAT CAUSE DISEASE

All of us carry both dominant and recessive genes. These genes control our individual characteristics, both those that are obvious, like hair color, and those out of sight at the level of chemical molecules. A gene may cause a characteristic harmful to its bearer — in other words, a disease. The disease-causing gene may be either dominant or recessive, and it may be located on the sex chromosome or on an autosomal (non-sex) chromosome. An example of a dominant gene is the one that determines *retinoblastoma*, a cancer of the retina of the eye. Dominant conditions carried on the autosomal chromosomes (those not linked to sex) are the most frequent types of inherited disorders. About 1500 have been identified. The usual criteria are: (1) The trait appears in each generation; (2) The trait is transmitted by an affected individual to approximately half of his or her children regardless of sex; (3) Unaffected individuals do not transmit the trait to their children; (4) Males and females are equally likely to have the trait and to transmit it. (The related topic of dominant genes linked to sex chromosomes is discussed below.)

When a disease-determining gene is recessive, one recessive gene from each parent is required in order to produce the disease in question. The most common recessive genes are located on autosomes, but recessive genes can also be carried on the sex chromosomes. Many recessive genes are lethal; when one is matched with another they produce a fertilized ovum so defective that it cannot survive. Such defective conceptions account for a significant percentage of spontaneous abortions (miscarriages) (see p. 305).

A person who carries the recessive, disease-causing gene, along with a different, dominant gene, is said to be a *carrier* of the gene. While most recessive, disease-determining genes do not cause difficulties in the carrier (heterozygote), this is not always the case. For example, in one inherited disorder of blood fats, the person with two genes for the disease (homozygote) is at increased risk for having a heart attack before the age of twenty. Yet the more mildly affected carrier does not develop problems until a later age — in the forties or fifties. The carrier for sickle-cell anemia usually has no problems. However, in unusual circumstances of low oxygen, such as are found at high altitudes (in nonpressurized airplanes, for example), the carrier's blood cells can also undergo sickling (collapsing into the shape of a sickle) and cause symptoms. It is crucial to understand the difference between being a carrier of a disease and actually having the disease. The carrier usually (but not always, as we saw above) has no symptoms, while a person with the disease is symptomatic in some way.

(:

A very important point in understanding the role of recessive genes in reproduction is that the outcome in the offspring is determined *by chance*. Consider the marriage of two people, each a carrier of the gene for sickle-cell anemia. Each child would have a one-in-four chance of being homozygous and having the disease. The fact that the first child was or was not affected does not alter the chances for the next child. Some families could have four affected children and some none. But overall, in the population at large, one out of every four children born to all carrier couples would have the disease.

In summary, the characteristics of autosomal recessive genes are:

1. The condition determined by the gene appears only in siblings and not in their parents, offspring, or other relatives.
2. On the average, one quarter of the siblings will be affected, which is the same as saying that the recurrence risk is one-quarter for each pregnancy.
3. Males and females are equally likely to be affected.
4. With especially rare disorders, the likelihood is that parents are blood relatives, a factor in the occurrence of certain diseases in isolated and inbred groups.

The frequency of recessive genes in a given human population varies according to the disease in question and the population. Some recessive genes are very common in certain groups. For example, take the gene for *sickle-cell anemia* in blacks. It has a frequency of 10 percent; that is, one out of ten blacks carries the recessive gene for sickle-cell anemia. A random marriage between any two blacks, thus, has a one-in-one-hundred (or one-tenth of one-tenth) chance of bringing two carriers together. Each child of such a marriage of carriers has a one-in-four chance of being homozygous and having the disease of sickle-cell anemia.

In the case of *Tay-Sachs disease*, one in every thirty Ashkenazic Jews (Jews of Eastern European descent) is a carrier. A random marriage of any two individuals from this ethnic group has a one-in-nine-hundred chance of uniting two carriers. Each child born of such a marriage has a 25 percent chance of being homozygous and having the disorder.

In *cystic fibrosis,* a disease involving abnormal production of mucus in the lungs, intestines, and other parts of the body, somewhere between one in thirty and one in sixty individuals is a carrier. Thus, one in 900 to 3,600 random marriages is likely to bring two carriers together, with a one-in-four chance of each child being affected.

The gene for *thalassemia* (or Cooley's anemia) occurs in about one in 30 to one in 12 people whose origins are in the Mediterranean basin (primarily Greeks and Italians), Africa, and Asia. This means that random pairings have a one in 900 to one in 144 chance of bringing together two carriers. Again, the chance for each one of the off-spring to be affected is one in four.

A recessively transmitted disease which is routinely checked for in newborns is *phenylketonuria* (or PKU). It occurs once in every 10,000 births and is amenable to treatment with a special diet (see p. 265). *Galactosemia,* another rare, recessively inherited disease, occurs perhaps only once in 100,000 births. This condition, which involves the lack of an enzyme that normally orders the conversion of galactose, a common milk sugar, into glucose, causes brain damage, liver disease, and cataracts. The treatment is a diet free of galactose.

Another relatively common disorder recessively inherited is deficiency of the plasma protein *alpha antitrypsin,* which leads to chronic lung disease (emphysema) and liver disease (cirrhosis). About one in 2,000 whites have this disorder, and 14 percent of these can be expected to die in early infancy.

The exciting news about genes is that more and more can be identified, making it possible to spot an affected fetus early in pregnancy. Among detectable genes are those for Tay-Sachs disease, sickle-cell anemia, thalassemia, cystic fibrosis and the most common forms of muscular dystrophy and hemophilia. Although no intrauterine treatment for these disorders is available yet (and as a result, most couples resort to abortion), the day may not be too far off when cure will become possible.

Genes are looked for in fetal cells obtained mainly from amniocentesis (p. 130) or chorionic villous sampling (p. 132). At present the characterization of a fetus' genes is undertaken when there is a family history of an identifiable disorder or if the parents are proven carriers.

POLYGENIC INHERITANCE

Many important characteristics (such as height, intelligence, and special aptitudes) appear to be transmitted, not by one, but by several genes. These characteristics are said to be *polygenic* in origin. In predicting the outcome of mating when multiple genes are involved, we follow the Mendelian laws. But we find that the problem rapidly becomes very complex as the number of possible combinations soars.

Most congenital abnormalities are polygenic. They include congenital heart disease, club foot, congenital dislocations of the hip, cleft lip and palate, and open neural tube defects. The last group includes *meningocele* (failure of closure of the back of the spine, with a sac-like protrusion of the membrane that covers the spinal cord), *meningomyelocele* (a meningocele containing the spinal cord and nerve roots), and *anencephaly* (failure of formation of the brain). When the spinal cord, or nerves, is involved in a meningomyelocele, there is usually an associated neurological defect, like paralysis of the legs or bladder.

Couples at risk for these disorders are usually identified through a review of their family histories. Genetic counseling in these situations must be highly individualized. Although the prevention or cure of most polygenic disorders prenatally is not yet possible (see p. 149, "Treating the Fetus"), prenatal diagnosis of serious congenital abnormalities (like meningomyelocele and hydrocephalus) can provide couples with information on which to base the decision whether or not to continue a pregnancy. For example, prenatal diagnosis of open neural tube defects is already available with considerable accuracy, beginning with the measuring of *alpha fetoprotein* (AFP) levels in the blood of pregnant women. (See p. 54, laboratory tests, and p. 130, "Amniocentesis.")

MUTATIONS

Occasionally genetic information changes when it passes from parent to child. Consequently, the offspring has characteristics different from those of either parent and his or her ancestors. Mutations are permanent, transmissible characteristics in the offspring. Should the right mutation occur, it would be possible, at least in theory, for a couple of redheads (from families in which no one but redheads had ever been born) to produce a child with black hair. The children of this child would receive the gene for black hair also.

Mutations occur all the time in each of us. They can account for the spontaneous appearance of some diseases, known to be hereditary, for which no previous family history can be found. While some mutations are beneficial or neutral in effect, the majority are detrimental and interfere with normal structures and functioning. Many are lethal. Cancer is a mutation of certain body cells. On occasion, a favorable mutation will occur and a superior individual may result. According to the principles of Darwin, the natural selection of favorable mutations is responsible, at least in part, for the gradual evolution over millions of years of all living species on earth.

While we know little about why mutations occur or how to control them, we know that their rate can be increased by exposure to certain factors like radiation and chemicals and, possibly, some viruses. In experiments with fruit flies it has been shown that exposure to radiation increases the rate of mutation, and that the rate of mutation is directly proportional to the amount of radiation exposure — the greater the level of radiation, the higher the mutation rate. While this possibility does not suggest that X rays and other necessary sources of radiation should be avoided, it does suggest that the amount of exposure of pregnant women, or of those of childbearing age, be carefully controlled. (See also p. 152, "Protecting the Fetus.")

CHROMOSOMAL ABNORMALITIES

Ordinary cell division is called *mitosis*. By splitting in two, each chromosome makes a copy of itself, one copy going to each of the two daughter cells produced by the division. Each daughter cell thus receives exactly the same number and kind of chromosomes the parent cell had. In the formation of egg and sperm cells, however, a different and unique type of division occurs, called *meiosis*. In meiosis, each daughter cell receives only half the number of chromosomes, one from each of the paired parental chromosomes. Human egg and sperm cells have 23 chromosomes each. When they combine, the new individual formed by their union has 46, the characteristic number for the human species. (If the chromosomes were not halved before fertilization, they would double with each succeeding generation.)

On occasion in meiosis there is an uneven apportioning of chromosomes to the daughter cells, causing them to form with an extra or missing chromosome. This is called *nondisjunction*. Another accident that may happen in meiosis is *translocation*, in which a segment of one chromosome shifts to another chromosome. Egg and sperm cells that have experienced either nondisjunction or translocation may be incapable of fertilization. Or, if such a germ cell participates in fertilization, the combination may give rise to a defective fetus which is spontaneously aborted (see p. 305); to an abnormal individual such as one with Down syndrome; or to an individual who is normal in appearance (phenotype) but who carries the rearranged chromosomal material in a *balanced translocation*. The fetuses produced by such an individual are at risk for abortion, for Down syndrome and other chromosomal syndromes, and for carrying balanced translocations themselves. The couple with frequent (three or more) spontaneous abortions (miscarriages), or one spontaneous abortion and a malformed still- or live birth, is at increased risk for having a translocation and should be studied for it (see p. 305).

The study of chromosomal conditions is called *cytogenetics*. In recent years knowledge in this field has grown enormously. Newer chemical methods of separating and staining enable geneticists to work from photographic prints of the chromosomes enlarged 3,000 to 4,000 times. The pairs of chromosomes are assigned numbers (from 1 through 22) according to the length and position of the *centromere*, the sharply constricted region which joins the halves of each pair. Pairs 1 through 22 are the *autosomes*, or non-sex chromosomes. In addition, there are two chromosomes which determine the sex of the individual, making the total of 46 chromosomes per person.

The sex chromosomes are of two types, X and Y. The female has two X chromosomes, the male an X and a Y. In meiosis, one of the mother's X chromosomes goes to each daughter cell (egg). The father's sperm cells are equally divided between those carrying an X and those carrying a Y chromosome. The union of a Y-bearing sperm with the X of the mother produces a male. The union of an X-bearing sperm with the X-bearing egg produces a female. Thus, it is the father who determines the sex of the baby.

The X chromosome is longer than the Y and contains more genes. In males, the genes on the X come from the mother only. If a recessive gene on that part of the X chromosome that is unopposed by the shorter Y chromosome is abnormal, there is no dominant gene to oppose it and the male will be affected with the disease. In the female, the action of the sex chromosomes is more complex. One of the two X chromosomes that exist in every cell in her body (except the egg) will become inactivated early in fetal development. This happens on a chance basis; in other words, about half of her cells will have an active X chromosome inherited from her mother, the other half an active X chromosome inherited from her father. Therefore, in an *X-linked chromosomal disorder*, the female will be only partly afflicted. She will, however, be a *carrier* of the abnormal gene, capable of passing it on to her children. Therefore, the characteristics of an X-linked recessive gene are:

1. The incidence of disease is much higher in males than females. If affected, females are rarely affected to as serious a degree.
2. The trait is never directly transmitted from fathers to sons.
3. The trait is passed from an affected male through all of his daughters, and from her to half of her sons.
4. The trait may be passed "silently" through a series of carrier females before manifesting itself in affected males.

X-linked dominant conditions also occur, but are rare. Many of the *hemophilias* follow this X-linked recessive inheritance, with females as carriers who do not show symptoms and males who have the disease. On an average, one-half of the male offspring of a mother who carries the defective gene will have hemophilia. The other half, having received a maternal X chromosome which does not contain the abnormal gene, will be normal. On an average, one-half of the female offspring of such a mother will be carriers like the mother and the other half normal noncarriers.

All the genetic diseases now known to be associated with chromosomal abnormalities appear to stem from either too much or too little genetic material. The most common of these is *Down syndrome*, also known as *mongolism*, in which chromosome pair 21 is involved. Individuals with Down syndrome have physical characteristics that make early recognition possible — they are invariably retarded and many have associated heart anomalies. It appears that this abnormality arises during meiosis. Instead of half the chromosomes going to each daughter cell in the normal manner, an ovum or sperm is formed which has two number 21 chromosomes. When this abnormal germ cell subsequently joins with its counterpart to receive another number 21 chromosome, the result is a cell with three number 21 chromosomes instead of the normal pair. In this most common form of Down syndrome, known as the *nondisjunction type*, the mother and father are cytogenetically normal by our present measurements.

Although we know how Down syndrome comes about, we still do not know why it happens. In the nondisjunction type the abnormality in the ovum is more common with increase in the age of the mother, particularly over thirty-five, but abnormal sperm appear to be less related to a father's age. While either parent can contribute the extra chromosome at any age, the older a couple is, the more likely the contribution is made by the mother.

The risk for Down syndrome varies according to maternal age as follows:

	Age		
	20–24	*25–29*	*30*	*33*
Live births	one per 1,352	1/1,133	1/885	1/592
	35	*37*	*40*	*42*
Live births	1/365	1/225	1/109	1/67

Despite the increasing incidence with maternal age, most Down syndrome babies are actually born to younger women. Even though the odds of any particular younger woman giving birth to an affected child are lower, more women have babies early in their childbearing years. Thus, performing *amniocentesis* (see

p. 130) after age thirty-five is far from a complete answer to effective prenatal screening for this disorder.

The age of thirty-five has been chosen as the usual cut-off point on a cost-benefit analysis. This analysis takes into account the costs, to society as a whole, of screening and therapeutic abortion of affected fetuses (as well as the risks of the procedure itself; see p. 305) as balanced against the costs of lifetime care for affected individuals. The ethical basis for such an analysis can be questioned, and couples should clarify their own values on this issue. Some, for example, to whom the burden of bearing an afflicted child outweighs the risk of testing and abortion might choose to do a chromosomal analysis even if the woman is under thirty-five. Other couples of any age might welcome the arrival of any child, Down syndrome or normal, and forego testing entirely.

Some recent developments in genetic testing may have an impact on the decision of the younger woman regarding chromosomal studies. Low maternal serum alpha protein levels (AFP) (see p. 59) are associated with an increased risk of chromosomal abnormalities. Combining maternal age with AFP is a better predictor than either alone and helps to identify risk in women under 35 years old. Also, *chorionic villous sampling* (see p. 132) offers the possibility of diagnosis earlier in pregnancy and quicker availability of results.

In about one Down syndrome child in fifty, a different type of chromosomal abnormality has occurred, indicating that one of the child's parents is a carrier of a *balanced translocation* (see above, p. 124). In this particular type of translocation, part of one of the number 21 chromosome pair has split off to join another chromosome.

When a Down syndrome child is born, cytogenetic analysis of the child is required to determine if the nondisjunction type or the translocation type is involved. If the translocation type of chromosomal abnormality is found, the parents and their close relatives should also be checked to see if they, too, have the translocation. In either situation, the parents need genetic education and counseling to understand their child's condition and to plan for future pregnancies.

There are several other well-recognized chromosomal abnormalities. In the disorder known as *Klinefelter's syndrome*, males have an extra X chromosome. Instead of being XY, they are XXY. The disorder becomes manifest usually in adolescence, when the testes fail to develop and growth of the breasts occurs. Puberty may be delayed. The abnormal testes produce neither sperm nor testosterone, the male sex hormone. About 8 to 10 percent of these boys are mentally retarded (usually mildly). Treatment consists of psychological counseling and the administration of sufficient male sex hormones to promote sexual development. Klinefelter's syndrome occurs in about two males per 1,000 in the population and is more common in the pregnancies of women over forty.

In *Turner's syndrome,* which affects females, an X chromosome is missing; such girls have only one X instead of two. The disorder occurs in about one in 2,500 live-born females and in about 5 percent of aborted fetuses. Individuals with Turner's syndrome fail to mature sexually at puberty because their ovaries do not develop.

A recently discovered chromosomal disorder, which now appears to be second only to Down syndrome as a cause of mental retardation, is the *"Fragile X syndrome."* In this abnormality an X chromosome is normal in appearance, except that one or both tips of its long arms appears either partly or completely detached from the rest of the chromosome. Whether these "fragile sites" contain one or more genes that cause the retardation, or are closely linked "markers" for its presence, is not yet understood. Since this is an X chromosome sex-linked disorder, males are more often and more severely affected than females. Characteristics of affected individuals include: large testes (three to four times normal size), a prominent chin bone, large ears, and normal-to-enlarged head size. Work is in progress to identify the affected fetus prenatally through chromosomal analysis, and to identify women who carry the abnormal chromosome. Although it is too early to be sure, there is some evidence that the B-vitamin folic acid is involved with this syndrome in an as yet unidentified way.

To complicate matters further, recent studies have indicated that there may be a significant number of nonretarded males with fragile X. Thus, analysis of the chromosomes of a fetus that reveals fragile X may suggest the definitive possibility of mental retardation *only* in families that have a previously known pattern of fragile X-linked mental retardation.

GENETIC COUNSELING

Genetic counseling involves knowledge of both the principles discussed in this chapter and the principles of making decisions under conditions in which outcomes are uncertain. This kind of decision-making involves knowing the probabilities of outcomes and how they mesh with one's values (see p. 29).

Questions involving genetics arise in families in several ways. When a baby with a congenital abnormality is born, or when there is a stillbirth, parents understandably seek to find out the cause of the defect and the chances of recurrence. Recurrent miscarriages also raise the question of a genetic cause. Those who should seek counseling include:

1. Couples who already have a child with some serious defect such as Down syndrome, spina bifida, congenital heart disease, malformed limb, or mental retardation.
2. Couples with a family history of a genetic disease or mental retardation.
3. Couples who are blood relatives (first or second cousins).
4. Blacks, Ashkenazic Jews, Italians, Greeks and other high risk ethnic groups.
5. Women who have had a serious infection early in pregnancy (rubella or toxoplasmosis) or who have been infected with AIDS (p. 159).
6. Women who have inadvertently taken some potentially harmful medication early in pregnancy, or who habitually take certain drugs (p. 153), including alcohol (see p. 171).
7. Women who have had X rays taken early in pregnancy.
8. Women who have had two or more of the following in any combination: stillbirths, deaths of newborn babies, miscarriages.
9. Any woman thirty-five years or older (see p. 127 for full discussion).

Ideally, a careful genetic history should be part of every premarital health checkup before children are planned. It should be done, at the latest, early in the first pregnancy. Certainly, the birth of a baby with a congenital problem should occasion a careful family history. The study of any stillborn baby for genetic defects is also important. We can improve the quality of our genetic histories by preparing and keeping up-to-date family trees and family medical histories. The better the data, the better the genetic counseling and prediction that can be offered. (See p. 37, "Your History.")

Genetic counseling may be obtained at most large medical centers and, without exception, at university teaching hospitals. Family physicians, pediatricians, and obstetricians are all good sources of information on genetic disorders and possible courses of action. A registry of counseling centers is maintained by The March of Dimes (see Appendix B).

The discussion of specific genetic disorders given in this chapter is far from exhaustive; only the more commonly encountered problems have been considered. (See Appendix D for further reading.)

Tests

AMNIOCENTESIS

Amniocentesis is the procedure of passing a needle through the abdominal wall into the uterus and amniotic cavity of a pregnant woman to obtain amniotic fluid for study. By means of amniocentesis it is possible to identify a fetus afflicted with certain inherited disorders (p. 117); to assess the maturity of the fetal lungs when preterm delivery is under consideration (p. 318); and, in some cases, to provide medical treatment before birth (see p. 149).

Amniocentesis for inherited disorders is generally performed between fourteen and sixteen weeks. At this time there is sufficient amniotic fluid to sample and the fetus is still quite small and unlikely to be stuck by the needle. Enough time remains to permit the abortion of an abnormal fetus. When amniocentesis is performed to test for amniotic alpha fetoprotein (see p. 59), it is usually done between sixteen and eighteen weeks because of increased validity of the chemical tests after the sixteenth week.

Before performing an amniocentesis, the uterus and fetus are examined with ultrasound to find the site of the placenta (to avoid puncturing it), to check for the presence of twins (each of whose sacs may need to be entered), and to verify the gestational age of the fetus. The woman's abdomen is washed with antiseptic solution and draped with sterile towels. The skin is numbed with a local anesthetic. Under ultrasonic guidance, to avoid hurting the fetus or the placenta, a hollow needle 3 to 6 inches in length is passed into the uterus. Amniotic fluid is withdrawn through a syringe attached to the needle. Occasionally no fluid is obtained after the first pass with the needle and another attempt is made. If the second pass also fails, the usual policy is to stop and wait a week before trying again.

When amniocentesis is peformed for chromosomal and gene analysis, the amniotic fluid obtained is separated in a centrifuge into cell-rich and cell-free layers. The cell-free layer is subjected to biochemical tests and may be cultured for microorganisms. The cell-rich part, containing about 10 to 100 living cells, can be studied directly to determine the sex of the fetus and the presence of certain enzymes. More often the cells are cultured; in a few weeks the harvested cells can be studied biochemically and genetically. Two million cells are required for certain biochemical tests, while 100,000 are enough for chromosomal analysis.

In about 10 percent of women more than one amniocentesis must be done, either because of failure to obtain fluid on the first attempt or technical failure of the laboratory to process the sample. If the fluid contains blood, it may be unsuitable for certain analyses, and a new sample will have to be obtained.

Minor complications occur in about one out of 100 procedures: uterine cramping, vaginal bleeding (from the uterus), and leaking of amniotic fluid through the vagina. In the rare event that the fetus is pricked, the result can be a permanent skin dimple.

More serious complications can occur. Even in the most experienced hands, amniocentesis appears to carry the risk of about one-quarter of 1 percent for miscarriage, maternal bleeding at birth, or injury to the fetus. However, some researchers doubt that amniocentesis actually increases the rate of spontaneous abortion at all. Although different studies reach different conclusions, nine recent studies showed no increased risk for loss of the fetus as a result of amniocentesis. In any case, for women over thirty-five, the risk of the fetus's carrying a chromosomal abnormality is between two to five times the highest estimated risk of pregnancy loss as a result of amniocentesis.

The inadvertent puncturing of the placenta may lead to transfer of fetal red blood cells into the mother's circulation. If the mother is Rh negative and the fetus Rh positive, the mother can be stimulated to produce antibodies to the transferred fetal cells (p. 56), which can destroy the baby's red blood cells. Because of this potential complication, all Rh negative mothers of Rh positive fetuses are considered candidates for Rhogam, the anti-Rh antibody which binds to Rh positive fetal cells in the mother's circulation, causing their removal before maternal sensitization.

Several problems in chromosomal analysis may lead either to no answer or to an uncertain result after amniocentesis. For one, the cell culture may fail altogether. Few good laboratories have failure rates exceeding 5 percent. If cells from the mother have been shed into the amniotic fluid, these may grow out in the culture and be mistaken for those of the fetus. This problem occurs in about one to two per 1,000 studies. If male cells are grown from the fluid, they must of necessity be from the fetus; but if female cells grow, there is a possibility that they are those of the mother rather than those of the fetus. Accordingly, a separate chromosomal analysis of the mother's blood cells is recommended for comparison with the chromosomes of the cells grown from the amniotic fluid. (Another way of identifying a male fetus is measuring testosterone levels in the amniotic fluid.)

Laboratory errors are not completely avoidable, even in the best of hands, and can result in aborting a normal fetus or allowing an abnormal one to continue to term. The error rate for prenatal diagnosis, however, is remarkably low, ranging from 0.2 percent to 0.6 percent. For many couples, the waiting period — one and one-half to two weeks — is a time of increased anxiety. For most, however, their risks and anxiety are well balanced by their peace of mind when certain very serious abnormalities of the developing fetus have been ruled out.

CHORIONIC VILLOUS SAMPLING

Chorionic villous sampling (CVS) is a painless procedure which can be performed in the hospital or a doctor's office as early as the fifth week of pregnancy. In the most common approach, a thin hollow tube (catheter) is inserted into the uterus through the vagina and guided by ultrasound or by hysteroscope (a fiberoptic viewing tube) into a position between the uterine lining and the *chorion*, a tissue layer that surrounds the embryo for the first two months of its development and then develops into the placenta. A syringe attached to the tube sucks up several of the *chorionic villi*, projections of tissue that transfer oxygen, food, and waste between the mother's circulation and that of the embryo and are genetically identical with the embryo. Analysis of the cells of the villi thus reveals the genetic endowment of the fetus. Certain kinds of analysis can be done on the same day, thereby enabling couples at times to avoid the anxiety of the long wait for the results of amniocentesis. And, should a couple choose to terminate a pregnancy, abortion at seven to nine weeks can be readily arranged as an out-patient procedure, rather than the more difficult and stressful type of abortion done in the hospital after five months.

CVS is under study as a replacement for amniocentesis as the first-line test for most genetic analyses. More subtle chromosomal abnormalities are not detectable in chorionic villi testing, and amniocentesis will still have a role in checking for these and confirming unclear findings from CVS.

Only a few centers in the country currently perform CVS. The major risk is abortion which, at present, occurs in about 0.2 percent of the cases studied.

WHAT A WOMAN CAN TELL

Lately, doctors and other birth attendants have shown renewed interest in the validity of observations a woman herself can make about her baby's activity in utero, and several investigators have looked at their predictive value. In one study, after the thirty-sixth week of pregnancy, women were asked to identify the time of day their babies were usually most active. During such active periods, the woman would lie quietly on her side for one hour and count the number of fetal kicks, excluding flutters and hiccups. A rate of more than three to four kicks per hour correlated well with other tests of fetal well-being.

It is not clear yet whether such measured self-monitoring should be included in a woman's caring for herself during pregnancy. More studies on this question are needed to determine whether standards can be established. Research is underway to establish whether the mechanical recording of fetal movements (with a sensing device placed over the uterus) can give more precise and useful information.

We suggest that any woman who notices a *significant decrease in fetal activity,* even if she "cannot put a number on it," report this promptly to her doctor or birth attendant. An increase in activity, on the other hand, is probably a good sign and has not been shown to predict fetal problems.

PRINCIPLES OF FETAL MONITORING

Because there is some controversy surrounding fetal monitoring, it is good to know a few basic facts about its methods and purpose. Heart rate and oxygen supply are the main concerns:

1. The fetal heart rate reflects fetal oxygen supply, which depends on the delivery of oxygen to the placenta from the mother's circulation and the function of the placenta itself.
2. Contraction of the uterus temporarily cuts off the blood supply to the placenta, enabling the fetus to draw only on oxygen already present in the placenta at the time of onset of the contraction.
3. The fetus whose oxygen supply is already borderline when the uterus is not contracting will be tipped into a state of oxygen deprivation during a contraction. This lack of oxygen will be reflected in a prolonged slowing of the fetal heart rate with slow recovery.

During a uterine contraction the fetal heart rate normally slows in response to pressure on the fetal head and returns to its baseline as the contraction ends. In monitoring terms, this is called an *early deceleration.* However, given an inadequately functioning placenta and a marginal oxygen supply to the fetus to begin with, a contraction will tip the fetus into a state of oxygen deprivation and the heart rate will drop. It will not recover until well after the contraction is over. In the language of monitoring, this is called a *late deceleration.* A third kind of deceleration, called *variable deceleration,* bears no consistent relationship to uterine contractions. It is believed that this pattern is caused by compression of the umbilical cord due to pressure by the baby or twisting. The precise mechanism of these three most important monitor patterns is not entirely clear.

Normally, the fetal heart beats at a baseline rate of between 110 and 150 to 160 beats per minute. A rate of 100 to 110 is termed *mild bradycardia* (literally, "slow heart"), and a rate less than 100 is called *marked bradycardia*. *Tachycardia* (literally, "fast heart") is termed "mild" if heart rate ranges from 160 to 180 and "marked" if it is greater than 180.

Tachycardia alone is not an indication of fetal distress, since it may be due to maternal fever, drugs given to the mother, or intrinsic abnormalities in the rhythm of the fetus's heart. Similarly, mild bradycardia without other changes is not necessarily a sign of fetal distress. Severe bradycardia has several causes, among them congenital heart defects in the fetus, sudden lowering of the blood pressure in a pregnant woman with hypertension, or decreased oxygen supply to the fetus.

Another term used in connection with monitoring is *variability*. Variability refers to the variation in heart rate from beat to beat. When a fetus is awake and healthy, its heart rate speeds up and slows from second to second. Although these changes are probably too subtle to detect simply by listening to the heart with a stethoscope, the internal fetal monitor, which produces a printout of the fetus's electrocardiogram (see below), graphically displays variability. Decreased variability is observed in a fetus that is asleep, in an otherwise normal premature infant, in babies whose mothers are medicated with drugs such as Demerol, morphine, and Nisentil, and in those who are experiencing distress.

MONITORING WITH A STETHOSCOPE

The traditional way to monitor the fetal heart rate is to listen with a stethoscope for thirty seconds immediately following a uterine contraction. Listening is done every fifteen minutes during the first stage of labor, every five minutes during transition, and following each contraction during the second stage. With practice, skilled attendants can use a stethoscope in much the same way they can an electronic monitor. They can follow heart rate patterns through a contraction and thereby identify the normality or abnormality of the pattern. Monitoring with a stethoscope can also be used in the non-stress test, as described below on p. 141.

Advocates of low-technology births, whether in the hospital, birthing center, or home, point to studies that show that frequent and careful listening with a stethoscope to the baby's heart in low-risk labors is as effective in detecting abnormalities as is continuous electronic fetal monitoring (see below). But not all obstetricians agree with this interpretation of current data. They cite other evidence, not completely confirmed, that deaths of infants, otherwise at low risk, but not monitored electronically, may be as many as one in 1,000. On theoretical grounds, obstetricians argue that, if electronic monitoring is not done, the condition of the primary "patient" in childbirth (the baby) is, for all practical purposes, unknown. They believe that stethoscopic monitoring is often hampered by shortages of staff to carry it out and by long silent periods during which contact with the baby is lost. The latter is a situation unique in clinical medical practice, for, as a prominent obstetrician once said, "Think of any other situation where as a physician you're expected to treat a patient about whom you are given or are able to obtain so little information."

Many obstetricians also take issue with the concept of "low risk," pointing out that a fetus allegedly at low risk at the onset of labor can turn into a high-risk patient within minutes, and one would surely want a monitor in place. The rejoinder is that, even with high-risk fetuses, the case for electronic surveillance has not been tightly proven.

Based on available evidence, our opinion on the monitor issue is that women entering labor at the end of low-risk pregnancies take, at most, a small risk in choosing a stethoscope instead of the electronic fetal monitor. This assumes, however, that the attendants have the *time* to follow the listening protocol as described.

ELECTRONIC FETAL MONITORING

Electronic fetal monitoring records uterine contractions and the fetal heart rate over time. The uterine contractions are measured by a pressure gauge strapped to the mother's abdomen. The changing shape of the uterus during a contraction is sensed and transmitted as electrical signals, activating a needle which imprints a lumpy line (blip) on a rolling strip of graph paper. The fetal heart rate can be picked up either by an *external* ultrasound monitor placed on the abdomen over the uterus or *internally* by a wire — leading through the vagina and attached to the fetal scalp — which produces an electrocardiogram tracing. (The electrical impulse associated with heart contraction spreads throughout the fetus's body. A sensor placed on any part of its body — in this case, the scalp — detects the impulses generated by the heart and provides accurate information about heart rate.) In measuring the variability of the heart rate, the internal (EKG) monitor has a decided advantage over the external (ultrasound) monitor.

The electrode commonly used for internal monitoring is attached to the fetus by twisting the corkscrew-shaped wires at its tip into the scalp. It is likely that the baby feels this jab, although we know, from observations made on newborns receiving injections or having blood drawn, that the pain is probably experienced for only a short time.

EVALUATING INTERNAL ELECTRONIC FETAL MONITORING

Internal electronic fetal monitoring (EFM) is widely and increasingly used during labor. The idea of maintaining constant surveillance of the fetus during the stress of labor has an obvious appeal. However, the contribution that EFM makes to better outcomes in terms of survival and short- and long-term well-being is as yet unclear, even confusing, and certainly controversial.

In 1979 a panel of experts, convened by the National Institutes of Health (NIH) to study the effectiveness of EFM, concluded that there was no evidence at that time that electronic monitoring of the *low-risk* woman during labor, in comparison with periodic listening to the fetal heart rate with a stethoscope, contributed to increased fetal well-being. Most obstetricians, however, did not agree with the recommendations of this report and had a different interpretation of the data. They put the cost of not using the electronic fetal monitor in terms of the death of one baby per thousand, in addition to a yet undetermined and unproven cost in terms of nonfatal, long-term, handicapping conditions. Advocates of family-centered maternity care, on the other hand, who have viewed routine EFM as an unnecessary and expensive intrusion of high technology on the natural processes of labor and delivery, were cheered by the NIH report.

Five randomized, controlled studies of internal EFM, published before 1984, while flawed because of the small number of labors involved, showed no advantage of EFM over traditional monitoring with the stethoscope in low-risk pregnancies.

An important study comparing EFM to listening with a fetoscope (auscultation), first reported in 1984, involved almost 13,000 women at the National Maternity Center Hospital in Dublin, Ireland. In this hospital, a policy of "active management of labor" is pursued. This involves (1) artificially rupturing the membranes (see "Labor," p. 183) on admission of those women in whom rupture has not occurred spontaneously; (2) use of Pitocin to stimulate labors not showing cervical dilation of at least 1 cm. per hour; and (3) cesarean section if delivery has not occurred in about twelve hours. A single nurse midwife stayed with each laboring mother until delivery, which was usually accomplished with women lying on their backs (see p. 211).

Women were eligible for inclusion in the trial if (1) they had a live fetus of at least twenty-eight weeks gestation (which meant that prematures were included); (2) they were in labor; and (3) no meconium (the stools of the fetus) staining of the amniotic fluid was present. These women were then randomly allocated to two groups, one of which was monitored electronically and the other by auscultation.

While this study included many details not discussed here, the major findings reported:

1. No difference in deaths of babies (2.1 per thousand in each group)
2. No differences in Apgar score (see p. 229) at one minute following birth
3. No difference in admissions to neonatal intensive care
4. No statistically significant differences in cesarean section rates (under 5 percent) (which are astoundingly low by U.S. standards).

The major difference observed was that more convulsions (seizures) occurred in newborns of the auscultated as opposed to the electronically followed labors, twenty-seven versus twelve, a difference seen, however, *only* when oxytocin was used. Nine of these thirty-nine babies died, but the deaths were not significantly greater in one group than the other. The thirty surviving babies were evaluated at one year of age, when six were found to have cerebral palsy, three in each group. Further follow-ups on the development of the surviving babies are planned and will be very important in drawing conclusions.

It can be argued that the Dublin study, by including women who by our standards would have been considered at increased risk and therefore electronically monitored, merely confirmed that EFM is advantageous in high-risk labors, a point about which there is little argument.

Another large scale study involving 34,995 labors at Texas Southwestern Medical School in 1986 showed no differences in electronically monitored low-risk pregnancies in terms of still-births, low Apgar scores, admissions to the neonatal intensive care unit, neonatal seizures, or assisted ventilation of the new-born.

The situation is further complicated by a lack of consensus on the criteria for defining abnormal patterns. A 1982 study involving twelve authorities on EFM revealed important areas of agreement and disagreement in their interpretation and use of the method. The less-than-perfect predictive value of EFM for fetal distress, even among acknowledged experts, very likely results in unnecessary cesarean sections (as many as six per 100 births, according to some estimates); thereby subjecting some mothers to increased risk of illness and death to say nothing of the increased cost of medical care and the inconvenience and discomfort of the procedure. On the other hand, this "overshoot" may be the unfortunate price we pay at this time in history if we are to avoid missing the fetus truly at risk.

One disadvantage of internal EFM monitoring is that the amniotic membranes must be ruptured to permit attachment of the electrode to the baby's scalp. The unnatural, unphysiological environment created when the membranes are ruptured results in more pressure on the fetus during uterine contractions than would be the case if the cushioning effect of the amniotic fluid were preserved. Thus, the very procedure designed to identify the fetus at risk for distress may contribute to the fetal distress. It is not yet clear how much of a problem this loss of amniotic fluid is, but there is some evidence that babies whose membranes are ruptured early in labor show more misalignment of the cranial bones and swelling of the scalp (caput). The possible long-term significance of these findings is not yet known.

Complications of internal fetal monitoring are rare but not insignificant. They include: infection of the scalp of the fetus at the site of attachment of the electrode; damage to fetal blood vessels, with resulting hermorrhage in the case of low-lying placenta (see p. 312 on placenta praevia); and an increased risk of infection within the amniotic cavity.

An important practical issue connected with internal fetal monitoring is that the woman must lie in bed for as long as the wires are attached. Telemetry systems, in which the fetal heart rate is broadcast to the monitor without maintaining connections by wire, have been developed, but such attractive systems are not widely available.

EFM has become increasingly routine throughout the industrialized world, even for low-risk pregnancies. In part, this trend seems to be related to obstetricians' justified fear of malpractice suits (which, in the United States, have increased to an alarming degree) that stem from almost any neurological damage in a baby. If a fetus was not electronically monitored during labor, the suits assume that monitoring would have inevitably led to action to prevent the mishap. The more monitoring is used, the more the courts view it as a standard for care, and, in turn, the more it will be used. In fact, the swing toward use of EFM has been so strong that it seems likely that further studies will be deemed "unethical" if they withhold EFM from a control group.

Our own reading of the evidence is that, in a low-risk birth, a woman cared for by a doctor, nurse, or midwife accepts at the very most a marginal risk if she asks not to have EFM, particularly if the birth is likely not to involve much intervention. We also laud the flexible approach of many doctors and midwives who, when dealing with a fetus that is otherwise doing well, use external EFM (through the wall of the mother's abdomen) only for several minutes on admission to the labor room and periodically thereafter. This approach seems to combine the advantages of both techniques and helps identify immediately the 3 to 4 percent of babies who might be in difficulty in early labor.

NON-STRESS TESTING AND
FETAL BIOPHYSICAL PROFILE

The basic principle of non-stress testing (NST) is that a healthy fetus's heart rate will increase in response to movement of the body. In the standard method of performing the test, an external fetal monitor detects the fetus's heart rate by ultrasound while a continuous recording of the heartbeat over twelve minutes is printed out on a moving strip of paper. When the mother feels a kick, she depresses a switch, which identifies the movement on the paper with a mark that can be related to the fetal heart rate at the time. The most widely accepted standard of normality is two accelerations of fifteen beats per minute lasting fifteen seconds per ten minutes. A normal test is known as "negative," or "reactive." An abnormal test is also known as "positive" or "non-reactive."

Another version of this test involves simply clocking the fetal heart rate with a stethoscope over five minutes. The fetus is considered to be reactive when a single acceleration of fifteen beats per minute lasting ten seconds is observed. This form of the non-stress test is less expensive than ultrasound monitoring and more readily available. It may also have advantages over the use of ultrasound in women with obesity or hydramnios (p. 300), in which the ultrasound waves are dampened by the intervening fat and/or fluid.

The non-stress test is a reasonably good screening test for fetuses at low risk for distress. In fetuses at high risk, it is usually combined with ultrasound assessment of amniotic fluid volume along with fetal body tone and limb and breathing movements into what is called the Fetal Biophysical Profile. This study is considered to predict fetal well being as accurately as the Contraction Stress Test (discussed below) and is much easier to administer.

CONTRACTION STRESS TESTING

Contraction stress testing involves monitoring the fetal heart rate with an external monitor while the uterus contracts spontaneously or is stimulated to contract with intravenously administered oxytocin. (Remember that internal fetal monitoring is used only with women in labor, because of the necessity of rupturing the amniotic membranes.) The contraction stress test is done in the labor and delivery sections of hospitals and is usually performed on women and fetuses who have failed the non-stress test. It takes from one to two hours. For fifteen to thirty minutes, "baseline" uterine activity and the fetal heart rate are recorded along with fetal movements. If spontaneous uterine contractions lasting 40 to 60 seconds occur approximately three times in ten minutes, the test can be done without oxytocin stimulation. In the absence of demonstrable uterine activity, oxytocin is infused to produce such contractions. Or, in a still somewhat experimental procedure, the nipples are stimulated to cause the woman to produce her own oxytocin, which results in contraction of the uterus. In positive tests, late decelerations (p. 134) accompany more than 50 percent of contractions.

The correlation between a negative contraction stress test and a favorable outcome is good. Positive contraction stress tests are divided into nonreactive and reactive groups. Both experience a significant increase in the incidence of intrauterine growth retardation, low five-minute Apgar scores (see p. 229), and fetal distress during labor in comparison with fetuses whose contraction stress tests are negative.

If the test is positive, labor can still be normal and, on the average, will be so about 25 percent of the time, depending on the study reviewed. About 7 percent of tests do not yield clear-cut results and must be repeated the next day. Whether non-stress and contraction stress tests help make pregnancy safer is not clear, despite their widespread use.

ULTRASOUND

Ultrasound (sonography), a relatively new and constantly improving diagnostic technology, is having a major impact on maternity care and medical practice in general. Its origins date to World War II, when high-frequency sound waves were first used to detect enemy submarines. The echoes of sound waves beamed into the water were reflected back from any object encountered, to be "heard" by electronic sensor.

The use of sound waves in medicine follows the same principle. Intermittent high frequency (inaudible to the human ear) sound waves are generated by applying an alternating current to a device known as a transducer. A transmitting solution like mineral oil is placed on the skin and the transducer is applied. In its use in pregnancy, the transducer sends pulsations of sound through the mother's abdomen to the interior of the uterus.

As the sound waves penetrate tissues of different composition (fetal skull and brain or amniotic fluid and fetal skull, for example), some of the sound energy is reflected (echoed) back to the transducer. The transducer alternates rapidly between emitting (sending) and receiving (listening) states. In the listening state, the echoes received generate a small electrical voltage, which is amplified and displayed on a black and white television screen. Thus the ultrasound technique identifies the location of anatomic structures by measuring how long it takes for ultrasound waves to reach them, be reflected at the interface between them and other structures, and return to the sensor. The echoes can also be converted into sounds, making it possible to "hear" the beating of the fetal heart.

Ultrasound can be used in several ways. It can measure the size of a structure such as the fetal head, which is useful in dating a pregnancy, and it can follow the growth of the fetus. It can produce a cross-sectional picture or "slice" of the fetal body. A "slice" through the fetal abdomen can show the size and location of the organs inside. A "slice" through the brain can identify the ventricles (fluid-filled cavities), providing information about their normality or enlargement (*hydrocephalus*). Ultrasound can be used to observe actual movements of fetal structures such as the beating of the heart, emptying of the bladder, movements of the chest, and thumb sucking. (See Fetal Biophysical Profile p. 141)

The clinical applications of ultrasound include:

1. identifying an embryo in order to diagnose pregnancy
2. monitoring the growth of the fetus
3. determining whether a fetus has or has not been aborted (p. 305)
4. determining a tubal (ectopic) pregnancy (p. 293)
5. identifying multiple pregnancies (p. 331) and fetal position (see p. 271, "Breech Presentation")

6. identifying fetal abnormalities such as meningomyelocele, hydrocephalus, or limb defects (p. 122)
7. locating the placenta and determining placental abnormalities (p. 312 on placental praevia)
8. measuring the amniotic fluid (see p. 300 on hydramnios and oligohydramnios)
9. guiding needle insertion in amniocentesis (p. 130)
10. measuring the fetal heart rate during prenatal visits (p. 80), stress and non-stress tests (p. 141), and labor
11. treating the fetus before birth (p. 149).

A still experimental use of ultrasound is measuring the pulsations of the mother's arteries, which deliver blood to the uterus and placenta, and of the fetal arteries in the umbilical cord, which deliver blood from the fetus to the placenta. Measurement of what is called the "velocity wave force" of these arteries holds the promise of being one of the best ways to identify fetuses at risk for illness in utero.

Despite the many applications of ultrasound, there is still no evidence that its routine use in low-risk pregnancies makes a measurable difference in outcome for babies. The one random controlled study reported, as of this writing (from the University of Trondheim in Norway), showed no differences in survival or illness at birth for babies of low-risk pregnancies, who had been examined with ultrasound at nineteen and thirty-two weeks' gestation, in comparison with those who had not. There was, however, earlier recognition of twins, and there were fewer inductions of labors for post dates (see p. 314) and fewer low birth weights in the ultrasonically examined babies, although not to a statistically significant degree.

The most skillful ultrasonographers will argue, however, without substantiating data, that, because of the high frequency with which fetal problems exist in pregnancy, routine examination can only be beneficial to the baby. These assertions will have to be backed up by controlled studies. As it is now, ultrasound is being more and more widely used without specific reasons and may soon become a routine part of care. The alarming rise in malpractice suits involving babies who have almost any neurological or developmental abnormality is putting pressure on doctors to leave no stone unturned in looking for problems early on. In addition, for doctors working on the basis of fee-for-service, there is a strong incentive to use rather than not use ultrasound.

The question of the safety of ultrasound is also of concern. All that can be said to date is that there is no evidence of fetal abnormalities related to its use. Nor have changes been observed in living cells in tissue culture after exposure to the doses used in humans. However, ultrasound has been in use in pregnancy in a major way only for the last ten years or so, a relatively short period for follow-up studies. Concern has been expressed about possible harm not only to the developing fetus, but also to the ovaries of the mother and the ovaries of the female fetus as well. These concerns are at present hypothetical and not based on any evidence. Nevertheless, some parents and doctors have decided to use ultrasound only when it seems clearly indicated, even though an increasingly strong case can be made for using it routinely in prenatal care, so rich are its applications.

If ultrasound is to be used, the growing consensus is that it be used only by physicians and/or technicians who are qualified to assess the normality of fetal structures as well as the gestational age of the fetus and the number of fetuses present. This capability does not exist in all settings. Women who are undergoing ultrasonic examination should check to see whether the examiners are qualified to detect significant fetal abnormalities, such as those of the spinal cord. These practitioners should be asked if they can meet the minimum standards of the American Institute of Ultrasound in Medicine. If the technology of ultrasound is to be used and its potential risks accepted, we believe that it is unacceptable to use it incompletely, overlooking important findings that might bear on the outcome of the pregnancy.

In 1984 the National Institutes of Health convened an expert panel, which, after much study, issued a consensus statement on ultrasound. The panel's summarized conclusion was, in part, as follows:

> From the body of information reviewed, taking into account the available bioeffects literature, data on clinical efficacy, and with concern for psychosocial, economic, and legal/ethical issues, it is the consensus of the panel that ultrasound examination in pregnancy should be performed for specific medical indication. The data on clinical efficacy and safety do not allow a recommendation for routine screening at this time.

Ultrasound examinations performed solely to satisfy the family's desire to know the fetal sex, to view the fetus, or to obtain a picture of the fetus should be discouraged. In addition, visualization of the fetus solely for educational or commercial demonstrations without medical benefit to the patient should not be performed.

Prior to an ultrasound examination, patients should be informed of the clinical indication for ultrasound, specific benefit, potential risk, and alternatives, if any. [This should also apply to the choice of using ultrasound or stethoscope in monitoring the fetal heart rate during prenatal visits and in labor.] In addition, the patient should be supplied with information about the exposure time and intensity, if requested . . . .

These guidelines (with our comments in brackets) are useful to remember in discussing ultrasound with your physician.

FETAL SCALP BLOOD PH TESTING

One measure of the well-being of the fetus is the amount of oxygen in its blood, supplied by the placenta. Since the fetal heart rate reflects oxygen supply to the heart, it is a good, although indirect, measure of blood oxygen. More precise monitoring would measure oxygen level itself. While work is underway to use the internal fetal monitor to obtain such data, at present the closest measure of fetal oxygen is the closely related acidity of the blood, measured by what is called the pH.

In order to perform this test, an endoscope (illuminated tube) is inserted through the cervix and pressed against the baby's head. The skin is then wiped clean with a cotton swab, sprayed with ethyl chloride to stimulate increased blood flow, and coated with a silicon gel to cause the blood to coalesce as easily collected globules.

Immediately after a uterine contraction, one or two tiny cuts are made through the skin to a predetermined depth. The blood is collected immediately in a long, pointed glass tube and analyzed.

In general, a pH reading of 7.25 or greater (i.e., more alkaline, as opposed to acid) is considered to be normal, 7.20 to 7.24 borderline, and less than 7.20 abnormal and indicative of too little oxygen in the blood. In general, the baby should then be delivered promptly. However, the test is not always reliable. pH results with "high" readings can be, rarely, associated with hypoxia, and some "low" ones can be associated with normal oxygen values. A deceptively low reading, which indicates danger when there is none, can occur when the baby's scalp is swollen and the blood is not circulating well, when the blood of the mother is too acid, or when the blood sample is inadvertently taken from the mother rather than the fetus.

The pH can be deceptively normal under the influence of pain medications and anesthetics given to the mother, as well as when infection is present, when the blood of the mother is alkaline, when the baby has certain congenital anomalies, and when the blood sample is obtained at times other than immediately after a contraction.

Overall, if a fetus's scalp blood pH is normal, there is an 80 percent chance of a good Apgar score (see p. 229) after delivery and a 20 percent chance of a low Apgar score. On the other hand, if the pH is too low, there is a 60 percent chance that the Apgar score will be low. Thus, while the scalp blood pH test is very useful, it is far from a perfect means of identifying babies who are stressed.

At present, pH testing is used to check babies with abnormal fetal monitor traces and as a result, improves the ability to detect the fetus at risk. Not all hospitals are equipped to perform this test.

URINE ESTRIOL DETERMINATION

Estriol is a hormone which the placenta produces using chemical building blocks (*precursors*) that are made in the adrenal gland of the fetus. Measuring estriol in the mother's blood or urine is another indirect way of judging the well-being of the fetus and placenta.

The 24-hour maternal urine estriol excretion has not proved to predict fetal well-being as accurately as was once thought. However, the ratio of estriol to creatinine (the breakdown product of muscle metabolism which is excreted from the blood into the urine) has been found to be highly sensitive in predicting the postmaturity syndrome (see p. 302), but not very good at predicting either tolerance of labor by the fetus or the occurrence of stillbirth.

THE L/S RATIO

Late in normal pregnancy certain cells in the fetal lung produce fat-rich chemicals which coat the inner walls of the air sacs. This coating prevents them from collapsing by sticking together after respiration begins following birth. A major problem for premature babies, particularly those of less than thirty-two weeks' gestation, is that these surface chemicals have not yet been produced. Such babies develop *respiratory distress syndrome.*

Some of the surface chemicals produced by the fetal lung are washed up through the airways to the mouth and out into the amniotic fluid, which can be examined by amniocentesis (see p. 130). Two of the chemicals secreted are lecithin (L) and sphingomyelin (S). The ratio between these two (the L/S ratio) is a good predictor of maturity of the lungs.

An L/S ratio of greater than 2.0 indicates that the risk of respiratory distress is slight, unless the mother is diabetic, the fetus has an illness caused by incompatibility between its blood type and that of its mother (see p. 56), or the fetus is very sick for any reason at the time of testing. In newborns, for whom the L/S ratio is 1.5 to 2.0, respiratory distress will occur 40 percent of the time; if it is below 1.5, distress occurs 73 percent of the time.

Thus, the L/S ratio is a useful although imperfect measure of fetal lung maturity. Whenever pre-term delivery is considered, as, for example, in suspected intrauterine growth disturbance (see p. 301), the risk of continued intrauterine life must be weighed against the dangers of prematurity, particularly the respiratory distress syndrome. The L/S ratio helps in this decision. Babies who are candidates for early delivery but whose lungs are immature can be treated with steroids to hasten maturation of the lungs (see p. 319).

Work is now in progress to determine whether ultrasound measurements of fetal growth can be used to predict fetal lung maturity; thus, in some cases, avoiding the more invasive and risky procedure of amniocentesis. It appears that in uncomplicated pregnancies, ultrasound is highly predictive.

FETOSCOPY

Fetoscopy is a technique of directly visualizing the fetus in utero. A flexible tube with a fiberoptic light system is passed through the abdominal wall via the umbilicus into the uterus. By means of this tube, the physician can see a circular area of 2 to 4 centimeters diameter, enough to permit a trained observer to detect gross congenital abnormalities in the fetus. It is possible to obtain a minute sample (biopsy) of the fetal skin for chromosomal or biochemical analysis, or to draw a sample of fetal blood from a blood vessel in the placenta. This blood can be tested for hemophilia or sickle-cell or related anemias while the fetus is still in the uterus (see also "Treating the Fetus," below). The risk that this procedure will cause an abortion is from 2 to 5 percent.

NUCLEAR MAGNETIC RESONANCE

Nuclear magnetic resonance (NMR) is an exciting new diagnostic technique. It reveals body structures based on the detectable electromagnetic waves that they emit when exposed to a magnetic field into which low frequency radio waves are beamed. It is finding increasing application in medicine and is now being studied with respect to its use in pregnancy. NMR is non-invasive and appears not to alter the organs studied, an important safety consideration.

Exactly what place NMR will take in diagnosis in pregnancy remains to be seen. Several studies are underway at the time of this writing.

Treating the Fetus

Of all recent developments in prenatal care, one of the most exciting is that of actually treating an ill fetus. As we have seen in the preceding section, our capacity to judge how well the fetus is developing and to take action, or to leave things alone, based on the information obtained, has grown enormously in recent years. We can now begin to speak of the field of *fetal medicine* with some justification. In the following discussion we will touch upon the highlights of this developing field, focusing on the active treatment of the unborn.

One of the oldest treatments involves the fetus whose survival is threatened by anemia and heart failure, most commonly caused by incompatibility of the blood factors of mother and fetus (p. 56). Such a fetus can be saved by blood transfusions performed in utero. Blood cells are injected into the fetus's abdominal cavity or into an umbilical artery through a needle which has been passed under ultrasonic guidance through the mother's skin, abdomen, uterus, and amniotic fluid. Several such transfusions may be needed to assure the survival of the fetus.

Treatment of the fetus can involve medication. For example, antibiotics are used to treat a mother and fetus with syphilis (p. 166). Fetuses with heart failure (also detectable by ultrasound) caused by rapid heart action (*tachycardia*) have been treated successfully by giving digitalis, which slows heart rate, to their mothers. The digitalis crosses the placenta to the fetus. Fetuses with underfunctioning thyroid glands (*hypothyroidism*) and goiter (enlargement of the thyroid) have been successfully treated by injecting thyroid hormone directly into the amniotic fluid. In swallowing the amniotic fluid the fetus also swallows the hormone, which is absorbed into the body. Similarly, overfunctioning of the fetal thyroid gland (*hyperthyroidism*) has been prevented by administering to the mother (and thereby to the fetus) a drug to decrease thyroid activity. If birth is imminent, the lungs of a premature fetus can be matured to a more functional level by giving the mother hydrocortisone-like hormones. (See p. 318 on premature labor and p. 148 on L/S ratio.)

The fetus in severe distress during labor (as detected by fetal monitoring and scalp pH sampling) can be resuscitated prior to an emergency cesarean section with oxygen given to the mother (and hence to the fetus), terbutaline (see p. 155) to stop uterine contractions, and positioning the mother to roll the uterus off her major abdominal blood vessels, thereby increasing blood flow and oxygen supply to the placenta and baby.

Prenatal treatment for problems which, if left uncorrected, would damage the fetus, is in its infancy. For example, with ultrasound it is possible to detect obstructions of the urinary tract, which, if uncorrected, can lead to stretching and progressive destruction of the kidneys. At several medical centers, operations have been performed to relieve such obstructions by passing a plastic catheter (small thin tube) through the fetus's abdomen into the bladder to drain off excess urine into the amniotic fluid. The tube is left in place to provide continuous drainage. Otherwise, the approach to this problem is to deliver the baby prior to term before intensive kidney damage has occurred. A combination of these approaches is also possible.

Prenatal treatment has also been employed in several centers to treat hydrocephalus, in which cerebrospinal fluid from the fluid-containing cavities within the brain (ventricles) cannot drain properly, resulting in stretching and damage to the brain itself. In this case the needle is inserted into the ventricle to drain off the excess cerebrospinal fluid. In treating urinary tract blockage and hydrocephalus, the goal is to interrupt the progress of the disease before irreversible damage has occurred. In the past, the recognition of these conditions has usually been delayed until the time of birth, often too late to save either the kidneys or the brain. But the results to date, however, have been generally disappointing.

Even if intrauterine treatment is not currently possible or desirable, the detection of problems in the fetus makes possible judgments about the timing and method of delivery (vaginal or cesarean section) and the preparation of the attending staff for promptly dealing with a sick baby. For example, it is safer to deliver a baby whose head is enlarged with hydrocephalus by cesarean section than by the vaginal route.

The most recent development in prenatal treatment is actual surgery on the fetus. In San Francisco doctors have treated a twenty-one-week fetus whose urinary system was blocked by partially removing the fetus from the womb and operating on it while it was still attached to the umbilical cord. Both mother and fetus were anesthetized with general anesthesia. The fetus's blocked ureters (tubes draining the kidneys) were opened to the skin, allowing urine to drain out into the amniotic fluid. It was then returned to the womb and the pregnancy allowed to proceed to term. The plan was to close the ureter drainage sites after birth. In this case, unfortunately, the baby died twelve hours after birth, not because of failure of the surgery but because its lungs had failed to grow as a result of the early lack of amniotic fluid directly caused by the urinary tract obstruction. Enough damage had already been done to the lungs so that even this most unusual and successful operation was to no avail.

In an article in *The New York Times Magazine* of February 28, 1982, author Robin Marantz Henig summarized these exciting and problematic developments as follows:

> Fetal surgery at this moment resides in an ethical grey zone, not quite research and not quite therapy. Doctors are now grappling with the question of just which fetus to treat and when. They do not know yet whether they are salvaging fetuses that will become profoundly retarded or otherwise handicapped children, whether they are operating on fetuses that would have survived intact without their help, or whether they are doing what they hope they are doing — producing healthy, normal children that otherwise might have died.

Currently, the conventional medical response to most detectable severe fetal abnormalities is abortion. If during the next five to ten years fetal surgery becomes the treatment of choice, new ethical and legal issues emerge. For example, who is to decide whether or not to treat a fetus? Does the fetus have rights independent of the mother's wishes? How can the interests of the mother and fetus be balanced when they are in conflict? As our technical sophistication increases, we will be challenged to upgrade our decision-making skills accordingly.

Protecting the Fetus

Every day, it seems, the list of things known to harm the growing fetus increases, so much so it may seem that "nothing is safe any more." In this section we present what is really known about drugs in pregnancy, vaccines, infections in the mother, addictive substances, and environmental poisons and hazards.

In general, we advise a conservative approach to drugs, vaccines, and other outside influences that may be harmful to the fetus. If a medication or vaccine does not directly benefit the fetus, we advise you to avoid it if at all possible. If you cannot, try to minimize exposure. Confine drug treatment to drugs that have never been shown to harm the fetus.

The climate of suspicion that surrounds drugs makes it difficult to study their effects during pregnancy. Since effects may not be apparent until many years after the drugs are taken, causal connections between a problem and prior drug exposure are often hard to draw. A prime example is the hormone diethylstilbestrol (DES), taken by many women a generation ago to prevent miscarriage. Years later a small percentage of their offspring in their teens and twenties were discovered to have abnormalities of the genitalia.

While reading this chapter parents-to-be would do well to remember that most babies are born healthy, as they have been for thousands of years. Worrying over imaginary or exaggerated hazards will help neither mother nor baby. After following sensible precautions, such as those outlined here, parents should try to relax and put their confidence in the age-old natural process of childbearing.

DRUGS DURING PREGNANCY

Although only a few drugs have been proven to harm the fetus, all drugs can, at least potentially, cause problems. The best overall policy is to use drugs in pregnancy only if there is no alternative and the symptom is extremely annoying, disruptive, or dangerous. Both prescription drugs and over-the-counter preparations should be treated this way. If you normally take either category of drugs for a condition that existed previous to pregnancy, or if during pregnancy you intend to use drugs you have not used before, or use infrequently, the best course is to consult your doctor or other medical professional.

In recognition of the potential harm drugs pose to the fetus, the U.S. Food and Drug Administration announced that, by 1984, many over-the-counter drugs taken by mouth will be required to carry warning labels. The labels advise pregnant women and nursing mothers to consult their doctor or nurse before using the drug. The manufacturer can omit warning labels only if the drug can be shown not to harm mother or baby.

The list of drugs in Table 4 summarizes what we know about those most commonly taken. Note especially that, as far as we know, most antibiotics can be used safely in pregnancy. While

Table 4. Drugs in Pregnancy

Type of Medication	"Safe" to Use in Pregnancy[a]	Relatively Safe (Limited Information)[b]	Some Risk Associated[c]	Contraindicated in Pregnancy[d]
Analgesics	acetaminophen meperidine[e,f] morphine codeine	Percodan[e,f] hydromorphone[e,f]	salicylates indomethacin[g]	
Antibiotics	ampicillin erythromycin isoniazid miconazole penicillin	amikacin amphotericin B carbenicillin cephalosporins clindamycin gentamicin kanamycin methicillin nafcillin oxacillin, dicloxacillin tobramycin	chloramphenicol[h] lincomycin nitrofurantoin[i] streptomycin[j] sulfonamides[k] Septra, Bactrim[l]	tetracycline
Anticoagulants	heparin[m]	dipyridamole	warfarin[n]	
Antiemetics	Bendectin*	trimethobenzamide hydroxyzine prochlorperazine		

Bronchodilators	aminophylline	terbutaline° cromolyn sodium beclomethasone		
Cardiac drugs	digoxin atropine lidocaine	procainamide disopyramide quinidine		
Cough preparations	Robitussin DM, CF	terpin hydrate		
Decongestants	diphenhydramine pseudoephedrine	Dimetapp Actifed all other over-the-counter cold pre-parations[p]		
Hypoglycemics		Use insulin only for optimal control Oral hypoglycemic agents are not indicated[q]		
Diuretics		hydrochlorothiazide[r] ethacrynic acid[r] furosemide[r]		
Antihypertensives	hydralazine methyldopa	metaproterenol clonidine prazosin propranolol	diazoxide[s]	reserpine

Table 4. Drugs in Pregnancy, *continued*

Type of Medication	"Safe" to Use in Pregnancy[a]	Relatively Safe (Limited Information)[b]	Some Risk Associated[c]	Contraindicated in Pregnancy[d]
Laxatives	Milk of Magnesia	Metamucil Colace		
Sedatives	barbiturates	flurazepam	diazepam[f]** chlordiazepoxide[f]	
Thyroid preparations	thyroxine		methimazole[t]	
Other drugs	vaccines (polio,[u] tetanus, rabies, influenza[v]) probenecid Kaopectate ferrous sulfate	cimetidine allopurinol primidone ethosuximide	phenytoin metronidazole trimethadione methadone[e,f] corticosteroids[w] phenothiazine tricyclic anti-depressants[e]	antineoplastic drugs diethylstilbestrol lithium estrogens vaccines (rubella, mumps, measles) isotretinoin (Accutane)

* Removed from production in 1983

** Diazepam (Valium) has been associated with fetal abnormalities including cleft lip.

[a] Although no drug can be used with certainty that there will be no adverse side effects associated, drugs listed in this column are used on a routine basis at this institution [Washington University School of Medicine].

[b] Many drugs in this column are relatively new, but no consistent adverse effect has been attributed to their use. Data on these drugs are limited.

c These drugs have some associated risk when used in pregnancy. The use of these drugs should be weighed against the possible adverse effects.

d These drugs have been well documented to have adverse fetal effects and should not be used in pregnancy.

e Possible neonatal addiction and withdrawal with long-term use.

f Possible neonatal depression when used intrapartum [during labor].

g Prostaglandin-synthetase inhibitors possess the pharmacologic ability to inhibit premature labor. When salicylates are used by a pregnant patient over long periods at high doses, pregnancy can be prolonged, postpartum blood loss increased, and the incidence of neonatal hemorrhage elevated slightly above that of controls. These adverse effects have not been reproducible. In general, salicylates have no known teratogenic [defect-causing] effect.

h Can cause [a serious combination of symptoms known as the] "gray syndrome" in neonates when used near term. Avoid third-trimester use unless absolutely necessary.

i Possible hemolytic [blood-damaging] disease in the newborn with glucose 6-phosphate deficiency. Avoid use at term.

j Can cause ototoxicity [hearing damage] in utero.

k Compete with bilirubin for binding sites on albumin, and thus third-trimester use should be avoided.

l Not to be used routinely in treating urinary tract infections. Use only in recurrent or resistant infections.

m Drug of choice for anticoagulation at any time during pregnancy. Does not cross the placenta.

n Has been associated with congenital anomalies in humans when used in first trimester. Crosses the placenta and thus leads to anticoagulation of the fetus. Should be stopped at week 36 of gestation or whenever delivery is imminent, in order to prevent hemorrhage complications during delivery. Under these circumstances, full anticoagulation of the mother can be carried out with heparin.

o Inhibits uterine activity in second and third trimester and can be used to manage premature labor.

p Up to 12 weeks, very few drugs, if any, should be used because this is a period of major fetal development. After 16 weeks, most drugs listed as safe or relatively safe can be used fairly safely.

q There is no place in the modern management of diabetes in pregnancy for oral hypoglycemic agents. Insulin and diet control are indicated to bring blood sugar under as rigid control as possible in order to ensure a satisfactory outcome of the pregnancy.

r Can deplete maternal intravascular volume and, in rare instances, be associated with neonatal thrombocytopenia [low blood platelets in the newborn]. Diuretics are not indicated in pregnancy-induced hypertension.

s Sudden drops in blood pressure in a hypertensive pregnant patient can precipitate fetal distress.

t When used judiciously and with close follow-up, these drugs are useful in treating the pregnant woman with Graves' disease. Risks involve neonatal goiter and hypothyroidism.

u Not recommended for routine prophylaxis [treatment] in pregnancy.

v Recommended only for the patient with serious underlying illness.

w Neonatal adrenal suppression can occur with long-term use. These drugs can be used to accelerate pulmonary maturity in utero in the fetus destined for a pre-term delivery. Corticosteroids are also very potent inducers of cleft palate in laboratory animals, but there is no reproducible evidence that this occurs in humans.

Source: J. Freitag, and L. Miller, *Manual of Medical Therapeutics*, 23rd edition. Boston: Little, Brown and Company, 1980.

the common over-the-counter drugs acetominophen (Tylenol) and Robitussin (a common cough medicine) have not been shown to be harmful, aspirin is related to heart defects and is known to affect the blood-clotting factors of both mother and baby. It should be avoided. (See also p. 203 on the question of using anesthetics and analgesics in labor and p. 70 on the problems of morning sickness.)

A common question that arises, with respect to drug safety, concerns oral contraceptive pills taken during early pregnancy, before a woman realizes she is pregnant. The best information to date is that oral contraceptive use is not associated with congenital malformations in the fetus. At the same time, it is important to stress that such contraceptives should be avoided during pregnancy if at all possible.

VACCINES

Vaccines are of two types: those containing dead and those containing live microorganisms, usually viruses. *Live virus vaccines* are generally avoided in pregnancy for fear of infecting the fetus. The most commonly used live virus vaccines are those against measles, rubella (German measles), mumps, and polio (the widely used Sabin vaccine).

Of these vaccines, *the polio vaccine only* can be given with relative safety during pregnancy. Even so, its use is recommended only during polio epidemics in which the risk of contracting paralytic polio clearly outweighs the risk of any complication associated with taking the vaccine, however small.

The *rubella vaccine* currently used (RA 27/3) can infect the fetus in a minority of exposures, but to date no cases of congenital rubella syndrome (see p. 166) have been reported after its use. The risk of vaccination within three months of conception appears to be so small as to be almost negligible. Thus, the rubella vaccination of a pregnant woman should not in itself be a reason for therapeutic abortion, even though the final decision is of course an individual matter. Despite this reassuring information, we recommend a conservative course of action. Pregnant women should avoid the rubella vaccine, and nonpregnant women should not become pregnant for three months following vaccination. Women whose blood antibody levels show that they are not immune to rubella should receive the vaccine prior to pregnancy.

In contrast to live vaccines, *killed vaccines*, which contain no living microorganisms, can be used safely as needed. The most commonly used killed vaccine is directed against tetanus and diphtheria and is recommended to be administered to adults every ten years up to the age of sixty-five. The "flu shots," made available to protect against the three strains of influenza expected to be common in any one winter season, are also killed vaccines, as is the Salk vaccine for polio and the vaccine against hepatitis B (see p. 163).

INFECTIONS

The fetus is generally well protected from infection in the mother contracted during pregnancy or before. Common colds, flu, stomach viruses, strep throat, sinusitis, and even pneumonia will not harm the fetus. There are, however, important exceptions to this general rule, and these are presented here.

AIDS. The virus which causes the notorious acquired immune deficiency disease, or AIDS, can be transmitted from an infected mother to her fetus. As there is no cure for this disease, women who are known to be infected should consider aborting their fetuses to prevent tragic illness in their offspring. Women at high risk for AIDS should undergo testing.

Chlamydia. Chlamydia, a bacterium little known to the public, causes more infections in the newborn than any other infectious agent. Like gonorrhea, Chlamydia inhabits the mother's cervix and is picked up by the baby as it passes through the birth canal. Up to 10 percent of all women harbor the bacteria, and 50 percent of the babies of these women will pick it up, although not all will show symptoms. About one-third of exposed babies will develop conjunctivitis if preventive treatment is not undertaken. Although Chlamydia conjunctivitis is not well prevented by the silver nitrate eyedrops traditionally used, it is both prevented and treated with erythromycin eye ointment.

Chlamydia can also cause pneumonia in infants less than three months old (with peak occurrence between four and twelve weeks). Erythromycin taken by mouth is the antibiotic proven most effective to date in treating conjunctivitis and, probably, pneumonia.

At present, there is no effective way to prevent this common bacterium from colonizing the newborn. It is not yet known if antibiotic treatment of the mother would be an effective preventive measure, or whether reinfection would still be a problem.

Cytomegalovirus. Discovered only recently, Cytomegalovirus (CMV) is a virus most people know little or nothing about. Recently revealed as the leading congenital infection in man, it infects 1 percent of all babies. Thus, of the approximately three million births annually in the United States, 30,000 newborns are infected. About 3,000 of these are obviously sick at birth, and about 600 actually die of the illness. The remaining 2,400 recover, but are likely to suffer nerve deafness, eye impairment, mental retardation, and stunted growth. Of the 27,000 infected infants who appear well at birth, between 2,700 and 7,600 will eventually develop hearing impairment, inflammation of the eyes and perhaps impaired vision, tooth infections that cause loss of baby teeth, and intellectual handicapping.

Infected newborns can harbor and excrete CMV for months, perhaps years, and so are a reservoir for the spread of the disease throughout the community. Day-care centers in particular are notorious in this process. Since the infected babies who play an important role in the cycle of CMV infection do not usually appear ill, pregnant women, women who could become pregnant, and those who work in these centers should observe careful handwashing techniques after handling the babies or their diapers.

In the older child or adult, CMV infection can take the form of a subclinical infection that produces no symptoms at all. Or it may cause symptoms similar to those of infectious mononucleosis — sore throat, fever, swollen glands, enlarged liver. Fortunately, CMV infection after infancy does not appear to have the risks of handicapping associated with the disease in the newborn.

Like the herpes virus discussed below, CMV can remain in the body indefinitely, perhaps for life. Periodically it becomes active, spreading throughout the body without necessarily causing symptoms. When a pregnant woman experiences such a flare-up or especially when she is first infected early in pregnancy, the virus can spread across the placenta to the fetus before birth, or from the cervix to the baby during birth. The risk to the fetus of such reinfections does not appear to be as great as an initial infection of the mother, insofar as serious illness at birth is concerned. Apparently the previously infected mother has produced antibodies that protect the fetus (and later the baby) from damage by the virus. Nonetheless, chronic subclinical infection and contagiousness do occur, and the long-range consequences to the child of such reinfections are not yet known.

CMV can also be present in breast milk. In such cases the baby may be immune, because antibodies to CMV have been transmitted from the mother across the placenta before birth. Transmission of CMV via breast milk is a strong argument against pooling the milk of several mothers into a milk bank to feed a premature infant who may lack maternally transmitted immunity.

To date there is no drug to combat CMV. A vaccine now under development offers the most likely long-range solution to this major health problem, but no quick solutions seem likely.

Gonorrhea.   Since germs that cause gonorrhea are present primarily in the cervix, gonorrhea infection is more a problem for the newborn, who can pick up the germs during passage through the birth canal, than for the fetus in utero. Gonorrhea can infect the baby's eyes, causing a virulent conjunctivitis which can sear the corneas and even cause blindness if it is left untreated. Gonorrheal conjunctivitis is prevented by routinely treating the eyes of the newborn with silver nitrate, tetracycline, or erythromycin very soon after birth (see p. 264).

On the expectant mother's first prenatal visit, a culture of the cervix is performed to detect possible gonorrhea infection. If the culture is positive, the woman is treated with antibiotics. But the eradication of gonorrhea early in pregnancy does not guarantee that the mother will not become reinfected. For this reason the eyes of the newborn are treated routinely, regardless of the mother's medical history.

Group B Streptococcal Infection.   In recent years it has been discovered that Group B streptococcus (different from the bacterium that causes the familiar "strep throat") is responsible for between 12,000 and 15,000 infections in newborns per year in this

161

country, affecting two to three babies per thousand. Without prompt recognition and treatment of the disease, about half the infected newborns will die; and half of those who become ill and develop meningitis will show long-term neurological effects. Despite the commonness of this infection, it has received scant public attention.

The Group B streptococcus is carried in the intestines of about 10 percent of women and spreads from the anus to the vagina. As far as is now known, it causes no symptoms in the woman. The baby picks up the bacteria during passage through the birth canal and can also acquire it after birth. About 40 percent of infected mothers transmit the bacteria to their babies.

The signs of illness in the newborn are nonspecific. They include irritability, fever, vomiting, lethargy, and labored breathing. Even mild symptoms may signify the potentially lethal spread of the bacteria throughout the baby's body.

Several approaches to this serious public health problem are under study. One is to take cultures from both the vagina and cervix of the pregnant woman as she begins labor. At the first sign of infection, which usually becomes apparent in the baby one to three days after birth, the baby of each mother from whom the organism is recovered is widely cultured (samples of blood, stool, urine, etc., are taken) and immediately treated with antibiotics. A second very promising approach involves culturing women who are at high risk late in pregnancy and treating those having positive cultures with intravenous antibiotics. A third approach involves culturing women late in pregnancy and treating those with positive cultures, together with their male partners, with antibiotics orally. A fourth approach focuses on the routine treatment of all babies born in nurseries in which there is high incidence of Group B streptococcal disease.

Some evidence has been found to link Group B streptococcus with premature labor (p. 503) and premature rupture of membranes (p. 320). If this association is shown to be valid, treatment of the pregnant woman who carries this germ may help prevent premature birth. And because women with premature rupture of the membranes and premature labor may be at higher risk for carrying Group B streptococcus, the argument is made for treating such high-risk mothers with antibiotics during labor. This therapy is now being studied.

The threat of Group B streptococcus to the newborn has only recently been recognized and come under study. While the solution to this serious health problem is yet to be found, it is likely that more and more women will be hearing about this disease and participating in some preventive action against it.

Hepatitis. The newborn whose mother is a carrier of Type B chronic viral hepatitis is likely to become infected at birth and become a carrier. In addition, such an infant is at significantly increased risk for developing chronic liver infection, with eventual cirrhosis and cancer of the liver. For this reason it is currently recommended that these infants be given special immune gamma globulin at birth and receive hepatitis vaccine within one week of birth and then at one and six months, to stimulate the production of protective antibodies before the infection takes hold. This combined therapy offers a 90 percent chance of preventing infection and its dire future consequences (Note: about 5 percent of infections occur in utero and cannot be so prevented).

In addition to mothers who are known carriers, the group of women identified by investigators as being at greatest risk for carrying hepatitis are:

1. health care professionals frequently exposed to blood or blood products
2. immigrant or U.S.-born women of Asian, Sub-Sahara African, Pacific Basin, or Haitian background
3. individuals who use mood altering drugs intravenously
4. prostitutes
5. those with previous undiagnosed jaundice, or with chronic liver disease of unknown cause
6. those who have received multiple blood transfusions (three or more, especially prior to 1975)
7. dialysis or renal transplant patients and staff who work with such patients
8. those who work or reside in institutions for the retarded
9. household contacts of hepatitis B carriers or chronic renal dialysis patients.

Such at-risk women should be studied in pregnancy for evidence of the carrier state, and their infants treated accordingly.

If a woman is exposed during pregnancy to someone who is infected with hepatitis B either acutely or chronically (carrier), she is a candidate for receiving gamma globulin and hepatitis vaccine even while pregnant. If such an exposed woman becomes infected (after an incubation period of about sixty days), there is a high likelihood of transmission of virus to her fetus before delivery as well as considerable risk to herself.

Herpes. The herpes virus occurs in two varieties, *Type One* and *Type Two*. *Type Two* produces the cold sores commonly encountered on the mouth and lips. *Type One*, which causes blisters on the genitalia of men and women, has recently become a frequently occurring sexually transmitted disease. After the first outbreak of infection, herpes virus can remain in the human host indefinitely, erupting periodically to cause visible, painful lesions. During such a herpes flare-up the virus can be transmitted to others. Thus, herpes virus present in a woman's birth canal can be picked up by her infant during labor and delivery.

Herpes infection of the newborn can be fatal or disabling, even with the partially effective drug therapy now available. To date, there is no vaccine against herpes, and a new promising drug treatment for the disease has not been tested in pregnant women, out of concern for possible harmful effects on the fetus from the drug itself.

At present, the best way to keep a baby from getting herpes is to prevent its exposure to the virus. When herpes virus is present in the cervix and vagina, the baby is kept away from this infective environment by being delivered through cesarean section. For this preventive approach to work, the amniotic membranes must either be intact or have been broken no more than four to six hours before the operation is performed.

Any woman who has herpes sores at the time of labor is a candidate for cesarean section. However, the absence of apparent sores, blisters, lesions, or any other symptoms does not guarantee that the virus is absent from the vagina. For this reason, it has been recommended that any woman with a history of herpes infection obtain cultures at thirty-two, thirty-four, and thirty-six weeks, and weekly thereafter until delivery. A woman could consider a vaginal delivery to be of low risk if virological studies were negative on two successive examinations (the second done within one week of delivery).

While there is an appealing logic to this rather expensive approach, it was seriously challenged in 1986 by researchers at Stanford University who have shown that there is no correlation between viral shedding at birth and detection of virus according to the protocol described. Newer approaches to this important health problem are clearly needed.

If the pregnant woman's partner has a documented herpes infection, it is recommended that the couple avoid genital contact in the last several months of pregnancy. If the partner has cold sores of the mouth (caused by Type Two herpes virus), oral-genital contact should be avoided, since herpes Type Two can infect the genitalia and is transmissible to the infant. After the birth, people with cold sores of the mouth or lips should avoid kissing or nuzzling the infant, cover any exposed lesions, and wash their hands before handling the baby.

Listeria monocytogenes. *Listeria monocytogenes* is a germ that can infect the pregnant woman and the newborn, leading to spontaneous abortion, stillbirth, and serious illness in the neonate. The germ is widespread in streams, sewage, silage, and soil, and infects primarily farm animals. It is passed in their stools, from which it can contaminate vegetables grown with infected manure. Thorough washing or cooking of vegetables should be preventive. Pasteurization of milk usually destroys this organism.

Monilia. *Monilia,* a yeast commonly present in the vagina, can cause vaginal infections in the mother and a condition known as *thrush* in the newborn. While many women with monilial infections have an itchy vaginal discharge, which leads to early diagnosis and treatment, monilial infections may also be silent (with no obvious symptoms) or go unnoticed. The vaginal speculum examination usually performed late in pregnancy is done in part to detect monilial infections. Treating the infection minimizes the possibility of transmitting the yeast to the baby.

If a baby picks up the yeast in the birth canal it can infect his or her mouth or tongue, causing the white coating known as thrush. Although troublesome, thrush is easily treatable.

Rubella.   *Rubella,* or *German measles,* usually a mild childhood infection, can have severely damaging effects on the growing fetus. In fact, the capacity of some viruses to damage the fetus was first established in connection with rubella. Investigations noted that epidemics of rubella preceded the birth of a significant number of babies with a group of birth defects known as *congenital rubella syndrome* (these include deafness, a small brain, and mental retardation).

The development of an effective vaccine (see p. 158) against this virus was given impetus by the serious problem of infection of the fetus. Now girls and women are routinely immunized against rubella, and the occurrence of rubella-induced birth defects has been virtually eliminated (see also p. 58 on test for rubella immunity).

Syphilis.   Syphilis is caused by a corkscrew-shaped microorganism which can reach the fetus of an infected woman by crossing the placenta from the mother's blood to that of the fetus. Infection can cause widespread and progressive damage to any part of the body of the fetus, including the brain, eyes, and bones. Although treatment with antibiotics can arrest infection of the fetus, the damage already done cannot be reversed. Because of the danger of syphilis, women are checked for the presence of the disease with a blood test at their first prenatal visit, and, if they are infected, are treated at once. (See p. 55.)

Toxoplasmosis.   Toxoplasmosis is an infectious disease caused by a one-celled organism called *Toxoplasma,* which resembles an amoeba. Commonly found in the feces of cats, it is also encountered encysted (in dormant form) in the raw meat of several animals, especially pigs. Up to one-fourth to one-third of all people have contracted this infection at some time in their lives, usually without being aware of it, and have measurable antibodies to *Toxoplasma* in their blood. Infected human beings harbor the cyst form of this organism in their tissues, apparently without ill effect.

If a woman becomes infected during pregnancy, the fetus can become infected in turn, suffering possible widespread damage, especially to the brain and eyes. Without treatment, it can suffer mental retardation, epilepsy, and blindness. The infected woman herself may show symptoms that resemble those of infectious mononucleosis: sore throat, fever, enlarged lymph glands in the neck; or she may have no symptoms at all.

The pregnant woman can best avoid exposure to *Toxoplasma* by not eating raw meat, especially pork; by washing her hands carefully after handling raw meat, and by avoiding contact with stray cats. If she has a pet cat, she should wear disposable gloves and a face mask (against dust) while changing the litter box, or delegate this task to someone else for the duration of the pregnancy. Litter should be changed daily to prevent *Toxoplasma* larvae from maturing to the stage of infectivity. The pet cat should be confined to an area where it cannot hunt birds and rodents, kept away from the stool of other cats, and fed canned or cooked food rather than raw meat.

Another approach to prevention is to check the woman's blood level of antibodies against *Toxoplasma* early in pregnancy to determine her immune status. If the level of antibodies is high enough to indicate immunity, she can be less strict in following the precautions mentioned above. If the level is low, she should carefully follow the precautions. The flaw in this approach is that an elevated level of antibodies may reflect an infection that is in progress, rather than one that has occurred in the past. Therefore physicians should be alert in this case for infection in the newborn.

DIABETES

Although diabetes and pregnancy do not mix well, attentive care can do much to reduce risks to the mother and the developing fetus. Pregnancy intensifies the metabolic derangement in this disorder. Thus, pregnancy can "bring out" diabetes in a woman with an underlying tendency to it, even though she has shown no signs or symptoms of the disease. During pregnancy such women may develop symptoms such as weakness, weight loss, increased thirst, and increased urination, or merely show an impaired ability to process glucose (sugar), as detected by testing.

The effects of diabetes on pregnancy include:

- increased risk of preeclampsia and eclampsia (see p. 315)
- increased susceptibility of the pregnant woman to infection

- increased size of the fetus, which may complicate delivery (see p. 325, "Shoulder Dystocia," and p. 293 on cephalopelvic disproportion)
- increased likelihood of cesarean section (see p. 278)
- increased incidence of polyhydramnios (see p. 300)
- increased incidence of congenital abnormalities (birth defects)
- problems for the baby at birth, such as low blood sugar, respiratory difficulties, and excessive jaundice.

The less severe the mother's diabetes and the better the control over it, regardless of severity, the less serious the problems will be for mother and baby.

Women at risk for diabetes during pregnancy include those who:

- demonstrate glycosuria (glucose in the urine), especially on more than one occasion (see p. 54, "Laboratory Tests")
- are obese (e.g., shorter than 5'5" and weigh more than 150 pounds; or taller than 5'5" and weigh more than 180 pounds during or prior to the first trimester)
- have had a previous infant weighing over nine and a half pounds
- have had a stillbirth
- have a family history of diabetes in parents, siblings, aunts, or uncles.

These women are candidates for the measurement of blood glucose after fasting or, as is more often done, after a test oral dose of glucose. Or, if diabetes is strongly suspected, they are given a glucose tolerance test, which measures blood glucose levels before, and at several hourly intervals after, ingesting a standard amount of glucose solution. Increasingly, blood testing is becoming routine in all pregnancies.

The treatment of diabetes varies with its severity. At one extreme is the severely diabetic woman who required insulin prior to pregnancy. She will certainly continue to need it while pregnant. Women with severe diabetes may require hospitalization to achieve optimal control over the disorder. At the other extreme is the woman whose diabetes is present only in pregnancy (gestational diabetics) and is detectable only as a change in the blood level of glucose before symptoms develop. Such a woman may be able to control her diabetes through proper diet alone, or she may need insulin as well. However, since the mildest case of diabetes can grow worse as pregnancy progresses, close monitoring of urine, and especially blood glucose, is necessary.

There is growing evidence that the first trimester (the period of organ formation in the fetus) is the time of greatest risk for the development of birth defects in the fetus of a diabetic woman. But, at this crucial time, she may not even know that she is pregnant. A study is underway, at a number of university medical centers, seeking the earliest possible identification of pregnancy in diabetic women through basal body temperature measurements. Pregnancy is suspected when the temperature is elevated over normal for sixteen days or more. Once pregnancy is diagnosed (see p. 39), the women being studied are hospitalized for instruction in tight diabetic control. They are taught to pay careful attention to diet, test their blood glucose at home, and use a self-regulated insulin pump to provide a continuous infusion of insulin which is adjusted throughout the day according to the body's needs. This pump delivers insulin into the skin of the abdomen through a needle, which can remain in one place for several days before a change of site is needed.

The optimal timing for a diabetic pregnant woman to give birth depends on several factors: the severity of the diabetes and the quality of control over it, the maturity of the fetus and its ability to survive outside the womb, the health of the fetus, and the risk of stillbirth. If labor does not occur spontaneously at term, delivery is usually accomplished either by induction or cesarean section. The woman who was diabetic prior to pregnancy may require hospitalization during pregnancy late in the third trimester, if not earlier. The infants of insulin-dependent diabetic women require observation for the development of such problems as low blood sugar and jaundice.

In general, the care of the diabetic pregnant woman, by emphasizing close (tight) control of blood glucose, has vastly improved outcomes in recent years. For example, in the group of women who develop diabetes during pregnancy, it is now possible through tight control to have just the same proportion of normal healthy newborns as in any nondiabetic group.

TOBACCO

Concern for their unborn baby can be a powerful motivation for a pregnant woman and her partner to stop smoking. Cigarette smoke that reaches the fetus by way of the mother's blood is now recognized as a hazard to its health. The babies of smokers are likely to be smaller and lighter in weight than those of non-smokers, to be born prematurely, and to have more respiratory problems after birth. Exposure of the pregnant woman to smoke in the air, produced by others, contributes to the smoke levels in her blood, although not to the same degree as would her own smoking. Tobacco products (*thiocyanate*, for example) are found in the cord blood of the baby at birth, even in mothers "passively exposed" to cigarette smoke.

Complications in pregnancy are also more common in women who smoke than in nonsmokers. They include spontaneous abortion (see p. 305), placenta praevia and abruptio placenta (p. 312), premature rupture of the membranes (p. 320), and bleeding in labor.

The intensity of cigarette addiction should not be underestimated. Even though a smoker knows intellectually that cigarettes are dangerous to health, she may deny that the risk applies to her personally. If she decides to stop, her major difficulty lies in dealing with the addiction itself.

Effective newer approaches to stopping smoking begin with the recognition of the hard plight of the cigarette addict and include strategies for coping with withdrawal symptoms and continuing cravings for nicotine. Doctors, midwives, clinics, hospitals, and local affiliates of the American Cancer Society can direct smokers who wish to quit to appropriate resources in their communities. Materials that may prove useful include the self-administered questionnaire, "Why Do You Smoke?" and the follow-up booklet, "Calling It Quits. The Latest Advice on How to Give Up Cigarettes." This literature can be obtained from the Office of Cancer Communications of the National Institutes of Health, Bethesda, Maryland 20014. Refer to DHEW publications (NIH) 79–1822, 1823, and 1824.

Bear in mind that there is good evidence that children of smokers show greater susceptibility to respiratory infections during childhood, and are more likely to take up the habit themselves in later life, than the children of nonsmokers. By stopping during and after pregnancy, parents become positive role models for their children.

ALCOHOL

Among the growing number of possible dangers to the fetus, alcohol may come as something of a surprise — particularly to the many women accustomed to a glass of wine with dinner or a highball after work. Just how dangerous is alcohol?

The question can be answered only partially and tentatively, but several things are clear. First, the babies of women who are active alcoholics during pregnancy tend to have widespread defects that are apparent at birth and may impair the child's functioning for life. The most severely affected babies have a cluster of defects known as the *fetal alcohol syndrome (FAS)*. They share three characteristics:

1. severe prenatal and/or postnatal growth retardation
2. central nervous system abnormality
3. multiple abnormalities of the head and face, such as an extremely small head, small eyes, a short distance between the corners of the eyelids, a poorly developed groove in the skin between the upper lip and the bottom of the nose, a thin upper lip, and/or flat cheekbones.

If the child at birth shows no evidence of the above defects, which are used as criteria for diagnosing FAS, but is still somewhat abnormal, the term *fetal alcohol effects (FAE)* is used. One example of such an effect, observed in some newborns, is their tendency to sleep less and awaken more often than normal infants. While we do not yet know fully about the mild physical and behavioral abnormalities of FAE, or how they affect children's intelligence or behavior over the long run, it seems likely that most children with FAE only will mature normally.

The degree of FAS or FAE appears directly related to both the quantity of alcohol consumed during pregnancy and the time it was consumed, but the details of these relationships are not yet well understood. It must be emphasized that FAS has been reported *only* in alcoholic women, some of them so severely addicted that they gave birth in the midst of delirium tremens or an alcoholic stupor. Even in alcoholic women, the effects on the fetus can be reduced if drinking is decreased. In a study at Boston City Hospital, the offspring of heavy drinkers who lowered their intake, or abstained before the last trimester of pregnancy, showed closer-to-normal fetal growth as indicated by weight, length, and head circumference.

For mothers who drink moderately during pregnancy, the evidence is incomplete, and existing studies are far from adequate. In one well-known report, 1,529 Seattle women in the fifth month of pregnancy were asked about their consumption of alcohol and other drugs during the month before they recognized that they were pregnant. Later, FAS was seen only in babies born to mothers who reported having had more than four drinks a day, and not in all the infants of such mothers. (A drink is defined as one-half ounce of pure alcohol, the amount present in 1 ounce of hard liquor, 5 ounces of wine, or 12 ounces of beer.) FAE was found in six of fifty-four infants of the mothers who had had two to four drinks per day, and in two of the ninety-three infants born to women who said they had had fewer than two drinks daily. Obviously, this study has methodological problems involving the accuracy of recall and reporting, but the results are worth bearing in mind when making a decision about drinking in pregnancy.

The interrelationship between drinking and other factors such as diet, caffeine, marijuana, and nicotine is also not known. It is, however, clear that *no completely proven safe dose of alcohol for the pregnant woman has been determined.* This is not equivalent to saying that there is no safe dose, only that no one can say what it is.

The chances of being able to identify a safe level of alcohol intake for all women (assuming that there is one higher than total abstention) are not very good. The dangers of alcohol to the fetus have been widely publicized, and few women are willing to take part in a study in which they volunteer to drink. We have never met a pregnant woman who, upon learning in detail about the risks of alcohol, did not desist completely, even though an occasional drink, or even one a day, probably carries little risk. Even the manager of a restaurant with whom we talked, who was responsible for tasting and selecting the wines offered each day, quickly got someone else to take over this part of her job until her child was born.

As a doctor, the most common alcohol-related problem I see concerns the social drinker who has been drinking moderately before she knows she is pregnant. What should she do? The available data suggest that it would be wise to terminate the pregnancy of a woman whose daily alcohol consumption has exceeded four drinks and who will not, or cannot, cut down, even when she receives counseling and other help. The chance that she will have an affected fetus is about 33 percent. Under two drinks per day, the odds are near zero for FAS, and, as has been discussed, the long-range outcome of FAE is not known. A woman who has one or two drinks a week probably has little to worry about. Thus, the woman who consumes between two and four drinks a day is in uncertain territory, with about a 10 percent chance that her infant will suffer FAE. There is no way to identify an affected fetus before birth as a way of assisting in the decision.

The response of women, who are regular drinkers, to the information we have presented varies with each woman's values and style of taking chances. It is not easy for anyone to compare the risk and trauma of bearing a child who has mild, perhaps temporary problems with the risk and trauma of aborting a normal fetus.

In conclusion, we feel it makes sense for women who think or know they are pregnant, or who want to conceive, either to avoid alcohol altogether (the safest course) or to limit their daily intake to two drinks or less. (Note that there is some evidence that suggests alcohol can be harmful to sperm; thus, men are advised to abstain from drinking while trying to conceive.) While the discovery of FAS and FAE poses many troubling, still unanswered questions, we should consider ourselves fortunate that this connection between alcohol and fetal well-being has come to light and that defects can now be understood and prevented.

CAFFEINE

Although caffeine in large doses has been shown to cause birth defects in experimental animals, no such effect has been demonstrated in infants born of mothers who consumed caffeine during their pregnancies, in the several studies that were done. For example, a 1982 report of more than 12,000 births at the Boston

Hospital for Women showed no correlation between caffeine consumption during pregnancy and birth defects in newborns.

Even with this reassuring information on the lack of toxicity of caffeine during pregnancy, many women will choose to avoid it nonetheless, a conservative policy with which we agree.

Bear in mind that caffeine is present not only in coffee but also in black tea, cola drinks, cocoa, and some headache remedies. You may need to read labels closely to discover the presence and amount of caffeine in some products. Substituting caffeine-free coffee, soft drinks, or herb teas for the "real thing" is a wise policy, whether you are pregnant or not, since high levels of caffeine consumption can cause anxiety, nervousness, sleeplessness, and other physical and mental disturbances. Hyperactivity of either the fetus in the womb or the nursing baby of a mother who consumes much caffeine seems to be related to the drug.

MARIJUANA

The impact of marijuana smoking on the fetus has been difficult to assess, partly because marijuana smokers also commonly drink alcoholic beverages (see above), smoke tobacco (see above), and are prone to have inadequate diets. Any defects noted in the babies of marijuana smokers may be the result of the interaction of several factors, making it difficult to isolate the specific contribution of marijuana.

With this cautionary note, the best available evidence is that marijuana is likely to result in smaller babies and ones who have features compatible with the Fetal Alcohol Syndrome (see p. 171). The best recommmendation, of course, is to avoid marijuana during pregnancy.

X RAYS

The possibility of harm to the fetus from diagnostic X rays has aroused great concern. Much of the concern over radiation originated in the aftermath of the atomic bombing of Japan, because of the increase in abortion and birth defects observed there. It is important to realize, however, that there is no reported case of a human birth defect caused by a diagnostic X ray study. Radiation to the fetus during diagnostic X rays, while hard to measure accurately, is without question significantly less than the dose received by some fetuses in Hiroshima and Nagasaki. Although it is also true that X radiation has been shown to be damaging in experimental animals, the doses used were far larger than those used in humans.

The risk of radiation exposure to the fetus from diagnostic X rays appears to be quite low, certainly not high enough to contraindicate medically needed X ray studies. Nevertheless, unnecessary exposure is unwise, especially in the first trimester. If a study can be delayed, so much the better. The following guidelines are suggested:

1. A woman in her reproductive years should assume that she is pregnant unless proved otherwise. Evidence of not being pregnant includes the following: onset of menses in the previous ten days, use of oral contraceptives, use of an IUD, no sexual intercourse since last menstrual period, having had surgical sterilization, or a negative result on a very sensitive pregnancy test (see p. 39).

2. If a woman known to be in the first trimester of pregnancy needs an X ray, the pelvis should not be included in the X ray field if at all possible.

3. Women should always wear a shield over the pelvis and abdomen when having X ray studies (including dental X rays), whether or not they are pregnant. These will offer some but not complete protection.

4. If there is medical indication to perform a diagnostic X ray study in pregnancy, the importance of the information to be obtained will generally outweigh the remote risk of harm to the fetus. However, each situation must be evaluated on its individual merits.

5. If a woman receives a relatively large amount of radiation (more than 5 rads) to the pelvis in the first trimester of pregnancy, she may have suffered an increased risk for birth defects, the exact percentage of which is not well understood, perhaps 1 to 3 percent. For some couples, such a risk may be enough to justify a therapeutic abortion after careful discussion with a physician.

6. With any X ray exposure during pregnancy, there may be a small increase in the incidence of leukemia during childhood, although this issue is not yet well understood.

The above discussion does not apply to the therapeutic use of X rays, administered in much larger doses, usually to treat cancer. These doses can be sufficient to damage the fetus.

AUTOMOBILE SAFETY

A woman of childbearing age is more likely to be killed or crippled by an automobile accident than by disease or other threat. Thus, if a woman could take only one preventive measure during pregnancy, she might be well advised to insist on using seat belts herself and demand that others in the car do the same. Both lap belts and shoulder harnesses can be used safely in pregnancy. To the extent possible, the shoulder harness should be used in the usual way, and the lap belt should be fastened tightly over the hips beneath the uterus. For maximum protection of the pregnant woman, all other passengers need to be restrained, too, since a crash can send unrestrained riders flying with unbelievable forces (over one ton at a car speed of 25 miles per hour) that can seriously harm themselves and others.

We also encourage expectant parents to plan ahead for their baby's car safety by obtaining a crash-tested infant restraint before the baby's birth, so that even the first ride will be a safe one. These restraints are held in place by the car's own safety belts. It is simply not safe to carry an infant or child on one's lap, even when sitting in the back seat. It is also best not to use the car's safety belts alone until a child weighs about 40 pounds. (If the alternative, however, is no restraint at all, the standard belt will do once a child can sit up alone.) More and more states are requiring child restraints by law.

Recently joining the campaign for the use of car seat restraints are the American Academy of Pediatrics and the American College of Obstetricians and Gynecologists, including its nursing association. The members of these professional groups, working in concert, are in a strategic postion to reach pregnant women and the parents of infants and children. They will be happy to inform you on the effective use of infant restraints and seat belts and recommend effective types.

Two other important activist groups concerned with automobile safety for all are MADD (Mothers Against Drunk Driving) and RID (Remove Intoxicated Drivers). These national organizations, together with their local chapters, complement each other by publicizing the major role of the drunk driver in highway accidents, lobbying for stiffer legal penalties and stricter enforcement of the law, and providing assistance to the families of persons killed by drunk drivers. Readers who want to contribute to solving one of our major health problems are encouraged to join these groups. (See Appendix B for further information.)

Another way of contributing to car safety is to fight for stronger legislation. One law often discussed would require that all new cars have automatically inflatable air bags. We as a society continue to delay such action — as of this writing — largely because of opposition by car manufacturers who fear loss of sales related to the necessary increase in auto prices to cover the costs of such devices. The manufacturers claim that the public doesn't want to pay for such a safety feature. Needless to say, the savings in death and disability measured in dollars alone would likely more than pay for the extra costs of the bags.

A less desirable automatic system involves automatic belts that move into position across the occupant as the car door closes. They have the major disadvantage of being disconnectable.

Another beneficial legislative move would be a requirement that all persons riding in cars wear seat belts. At the time of this writing, legislation to this effect has been introduced in many states. In New York State, the first to pass such legislation, the law went into effect in 1985. Ironically, car manufacturers are actively lobbying for such laws because their passage by two-thirds of the states will prevent air bags from becoming mandatory under current guidelines.

ENVIRONMENTAL POLLUTION

Of all the issues that concern protecting the fetus, none seems to us more frightening or more urgent than the growing worldwide problem of environmental pollution.

Our knowledge about the specific effects on the fetus of exposure to toxins in the mother, such as lead, mercury, cadmium, industrial toxins, pesticide residues, and low-level radioactive wastes, is as yet quite limited. There is, for example, some preliminary evidence that high lead levels in a pregnant woman may contribute to spontaneous abortion (miscarriage), stillbirth, premature labor, premature rupture of membranes, and infertility. In males, lead may be a factor in deficiencies and abnormalities in sperm production. Exposure to lead can occur in people employed as battery makers, paint manufacturers, glass makers, welders, and motor fuel blenders.

It is also known that toxins can be transferred to the fetus, and babies can begin life already endowed with the waste products of our industrial civilization. From the moment of birth, the infant shares in the environment of his or her family. In addition, some toxins in the mother are concentrated and excreted into the breast milk, to be ingested by the nursing infant. Little that is good can come from this chemical burden.

While the toxic effects of these chemicals in large exposures are well known, only now are we beginning to understand the consequences of low-level exposure to certain toxins. As an example, lead in body quantities less than that which cause encephalopathy (coma, convulsions, etc.) can cause poor school performance and behavioral problems. (After birth, children are exposed to lead in lead-based paints, fumes from cars that use leaded gasoline, water coming through lead pipes, and contaminated soil.) For most toxins, however, the significance of low body concentrations still remains unknown.

An important lead to the link between environment and fetal outcome has been provided by a recent study from the Harvard School of Public Health, which examined the impact on pregnancies of women in Woburn, Massachusetts, who were exposed to water supplies contaminated by toxic industrial wastes. There were significantly higher risks for perinatal deaths, eye and ear disorders, cleft palate, Down syndrome (see p. 125), and central nervous system disorders.

Cleaning up our environment, and preventing future pollution on a worldwide scale, poses enormous challenges that involve political and economic as well as health considerations. Although public awareness of these problems is growing, there is still little evidence of the kind of serious commitment required in this country, or the rest of the world, if we are all to avoid a public health catastrophe. In this country alone there are thousands of toxic waste dumps (future Love Canals) that will leak into water supplies and soil unless they are cleaned up. Many already have. We continue to support and export nuclear technology for the generation of electrical power, in spite of the fact that there is no secure disposal mechanism for the dangerous liquid wastes unavoidably produced, and there may never be. Some of these wastes retain their radioactivity for tens of thousands of years. Sooner or later, even in the absence of disruption of storage centers by human error, sabotage, war, or natural disasters like earthquakes, it is highly probable that such wastes will leak and further contaminate water supplies and food chains. The worldwide destruction of forests, which seems related to environmental contamination, should serve as a warning that we ourselves are next on the list of living things whose survival is threatened. The environmental time bomb is ticking away.

We urge all expectant parents (and everyone else) not only to care for their own health and that of their children, but to join the campaign for a clean environment for the sake of ourselves and future generations. (See Appendix B for a list of organizations working in this cause who offer information and opportunities to become active.)

As an example of an important small individual step, we recommend that you consider installing an activated charcoal filter in your drinking water supply to remove industrial and agricultural chemicals that are not ordinarily treated by municipal water works. At this time of uncertainty about the long-range effects of such products that can accumulate in the body over time, the wise course appears to be prevention. Other steps are many and include: reading labels carefully, seeking sources of unsprayed fruit and vegetables, and avoiding building materials containing asbestos and formaldehyde. The environmental groups listed in Appendix B are good sources of information on ways to protect family health.

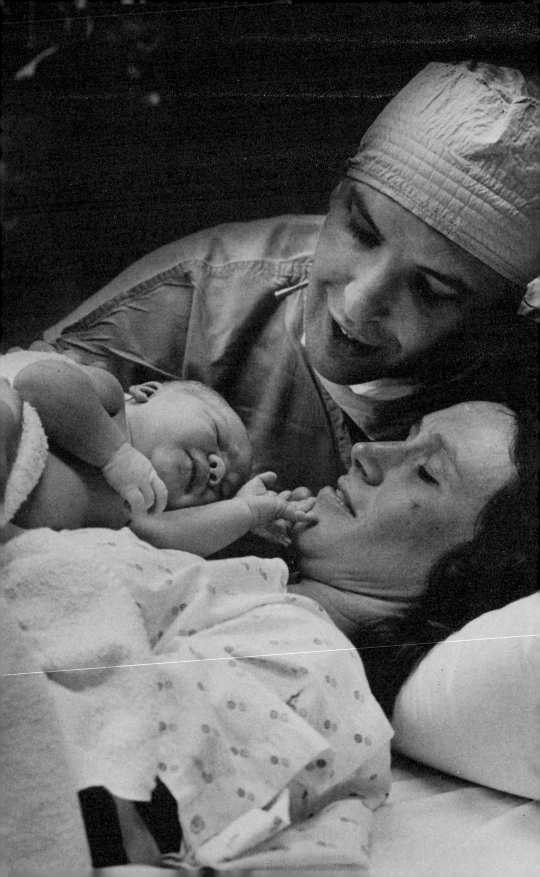

4

Choices in Childbirth

Where to Give Birth

Choosing where to have to have the baby is one of the most important decisions a pregnant woman and her partner must make. Their decision must be based on available local options. In Chapter 1 we saw two different approaches: a hospital birth and a home birth. As of this writing, only about 1 percent of all births in this country occur at home (a relatively stable figure during recent years), and only about 10,000 occur annually in freestanding birthing centers. (There are about 130 of these centers, and the number is steadily increasing.) Births in out-of-hospital settings, especially in the home, often meet with intense opposition from obstetricians.

At this point there are no randomized controlled studies of out-of-hospital versus in-hospital births, which means that existing data are less than satisfactory. However, there is a growing literature of European and American experiences with different birth sites. In order to help couples who want more information, we have given an overview of this literature in Appendix A.

Apart from medical considerations in hospital delivery, women who choose to have their babies in hospitals do so for many different reasons: a sense of security; access to a range of pain medication and technical backup; because the obstetrician they chose and trust works out of a particular hospital; or simply because a few days in the hospital would relieve them from the pressures and duties that surround them at home. Some husbands who feel more secure with the idea of their wives giving birth in a hospital encourage this choice.

Women who choose a home birth also have different reasons for their decisions: a preference for home-like surroundings; the chance to have children or friends present; a greater opportunity to make their own decisions surrounding the birth; a sense of intimacy; greater involvement of the father.

Shelia Kitzinger, in her excellent book, *The Complete Book of Pregnancy and Childbirth,* makes the point that choosing home birth means taking on added responsibilities. These include: an early start on prenatal care and screening for potential difficulties; the selection of a competent birth attendant; attention to nutrition; education on home birth; getting started in breast-feeding and the birth process itself; and finally, obtaining all the supplies needed by the birth attendant. Couples who choose home birth must be prepared to take on these added responsibilities wholeheartedly.

Our view is that, for a healthy, low-risk pregnancy, the probability of a complication (like fetal distress or severe postpartum hemorrhage) that would make the loss of time in transit to hospital a serious disadvantage in managing the labor is less than one in a thousand. Couples should be informed of this very small but real risk, which they must balance against the risk of excess intervention and the psychological risk incurred in the hospital. In our society large risks are taken for granted in automobile travel, alcohol and tobacco consumption, and dangerous sports. Pregnant women are only now legally required to wear seat belts in automobiles and not yet in all states. Against such a context, are the small risks of out-of-hospital birth unreasonable ones, in return for the perceived psychological benefits of a home or home-like atmosphere?

Citizens and professionals who are concerned by the risks of out-of-hospital birth can contribute constructively in two ways: by helping to collect data about home birth and by helping to create support systems to reduce the already minimal risks of home birth. Those who are concerned about the coldness and excessive technology of hospital birth can work to make their hospital a more humane setting for childbirth — a place where childbirth can be regarded as a normal, joyous process. Many groups have already accomplished much along these lines. They are listed in Appendix B.

Labor

By convention, labor is divided into three stages. The *first stage* begins with dilatation of the cervix and lasts until the cervix is completely dilated, marking the onset of the next stage. This first stage is divided into latent and active phases. We discuss these later on. The *second stage* of complete dilatation ends with the birth of the baby, as the *third stage*, the delivery of the placenta, begins.

The progress of the first stage of labor is judged according to the diameter (width) of the cervix. The size of the opening ranges from "zero" (completely closed) to "fully dilated," at an average of 10 centimeters (just under 4 inches) with a full-term baby. (See p. 184.) The smallest discernible dilation usually noted is a "fingertip"; that is, it allows for the introduction of the tip only of the examiner's finger. The cervix may be dilated several centimeters before labor begins, especially in first pregnancies.

The definition of labor encompasses regular uterine contractions and progressive cervical dilatation. For practical purposes, the cervix should open to 3 or 4 centimeters before it is concluded that labor has begun, even though the length of labor once in progress is timed from the onset of regular contractions. It is both possible and common for a woman with a slightly dilated cervix and the experience of contractions *not* to be in labor, since, during the latter part of pregnancy, uterine contractions that may be quite painful are common. These are known as *Braxton Hicks contractions*, after the physician who first described them. A run of Braxton Hicks contractions constitutes what is commonly called "false labor." These false labor contractions are usually irregular. They do change unpredictably in length, strength, or frequency and often stop with a change in activity. Shifting from standing to lying down (or vice versa) or taking a warm bath will often make them stop.

In contrast, "true labor" contractions increase in regularity, length, strength, and frequency. They do not subside, and grow stronger with activity. The onset of labor is often heralded by loss of the *mucous plug*, which fills the crevices in the cervical canal. Bloody mucus leaks from the vagina or is noticed on toilet paper. This "bloody show" may appear just before the onset of labor or may come intermittently over several days. One way or another it signifies that the time is drawing near.

Labor is announced in about 10 percent of pregnancies by the breaking of the "bag of waters" or *amniotic sac* (see p. 53), experienced by the woman as a slow leak or gush of warm fluid which she may mistake for urine. Such "premature rupture of the membranes" exposes the uterus and fetus to the bacteria naturally present in the vagina and calls for special care to prevent infection if labor does not proceed quickly.

The essential distinction between true and false labor is dilatation of the cervix. Many a woman has thought she was in labor, only to find out she was not. False alarms result in futile trips to the hospital and unnecessary anxiety. Because contractions do not always mean that labor has started, official admission to the hospital is delayed until the width of the cervix has been observed for a while.

During labor, or even some time before it begins, the cervix not only dilates but "effaces" or thins out. (See Figure 8.) This *effacement* is measured as a percentage of its full thickness — 25 percent, 80 percent, etc. At the onset of labor effacement of the cervix varies from zero to 100 percent. As a rule it is completed, at the latest, when labor enters its *active phase*.

Thus, before labor begins, the cervix may be said to prepare for the work ahead. This "ripening" of the cervix for labor consists of its dilatation, effacement, softening, and forward rotation as it shifts from a position facing the woman's spine to one facing forward.

Another important consideration in assessing the progress of labor is the location of the baby in relation to the birth canal. (See Figure 9.) The position of the leading edge of the baby, the part that first enters the birth canal (usually the head), in relation to the center of the mother's pelvis is known as the *station*. The midpelvis is called "station zero." When the head reaches station zero, it is said to be "engaged." (See also p. 44 on pelvic mea-

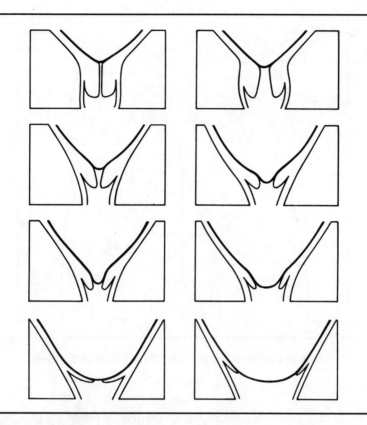

Figure 8. Dilatation and effacement (thinning) of cervix. Left-hand column shows cervix in a first birth; right-hand column shows the cervix after two or more births.

surements.) Above the level of the mid-pelvis the station is called negative; below the mid-pelvis, positive. "Plus one," then, means 1 centimeter below or beyond the mid-pelvis, while "minus two" means 2 centimeters above the mid-pelvis. Descent of the baby is recorded in sequence as "minus three," "minus two," "minus one," zero (at the mid-pelvis), "plus one," "plus two," and "plus three" (when the baby's head is visible).

In addition to determining where the baby is located, it is also essential to know what part of the baby will appear first — head, face, hands, buttocks — and how it is oriented in space. This can usually be determined during vaginal examinations. Determining

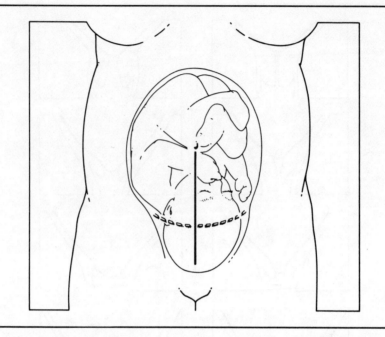

Figure 9.   Axis of birth canal (bold line). Mid-pelvis (dotted line)

the way the head, for example, is turned requires identification of its "landmarks," or topical characteristics, with reference to an imaginary line or axis passing through the birth canal. For example, *sutures,* or *fontanels,* distinguish the front from the back of the skull. These sutures are the grooves between the still unknit bones of the skull. The fontanels are the triangular spaces at the junctions of the sutures, a large one in front (anterior) and a smaller one in back (posterior). (See Figure 10.) Using these landmarks, it is possible to determine whether the head is facing forward, backward, or crossways. In medical terms, the location of the *occiput* (point of the head) is described as being to the left or right of center, pointing forward (anterior), backward (posterior), or crossways (transverse), 90 degrees to the right or left of the midline. Thus, "*LOA*" (left occiput anterior, the most common position), means that the occiput (the "O") is directed left and forward. For a summary of the various positions, see Figures 11 through 14.

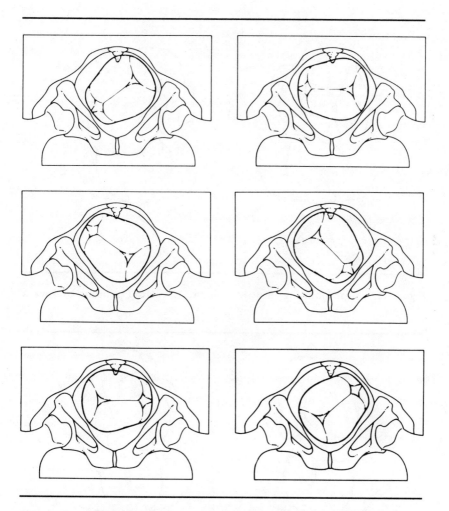

Figure 10. **Position of head in labor as seen from below, showing fontanels**

In touching the baby's head, the examiner determines whether or not the scalp is swollen. Swelling is called *caput succedaneum*, and a "caput" signifies that the ring of pressure exerted by the cervix on the scalp has interfered with the return of blood from the skin in the center of the ring. The presence of a caput (see Figure 15) suggests that the cervix is not yielding to pressure from the head and may mean some degree of obstruction to the descent of the baby. At times a caput can be several centimeters thick,

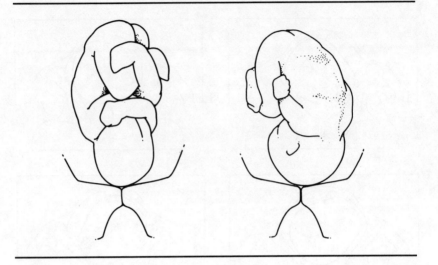

Figure 11.   Head pointing forward   Figure 12.   Head pointing backward

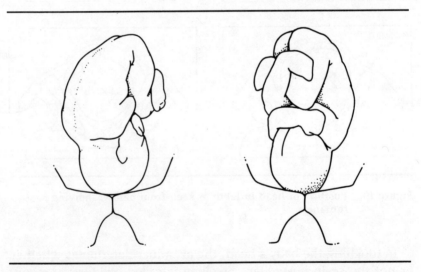

Figure 13.   Head pointing right   Figure 14.   Head pointing left

suggesting a misleadingly greater degree of descent than is the case.

Another effect of pressure on the baby's head is known as *molding*, referring to the shaping of the head by the architecture

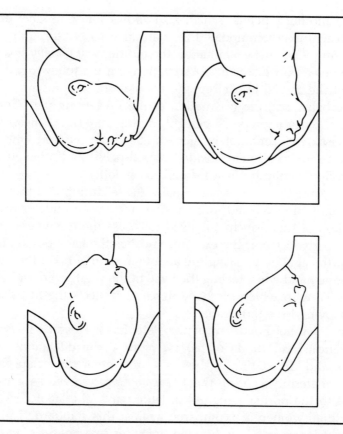

Figure 15.   Caput (swelling of baby's scalp due to pressure from the cervix or vagina)

of the birth canal. At birth a baby's head, unlike that of the adult or child, can be squeezed and elongated because the separate bones of the skull have not yet fused. (See Figure 10.) The seams are open and the bones can overlap. This overlapping of the bones can often be detected in a vaginal examination. Molding is seen at birth in the form of elongation of the head and usually reverses spontaneously within a few days. The capacity of the head to "mold" is an adaptation of our species to the stresses of labor. The "give" of the skull prevents it from cracking and permits a birth that otherwise would have been obstructed. The molding of the baby's head is complemented by the looseness of the joints of the mother's pelvis, which also allows for some give of the birth canal to accommodate the infant as it passes through.

During a vaginal examination the mother will usually hear the examiner report his or her observations on the following: dilatation of the cervix, its effacement, the station, the presenting part of the baby, and the orientation of the presenting part. For example, "6 centimeters, 80 percent, minus one, LOA" means that the cervix is 6 centimeters dilated, 80 percent effaced, and that the head is 1 centimeter inside the mid-pelvis and oriented with the occiput, pointing forward and to the left.

These measurements are usually made during a contraction, since they are expected to be at their maximum under stress. A variation of this principle is used to assess the roominess of the pelvis early in labor: the examiner pushes the baby down and to the birth canal by pressing the abdomen on the top of the uterus with one hand while feeling the head in the vagina with the other. The ease with which the baby descends reflects the fit between the baby and the birth canal.

Dr. Emanuel Friedman of the Beth Israel Hospital in Boston has studied hundreds of labors, plotting the dilatation of the cervix and the station against the amount of time elapsed. In many maternity centers the *Friedman Curve* serves as a useful guide to the normal progress of labor, since the labor curves of individual women are compared against this standard. The first stage of labor, as we mentioned, includes two phases of cervical dilatation, the *latent phase* and the *active phase*. The active phase is further divided into the *acceleration phase* and the *deceleration phase*. The latter part of the acceleration phase and the early part of the deceleration phase are referred to as the *transition*, that part of labor in which the cervix usually opens rapidly, from about 7 centimeters to full dilatation. Transition is often the hardest part of labor, and its pain may be unbearable. It is often accompanied by nausea and vomiting.

In first labors the latent phase normally lasts less than twenty hours; in second and subsequent labors, normally less than fourteen hours. In the active phase in first labors the cervix normally dilates about 1.2 centimeters per hour; in second and subsequent labors, 1.5 centimeters per hour. The latent phase is subject to many influences, such as drugs, and its duration (see below) has little bearing on the subsequent course of labor. A prolonged active phase, on the other hand, may mean a misfit between the baby and the birth canal (see p. 293 on disproportion).

Each stage and phase of labor has its own characteristics. A sensitive attendant, or the laboring woman herself, particularly if she has given birth before, can often tell the status of labor by the frequency, duration, and intensity of contractions, the presence or absence of pressure sensations in the birth canal, and the existence of associated symptoms such as nausea or vomiting.

Early in the latent phase of the first stage, contractions are five to thirty minutes apart and last from fifteen to forty seconds. They are often described as "mild cramps," "gas," "back pain," or "pressure." During the active phase, the contractions come two to five minutes apart, are forty-five to sixty seconds in duration, and are stronger, more intense. In transition the contractions occur one and one-half to three minutes apart, last for forty-five to ninety seconds, and are the strongest they will be during the whole labor. Often, one follows the other so rapidly that rest may be impossible. Once full dilatation is achieved, the contractions may then space out to three to five or more minutes apart, so that some women are able to doze off between them. The contractions are now less intense, and discomfort shifts from the uterus to the rectum and vagina and includes a sense of pressure and an "urge to push." As the baby descends to the perineum, many women report a "burning" sensation.

The second stage of labor, when dilatation is completed, usually lasts less than two hours. There is some controversy about the significance to the baby of a second stage that lasts longer, even in cases in which there is no obvious sign of fetal distress. The official view — but one that lacks substantiating evidence — is that the second stage should last no longer than two hours. The view of the authors is that, as long as progress is occurring and both mother and baby are well, no arbitrary limit need be set on the second stage.

Now that we have discussed the characteristics of an average labor, it is important to emphasize how variable labor can actually be. While we know the average first labor lasts about sixteen hours and average subsequent labors last six to eight hours, it is important we realize that these are averages only. Experienced birth attendants never cease to be amazed at the variability of the normal pattern. In my (Richard Feinbloom's) practice, I have seen first labors go on for two days, but I have also seen more than one first labor in which the cervix dilated from 2 centimeters to "full" in less than an hour. I vividly remember one woman who had irregular but distressing contractions without progress in dilatation for over forty-eight hours; no doubt, as I thought, a prolonged latent phase. To stimulate her labor, one of the midwives administered castor oil and an enema in the office. Within minutes this woman, who had never experienced labor before, felt the urge to push. My initial reaction was that the enema was working, and I suggested that she try using the toilet. When she was unable to produce a bowel movement, I suggested that she lie down in a chaise longue in our treatment room until the urge ceased. But the urge to push continued. I did a vaginal examination and found, to my utter disbelief, that she was fully dilated. There was no time to get to the hospital. We hastily pulled supplies together, and she had the baby right in the office. Both baby and mother came through in fine condition.

Each woman's labor is truly her own, and its particular course needs to be respected and attended to. Some common patterns, as well described by midwife Peggy Spindel, are as follows:

1. Some women go very slowly through early labor, then take off quickly when active labor is reached. This is the pattern described by Friedman as the norm.
2. Some women involuntarily "tighten up" and resist stronger contractions (especially at dilatation of 4 to 5 centimeters) to the point where those present begin to worry about the lack of progress. When these women seemingly can hold back no longer, and are able to "let go," they dilate very easily.
3. Some women progress in steps rather than continuously, resting as each new step is reached. It seems as if they successively interpret, integrate, then yield to each new set of sensations.
4. Some women resist when descent, with its strong genital sensations, begins to occur, even though they may have dilated rapidly until then (the late active stage) and pushing may be very slow.
5. Some women do not show their labor very much at all. It is

hard to tell when they are having a contraction and how strong it is. Vaginal examinations must be done periodically to assess progress. Often these women dilate quite well.

6. Some women stop their labor entirely at some point, either to deal with a problem, to rest, or seemingly for no apparent reason. This unusual variant of labor, while deviating from the norm, may still be compatible with a trouble-free birth.

The configuration of the birth canal varies along its course. It is not like a curved tube or tunnel with a constant diameter throughout. At the entry to the birth canal the widest measurements are the oblique distances running from the right back to the left front and from the left back to the right front. At the outlet of the canal, the widest dimension is from front to back, from the tip of the spine (coccyx) to the juncture of the pubic bone in the front. As the baby's body descends in the birth canal, it turns and twists to accommodate to these shifts in dimension. In the LOA position, the head approaches the perineum at an angle and then moves to a direct front-to-back orientation just as it is being born, while the shoulders and back, following behind higher in the canal, are still at an angle. When the head fully emerges, it immediately turns back into alignment with the rest of the body. As the shoulders are born, they move into a direct front-to-back position with one shoulder under the pubic bone as the other emerges over the coccyx. As the shoulders turn, the head turns with them and the baby's face looks directly to the side. (See Figures 16 and 17).

While the posterior position (occiput pointing to the back) is a normal but minority presentation from which babies are safely born, it is one that is often associated with the prolongation of labor and the experience of back pain. If a baby is posterior and progress in labor is slow, efforts are usually made to help the head (and the baby) to rotate forward, either by having the mother change position or by having the attendant turn the head manually in the vagina.

Prolonged early labor (or *prolonged latent phase*) is the term generally used to describe delays of twenty hours or more in first labors and fourteen or more in subsequent ones. Shorter delays are sometimes just called "pokey."

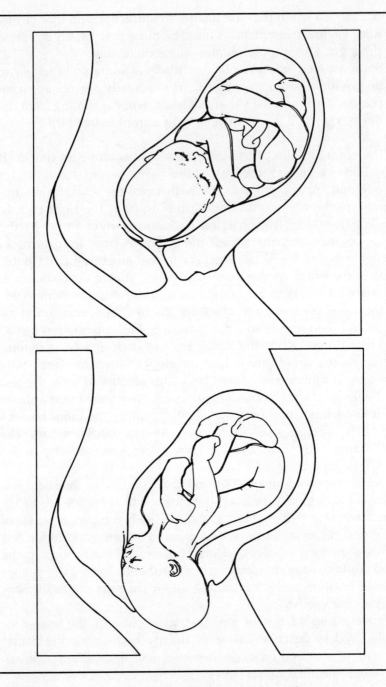

Figure 16. Descent and rotation of baby in birth canal

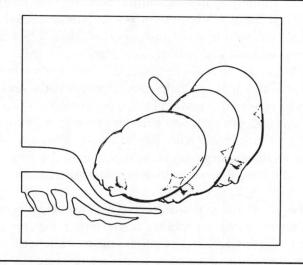

Figure 17. Rotation of baby's head during birth

A prolonged early labor can be a major source of distress to a woman, who may become discouraged and physically exhausted. Her condition is compounded by lack of sleep and dehydration. This "failure to progress" is usually why a home birth is transferred to the hospital.

Two basic approaches to this problem are to either stimulate labor or slow it down. The course to follow depends on how tired the woman is. She may need to rest for a while, or she may have enough reserve to get on with her labor after brief stimulation. If she has the will to move along, and still has some energy, there are certain measures that can pick up a labor; walking around; and, in the hospital, the use of Pitocin (trade name for *oxytocin*, a hormone that stimulates uterine contractions). (See p. 198.) In any case, she needs reassurance that failure to progress is not of her own doing, for a woman can do everything "right" and still have this problem. Reassurance from a trusted, familiar attendant that both she and the baby are basically well can bolster her flagging spirits.

An enema or a dose of castor oil are two generally effective ways of stimulating contractions. *Acidosis* (increased acidity) of the blood and urine, associated with *dehydration*, is believed to be a factor in inhibiting uterine contraction. In the hospital (and sometimes at home) dehydration is commonly treated with an intravenous infusion of a salt and sugar solution. Replacing fluids can reverse acidosis and reinvigorate uterine activity.

If the decision is to quiet the labor down and allow the woman to rest, measures that can help include warm baths and medications. *Hydroxyzine* (also known by the trade name, Vistaril) slows contractions and can be given either by mouth or by injection. It is sometimes combined with two shots of whiskey. Morphine sulfate in relatively large amounts is probably the most effective drug for allowing a woman to rest. Administered by injection, two doses fifteen to twenty minutes apart are usually required. It should be given only in the hospital. While most women fall asleep after receiving morphine, many report that they are still aware of their contractions but better able to tolerate them. At the very least, morphine does seem to permit rest and the recuperation of energy. Sometimes labor stops completely, to resume within several days; but more commonly it is only temporarily dampened.

A prolonged latent phase that cannot be reversed with the measures described raises the question of some other reason for the delay, such as disproportion (see p. 293), and calls for further investigation.

Fluids and Food

The basis for the usual recommendation — to avoid eating and drinking in labor and to rely on intravenous fluids (I.V.'s) exclusively — is that in an emergency, should a general (gas) anesthetic (see p. 209) be required to deliver the baby (usually by cesarean section), there is a danger that, during the induction of anesthesia, the woman will vomit and breathe the vomit into her lungs. This is a serious problem; chemical pneumonia, and even death, can result. A hospital policy of "nothing to eat or drink" during labor is not enough; few women's stomachs are empty before they reach the hospital. Other ways of minimizing the risk of chemical pneumonia during the induction of anesthesia are to compress the esophagus by pressure on the neck and to administer during labor drugs that reduce stomach acidity, since it appears that it is acid from the stomach that does most of the damage to the lungs.

Critics of the I.V. and the "no fluids by mouth" approach point out that the chance of requiring general anesthesia is actually very small and that policies affecting everyone should not be based on rare exceptions. Such critics suggest that alternative approaches to preventing chemical pneumonia, as described above, are available. They see the I.V. as an unnecessary intervention, which restrains a woman's movement and exemplifies the "medicalization" of childbirth. Most women, they feel, can sip fluids as needed. Proponents of I.V.'s and "no fluids by mouth" counter that the risk to the woman who suffers aspiration, although rare, is total — 100 percent. Furthermore, since the reduction in intestinal activity during labor may interfere with the absorption of fluids taken by mouth, an I.V. is a more reliable way to get fluids.

Each woman needs to consider the arguments on both sides of this issue in relation to the characteristics of her own pregnancy. In home births, the laboring woman is allowed to drink and eat. Experience has shown that she can tolerate certain categories of foods better than others. Easily digested carbohydrate foods — such as bread, fruit, rice, and pasta — and light protein foods — such as cheese and yogurt — can be taken as long as she wants them. As labor progresses, the emphasis should shift to high-calorie liquids. In general, water, Gatorade, iced tea, and non-citrus fruit juices are well tolerated. Honey or sugar can provide calories for women who want to drink plain water. Women should optimally consume 8 ounces of fluid and 200 calories an hour. (As examples of frequently used foods, a tablespoon of honey contains 64 calories; one cup of grape juice, 167 calories.)

Some attendants have noted that citrus and apple juices and dairy products can cause vomiting in heavy labor. They advise women to freeze cranberry or grape juice in ice trays to use in the event of nausea. Crushed ice from these juices, plain ice chips, or small sips of cool water tend to be kept down if taken in small amounts between each contraction. Dry toast or crackers also often help to reduce nausea.

Drugs That Contract the Uterus

Oxytocin (trade names Pitocin and Syntocinon), *ergonovine maleate* (Ergotrate), and *methylergonovine maleate* (Methergine) are drugs that stimulate contraction of the uterus. They play an important role in the care of women during and immediately after labor.

Oxytocin is the synthetic form of a hormone normally secreted by the pituitary gland to contract the muscles of the uterus and the glands of the breasts, leading to the ejection of milk. In the postpartum period, the secretion of this natural hormone accounts for the "after-pains" of uterine contractions familiar to nursing mothers, particularly with their second and subsequent babies. The secretion of natural oxytocin is stimulated by nerve impulses that reach the brain and pituitary from the breasts during nipple stimulation. Thus, stimulation can initiate and augment labor as well as initiate both the let-down of milk and the uterine contractions that help prevent postpartum hemorrhage. Because oxytocin is metabolized readily and lasts but a short time in the blood, it is ideal for artificially inducing uterine contractions in labor.

When used intravenously to enhance labor, an ampule of 10 units of oxytocin is thoroughly mixed with 1 liter of salt-sugar solution to produce a concentration of 10 milliunits (one one-thousandth of a unit) per milliliter of solution. Oxytocin is delivered intravenously through a constant infusion pump set to carefully regulate the amount of hormone entering the woman. When using oxytocin, attendants must be on constant guard to prevent the uterus from contracting either violently or for a prolonged period, lest it rupture or the fetus be harmed from poor circulation or head injuries. When oxytocin is being infused, the heart rate of the fetus is usually watched with an internal electronic fetal monitor (p. 136) or by careful external monitoring with a stethoscope. Oxytocin is immediately discontinued if worrisome heart rate patterns develop. Intrauterine pressure monitors inserted via a tube through the vagina are being used increasingly to measure the intensity of uterine contractions during oxytocin stimulation.

Oxytocin can be used only when there is reasonable evidence that the baby adequately fits the pelvis (see p. 44 on pelvic measurements and p. 293 on disproportion). Because of the risk of uterine rupture, oxytocin is generally avoided in cases of gross uterine overdistension, as in hydramnios (p. 300), twin pregnancies (p. 331), and in women who have had more than five full-term pregnancies.

Oxytocin is sometimes used to initiate labor. In the past, such "elective" inductions were routinely done for the convenience of the family and/or the obstetrician. Unfortunately, the price paid for this convenience was a prematurity rate of about 3.5 percent, due to errors in estimating gestational age. Nowadays elective induction is frowned upon; however, medical grounds for inducing labor *do* exist. For example, in intrauterine growth disturbance (p. 301) or preeclampsia (p. 315), induced delivery of the baby may be essential for fetal and maternal well-being. Nipple stimulation is also being tried as a "natural" alternative to the administration of synthetic oxytocin.

Finally, oxytocin can be used to help contract the uterus after delivery of the placenta. For this purpose it can be given by injection or added to an intravenous infusion already in place.

Multigravidas (women who have had more than two full-term pregnancies) seem to be more sensitive to oxytocin than women who are pregnant for the first or second time. They experience more cramping and pain from administered oxytocin or from the natural hormone they produce themselves. As mentioned above, their "after-pains" are characteristically more intense. For these reasons, oxytocin should be given to these women in lower doses.

Oxytocin is not always effective. The earlier in pregnancy, the less likely the uterus will respond or an "unripe" cervix will undergo dilatation. When labor must be induced to deliver an immature fetus that has died in utero, a prostaglandin (see below) is sometimes used instead.

There is also a limit to the amount of oxytocin a woman can tolerate before harmful side effects occur. Since the hormone inhibits the capacity of the kidneys to excrete water, an overdose can put a woman in danger of water intoxication.

Ergonovine is a chemical derived from the ergot fungus found in rye and other grains or produced synthetically in the laboratory. Used for centuries as a poison by murderers, it also causes unintentional epidemics of poisoning when people unwittingly eat foods on which the fungus has grown. In large doses far in excess of those used during pregnancy it can cause severe pain, convulsions, gangrene of the limbs, and death. In much smaller doses, it causes uterine contraction. Unlike oxytocin, the effects of ergonovine last for hours, making it unsuitable for use in labor but ideal for maintaining a contracted uterus after delivery of the placenta.

Ergonovine and *methylergonovine* are administered by injection after the placenta has been delivered and can be given in conjunction with oxytocin. They can also be given by mouth as needed to maintain the uterus in a contracted state. Both are commonly used to contract the uterus and prevent bleeding after a D. and C. (p. 310).

Undesirable side effects of ergonovine preparations include nausea and elevated blood pressure. If the recommended dosages are adhered to, however, these problems occur very rarely. Giving these long-acting drugs prior to the delivery of the placenta may entrap the placenta in the uterus, with serious consequences, and is to be avoided if at all possible.

Prostaglandins are another group of chemicals that cause uterine muscle contraction. They also cause ripening of the cervix. Recent studies in which they are administered as vaginal suppositories have shown them to be effective in inducing labor. They appear to have the additional advantage, in contrast to oxytocin, of being effective even when the cervix is initially unripe. (See also the discussion of the use of prostaglandins in abortion on p. 327.) It is likely that prostaglandins will be more widely used in the years ahead.

Pain in Labor

The pain of labor is different from other kinds of human pain because it signifies a normal physiological process, one of the few kinds of pain (besides teething) that does. Because we usually associate pain with a health problem, our first objective in dealing with labor pain is to break that association. Contractions mean progress; each labor pain means that the baby is one step closer to being born. While labor pain per se cannot be reduced, the fear that exaggerates it can be. Nor does pain in labor contradict the view of the female body as essentially healthy, designed to conceive and bear children. Instead, it may be seen as a prototype of the anguish and difficulty so often associated with the creative acts of all human beings. It is not coincidental that creative persons often liken their work to giving birth. A woman can use the pain of labor as an opportunity to come into touch with her own basic resiliency as a human being. Trusting in one's own body and self is the first step toward dealing with pain in labor in a nontechnological way.

Women with whom we have discussed the pain of labor point out that there are times when it seems impossible to cope with even one more contraction, when it truly seems as if she "can't go on" and would gladly accept "anything" to "end it all." Transition is usually the stage when this sense of impossibility arises. We like to point out that it is when a woman feels worst that she has just about reached the top of the mountain. At this point she needs to mobilize all her resources to make it to the summit. Awareness of this paradoxical mixture of pain and progress can inspire her to continue.

Another useful perspective on pain in labor is to consider its duration: only a few hours out of a lifetime are at stake. After an unmedicated birth, despite her protest at the time, no woman, in our experience, has ever expressed regret at having been able to deal successfully with the pain without the aid of technological intervention. Overcoming pain in labor can contribute to a woman's sense of achievement, fulfillment, and satisfaction with her own capacities and can bolster her physical and emotional integrity.

Such an ideal, however, must not be so rigidly adhered to that it inappropriately deprives a woman of needed pain relief. There is a distinction here between heroism and martyrdom. The use of anesthesia or analgesia may represent the best decision and need not be regarded as a sign of inadequacy or failure. Pain in labor, if it overwhelms and terrifies the woman, may inhibit the strength of uterine contractions and decrease the flow of blood to the placenta, putting the baby in jeopardy. Every birth attendant has seen an injection of epidural anesthesia convert a labor that was becoming a nightmare to an exhausted, frightened woman into a satisfying birth experience. In many situations, analgesia or anesthesia can be a blessing. Even women who are most committed to unmedicated birth find support in knowing that these technological measures are available if needed and that they need not feel abandoned to useless suffering when other "natural" measures have failed.

One of the hardest judgments an attendant must make during natural childbirth is whether to be firmly encouraging ("Remember how much you wanted a natural childbirth. We're going to help you do it. You are doing very well, let's keep it up!") or to decide to intervene technically. The woman herself may not be the best judge, for there are few women who, while suffering the intense pain of labor, would refuse medication if offered. Yet the experience of many attendants and pregnant women shows time and time again that motivated women with the right kind of support can pull themselves together and go on to deliver without medication. Knowing the woman well helps attendants make such distinctions. Midwives often spend hours during the prenatal period getting to know their clients — their strengths, weaknesses, and coping styles. At the same time, of course, the clients are getting to know them. This mutual knowledge proves invaluable when decisions must be made in the intense atmosphere of labor. If it is unlikely that familiar people will attend a woman in birth, compensatory supports can be built in. Her partner may serve as labor coach, as in "husband-coached childbirth," or another relative or friend can perform this service.

The importance of trust and empathy also argues for the greater involvement of women as birth attendants, especially women who have themselves had babies. Women who have experienced childbirth have a built-in advantage over male doctors in terms of their capacity to empathize with the laboring woman. You will notice in both of our stories in Chapter 1 how inventive the midwives and nurses are. They seem to have an endless bag of tricks to draw upon to provide physical and emotional comfort and support.

Responding to the complaints of a woman in pain, as labor coaches and other attendants know, is complicated. Response is almost automatic. We want to reassure ("Everything's okay." "Don't worry."); to offer what relief we can; to assume responsibility ("If only I could do something for you . . ."); or to invalidate her experience ("Stop crying like a baby!" "Other women have done it, and you can, too.").

Real communication with a woman in pain begins with the recognition that it is *she* who is in pain and who needs first and foremost an acknowledgment of her feelings: "It sounds as if you're feeling that you can't make it one step further." This show of understanding serves to validate her experience and lessens some of her terror in feeling crazily outside the bounds of human experience. A woman in labor needs to know that, regardless of her bewildering feelings and embarrassment at not being able to cope, she can count on the unqualified support of others. Actively "being with" a woman in labor, quite apart from "doing for" her, such as supporting her in breathing through a contraction, is half the job of coaching.

On a more practical level, pain can often be reduced through a change in position. A woman in pain can try turning on one side or another, can sit up, stand up, or walk around, or can get down on all fours, until she finds what really works best. Back pain is often relieved by lying on one's side, by sitting upright, walking or getting on hands and knees. Firm pressure with the wrist or the palm of the hand against the most painful spot can help. Sometimes a light stroking motion feels better than pressure. Warm baths or showers also have a favorable effect on pain, as does massage, singing, or listening to music.

Relaxation and breathing techniques are now the classical approach to coping with the pain of labor. They have been featured in childbirth education classes for the past generation. Both are discussed in the section on prenatal exercise, along with the current rethinking of the role of breathing in labor. (See p. 88.)

Pain Relief

ANALGESICS

Analgesics and anesthetics are medications used for pain relief. Analgesics reduce pain to make it tolerable, while anesthetics are intended to eliminate it completely. Analgesics in everyday use include aspirin and acetaminophen (Tylenol). Among the stronger analgesics are codeine, Percodan, and some newer drugs like

Zomax. The strongest analgesics include morphine, meperidine (Demerol), alphaprodine (Nisentil), and hydromorphone (Dilaudid).

The most common analgesics used in labor are meperidine and alphaprodine. They are sometimes combined with the antihistamine promethazine to enhance their effect, producing a dose with more impact and greater effectiveness. These drugs are given by injection. In addition to relieving pain, they produce some drowsiness and euphoria (a feeling of well-being and tranquility). Many women find that these drugs help them regain their strength during a long, difficult early labor. Analgesics pass through the placenta to the fetus where they can depress those centers in the baby's brain that drive respiration, an effect of clinical importance only if the baby is called on to breathe on its own, not while the work of respiration is being done by the mother. Analgesics can also sedate babies, resulting in drowsiness which can interfere with the baby's responsiveness during the first few hours after birth, or even longer. Because of their depressant and sedative effects, these drugs are given in controlled doses long before the expected time of birth, and preferably only during the first stage of labor (see p. 183). Barring an unexpectedly rapid birth, as in an emergency cesarean, their effect on an infant's respiration should be well over before delivery. If the effect is not over, and if the baby's respiration is depressed, assistance can be provided as needed with a breathing bag and oxygen. The drug naloxone hydrochloride (Narcan) can also be used, administered to the baby as often as needed to reverse the respiratory depression effects of analgesics. Whether the effects of the drugs on the infant's responsiveness last longer than they do on respiration is a question still under careful study, and answers are so far reassuring. (See p. 242 on Bonding and Attachment.)

ANESTHETICS

Anesthetics are drugs that can altogether eliminate pain. Two broad classes are used — local nerve blocking agents (which prevent the nerves from passing messages to the brain), such as those used in dental work or in surgery of the skin, and gases that are inhaled through the lungs to affect the entire body. Lidocaine (Xylocaine) is a popular example of the former, and nitrous oxide, the latter. Another new and not yet understood type is acupuncture.

Blocking Agents.   It can be stated as a generalization that the nerve blocking agents are quite safe as currently used. One known drawback is that, even though the drugs are injected into a defined place in the body, they are absorbed into the mother's bloodstream in small amounts and passed through the placenta to the fetus. The issue of persisting drug effects in the baby after birth, especially as they affect its behavior during early parent–infant interaction, has largely been laid to rest.

Accidental injection of the blocking drug into the mother's blood, which sometimes occurs despite all precautions, may result in high circulating levels in the blood. The mother may experience light-headedness, dizziness, slurred speech, a metallic taste in her mouth, numbness of her tongue and mouth, muscle twitching, loss of consciousness, and, in the extreme, generalized convulsions. Her blood pressure may fall as a consequence both of the drug itself and from lying flat on her back, still a common laboring position for women who have received blocking anesthetics. Fetal distress may occur as a direct effect of the drug or as a result of decreased oxygen due to diminished blood flow to the placenta from the drug complications described in the mother. These rare problems of inadvertent overdose of the mother, which can occur even in the best of hands, are usually treated successfully, but obviously are best avoided altogether.

The blocking agents are most commonly given as *spinal* or *epidural anesthetics.* "Spinals" and "epidurals," as they are called for short, have the advantage of allowing the woman to remain awake and aware during labor and delivery. Both can be used for either vaginal or cesarean birth. Epidural anesthesia is used for pain relief during both labor and delivery, while spinal anesthesia is used only for delivery.

In *spinal anesthesia,* a needle inserted between the vertebrae of the lower back introduces the blocking agent into the spinal canal. The drug bathes the spinal nerves in the canal before they exit to pass to lower parts of the body. Both sensory and motor nerves are temporarily blocked so that the mother's pelvic area and legs are numbed and cannot be moved voluntarily. The "level" of anesthesia (that is, how high on the abdomen the anesthesia reaches) is largely determined by how much drug is given and by the position the mother assumes immediately following the injection. For a vaginal delivery, the goal is to anesthetize only the perineum and legs. For a cesarean section, anesthesia should be achieved to the level of the rib cage.

A spinal anesthetic can be given while the woman is either sitting or lying on her side. First the skin is cleaned with an antiseptic solution. Next a sterile drape with a central hole is placed over the lower back. The anesthesiologist numbs the skin with some of the blocking agent, infiltrating the solution down to the spinal column so that the "channel" between skin and spinal column is anesthetized. The woman is then asked to curl forward to open the spaces between the vertebrae. A thin hollow needle containing a removable stylet is pushed through the now numbed area until it enters the canal. The stylet is removed and the location of the needle in the spinal canal is verified by the return of clear spinal fluid. A syringe containing the anesthetic solution is then attached to the needle and the medication is introduced between uterine contractions. For a vaginal delivery the woman is asked to sit up for forty-five seconds to allow the medication to settle to the bottom of the spinal canal. For a cesarean section, the woman lies first on one side, then on the other, to allow the anesthetic to travel upward in the canal to block the nerves that supply the entire abdomen. The level of anesthesia is controlled to some extent by tilting the operating table either up or down as indicated. The anesthesiologist checks the level by checking the woman's response to the prick of a needle moved up or down the abdomen.

In vaginal delivery, spinal anesthesia causes the mother to lose the ability to bear down. The higher the level of anesthetic, the less voluntary control. In addition, spinal anesthesia decreases the force of uterine contractions. For both reasons forceps and an episiotomy (see p. 214) are almost inevitably needed. Because of these effects on the course of labor, spinal anesthesia is not given for vaginal deliveries until the cervix is fully dilated, at the onset of the second stage of labor (see p. 183), and delivery is usually accomplished soon after its administration.

Spinal anesthesia carries several risks. The most common is a drop in the mother's blood pressure due to a blockage of the sympathetic nerves that control the tone of muscles in arteries.

When the arteries dilate, the same volume of blood is contained in a larger volume of vessel, and thus the pressure of blood falls. This fall in blood pressure is made worse by the fact that a woman is very commonly flat on her back to deliver; in this position, the uterus rests on the large vein in the back of the abdomen (inferior vena cava), interfering with the return of blood to the heart and the pumping of blood from the heart. For this reason it is essential to avoid lying flat. Not all obstetricians recognize this danger, so it may be important for the informed pregnant woman to be mindful of this. (See p. 211 on position in labor.) Another way to minimize the fall in blood pressure due to spinal anesthesia is to give the woman a liter or more of intravenous sugar-salt solution before beginning the procedure. If a drop in blood pressure occurs despite fluids and avoidance of lying flat, medication to contract the dilated muscles in the arteries is administered. Because of the risk of low blood pressure, spinal anesthesia is not used when a woman's blood volume is already compromised; for example, when blood loss has occurred or when preeclampsia is present (see p. 315).

Another problem with spinal anesthetic, far less common today than it was in the past, is headache, often referred to as "spinal headache," which usually comes on several hours after the procedure. This pain is believed to be due to the slow leakage of spinal fluid through the puncture site, which results in loss of the cushioning of the brain that the spinal fluid provides. As a result, the brain tugs on its attachments, producing pain. Spinal headache is minimized by using a very thin needle which produces a very small hole. Bed rest and analgesics are helpful, and abdominal support with a girdle is also useful. If all else fails, a "blood patch," or injection of a few cubic centimeters of the woman's blood into the area just outside the puncture site, has proven effective in sealing off the tear. Occasionally spinal anesthesia causes temporary loss of control of the bladder, which may necessitate bladder catheterization during the first twenty-four hours after delivery.

A dreaded complication of the inadvertent introduction of an excessively large dose of anesthetic into the spinal canal is blockage of all nerves, which produces temporary total body paralysis. In this emergency, hypotension (low blood pressure) is treated by the measures discussed above and by elevating the legs to allow blood now needed elsewhere to drain back into the heart. The depressed respiration is treated by passing a tube through the mouth and into the airway to move oxygen in and out of the lungs with the use of a hand bag or respirator. Fluids and drugs to constrict blood vessels are also given. Spinal anesthesia is not used in women who have had allergic reactions to local anesthetics, whose skin at the injection site is infected, or who have chronic low back pain which could be aggravated by the spinal needle.

In the *epidural anesthetic,* the nerves are numbed after their exit from the spinal canal into the space just outside it, which is known as the epidural space. In this space, the sensory nerves that transmit external stimuli are less well insulated and more susceptible to blockade than are the motor nerves that govern movement. Thus, pain and other sensations are eliminated while voluntary movement is preserved, an advantage over spinal anesthesia. But because the woman's sense of position and tension is blocked, her use of these voluntary muscles is less effective. Unlike the spinal anesthetic, which is given only during the second stage of labor, the epidural can be given earlier. Usually, however, it is not given until the active phase of the first stage, because the anesthetic can stop labor altogether if it is administered during the latent phase. The procedure for performing an epidural is similar to that used in the spinal. Once the needle enters the epidural space, a thin plastic catheter is passed through it. Not uncommonly, the woman will experience a twinge of pain in her back or leg as the catheter touches a nerve. When the needle is withdrawn, the catheter is left in place and the anesthetic solution is injected into the space. The catheter is then taped in place on the woman's back until delivery. A major convenience of the epidural block is that additional solution can be introduced as needed.

Several uncommon problems may be encountered about one-half to 1 percent of the time. For one, inadvertent entry into the spinal canal, unrecognized before anesthetic injection, can result in a high level of spinal anesthesia, which can cause widespread temporary paralysis and respiratory and blood pressure problems similar to those described as possible consequences of spinal anesthesia. The resulting leak of spinal fluid may also cause a "spinal headache" (see above), even if no anesthetic was introduced. Also of major concern is inadvertent injection into the mother's bloodstream through a vein. Proper technique, which includes using small, safe test doses, can reduce these risks and minimize their consequences.

Epidural anesthesia is not always completely effective even in the most experienced hands. In one study, 85 percent of women were free of pain, 12 percent had partial relief, and 3 percent experienced no relief at all. An epidural given to relieve labor pain, with the catheter pointing upward (toward the head) to direct the solution to the nerves supplying the uterus, may not effectively numb the perineum during the second stage.

As with spinals, epidural anesthesia can produce a decrease in blood pressure. Much of this effect, as we pointed out above, is due to the once common practice of lying flat, with the resulting pressure of the uterus on the great blood vessels in the abdomen. It is essential that women with epidurals in place stay off their backs. (See p. 211 on position in labor.) Intravenous fluids are also used to prevent hypotension.

Epidural anesthesia has also been associated with a decrease in uterine contraction, slowing of labor, and the woman's inability to push effectively during the second stage. All these features necessitate an episiotomy and the use of forceps, and add up to a highly medical type of birth. However, some anesthesiologists have found that these problems can be avoided by allowing the anesthetic to wear off as soon as full dilation is reached, and also by keeping women on their sides. A more selective use of epidural anesthesia may be compatible with "natural" childbirth.

A less commonly used but available form of local anesthesia is the *pudendal block*. The pudendal nerves supply the perineum and can be blocked in the vagina. The injection is made into the side walls of the vagina. Blocking the pudendal nerves anesthetizes the lower vagina and perineum but does not interfere with the woman's ability to push.

Local anesthetic is also frequently used to numb the perineum as an episiotomy is performed, in suturing a perineal laceration, or in repairing an episiotomy incision. The anesthetic is injected directly into the tissues involved.

General Anesthesia.   While less commonly used in obstetrics than blocking agents, gas, or general anesthesia, still occupies an important place in labor and delivery. The great advantages are ease of administration and the rapid onset of effect. Thus, in emergencies in which time is critical, it is the anesthetic of choice. The great disadvantage of general anesthesia is that it passes directly to the fetus, anesthetizing it as well. This is rarely serious unless the fetus is threatened by some other problem. Of course, during labor under general anesthesia the mother is asleep or nearly asleep and misses out on much of the birth. The most serious problem of general anesthesia is the possibility that the laboring woman may vomit and aspirate the stomach contents into her lungs, producing a chemical pneumonia. (This topic is discussed more fully under Fluids and Food, p. 196.)

The most commonly used anesthetic gas is nitrous oxide, sometimes called "laughing gas," given mixed with oxygen. (In some hospitals women take several puffs of this mixture in the second stage of labor just before bearing down during a contraction. When used this way, the gas serves as an analgesic rather than as an anesthetic.) Methoxyflurane and halothane are other gas anesthetics sometimes given in addition to the nitrous oxide. Halothane is particularly useful for achieving uterine relaxation, for example when a placenta is trapped in the uterus and has to be removed manually (see p. 218). Fast-acting intravenously administered barbiturate drugs, of which thiopental is the best example, are used as adjuncts to general anesthesia. These drugs quickly put the patient to sleep while allowing the anesthesiologist to pass a breathing tube into the airway. Muscle relaxants are also used as needed.

Acupuncture. In the People's Republic of China, acupuncture is used for anesthesia during cesarean section, induction of labor, and prolonged latent phase. Few studies have been done to help us assess these applications of acupuncture. More are clearly needed to follow up on these promising leads from China.

Learning about Anesthesia. In some hospitals anesthesiologists meet with pregnant women and their partners to answer their questions about anesthesia and the role of the anesthesiologist. Some obstetricians routinely refer patients for these consultations, which may be regarded as part of childbirth education, being equally informative to both those who have definitely decided they want anesthesia and those who would use it only if needed. The topic of anesthesia is also covered in most childbirth education classes. Couples should inform themselves about anesthesia prior to rather than during labor itself when making decisions is more pressured. For further discussion of the topic of pain in labor and of alternatives to the use of drugs, see p. 200.

Position in Labor and Delivery

In a traditional hospital birth, a woman lies on her back with her legs in stirrups. This supine, or *lithotomy*, position is often associated with episiotomy and the use of anesthesia and forceps. It was designed primarily to allow the physician easier access to the birth canal and perineum for the manipulations that are often characteristic of this type of delivery. The supine position has come under considerable criticism for several reasons.

First, when women lie flat on their backs, the uterus presses down on the large artery and vein that run adjacent to the spine, interfering with the return of blood to the woman's heart, the outflow of blood from her heart, and blood circulation to the uterus, placenta, and fetus. Fetal distress (see p. 134) can result; moreover, the uterus, deprived of its normal circulation, is less able to contract, potentially interfering with labor. (In fact, many of the ill effects blamed on epidural anesthesia may be the result of the supine position. Getting women with epidurals onto their sides and off their backs can probably prevent most of these problems and even allow the women to push their babies out while anesthetized.) A second problem is that bearing down during the second stage is much more difficult and less effective when lying on one's back than when sitting up. Third, as Dr. Michel Odent, obstetrician of the famous birthing center at Pithiviers in France, claims, based on extensive clinical experience, tearing of the perineum may be reduced to a very low level in the upright position and episiotomies are rarely if ever needed.

Births in preindustrial societies have almost always been con-

211

ducted with women either standing or squatting, in both cases taking full advantage of the force of gravity to help push the baby out. (A similar effect was achieved by Andrea in our home birth story, when she sat on the toilet seat, an excellent place for a woman to labor in home or hospital.) Evidence in the form of X rays of the pelvis has shown that the area of the outlet of the birth canal is increased by 28 percent (almost a third) when the woman squats!

Another position that is more effective than lying on the back is sitting up, at least at a 45-degree angle, drawing legs up if desired to provide more effective pushing and possibly to enlarge the diameter of the birth canal. (The newer birthing chairs achieve this position very well.) Since the baby normally first moves downward, once the head is out (that is, toward the mother's back in whatever position she may be), the sitting woman either brings her buttocks to the edge of the bed or elevates her buttocks with a firm object (such as an inverted bedpan covered with a soft pad) in order to provide room for the emerging baby.

Another effective position is lying on the side with the upper leg held up by an assistant and the back and buttocks near the edge of the bed. The attendant stands behind the buttocks with one hand supporting the perineum and the other arched over the uplifted leg to control the baby's head. This position also helps the woman to see her baby emerging.

Our own view is that women should be in the upright (squatting or standing) or side position during delivery. If a woman is in bed during labor, she should not lie flat on her back. She should recline in a semi-sitting position with her back supported or lie on her side. Except for complicated deliveries, we believe that, in the absence of studies that show otherwise, deliveries should no longer occur lying flat, whether or not the woman has received anesthesia. The burden of proof should now be on those who claim otherwise.

The upright position (standing, sitting, or squatting) is also an excellent one in which to labor, especially if it relieves pain. This observation is based both on clinical experience and on studies that show a shortening of labor in the vertical position. One recent, small but controlled study from the University of Southern California showed that walking was as effective as oxytocin in stimulating labor. The upright position appears to be as advantageous in delivering the placenta as it is in delivering the baby. While there are no controlled studies yet, the evidence available strongly suggests an advantage in expelling the placenta while squatting.

Some women have also found it comfortable to give birth while on their hands and knees ("on all fours"). From the point of view of normal physiology, the "all fours" position makes good sense.

Forceps and Vacuum Extraction

Forceps are metal instruments like tongs with detachable blades that are designed to grasp the baby's head to pull it from the birth canal. In vaginal deliveries in which the head appears first, forceps are used for two reasons: when the mother's own expulsive forces are not enough; and when the baby is in distress. (The use of forceps in breech delivery is discussed on p. 271.)

Forceps should only be used when the head is visible in the vagina between, as well as during, each contraction. The occiput should be anterior. The position of the head must be precisely known so that the forceps blades can be applied properly, one at a time. Forceps are never used until the cervix is completely dilated and the amniotic membrane is ruptured.

The vacuum extractor, more widely used in Europe than in the United States, is an alternative to forceps that appears to be as effective and less traumatic to mother and baby. It consists of a plastic suction cup attached to a hollow handle and air pump. The cup is applied to the baby's scalp and a vacuum is created in the cup by a pump connected to the handle. This vacuum sucks the fetal scalp tightly against the interior of the cup (an effect similar to that produced by a toilet plunger), and negative pressure in the cup causes swelling of the skin of the fetal scalp ("caput"), which fills the hollow of the cup to form a firm seal. The handle can then be pulled to draw the baby down and out through the birth canal. The cup is usually applied during a contraction and released between contractions.

Sterile Technique

The two births described in Chapter 1 show two different approaches to the question of how sterile a birth should be. In the traditional hospital birth, surgical sterility is the goal, while in an at-home birth cleanliness is the standard, as is the case for many births in alternative birthing centers. While the traditional approach may make more sense theoretically, there is no evidence that actual incidence of infection in hospitals is reduced. However, in the hospital, where dangerous germs are likely to be present, additional precautions still make sense. At home, street clothes are worn by all, while in the hospital surgical scrub suits are required. The "prep" performed in the delivery room is completely bypassed at home. In both settings, however, sterile examining gloves are used to avoid introducing germs directly into the birth canal.

There is no evidence to suggest that the relaxation of sterile technique at home is associated with any increased risk to either the mother or the baby. From the point of view of the baby's health, it could be argued that the baby at home is born into the environment in which he or she is going to live, and for which he or she has adequate protection. This is one more issue for which there are no final answers.

Episiotomy

Episiotomy is an incision or surgical cut made with a sterile scissors in the perineum, the area between the lower junction of the labia and the anus, performed to widen the opening of the vagina to ease passage of the baby's head. It may be made in the midline (median) (more frequently done in this country) or angled to the side (mediolateral). (See Figure 18.) Usually an episiotomy is repaired (sewn up) following delivery of the placenta. Absorbable sutures that dissolve and so do not require later removal are used. Unless a spinal or epidural anesthetic has been administered, making and repairing an episiotomy are usually done under local anesthesia.

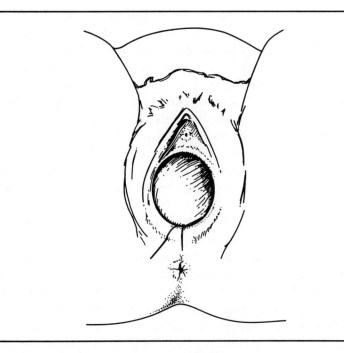

Figure 18.   Episiotomy: midline or angled to the side

The mainstream medical view of episiotomy, which supports its almost routine use, is described in a well-known textbook, *Williams Obstetrics*, as "the most common operation in obstetrics." It

> substitutes a straight, neat surgical incision for the ragged laceration that otherwise frequently results. It is easier to repair and heals better than a tear. It spares the fetal head the necessity of serving as a battering ram against perineal obstruction. If prolonged, the pounding of the fetal head against the perineum may cause intracranial injury. Episiotomy shortens the second stage of labor.

Episiotomy is alleged to prevent vaginal and pelvic relaxation following birth. It is also recommended during the birth of premature babies to minimize trauma to the fetal skull, which is more delicate than that of a full-term infant, or when there is a premium on rapid delivery because of a problem in the baby (see, for example, the discussion on shoulder dystocia on p. 325). When forceps or vacuum extractor is used, episiotomy is commonly performed to decrease resistance to extraction of the baby.

The topic of episiotomy can arouse strong feelings. Many prominent obstetricians say that they "*always* do an episiotomy." But Sheila Kitzinger, a well-known critic of contemporary childbirth practices, termed the procedure "ritual genital mutilation," in which males exert power over women's bodies and deny women the opportunity to experience birth as a sexual act.

Critics of routine episiotomy point to the pain of the healing episiotomy and its negative effects on lovemaking, urination, and defecation. These discomforts are far worse, they believe, than the pain of a "natural" and "more physiological" tear in the perineum. Indeed, several studies have shown that women who have episiotomies do report more postpartum pain and are slower to return to full activity, including sexual intercourse. The problem with such reports is that those women who had the procedure and those who didn't may have been different to start with. For example, it could be that only those most likely to tear badly received an episiotomy and would have been in even worse condition without it.

One study, in which women *at random* were allocated to either a restricted "conservative" or a "liberal" use of the procedure, was done by Dr. Adrian Grant of Oxford. The episiotomy rates of the two groups, who were otherwise similar in characteristics and were handled similarly in labor, were 10 percent and 51 percent respectively. Interestingly, there were *no* differences between the groups with respect to the amount of pain reported after birth, the time it took for the perineum to become pain free, or problems with controlling urination. The one difference in outcomes was that women who were in the restricted group were more likely to have resumed sexual intercourse within a month after delivery (presumably because it was less uncomfortable for them). Despite the differences in episiotomy rates, there was little difference in the frequency with which suturing of the perineum was required. The women who did not receive episiotomies were more likely to tear on their own, so that not having an episiotomy did not spare women from tearing and being sutured.

Our opinion is that episiotomy is not needed in the majority of births if labor is conducted in a manner that keeps the perineum from being stretched too abruptly. A number of measures appear to minimize the need for episiotomy. (None, we hasten to add, have been subjected to controlled clinical studies.) What follows is based on the experience of many colleagues.

1. As long as mother and baby are doing well, birth should be gradual and unhurried, in order to allow the perineum to stretch slowly and naturally. (There is little doubt that episiotomies facilitate quicker births, as do forceps, and so one inevitably wonders whether the time factor may not play a role in the popularity of this procedure with some obstetricians and their patients.)

2. In order to prevent undue stretching, the prepared mother can control pushing in part according to the status of her perineum. Attendants can give verbal feedback and show her the effects of her pushing with a mirror. If pushing causes too forceful stretching, the woman can stop pushing and allow her uterus to do the work alone. A gentle push between uterine contractions can then ease the baby's head out. In contrast, the breath-holding type of pushing in many traditional deliveries all too often resembles an athletic competition, with bystanders cheering the woman on to bear down as hard as she can.

3. Perineal massage is a time-honored technique used by midwives. Warm compresses are applied to the perineum (the theory is that the heat will increase blood flow and hence stretchability) and the perineum is stretched with the fingers.

4. Supporting the perineum is another way to minimize tearing. This is accomplished by maintaining constant counterpressure with the hands applied to the perineum as it gradually stretches.

5. Position in giving birth may also be important. There is accumulating evidence that the upright position, either standing or squatting, minimizes tearing, another good argument for avoiding lying flat on the back during delivery. Dr. Michel Odent, the director of the birthing center in Pithiviers, France, has stressed this point.

6. Preparation of the perineum through Kegel exercises, by its "toning" effect on the muscles and fascia, is believed to make them more stretchable and less likely to tear, a point analogous

to the minimization of muscle pain in joggers who stretch their muscles before running. (See p. 88 on prenatal exercise and p. 40 on the Physical Examination.)

The elements of this physiological approach presuppose that Pitocin, epidural anesthetics, and forceps are used only for specific medical indications, as each of them is more likely to make an episiotomy necessary. This approach to perineal care, both before and during labor, requires active participation by the woman and her attendant in the birth process. It should result in a need for episiotomies in less than 20 percent of births. There is no convincing evidence that such an approach results in more deep tears than occur when episiotomies are done. Women should at least question their obstetricians on the notion of the "routine" episiotomy, and become aware of the options available.

Some physicians and midwives as well are reconsidering their interpretation of vaginal tears and are recognizing that, in many cases, the vagina will repair itself very well without suturing. Again, more data are needed. Of course, deep tears such as those that extend to or into the rectum benefit from suturing, but physicians have probably sutured superficial tears more often than is necessary. The collective experience of many midwives and physicians suggests that, with small tears, healing occurs just as quickly, and with less discomfort, without sutures.

Delivery of the Placenta

The placenta usually delivers within minutes of the birth of a baby, clearly signaling the baby's separation from the uterus. First, the uterus becomes more globular and often firmer. Second, there is a gush of blood. Third, the uterus rises higher in the abdomen, displaced upward by the placenta. Fourth, more of the umbilical cord emerges from the vagina. Once the placenta has separated, gentle pulling on the cord can aid its delivery. Sometimes the placenta, encircled by the cervix, is caught high in the vagina. Under these circumstances it is often possible for the attendant to reach in, grasp it, and pull it out. The upright position of the mother, either sitting or squatting, also aids in expelling the placenta.

If the placenta fails to be delivered within one half hour of birth, or if there is brisk bleeding, it must be removed manually to prevent hemorrhaging. This is a painful procedure which is ideally done under anesthesia. Once removed, the placenta is carefully inspected. In the unlikely event that a large piece is missing, the uterus must be explored manually under anesthesia to identify and permit removal of the fragment left behind.

Following the expulsion of the placenta, it is important to keep the uterus well contracted to prevent further bleeding. One way to accomplish this is through massage. When contracted, the uterus has the consistency of a baseball. Women and their partners can learn to monitor the condition of the uterus and massage it as necessary. A natural way of causing the uterus to contract is through nipple stimulation, usually supplied by the suckling baby. If there is a need to cause uterine contraction and the baby is slow to suck, someone else (usually the spouse) can suck on the woman's nipples and achieve the same result. The oxytocic drugs usually used in hospital births (see p. 198) can also be used to bring about uterine contraction and are available for use in home births as well.

Once the baby has started to suck and the uterus is contracted, mother and baby have begun to recover from the birth and are on their way to a new life together.

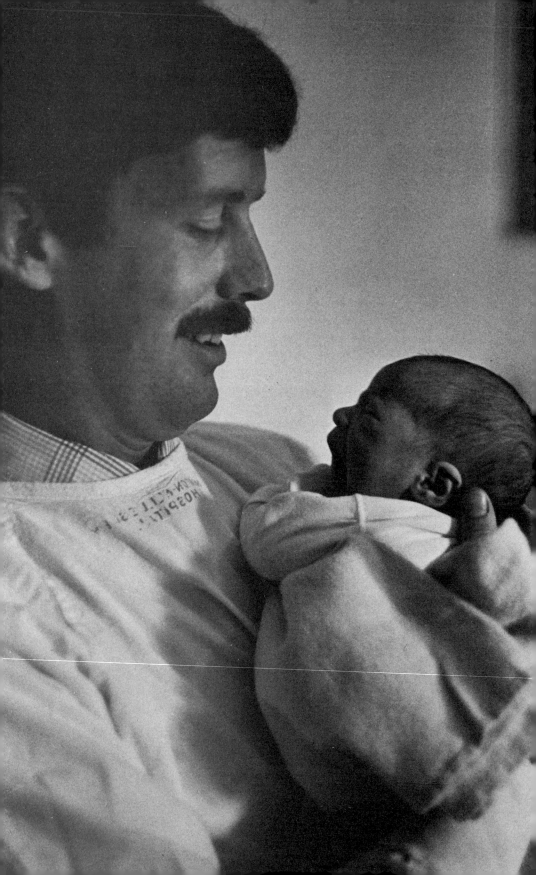

5

*After the Birth: Care of the Parents**

Postpartum Care

As more and more parents take their babies home soon after delivery, either in the hospital or in a birthing center, and as more women have their babies at home, they all have to rely more on themselves and less on professionals for dealing with common postpartum issues. Postpartum care includes the procedures outlined here.

Immediately after the birth the mother should be careful to *urinate frequently*, because a full bladder may keep the uterus from contracting as it should. To relieve stinging, dilute the urine by spraying warm water over the perineum with a squeeze bottle during urinating, or urinate while under the shower with water running over the body. Signs of possible urinary tract infection — elevated temperature, burning on urination in which the discomfort is "inside" the bladder rather than on the sore perineum — need to be noticed and treated (see p. 71).

The postpartum woman may not have a *bowel movement* for the first several days after birth. There is no need to strain, for it is not necessary to defecate immediately and straining may be harmful. Prune juice, increased fiber, and fluids can soften or stimulate

*This chapter is adapted in part from the publication, *Postpartum Care*, by Peggy Spindel, R.N.

stools. Hemorrhoids, which may have initiated during pregnancy, usually improve on their own after delivery.

The uterus should be checked every fifteen to thirty minutes for the first few hours and hourly for the rest of the first day. If it is not hard like a softball (or coconut), it needs to be massaged until it firms up. If massaging does not work, the midwife or doctor should be informed. Nursing can be expected to lead to uterine contractions, sometimes called "afterpains." Nature in her wisdom has linked the feeding of the infant with the tightening up of the uterus and the prevention of postpartum bleeding. The uterus should be monitored until it is too low in the abdomen to feel, about the tenth day after delivery. The vaginal flow (*lochia*) should not be greater than a heavy menstrual period. It should not be green or have a foul smell. By the tenth day it is usually just a light pink to brown discharge. Sanitary pads rather than tampons should be used for the first two weeks since tampons may introduce germs into the vagina and the uterus.

A woman may *shower* when she feels steady on her feet. Tub baths have traditionally been discouraged for two weeks, in the interest of preventing infection from bacteria washed into the uterus. The validity of this teaching has not been confirmed. Perineal pain may respond to hot sitz baths (one and one-half inches of water) several times a day. A strong brew of the herb comfrey (available in health food stores) added to the water is alleged by many midwives to promote healing.

Ice applied to the perineum during the first twenty-four hours will help reduce labial swelling. Crushed ice is packed in a rubber glove which is tied at its wrist, then wrapped in a sterile gauze pad. A sterile cotton ball soaked in refrigerated witch hazel can be placed under a perineal pad over sore regions — rectum, perineum, labia. The perineum should be inspected soon after birth and regularly thereafter to keep track of its healing.

For advice on *eating*, see p. 82 on diet during lactation. The new mother should not forget vitamin and iron supplements and should drink some liquid every time she nurses.

Kegel exercises (see p. 97) should be started immediately after delivery. Other exercises can and should be resumed gradually. Even if a woman feels full of energy, we recommend she take it *very* easy for two weeks and *a little bit* easy for four weeks more.

The exercises described in Chapter 2 on p. 88 are all useful, if gradually introduced as the new mother feels stronger.

Emotions

For parents, it takes time to incorporate the birth experience. Mothers and fathers describe three general emotional stages in the postpartum period.

The first may be called the "taking in" stage, after an extraordinary, possibly once-in-a-lifetime, experience. During this period mothers think and talk about the delivery a great deal and in detail. While taking stock, they work on resolving any mixed feelings. In this stage a mother can feel very focused on herself and inwardly directed and may even welcome being mothered herself.

The second stage, "taking hold," is a time when a mother feels motivated to take charge of herself and her new baby. She feels less dependent on her family and wants to move quickly into asserting the new role she sees for herself. The pitfalls of this stage of rising expectations and mobilized energy are overtiredness and anxiety about one's competence as a mother.

Last, there is a "letting go," or "settling in," phase, in which the transition represented by the birth experience is resolved and put away, when the baby's separateness is realized and enjoyed, and the parental role is incorporated into one's identity.

Women often report *feelings of grieving* after a birth. They discover that the sense of loss they experience is the loss of being pregnant. The special feeling of fullness within, the self-conscious pride, and the attention of others can all be sorely missed once the baby arrives and "steals the show." Mothers sometimes feel like a cross between an anonymous cow that supplies the milk and an ignored maid who cleans up the messes, while it is the baby who is the focus of everyone's loving attention. To prevent this, families should keep up a little extra loving and mothering of the mother for a month or so. The result is likely to be a mother who has plenty of love to give because she is receiving much love and who is strong and more confident because she feels valued.

During this time a father is called upon to provide a lot of extra attention and do extra work — and he deserves extra love, too.

Mothers often describe a feeling of "fluffiness in the head," as one postpartum mother put it, finding it hard to imagine a life separate from mothering. It is as if they have forgotten how to do anything except care for the baby. Especially troublesome is the inability to find or remember a word or carry on a coherent conversation. This state of mind is probably related to a combination of factors that include hormonal effects, lack of sleep, and the intense emotional involvement with the baby. Among the many reactions it can elicit from others in the family are amusement and annoyance. The "fluffiness," luckily, will soon pass.

Sexuality

During the postpartum period, the sexuality of new parents can take a special, less genitally focused form. Childbearing is so overwhelming a part of a woman's sexual existence that it can entirely overwhelm her libido. Birth and adjustments to the baby during the postpartum and nursing periods can be such powerful sexual experiences that for a time intercourse can feel like an irrelevant intrusion. Men, too, normally have fears and concerns about causing another pregnancy too soon, injuring or causing pain to the new mother, or pushing to have sex before the partners are ready. All of these factors can color sexual relationships and inhibit the expression of sexual feelings. The couple needs to take advantage of the opportunity these changes present for empathic communication. Each can come to understand how the other experienced the birth in terms of his or her own body and psychological makeup.

Genital sex is but one expression of intimacy, and it may be temporarily suspended during late pregnancy and after birth. Other forms of warmth and caring can flow in both directions — massage, mutual masturbation, showering together, for example — to take its place. Even when a couple is ready for genital sex again, they may not return immediately to the prebirth relationship, for physical or psychological reasons.

The timing of the reinitiation of genital sex is best left to the discretion of the couple. Traditionally, doctors have recommended abstention until the "six-week checkup." Although on theoretical grounds there would appear to be a heightened vulnerability to infection until the uterus is fully returned to its non-pregnant form, there is no data to support this concern.

If the vagina is dry or has tender spots, a water-soluble lubricant like K-Y jelly will help relieve irritation. Adjustments in positioning can help reduce pressure on a sore area. Many of the positions and other forms of intimacy suggested for late pregnancy are appropriate for the postpartum period, too. Milk ejection may occur spontaneously with arousal and seem bizarre and/or humorous to both partners.

Many couples report increased sexual enjoyment following birth, especially women after their first child. However, this may take several months to achieve, while the mother's body returns to normal and the baby's schedule evolves.

Although breast-feeding suppresses the mother's ovulation, it is *not* a foolproof form of contraception. Since ovulation occurs *before* the return of menstrual periods, menstruation is not a reliable guide to resumed fertility. The combination of a condom with contraceptive foam or jelly is a very effective contraceptive which can be used indefinitely or until other birth control arrangements are made.

Oral contraceptives (birth control pills) remain controversial during nursing because of reduced milk production, apparent alterations in the composition of milk, and the passage through the milk of some hormones to the baby. Most medical authorities (for example, the American Academy of Pediatrics) sanction the use of oral contraceptives after nursing is well established (six to eight weeks), while consumer groups like La Leche League discourage mothers from taking them. Nursing mothers might ask about the "mini-pill," containing progesterone alone.

Regarding the IUD (intrauterine device), some evidence points to an increased risk of uterine perforation in nursing women as opposed to non-nursing women. Until further studies are done, nursing mothers might be wise to avoid using an IUD. A diaphragm (refitted to suit the changed shape of the mother after birth) used with a contraceptive jelly is another good method, though not foolproof. A cervical cap, when available, is another. Check with your doctor regarding the most recent techniques.

Family Crises

Combinations of physical and psychological problems can precipitate genuine family crises in the days and weeks following birth. A sluggish baby who won't nurse, combined with a mother who is exhausted and whose breasts are painfully engorged with sore nipples, is one. Another is the combination of a screaming baby with well-meaning but intrusive and undermining grandparents and parents who feel frazzled and incompetent. The "superwoman" with older children, who refuses to stop waiting on everyone else long enough to care for herself, is a prime candidate for exhaustion and problems with the baby.

Such situations, which in the extreme can become nightmarish, call for active involvement by the doctor, midwife, friends, and others in the family's support network. Phone contact with the doctor (or midwife) is helpful, for he or she can assess the family's needs, provide loving support, and offer concrete suggestions. An exhausted mother should be encouraged to get into bed and take her baby with her. Relatives, friends, and fellow members of the prenatal class can be mobilized to bring cooked food, do laundry and shopping, and care for other children while the parents focus on themselves and the baby.

We vividly remember one mother who got into such a state of anxiety that her milk dwindled and her baby became dehydrated, almost to the point of needing hospitalization. A team of nursing mothers, who had used our practice, were quickly recruited to supplement this woman's depleted milk supply and to allow her to rest and successfully recoup her strength and confidence.

For those whose obsessive neatness is a barrier to their relaxation, the postpartum period offers an opportunity for them to learn that people can take priority over things. If a family is besieged by well-wishers, limited, brief visiting hours can be arranged and the phone taken off the hook. Public Health and Visiting Nurse Association nurses, supervised home health aides, and commercial homemakers can also provide support. Ask your physician or the hospital or birthing center about such resources.

Other formal support groups for the postpartum period include independent counseling services and childbirth preparation organizations, such as the local affiliate of ICEA and La Leche League. Help is usually available if one only asks for it. (See Appendix B for a list of resources).

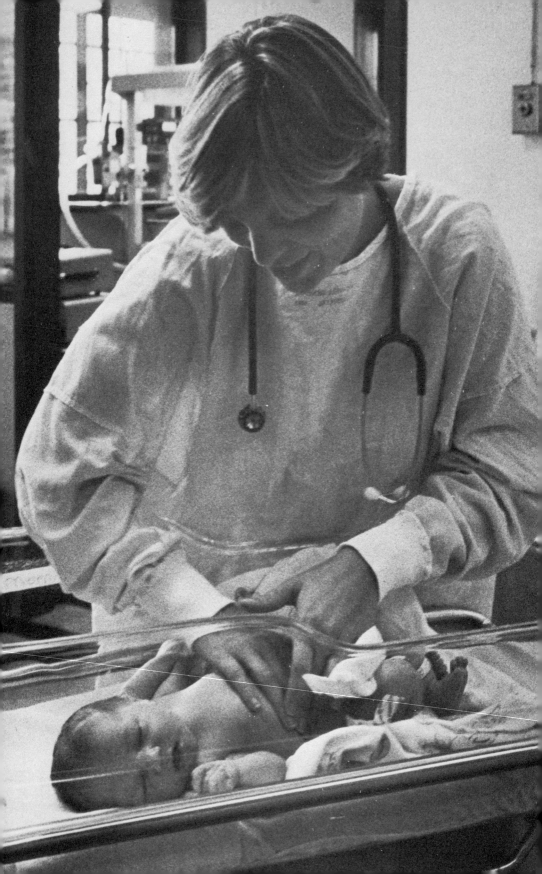

CHAPTER

6

After the Birth: Care of the Baby

The Apgar Test

Immediately after the birth the health and well-being of every newborn is judged according to a test named for Dr. Virginia Apgar, an American anesthetist who worked at Columbia Presbyterian Hospital in New York. She identified the critical nature of the several minutes immediately following birth and developed a rating scale to help attendants decide if resuscitative efforts are necessary.

The Apgar Test rates a newborn baby on each of the following five signs:

- appearance or color
- pulse (heart rate)
- grimace or reflex irritability
- activity
- respiration.

Sixty seconds after birth, the baby is rated on these measures using a scale of zero to two. In appearance, the newborn is given a score of two (the maximum) if the skin is pink all over; one if the body is pink but the arms and legs blue; and zero if the entire body is blue. A score of two is given when the pulse is greater than 100 beats per minute; one if it is less than 100; and zero if it is not present at all. An infant who cries vigorously when given a slap on the soles of the feet is scored two for reflex responsiveness; a grimace or slight cry counts for one; no response is zero. A newborn who makes active motions is scored two for activity or muscle tone; some movement of the arms or legs is rated one; while zero is the score if the baby is motionless and limp. Strong efforts to breathe, along with vigorous crying, count for two; slow, irregular breathing is rated one; no respiration, zero. The five components are totaled to give the one-minute Apgar score (maximum ten, minimum zero).

Most newborns score seven to ten points one minute after birth. Infants with scores of four, five, or six usually require immediate help and oxygen to assist their first attempts at breathing. Mucus in the throat, if present, must be suctioned before they can breathe adequately. A baby with an Apgar score of less than four is unresponsive, pale, limp, usually not breathing, and possibly lacks a heartbeat. The throat of such an infant requires immediate suction to clear the airway, and the lungs require external inflation. Several minutes of attention may be necessary before the baby can take over on its own. Premature infants and others with breathing difficulties may need continuous respiratory assistance in the intensive care nursery.

The Apgar scoring is repeated five minutes after birth, and both scores are recorded. Studies have shown that good scores, especially at the five-minute mark, are strongly predictive of the baby's chances for survival and normal development in early infancy. The one-minute score, on the other hand, alerts the attendants to the immediate, sometimes urgent, need for life support to protect the baby from either imminent death or lifelong neurological problems.

Behavior of the Newborn

In recent years scientific studies have greatly expanded what we know about the newborn's extraordinary capacity to interact with his or her environment. For example, a baby at birth can turn its head repeatedly toward the source of a human voice, its face assuming an alert expression as the baby searches it out. The baby will choose a female voice over any other and prefers human-like sounds to pure tones of an equivalent pitch range. A baby's response to sound can be measured by his or her sucking pattern. The baby pauses briefly after a pure auditory tone, then goes on sucking steadily. When the baby hears a human sound, however, it stops, then continues sucking in a "burst-pause" pattern, as though he or she were expecting something to follow, and pauses in sucking to hear more. The baby will notice and follow the picture of a human face, turning a full 90 degrees, but will not follow the picture of a "scrambled" face, although he or she will look at it wide-eyed for long periods. Babies prefer the odors of milk to those of water or sugar water, and they can taste the difference between human milk and a cow's milk formula designed to be identical to breast milk.

The remarkable complexity and individuality of the newborn is captured and made vivid by the Neonatal Behavioral Assessment Scale (NBAS) developed by Dr. T. Berry Brazelton of Boston. This scale recognizes six states of alertness, twenty-six items of behavior, and twenty neurological reflexes. The twenty-six items of behavior are grouped into six types:

1. *Habituation:* the infant's ability to shut out disturbing environmental stimuli
2. *Interactive* (orientation): the newborn's ability to notice and process both simple and complex events in the environment
3. *Motor:* the ability to maintain muscle tone, control motor actions, and perform integrated motor activities
4. *Range of state:* the intensity and variability of the infant's state of consciousness during the assessment
5. *State regulation:* the newborn's ability to control and modulate states while attending to social and inanimate stimuli

6. *Automatic regulation:* the newborn's vulnerability to such automatic behavior as trembling, startling, and changes in skin color.

The pediatrician may perform the NBAS (in whole or in part) and the general physical examination with the baby's parents present. This is a splendid opportunity for them to observe the remarkable capacities of their baby. By understanding his or her individual temperament or personality, parents are better able to care for the baby, to discriminate between themselves and the baby, and to gain some insight into the responses the baby elicits in them (and vice versa). For example, an intense, easily startled, hard-to-quiet newborn can be predicted to be a fussy, even "colicky" infant. Parents of such a child can expect a stressful start with great potential for self-blame and feelings of inadequacy, desperation, and depression. The frazzled parents risk playing into the infant's irritability, setting into motion a cycle of mutually stimulating and reinforcing negative behaviors. But with the insight derived from watching as the pediatrician examines the baby, it is possible for parents to discover how to help such an excitable infant to become calm. The examination, and/or the time the assessment scale is being carried out, are ideal times to build an alliance with the doctor — family practitioner or pediatrician — who will be caring for the baby.

The interactiveness of the newborn grows rapidly in complexity. For example, by the age of three or four weeks, clear differences in the baby's response to mother and father can be demonstrated. As Dr. Brazelton says in his book *Infants and Mothers:*

> With the mother in sight, it is the baby who is likely to set the pace of their interactions. His face will brighten, his hands and legs will "reach out" gently toward the mother moving smoothly back and forth in a rhythmic fashion. If we watch the baby's face and eyes, we see that they alternately brighten with an intensely interested look as his mother, responding, attempts to engage him, and then become dull as the child retreats into himself and his mother desists.
>
> Father and infant synchronize, too, though their rhythmic pattern is different from that between mother and child and it is the father who is more likely to "set the pace." In our studies we have found that fathers are likelier . . . to "jazz up" the baby. Exaggerated gestures or expressions seem to say, "Come! It's playtime!" At first the baby

will watch the father's antics as if trying to take them in and adjust to them. His shoulders will hunch, his eyebrows go up, his face show anticipation. Then the interaction will begin. As the baby gets older he will laugh out loud and bounce up and down in his eagerness to continue his games with his father.

Many of the visible and audible signs and responses of the newborn change over the first few days. After enduring the trying experience of birth and the one to two hours of intense alertness that follow, permitting peak interaction with parents (see p. 242 on parent-infant attachment), many babies withdraw into a state of toned-down activity or disorganization for the next twenty-four to forty-eight hours. The baby may not suck long or hard and appears to have little interest in eating. This normal withdrawal following delivery may confuse parents eager for interaction with their newborn. Nursing usually picks up once the milk comes in, on the third and fourth day, as though the baby's changing needs are timed to coincide with milk production. The nursing that occurs earlier, however, is very important for the baby, for he or she receives nutrition and immune factors from the mother to help ward off infection. This often low-level nursing is also essential for the mother because it stimulates milk production, promotes uterine contraction, and reinforces the closeness between mother and baby that nursing represents. So don't worry about pokey feeding in the first several days.

REFLEX BEHAVIOR

The newborn is endowed with certain coordinated patterns of behavior known as reflexes, which operate from circuits within the lower centers of the brain and have little to do with the process of rational thought or purposeful action.

Appropriate stimulation in the quiet alert state will automatically elicit these reflex responses. If the cheek of a sufficiently awake and hungry newborn is stroked, she will turn her mouth toward the stroking object, be it a finger or, as nature intended, the nipple of her mother's breast. This reflex is known as the *rooting response*. It is completely automatic and serves to orient the baby toward her source of nutrition before she "knows" where food comes from. Sucking occurs by reflex if something touches the lips, the mucous membranes of the mouth, or the soft palate.

If the newborn is startled by a loud noise or sudden change of position, particularly one with an element of falling, his arms and legs respond in a characteristic way. They move symmetrically first outward, then upward, and then inward. The hands first open, then clench tightly into a fist, as though the infant were echoing remote primate ancestors in trying to grasp a branch of a tree to prevent a fall. The legs go through a similar although less consistent sequence of movements. In addition, the baby's head bends down and forward. This reflex, known as the *startle* or *scare response* is named the *Moro reflex* after the neurologist who first wrote about it.

If pressure is applied by a finger to the palms of the baby's hands or to the balls of her feet, the fingers and toes will curl in to "grasp" the pressing object. The hand grasp is often so strong that the infant can be lifted out of her crib. This automatic response of hands and feet is known as the *grasp reflex.* If the soles of the feet are stroked, the foot will pull up, the toes fan out, and the large toe elevate. This response is known as the *Babinski reflex,* again for the neurologist who first described it.

If you support a baby by holding him under the arms and move him across a tabletop with his feet just touching the surface, his legs will make movements that are very similar to walking. This response to movement and pressure of the feet is reflexive and should not be confused with early walking.

There is a group of hand-mouth reflexes that can be elicited by stroking the cheek or the palm of the hand. The baby roots toward the stroking finger. Her arm flexes and she brings her hand to her mouth. She opens her mouth, puts in the fist, and begins to suck. Stimulating the baby at either end of the line, cheek or hand, leads to the same complex series of movements. (No doubt this reflex is a precursor of thumb sucking. Even in the newborn and fetus, nature has seemingly endowed the infant with a way to handle tension.)

If you place a cloth across the nose of a baby, he will first attempt to mouth it. When this fails, he will twist his head and flail with both hands in an effort to remove it. (This reflex makes it all but impossible for a baby to smother in his bedding.) If one leg is stroked, the other leg will move over by reflex to push the stroking finger away. Babies withdraw by reflex from such painful stimuli as pinches or pinpricks.

234

If a baby's head is slowly turned to one side while she is lying either prone or supine, the body will predictably assume the attitude of a fencer. The arm on the side toward which the head is turned will be extended and the other arm will bend at the elbow; the legs will move in exactly the reverse pattern, one bent, the other extended. This response of the extremities to head turning is known as the *tonic neck reflex*. If the baby is suspended in air by her feet (a position not harmful or bothersome to the infant), she will first assume the fetal position, flexing both arms and legs and curling into an upside-down ball. Then she will extend her legs and arms outward and arch her back, like an athlete in a swan dive.

Reflexes are part of the baby's equipment at birth. As the forerunners of voluntary control, they demonstrate that the "circuits" for complex movements such as walking have been laid down long before actual walking begins. The reflexes persist until voluntary control is developed to the point where it dominates behavior. Thus, when a baby begins to reach and grasp objects at the age of about three months or so, the grasp reflex disappears. When the baby becomes aware of his surroundings and visually searches out his bottle or his mother's breast, the rooting reflex vanishes. In the newborn, reflexes give information on the normalcy of a baby's nervous system. Not all of the reflexes mentioned above are routinely elicited in the normal newborn during a physical examination.

Appearance

To turn to the more physical aspects of the newborn, a great deal can be learned simply by looking. During the first day or two babies may have bluish *(cyanotic)* fingers and toes from a clamping down of circulation to their extremities, perhaps to conserve heat. The rest of the body is pink. This is quite normal. In a few days the fingers and toes will take on the same coloration as the rest of the body. If a bluish or dusky color remains, the doctor will check for heart or lung disorders.

The normal breathing pattern of newborns is variable. They may breathe as rapidly as 60 to 70 times a minute, then slow down to 20 or 30 times per minute, all within the space of two or three minutes. While breathing is noisy, it should not be labored or require hard work. A quality of struggle characterizes the breathing of babies with pulmonary difficulties and makes it different from normal rapid breathing. The vigor and quality of the baby's cry gives information about her airway, vocal cords, and general strength. When stirred up, she is apt to move all four of her limbs and thus give an observer an excellent opportunity to detect any impairments of motion. When she cries vigorously, her color usually changes from pale pink to a beet red.

A newborn's skin is usually dry and flaky, as though he were shedding his skin. The soft, lustrous appearance of the skin seen in pictures in baby magazines will take weeks to develop. At birth, the skin is covered with a greasy coating known as *vernix*. Even though most vernix comes off in the first sponge bath given, bits may remain behind the ears and in the folds of the buttocks. Actually, it is unnecessary to remove vernix at all; it may be massaged into the skin. It is thought to have antibacterial properties. The long hairs on a newborn's body are known as *lanugo*. They characteristically fall out over the first few weeks.

A baby's hands and feet will normally feel cool, while his or her body will be warm. There is no need to add clothing unless the baby seems uncomfortable.

Forceps used in a delivery may leave marks on the skin of the baby's face and head, but these fade within several days. The small yellow or white spots present on the noses, cheeks, or chins of many babies represent trapped collections of sebum, the fatty secretion of the sebaceous glands of the skin. These require no attention and disappear in a matter of weeks.

Small faint red spots or blotches are often seen on the upper eyelids, at the nape of the neck, and in a diamond shape over the bridge of the nose and the forehead. Clusters of tiny blood vessels (or capillaries) present in the immediate newborn period and early infancy account for these markings. Why they occur is not known. In the old days, marks at the bottom of the neck were often called "stork bites" (since the back of the neck was the part of the anatomy grasped by the beak of the mythical stork when he delivered the infant to his new home). "Stork bites" tend to blush and become darker when the baby cries. They disappear gradually over the first year. The diamond-shaped spot on the forehead fades with time, but in some individuals it may persist for life, barely visible except during emotional upsets, when it may flush.

The common *strawberry patch* is a mole *(nevus)* made up of blood vessels. Usually not present in the newborn, it shows up after the baby is brought home. A small bright red spot on the skin is the first sign of such a mark, which predictably will grow rapidly after the baby leaves the hospital. Such nevi enlarge over the first year and gradually resolve over the next several years. They do not usually require treatment.

The newborn's skin is very reactive. When a baby is excited by hunger or stimulated by the poking fingers of a nurse or doctor, large red blotches or mottling may appear over the body, sometimes more prominently in one part than another. Why babies are susceptible to this blotching and mottling is not known for sure, but it is thought to be related to immature regulation of the flow of blood to the skin. These irregularities of coloration have no medical significance, and in several months the exaggerated skin responses disappear.

A common rash seen after the first day or two, and for the next several weeks, is *erythema toxicum.* The characteristic spot of this rash (its exact cause is unknown) is a red blotch with a small white raised center. It resembles prickly heat, or heat rash, which is usually finer. The rash is more prominent on the face, neck, and trunk than on the arms and legs. It comes and goes right before one's eyes. Neither the cause nor the treatment is known, for the condition is so transient and harmless that it has not stimulated the interest of researchers.

Prickly heat or *heat rash* is caused by trapped sweat that accumulates deep in the skin and sets up an inflammation. It can afflict people of all ages but is more common in babies. Heat rash manifests itself in small, often pinpoint, red blotches with slightly raised whitish centers. The rash characteristically comes and goes with great rapidity; it may be present in the morning and gone by noon. It is a condition best left alone, since the application of powders and creams on the skin only aggravates the plugging of the sweat ducts and tends, if anything, to make the condition worse. Keeping the baby in a relatively cool environment will reduce heat rash but may not eliminate it altogether. Fortunately, babies seem to be less troubled by it than parents.

The head of the newborn often shows the effects of passage through the birth canal. If *molding* (see p. 188) has occurred, the result may be a transient lopsidedness. The bones of the baby's skull are not as tightly knit as they are in adults and can shift and overlap to a degree. Thus, the head can usually adapt to the squeezing at birth without injury. The normal separations between the bones *(sutures)* can be felt by running the finger over the head. You will have the distinct impression of a small groove separating one bone from the other. In the middle of the head toward the front is the major (anterior) *fontanel*, or soft spot. There is a smaller posterior fontanel at the "point" of the head in back. The coverings of the fontanels are very tough and can be pressed on without fear of damage. As the baby grows, the skull bones fuse, closing the fontanels and suture lines. For most infants, closure of the anterior fontanel occurs between six months and one and one-half years, while the posterior fontanel closes in a few weeks to months. The anterior fontanel in a quiet baby held in a sitting position sinks in somewhat. When the baby cries, the soft spot tenses. The veins of the baby's head are more prominent than those of adults because they are closer to the surface of the skin. Also, there is less hair to conceal them.

Swelling of the scalp from pressure of the cervix during birth is known as a *caput succedaneum* (see p. 187). It gradually resolves in twenty-four to forty-eight hours and is of no special significance. Trauma to the head during delivery may result in a linear crack (fracture) in the skull and lead to bleeding between the skull and the scalp. The accumulation of blood can be seen as a swelling over the side of the head and is known as *cephalohematoma*. It requires no treatment and gradually resolves over several weeks.

The eyes of the newborn are fully formed. The whites often have small reddish blotches which are tiny hemorrhages produced by squeezing of the head in delivery. These specks of blood clear in a week or so and have no significance. The color of the eyes is almost always blue. If there is to be a change of color it comes on gradually. The eyes are examined by a nurse or doctor with an ophthalmoscope, a special adaptation of a flashlight with a peephole and magnifying lenses, used to check the lenses of the eyes for cataracts and the retina (the sensing part of the eye) for its normal red color. If this red reflex is present, it excludes the possibility of congenital retinal tumors and other abnormalities.

Infants see more than was once thought. Infants can fix on a red or soft yellow object dangled before their eyes and follow it. Shining a bright light causes the lids to shut tightly. If we spin a baby about, her head will turn reflexively in the direction of the spin, and her eyes, in a rhythmical series of alternating fast and slow movements known as *nystagmus*, will try to keep up with the spin. When the baby stops short, the eyes continue quick, rhythmical movements in the direction of spin for several seconds. These reactions depend on the complex position-sensing connections in ear and brain. If you pull a baby up to sitting position by her hands, her eyes will open much as do the weighted eyes on old china dolls. This response is called the "doll's eye" reflex.

The ears are inspected for proper formation and normal location of the canals. Since vernix in the canal often blocks easy inspection of the eardrum, it is not routinely checked in the newborn. As for hearing, fully awake infants usually respond with a startle to any sudden loud noise. Immediate repetition of the noise usually elicits no reaction. The infant seems able to "shut out" the repeated stimulus as a kind of self-protection. (Might it even be that babies do not hear their own crying after a point?)

The lips and mouth, including the gums and palate, are examined for defects. In rare cases, babies are born with teeth, which usually will be "extras" rather than the standard primary and secondary teeth. The tip of the tongue is joined to the floor of the mouth by a little band known as the *frenulum*, which is sometimes quite short. In the past, short frenula gave rise to the concept of being "tongue-tied," and accordingly, many frenula were clipped. In point of fact, babies with short frenula rarely have problems with sucking or, later, with speaking.

A fuzzy white coating on the tongue, noticed usually after the third or fourth day, signifies *thrush*, a yeast or fungal infection with the germ known as *Monilia*. The baby picks up the yeast from the mother's vagina while passing through it before birth (see p. 165).

The neck is inspected and felt for masses. There are several kinds of congenital cysts, some of which may have sinuses, or small openings, in the skin. While they may require surgical removal, this is not usually done in the newborn period. The sternocleidomastoid muscles run from the mastoid bone of the skull just behind the ear down to the inner third of each collarbone and come into play when the head is bent forward or turned to the side. Bruises of this muscle, which possibly occur during or even before birth, may produce a swelling and later a scarring and tightening, the condition known as *torticollis*. When the neck is examined, the position of the windpipe *(trachea)* is checked. Normally in the mid-line of the neck, it may be tugged to one side in certain abnormalities of the lungs. The thyroid gland at the lower part of the front of the neck is also checked.

The chest should expand and contract symmetrically. Unequal movements of the two sides point to lung problems which require further investigation. Attached to the lowest point of the breast-bone just at the top of the abdomen is a distinct little bone known as the *xiphoid*. While it may be particularly prominent and slightly pointed in newborns, it has no special significance. The doctor listens to the chest with a stethoscope to check on the flow of air in and out of the lungs and to detect any fluid within the lungs.

The rhythm and rate of the heartbeat are also checked with the stethoscope. While heart murmurs are common in the newborn, the majority are normal and do not signify heart disease. Most disappear promptly. The explanation for murmurs lies in the radical reorganization of the circulation that occurs at birth. Before birth, blood almost completely bypasses the lungs; with the newborn's first breath, blood begins to circulate through them. This shift in blood flow is accompanied by the opening and closing of various channels within the heart and large blood vessels. The process of reorganization may not be complete for a few days, and blood flowing through partially opened or closed channels generates the noise called a murmur. Later murmurs, too, are in and of themselves not abnormal, for about one-third of normal children have murmurs that do not signify any heart disease.

Feeling the pulses in a baby's groin assures the examiner that there is no significant constriction of the aorta, the major artery leading from the heart to the body. Sometimes these pulses are difficult to feel in a newborn, but they can be detected later.

The stump of the *umbilical cord* is prominent and firmly attached to the *umbilicus* ("belly button"). The stump, shiny and moist for the first day or so, gradually dries, shrivels, and falls off in about ten to twenty days. More than a small rim of redness of the skin of the umbilicus signifies infection and requires medical attention. In newborns, unlike adults, the size and shape of the abdominal organs, the liver, spleen, and kidneys, can be felt under normal conditions. The examiner searches for abnormal masses, such as a blocked kidney. The bladder of the newborn normally rises up much higher in the abdomen than in the adult and can be felt when full of urine. If stools are being passed normally, no examination of the anus or rectum is called for beyond mere external inspection.

The skin of the *scrotum* reflects the maturity of the baby boy. The normal rough appearance develops only in babies whose gestation was close to term. In premature infants the scrotal skin is likely to be smooth and shiny. The testes should be present in the sac. Hernias and hydroceles (fluid accumulations) can be detected as swellings in the scrotum, and hernias require repair even in the newborn period. The urethra, the thin tube that runs the length of the inside of the penis, should open at its tip. In a noncircumcised infant, the foreskin may conceal the urethral opening *(meatus)*. Seeing (or feeling) urine shoot out in males assures that there is no obstruction to the lower urinary tract.

The legs of the newborn are normally bowed from the curled-up position in the womb, and the feet are likely to be turned inward as they were in utero. Both bowing and in-turning of feet persist until the child walks, demonstrating the principle that the shape of the bones depends largely on the forces they sustain. Until the stress of walking is put on them, the legs remain bowed because nothing has stimulated them to change. The legs and feet of babies born by breech (see p. 271) may show the effects of their uterine position. The legs turn outward, with the kneecaps touching, and the feet may also turn outward. In time, these effects disappear.

The hips are checked for dislocation, since congenital dislocation of the hip is a progressive condition, and success in treatment depends mainly on early recognition. Careful note of the hips should be taken at all examinations in infancy, for dislocations may make their appearance only after several months and even as late as a year after birth.

Bonding and Attachment

Both of our birth stories in Chapter 1 demonstrated the importance of keeping parents and infants together immediately after birth. This commonsense practice was neglected earlier in this century as birth moved from home to hospital. Although we are again taking it for granted, only recently have hospitals "permitted" fathers to be with their partners at birth, and "rooming in" is not a universal practice in hospitals.

Midwife Raven Lang studied a group of mothers having home births in California and identified a seemingly "species specific" behavior in mothers who have access to their babies immediately after birth. Even before delivery of the placenta, the mother, in an apparent state of ecstasy, turns, picks up her infant, and often assumes a "face on face" posture. After the infant quiets down, she almost always rubs her baby's skin with her fingertips in a gentle stroking motion, beginning with the face. Most of the parents talk to their infants in high-pitched voices, and all other participants are drawn to the infant as well (see p. 107, "Children and Birth"). Breast-feeding begins within minutes as the infant licks the nipple. As we saw above, this sucking leads to contraction of the uterus, reducing bleeding. At the same time the colostrum delivers nourishment to the baby along with antibodies and antibody-producing cells to help ward off infection.

During the hour or so following birth, the baby is alert to interactions with its parents. This availability must be taken advantage of before the baby becomes sleepy. The richness of the newborn's psychological skills have only recently been described by researchers (see p. 231), even though it is likely that mothers have always known that their babies recognized them. In the parents and other participants, these interactions are accompanied by the welling up of intense, at times overwhelming, feelings of warmth and love for the baby and a desire to nurture him. Thus it is that "babies will make parents of us all."

The effect of medication on the baby's alertness and responsiveness after birth (see p. 203 on analgesics and anesthetics in labor) is of continued interest. In the safe doses currently used, they do not interfere with early bonding between infants and parents. The answer to this question is obviously of great importance, since it will affect decisions about the use of these medicines, and will influence the question of how parents can understand and "correct" for possible drug effects when responding to their baby's early behavior.

Follow-up studies of the interactions between parents and infants who had and who did not have early contact with one another suggest some interesting differences. In one study, for example, mothers who played with their nude babies soon after birth spent much more time with them during the first three months than mothers who did not. Mothers who had early contact spent more time with the baby during the first month, stood closer to and soothed the baby more during an office visit to the doctor, and came to the baby's aid more readily in a stress situation (such as vaccinations). Two years after the birth, they spoke to their babies differently, asking more questions, making fewer demands, and using more adjectives and adverbs. A study of premature infants who had contact with their mothers on the first day as opposed to the twentieth day showed a significantly greater developmental quotient at four years of age. Not all studies, however, show such effects, and even those that do can be faulted, because they involved small numbers of mothers and infants. Nevertheless, the burden of proof seems to be on those who claim no differences in behavior and argue (if any still do) against early parent and infant contact. The "obvious" human advantages of having infants and parents together seem to override any objections.

Drs. Marshall Klaus and John Kennell, who have done important work on parent-infant bonding, have identified seven principles of attachment:

1. There is a "sensitive period" during the first minutes and hours of life in which the close contact of the mother and father with their newborn, in a private situation, is desirable in order for optimal later parental behavior to develop.
2. There appears to be species-specific behavior in the human mother and father when they are first given their baby.
3. The process of attachment is structured so that the father and mother will become attached to only one infant at a time. With twins, this explains why mothers dress them alike, and it also argues for keeping twins together and discharging them together from the hospital, even if the larger one must wait.

4. During the process of a mother's attachment to her infant, it is necessary that the infant respond to her with some signal. The mother needs feedback from the baby in order to invest her love and nurturing efforts. Babies, it has been demonstrated, follow and attend to spoken words for short periods even on the first day after birth.
5. People who witness a birth process become strongly attached to the infant.
6. The processes of attachment and detachment are mutually incompatible. Thus, it is difficult to go through a process of attachment to one person while mourning the loss of another person. For example, if a mother loses a baby, she should get over the process of the loss (which might take seven to eight months) before she becomes pregnant again.
7. Early events can have long-lasting effects. Anxiety about the well-being of a baby with a temporary disorder may result in enduring concerns, which may adversely shape the development of the child.

Even though bonding is a real and important process, it should not be interpreted too rigidly or literally. We would like to add several strong notes of caution.

First of all, bonding and attachment take place over a long period of time. They can start slowly and gather strength. There is no evidence that infants and parents, whose normal contact is disrupted for any reason (say, for example, the need for a premature infant to be put in an incubator in an intensive-care nursery), are unable to recoup and proceed with normal subsequent development. It would be tragic if parents separated from their infant at birth believed that what they had lost could never be regained, and there is certainly no support for such a conclusion.

While early contact is highly desirable and should be encouraged whenever possible, dire consequences are not likely if it cannot occur. There are no rules about human development; except, perhaps, for its extreme plasticity. We must guard against the "tyranny of the normal," which can be as destructive as the practices it seeks to correct.

Most parents would agree that bonding proceeds over many days, if not weeks and months, and is a very individual matter. Not all mothers or fathers experience an instantaneous rush of love for the infant. Some work their way slowly into attaching to the baby — in stages, with occasional steps backward, too. For all parents, there will be ups and downs and much room for patience and steady caring. As Dr. T. Berry Brazelton says in his book, *On Becoming a Family*, "Falling in love with a baby may well happen at first sight, but staying in love is a learning process — learning to know oneself as well as the baby."

It is important for parents to follow their own feelings and not be too caught up in expectations of what should and shouldn't happen. If there is any "should" in this discussion at all, it is that hospitals should adopt policies that permit parents unlimited and free access to their newborns from the time of birth onward.

Another misconception that can interfere with the pleasures of early parenthood is the notion of "spoiling." This is a concern of many parents. All of us want babies to grow up to be self-reliant, independent individuals who do not need or expect to be coddled. However, such worries are completely irrelevant when it comes to the newborn baby. Lavish all the love and affection you can muster and do it unstintingly. There is no more important contribution to a baby's well-being than giving him or her a sense of self-worth and lovableness and trust in parents and home environment. As long as a baby responds positively, it is hard to see any problem in extensive physical contact, including keeping him or her in bed with you. There will be time later in the first year to begin the important job of setting limits.

Nursing

While we strongly urge women to breast-feed if at all possible, and to take advantage of all available supports for nursing, the woman who chooses not to should not feel guilty or inadequate. Thirty-five years ago an American woman was looked upon as odd if she nursed. Today, with the recent return to breast-feeding as a more "natural" alternative, we may have shifted 180 degrees to a position where we now frown on the woman who does not. Both extremes have an element of tyranny in them. We suggest that women read as much as possible about breast and bottle feeding (see Appendix D) and then make an informed choice, just as they have about all other issues raised by their pregnancy.

A mother who chooses to breast-feed needs to nurse the baby as soon as possible for a few minutes at a time at each breast. Doing this often helps prevent soft sore nipples, gets nursing firmly established, and helps keep the uterus contracted. She should alternate the breast she starts each session with, realizing the more she nurses, the more milk she will have. To increase the supply, she should put the baby to the breast more often. If the nipples get sore or cracked, they should be rubbed with lanolin, vitamin E, or some other pure oil and exposed to air and sun (see p. 66 on toughening nipples prenatally).

The *colostrum*, a thick yellowish-white substance produced before the milk, is full of nutrients and antibodies. When milk comes in on the second or third day, the breasts may feel very full and hard for a day or so. If they are uncomfortable, hot wet compresses or a hot shower can be soothing. The nursing woman may have to express a little milk with her hand before the baby can grasp the nipple (see Figure 19). (A woman experienced in breast-feeding can demonstrate the technique of manual expression.) Mothers should make sure to wash their hands before handling their breasts, especially after changing diapers.

If a tender lump develops, it is likely to be due to a plugged duct. Massaging the lump toward the nipple and nursing in a different position should cure the problem. The symptoms and signs of a *breast infection* (mastitis) are pain, swelling, redness of the breasts, general malaise, chills, and headache. If these are present, a woman should promptly go to bed with the baby and nurse every one to two hours, favoring the infected side. She should increase her intake of fluids and apply heat to the sore breast. If symptoms do not lessen in a few hours, the doctor should be called. Dicloxacillin and erythromycin are two antibiotics that work well against staphylococcus, the bacterium usually responsible. It is important to continue nursing, noting that neither the infection nor the antibiotic in the breast milk is likely to harm the baby.

Most drugs taken by the mother will to some degree pass through the breast milk to the baby. The risk to the baby of any given drug must be weighed against the advantage of the drug to the mother and the desirability of continuing breast-feeding.

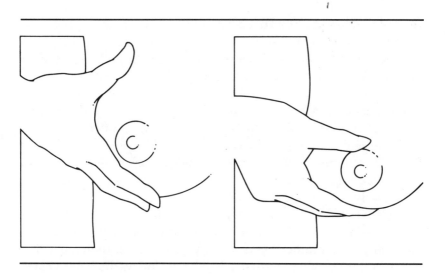

Figure 19. Expressing milk with the hand

An individual consideration must be made in each case. La Leche League, a very valuable resource for nursing mothers (see Appendix B), maintains up-to-date information on this topic.

In general, the most common drugs a mother may require, including the usual antibiotics and over-the-counter analgesics like aspirin and acetaminophen, exert no demonstrable harm to the baby, even though they pass into the milk and thereby into the baby. (For a discussion of the effect of oral contraceptives, see p. 224.) If a particular drug is harmful for the baby but needs to be given only for a defined period, one acceptable approach is to discontinue breast-feeding, pump the breasts to maintain milk production, and use a formula until the course of drug treatment is complete. Breast-feeding can then be resumed.

During their first few weeks babies nurse eight to twelve times a day, about once every two or three hours. Feedings may cluster at certain times and become more spaced out at others. The baby's cues should be closely followed. Since little uninterrupted time is available for the nursing mother to sleep, it is important for her to protect herself from the telephone and other possible interruptions during the brief periods when she is not feeding the baby.

La Leche League recommends that, during the first few weeks, a baby be fed at least every four hours, even if this means waking the baby. They cite the need to build up the milk supply, also pointing out that an overly hungry baby's eager sucking can traumatize the nipples. Some mothers use the fullness of their breasts as well as the baby's cues as a guide for when to nurse.

During the first two or three days the baby may not be very interested in nursing. After the wide-eyed alertness of the first one to two hours after birth (see p. 242), babies often withdraw to recharge their energy. The mother should be prepared to adjust her expectations to the baby's behavior during this period of erratic feeding, for soon the baby will suck eagerly and more predictably.

A little practice is usually needed in getting used to each other before settling into a smooth breast-feeding or bottle-feeding relationship. The mother needs to be patient, relax, remember that she is built to be able to nurse a baby, and follow the baby's cues. The following techniques may also help.

If you touch a baby's cheek she will turn toward the area touched. This is called the *rooting* reflex, as mentioned earlier, and can be used to direct the baby to the breast nipple or to the nipple of a bottle. If the nipple is large in relationship to the baby's mouth, it may have to be squeezed between two fingers to make it smaller and to keep the breast from blocking the baby's nose. The mother may try various positions — sitting, lying on her side, or leaning over the baby, perhaps making herself comfortable with pillows, blankets, and other supports. (See Figure 20.) At the end of nursing the mother may have to place the tip of her little finger between the baby's lips to break the suction.

Many mothers find they can use their breasts as *pacifiers*, allowing the baby to suck for pleasure, beyond satisfying his or her need for food. As long as the nipples hold up, there is no harm in this practice, and much to recommend it. A rubber pacifier or a rubber bottle nipple stuffed with cotton will also keep the baby busy. If left alone, most babies will gratify their need to suck by chomping on their fists (something they do in utero as well).

The answer to a *hungry baby* is more nursing, not a bottle. The same principle applies to a baby's excess hunger after the newborn period. As they grow, many babies temporarily outstrip their mother's milk supply and let it be known by crying. The extra sucking and emptying by more nursing stimulates increased milk production, and a new balance between demand and supply is

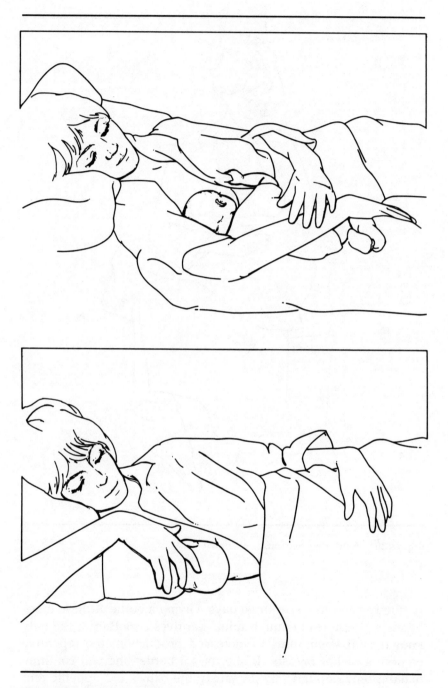

Figure 20. Nursing positions

Figure 20. **Nursing positions,** *continued*

reached in about two to three days. Giving a bottle at these times because "there isn't enough milk" deprives a mother of the only known natural stimulus to increased production, the repetitive emptying of her breasts. If she uses a bottle, she will continue making only enough milk to satisfy the baby's old appetite and thus become increasingly dependent on supplementary formula.

Occasionally, if milk production lags markedly behind demand, it may be appropriate to use small amounts of supplementary formula after nursing, or to recruit another woman to nurse the baby while the mother rests. Midwives, doctors, or La Leche League can advise a suitable approach. Several recent reports describe a new drug, metoclopromide, which has been shown to stimulate milk production by increasing the release from the pituitary of prolactin, the milk-producing hormone. While further studies are needed to determine the effects and possible side-effects of this drug, it may prove useful to the mother with low milk supplies.

After the first few weeks, there is one practical reason to introduce the bottle to the nursing baby. Babies may be likely to refuse bottles altogether if they are not introduced to them until they are several months old. We have seen a number of older babies who, even with much coaxing, have been unable to cope with a bottle at all. Without resumed nursing, or, in some cases, spoon-feeding, it seems these babies would rather go hungry than give in to anything but a breast. It is worth noting that the muscle movements involved in breast-feeding and bottle-feeding are different. The action for nursing is biting with the gums (or chomping), while that for bottle-feeding is truly sucking. It's understandable that an infant might not be able to do both. The refusal of bottle-feedings can occur whether formula or expressed breast milk is used. It is also often the case that the bottle-fed infant will not easily transfer to the breast.

As attached as most mothers are to their babies, there are many situations when a bottle might be helpful. One of these is to give the mother a break, allowing the father to participate more actively in the fun of feeding. Our advice is to offer one small "get acquainted" bottle feeding per day after the first two weeks. This can be water, juice, expressed breast milk, or formula.

Babies regularly swallow air with feedings and usually *burp* it up. Sometimes they seem uncomfortable before burping, as though their stomach is too full. Since air rises, the upright position is the best one to facilitate burping, traditionally assisted with a gentle pat on the back. Along with burping, many babies bring up ("spit up") some milk, which may exit through their nose as well as their mouth. Spitting up is of no consequence to the baby. It is likely that whenever a baby burps, some milk enters the esophagus (food tube). Since the distance from stomach to mouth in a baby is a matter of mere inches, it does not take too much extra force to bring the milk all the way up and out. If spitting up is bothersome, burping midway through a feeding, and letting up on nursing as soon as the baby slows down, will avoid giving more milk than he or she can hold and thus will tend to prevent spitting up.

Babies also *hiccup*. They even have hiccups in utero, which mothers can often distinguish from kicking. Hiccups seem to bother babies little if at all, and most will merrily hiccup their way to sleep. There is no need for concern.

Babies have no need for *solid foods* for at least the first four months, and preferably six. Certainly they need not be given them until they can take them from a spoon. There is no evidence that the earlier introduction of solid foods reduces the number of nighttime awakenings.

Bottle Feeding

Even though formula lacks some special features of human milk, such as germ-fighting antibodies and white blood cells, babies do very well on it. In the relatively sanitary conditions in the United States today, such advantages of human milk are less important than in underdeveloped areas of the world.

TYPES OF FORMULA

The various commercial infant formulas so popular today (Similac, Enfamil, etc.) are, for all practical purposes, interchangeable. They come as powders, to which water is added, or as liquids that are either ready-to-use or diluted with water. These formulas are as close in composition to breast milk as modern industry can make them. The advantage of the powdered formula is that a small amount may be used while the rest is refrigerated and can be kept up to at least a week.

Commercial formulas are almost the rule today, but their alleged superiority over evaporated and whole milk formulas has never been proven. Theoretically, at least, they are closer in composition to breast milk, and they substitute allegedly healthier vegetable oil for the saturated milk fat of cow's milk formulas. But they cost about twice as much.

An acceptable whole milk formula is

Whole milk........	20	ounces
Water	10	ounces
Sugar	2	tablespoons corn syrup (Karo) or
	4	tablespoons dextrin-maltose powder

The sugar syrup or powder is used to add back the calories diluted out when water is added to decrease salt and protein concentrations.

A similar formula using evaporated milk is

Evaporated milk...........	10	ounces
Water	20	ounces
Sugar	2	tablespoons corn syrup or
	4	tablespoons dextrin-maltose

Both of the above formulas are usually deficient in vitamin C, so this may have to be supplemented (see p. 258).

Evaporated milk has the following advantages over whole milk: smaller curd formation in the stomach (because it has been previously cooked), leading to possibly greater digestibility, and indefinite shelf life.

EQUIPMENT

The preparation of formulas requires a small amount of equipment, some of which can be adapted to other uses when the baby is weaned. Nursing bottles come in two sizes, four-ounce and eight-ounce. The baby will begin with the small ones and grow into the larger size. You will need about eight of each. Bottles should be of heat-resistant, unbreakable glass or clear plastic, smooth inside, with a graduated scale in ounces plainly marked on the outside. This scale is needed to indicate the amount of formula poured in. If you buy a six-pack of commercial formula early on, the bottles may be reused for formula prepared at home.

Rubber or plastic caps, collars, and nipples for the bottles are required. All can be bought separately. In all, a dozen nipples should be available. The U.S. Food and Drug Administration recommends boiling new nipples five or six times, using fresh water for each boil, before using them. This process removes nitrosamines, chemicals that may be harmful to the baby. Extra collars, with the little disks that convert them into caps, are always handy. Bottles with plastic bag inserts are said to minimize air swallowing. Whether or not this is true, these bags are good for storing and freezing both breast milk and formula with a minimum of bacterial contamination.

A nipple should not be so long that it reaches the back of the baby's throat and causes gagging. A premature baby, or one who lacks the strength to suck, may need a softer nipple, the so-called "preemie nipple." The flow of milk from the bottle should be neither too slow nor too fast. Either extreme can lead to swallowing excess air. A good rule of thumb is that the milk should drip out slowly and steadily, a drop at a time, when the bottle is held upside down. To tell whether the baby is getting the milk, watch for bubbles on the surface of the milk still in the bottle. Nipples harden under repeated boiling, so old nipples may have openings that are small. Either enlarge the opening with a needle or discard the nipple. If a new nipple has too large an opening, boiling it a few times may help. You will want a bristle brush for scrubbing the bottles and a pair of metal tongs for handling them. You will find use for a heat-resistant glass measuring cup, measuring spoon, glass funnel, can opener, standard tablespoon, strainer, and glass jar with a tightly fitting screw top to keep sterilized nipples and collars uncontaminated.

The sterilizer, of course, is the main piece of equipment. This contraption need be nothing more complicated than a deep aluminum or porcelain-coated kettle with a lid and rack for bottles. Sterilizers come in a variety of styles and prices to suit your own taste and pocketbook. When the baby is weaned, add the sterilizer to your collection of pots and pans. Even the bottle rack is worth keeping — you can use it for steaming asparagus.

STERILIZATION

Old ideas about sterilizing formula and utensils have undergone recent modification. When bottle feeding first became prevalent, infections among newborn babies constituted a serious health problem. Since those days, we have developed effective inocula-tions and medicines against most dreaded infections and greatly improved the sanitation of our water supplies. Under conditions of ordinary cleanliness, most American babies could probably get by today without any sterilization of their bottles or formulas, but there is no point in subjecting them to needless risk. Unless your own doctor advises otherwise, you should sterilize for at least the baby's first two months.

The procedures for sterilizing are quite simple. When the baby has finished a bottle, rinse the bottle, collar, and nipple under the faucet. Either wash the bottle immediately or leave it filled with water until you do. For washing, use either soap or a dishwashing detergent. Scrub the inside of the bottle and the screw threads of the collar thoroughly with the bristle brush. The brush will be more effective for digging into nooks and crannies if it has a hook on the bristle end. Wash the nipples by forcing soapy water through them. Hold the nipple between your first two fingers, fill it with soapy water, then press down with your thumb. The water will shoot out in a fine stream. Use the same trick with clear water to rinse. Be thorough about rinsing bottles, nipples, and collars.

Once bottles, nipples, and collars are washed clean, you have a choice of two methods for the sterilization proper. You can boil the utensils and the formula separately; or (the simpler way) you can fill the bottles with the mixed formula and boil. The first method is called *presterilization*, the latter, *terminal sterilization*.

In presterilization, simply put all the equipment — bottles, col-lars, caps, and mixing utensils — into the sterilizer and boil them for at least ten minutes. Boil the nipples less than five minutes. They will harden and crack if boiled longer. After washing your hands thoroughly, measure into a saucepan the amount of water needed for the formula, plus an extra half ounce to allow for evaporation, and bring it to a boil. If you are using whole milk, shake the bottle or carton to mix the contents and wash its top well with warm water before opening it. When the water in the saucepan has come to a full boil, add the required amount of milk and, stirring constantly, let the milk and water boil for five min-utes. Then add sugar, if the formula calls for it. If the formula specifies evaporated milk or either powdered or liquid commercial premodified milk, wash the top of the can well with soap and water and rinse thoroughly before you puncture the lid to pour. These products are already sterile, so no further sterilization is necessary. Just pour the milk into the pan of water you have been boiling. Add the sugar if necessary. The formula is then ready for bottling and capping with clean hands. Don't touch the part of the bottles that come in contact with the formula.

In terminal sterilization, wash all the utensils well but don't boil them before mixing the formula. Pour the mixed formula into the clean bottles. Place caps loosely on the bottles, but don't tighten them. Loosely place the screw-type lid on the empty glass container which, following sterilization, will be used to store the nipples. Now put the bottles of formula in the rack in the sterilizer along with the container for the nipples and pour in enough water to cover them half way up. Cover the sterilizer, bring to a boil, and boil gently for twenty-five minutes. Remove the bottles with tongs, placing them in a container of cool water, and tighten the caps securely. Then put them in the refrigerator. The usual sterilizer will have room enough for tongs, spoons, and the screw-top glass jar for nipples, in addition to the load of formula bottles. The easiest procedure for the nipples is to boil them separately after fitting them to collars. Five minutes in boiling water will be enough. Then remove them with tongs to the sterilized jar and cover tightly. When it's time to fix the baby's bottle, all that remains to be done is to take the cap off the bottle and replace it with a sterilized nipple. It goes without saying that you should wash your hands well with soap and water before handling any of the utensils or equipment for the baby's food.

Cans of formula base (including evaporated milk) come in the right size for making single batches of formula. If you have some left over, you can store it safely in the refrigerator for forty-eight hours, covered tightly with plastic wrap. The bottled formula also can be kept safely in the refrigerator for forty-eight hours. A bottle can stand at room temperature for an hour without spoiling and, if unopened, go back in the refrigerator. If, however, the baby has taken some formula from the bottle, the remainder should not be kept for more than an hour (half hour in a hot climate) and should not be returned to the refrigerator.

Up until a few years ago it was taken for granted that the baby's bottle had to be served up warm just like breast milk. Then a venturesome study demonstrated convincingly that there is no apparent medical reason to warm the milk. Not only can babies take cold milk without flinching, many of them seem to enjoy it. Nevertheless, since the baby's natural milk would come warm from the breast, and since so little effort is involved in taking the refrigerator chill off the bottle, why be innovative just for the sake of innovation? Ordinarily we recommend giving formulas at room temperature or a little warmer.

Styles of Feeding

Dr. Anton Lethin and colleagues at Yale University, in a 1953 article in the *Journal of the American Medical Association*, identified five ways babies feed. While the descriptions were based on nursing babies, they apply equally well to bottle feeders. All are within the range of normal nursing behavior.

1. "Barracudas." When put to the breast, these babies vigorously and promptly grasp the nipple and suck energetically for ten to twenty minutes. They do not dally. Occasionally they put too much vigor into nursing and hurt the nipple.
2. "Excited ineffectives." These babies become so excited and active at the breast that they alternatively grasp and lose it. Then they start screaming. Often the nurse or mother must pick up the baby and quiet her, then put her back to the breast. After a few days, mother and baby usually become adjusted to each other.
3. "Procrastinators." These babies often seem to put off until the fourth or fifth postpartum day what they could just as well have done from the start. They show no particular interest or ability in sucking in the first few days and wait until the milk comes in. It is important not to prod or force these babies when they seem disinclined, for they do well once they start nursing.
4. "Gourmets" or "Mouthers." These babies insist on mouthing the nipple — tasting a little milk and smacking their lips — before starting to nurse. If hurried or prodded, this sort of

"Styles of Feeding" is adapted from G. Barnes, A. Lethin, E. Jackson, *et al.* "Management of Breastfeeding" appeared in the *Journal of the American Medical Association* (151: 192, 1953). Copyright © 1953 American Medical Association.

infant becomes furious and begins to scream. Left alone, he settles down and nurses very well after a few minutes of mouthing.

5. "Resters." These babies prefer to alternate a few minutes of nursing with a few minutes of rest. If left alone, they often nurse well, although the entire feeding procedure takes much longer for this type than for the other types. They cannot, however, be hurried.

Vitamins and Minerals

Babies, like people of all ages, require vitamins. The official recommendation is to supplement the diets of infants with 400 milligrams of vitamin D and 30 to 50 milligrams of vitamin C daily. Manufacturers add these vitamins to commercial formulas. Breast-fed babies, according to the American Academy of Pediatrics, should be given drops containing vitamin C and D, because breast milk does not transfer them well. In point of fact, we have never encountered a baby who was breast-fed without vitamin supplementation who showed any signs of either vitamin D or vitamin C deficiency. Moreover, present evidence suggests that breast milk normally contains a very active form of vitamin D, different from that traditionally measured. This variety, it now appears, suffices to meet the baby's needs. For extra insurance, we suggest that the mother continue taking her prenatal vitamins.

Vitamin K is necessary to the production of blood clotting factors. Without it, there is widespread bleeding throughout the body. Newborns have only small amounts of this vitamin and require about a week to make enough on their own to facilitate normal clotting. Therefore, vitamin K is routinely administered at birth to boost the level immediately.

Vitamin K is traditionally given by injection right after delivery. It is also possible to give it to the baby by mouth. It may be given prenatally by way of the placenta. The mother takes 5 to 10 milligrams daily, beginning fourteen days before the estimated date of birth and continuing until birth. These methods have the advantage of being painless, but have not yet been carefully studied.

Fluoride is of proven benefit in preventing dental cavities. Populations of children exposed to fluoride, either in the water supply or as supplements, show a 50 percent reduction in cavities. Fluoridation of water has proved to be one of the most effective of all public health measures. Fluoride is incorporated into growing teeth and can also be applied to the surface of teeth with, for example, a fluoridated toothpaste or a special fluoride solution. Since fluoride passes poorly through breast milk and is not added to prepared ready-to-use infant formulas, parents will need to give it directly to the baby. If your town water supply is fluoridated and you are bottle-feeding, using the water to prepare formula, you will not need to give fluoride drops. Too much fluoride stains the teeth. As the breast-fed baby grows older and takes more town water, directly or in foods, taper off the supplements. By a year they are probably not needed. Check with your doctor or nurse about obtaining fluoride drops and the proper doses to use.

Sleep and Crying

Sleeping patterns vary widely. Your baby will give you plenty of clues about what his or her schedule is. Most babies sleep twenty out of twenty-four hours in the first week or two and slowly taper off to sixteen to eighteen hours by the end of the first month. Some infants have predictable sleep/wake patterns; other babies are much more irregular. Some sleep more at night, while others catnap during the day in a variable pattern. Most infants do not sleep through the night until four or more months, although you can count on hearing about the exception who does so within the first one to two weeks. Many infants seem to mix up nights and days during the first several weeks of life. The introduction of solid foods does not affect the age of "sleeping through."

Light and noise do not usually bother infants, but if your baby startles easily, or is a restless sleeper, you may have to arrange some dark and quiet spot. Laying the baby on her side or stomach has the advantage of allowing gravity to assist her in handling spit-up stomach contents and will make her more comfortable, perhaps inducing her to fall asleep more easily.

If you are breast-feeding a fussy, wakeful baby and are drinking caffeine-containing beverages (coffee, tea, cola drinks), prudence suggests stopping, since there is evidence that caffeine that reaches the baby through breast milk acts as a stimulant to keep her awake, active, and irritable.

Crying is an infant's major means of communication and expression. It can mean "I'm hungry," "I'm tired," "I'm uncomfortable," "I'm letting off steam," or "I'm bored." Not all crying can be readily explained, and, of course, a baby cannot be asked about his or her inner experience. Many babies will cry without obvious cause for up to several hours a day, often in the late afternoon and early evening (one hopes not in the middle of the night). Do what you will, feed, change, rock, swaddle, hug, coo, nothing works for long. Interestingly, babies of all cultures and childrearing practices show this common behavior, meaning that the source probably lies within the infant rather than his or her environment. (In other words, it's not your fault.)

An extreme degree of inconsolable crying, when a baby seems truly miserable, is known as *colic*. Colic is believed to be related to intestinal cramps, but no one knows for sure. Researchers now report that hormone levels in the brain may play a role.

Babies who cry swallow air. It rumbles through their stomachs and intestines and is passed through the rectum. It is possible that the air contributes to intestinal cramps and leads to still more crying, more air swallowing, and so on. It is also possible that babies cry when they hear themselves cry, in a kind of self-imitation or contagion of sadness.

When all else fails, you may have to let a baby "cry it out." Pick him up every fifteen minutes to see if you can comfort him. If not, put him back to bed, close the door, and cover your ears. If the crying is driving you up the wall, ask someone else to take over while you go for a walk. A rested person with a fresh point of view may be able to figure out a few tricks that have eluded you — little ways of working around a baby's individual quirks.

There are few forces on earth that can make one feel more inadequate, or so undermine one's self-confidence, as the crying of a baby who cannot be comforted. Don't be surprised if you feel a little helpless, incompetent, or guilty in dealing with this behavior — you are not alone. And you can reassure yourself that, as far as anyone can tell, colicky crying leads to no permanent physical or emotional scars. Such babies grow up well anyway. Another piece of good news about even the worst colic is that it does not go on forever. By three months, or four at the outside, it is only a memory. (See Appendix D for books on babies in the first year.)

Bathing and Diapering

Young babies do not need baths. They are not dirty at birth. *Vernix* (see p. 236), which coats the skin in utero, is healthy for the skin and may protect it against infection. If vernix accumulates in the skin folds, spread it around and rub it in like lotion. Wash the baby's bottom with warm water on a soft cloth.

Traditional practice directs that, until the stump of the umbilical cord falls off, the baby should be sponge bathed with warm water and not immersed — presumably to prevent infection of the cord. To our knowledge, however, this has never been critically studied.

The bathing procedure is simple. Wash the eyelids with a clean cloth or cotton ball. While a Q-tip can be used to remove visible ear wax, it should not be used to dig into the ear canal. (Ear wax is normal. It becomes a problem only when it blocks a doctor's or nurse's view of the eardrum, when *otitis media* is suspected.) Use a mild soap to wash the baby from neck to feet, soaping the creases in the neck, under the arms, and in the groin. Wipe a girl's genitals from front to back to minimize the chance of a urinary tract infection. (This practice should be followed by the girl herself later in life when she begins using toilet tissue.) Use mild shampoo or soap for the scalp. Remove head scales ("cradle cap," or *seborrhea*) by rubbing with a cloth. If the scales are particularly resistant, soften them first with some baby oil. You may have to rub hard to get them off.

When using a baby tub, support the infant with one arm. You can also use a shallow bath tub. *Never leave an infant alone or unsupported in the water.* Since babies usually enjoy being bathed, a bath is a nice time for socializing and a useful diversion during fussy periods.

The *umbilical cord* stub should fall off on its own in seven to fourteen days. Do not pull it off. Until the cord falls off, keep the diaper rolled down under the navel. Dabbing a small amount of alcohol on the stump at each diaper change may hasten drying and keep the area clean, but it is not necessary. If more than the rim of the skin around the base of the cord becomes red, call the doctor promptly, since this could mean infection. Following the separation of the cord, the umbilicus ("belly button") may be wet and red, and the raw area left behind may bleed when touched. This area will usually heal within a few days. If it does not, the doctor or nurse can treat it by applying silver nitrate on the end of what looks like a long match stick.

The baby should urinate and have a *bowel movement* within twenty-four hours. The first stool, called *meconium*, is black and sticky, almost like tar. The appearance changes first to a "seedy" yellow, then finally to a golden yellow with the consistency of scrambled eggs after the mother's milk comes in.

Bowel patterns vary from infant to infant. Some babies will have a bowel movement with every feeding, while others will have but three or four a week. Breast-fed infants are notorious for skipping days, and may even go a week, between stools. The stool pattern may change dramatically after the first few weeks, from six stools a day to one every other day. We know of one record-holder who went three weeks between stools and was perfectly well!

Babies commonly strain and turn brick red when passing stools, but their discomfort usually lasts no more than a few minutes. None of this straining means that the baby is constipated. *Diarrhea* is characterized by frequent, watery, sometimes foul-smelling, sometimes green, loose stools. The doctor should be called if your baby develops diarrhea. (The green color, incidentally, comes from bile that has not undergone processing because of the rapid passage of the stool through the intestine.)

A baby boy's *foreskin* will not retract completely at birth. Retractability increases with age and is usually not complete for several years. During baths it is not necessary to retract the foreskin over the head of the penis for cleaning. Periodically gently test the foreskin for retractability; *do not* force it.

A *circumcision* takes about ten days to heal. Wash the area with warm water on a cotton ball at each diaper change.

Regarding the necessity of circumcision, there is no medical argument for it and there are risks which should be faced. We strongly advise against routine circumcision. If the procedure must be done, a local anesthetic should be injected at the base of the penis to minimize pain to the baby.

Pink-colored urine is common during the first few weeks, particularly in baby boys. The pink stain, lighter in color than blood, is often noticed on the diaper but is no cause for alarm. The color comes from urate crystals and is of no special significance.

A baby girl may have a *pink-tinged vaginal discharge* during the first ten days. This is caused by the withdrawal of stimulation of her uterus by maternal hormones which passed via the placenta to her body. It is a normal response.

Babies of both sexes may temporarily have *swollen breasts* and nipple secretions caused by the transfer of hormones from the mother across the placenta. This swelling disappears in seven to ten days.

An accumulation of *mucus* in the corner of the eye, particularly in the morning on awakening, is very common. It probably represents a transient partial blockage of the duct that drains tears from the eye into the nose. Wipe the mucus away with a moist washcloth or cotton ball. Redness of the whites of the eye (except for red spots present at birth, mentioned earlier on p. 236) signifies infection (*conjunctivitis*) and should be reported to your doctor or nurse.

Diaper rash is the almost inevitable result of using diapers, a price we seem willing to pay for the convenience of dry sheets, clothes, and laps. For an infant, wearing wet diapers is analogous to an adult's having a wet bathing suit on most of the day. Since infants vary in their susceptibility to rash, care of their bottoms can easily be individualized.

The following procedures will prevent rash and help clear up rashes in progress:

1. Change diapers as soon as they are wet, or at least every two to four hours, including a change at night. Gently rinse the skin with clear water, allowing it to air dry as much as possible.
2. Avoid overnight use of plastic pants over a cloth diaper. Instead, use a "triple diaper" made of cloth diapers and a rubber pad to protect the bed.

3. In washing cotton diapers, use an extra rinse with diluted vinegar added.
4. For babies with sensitive skin, consider using disposable diapers. They absorb more water than cloth. The so-called new disposable diapers are even more absorbent than the conventional disposables.
5. Use ointments to protect the skin. These are probably better as preventives than as treatments for established rashes. Zinc oxide, A and D, Desitin, and Vaseline Intensive Care all will do. Air exposure will also reduce rash.
6. Check with your doctor or nurse about any rash that resists your efforts to clear it up. Medicated creams or ointments may be required.

Preventing Eye Infection

In the United States all states mandate by law the treatment of the newborn's eyes to prevent gonococcal infection (see p. 161). Some states follow the standards of the Federal Center for Communicable Diseases in allowing a choice between silver nitrate and an antibiotic ointment (erythromycin or tetracycline), while other states restrict treatment to the traditional silver nitrate solution.

Some parents object to the use of silver nitrate. The swelling conjunctivae and eyelids that result interfere with the infant's ability to open her eyes. It therefore disturbs the family's earliest hours together and the bonding process which is enhanced by eye-to-eye contact (see p. 242). Antibiotic ointment does not cause as much inflammation and is preferable to silver nitrate in this regard. When silver nitrate is used, its application can be delayed one or more hours after birth, in order not to interfere with initial parent-infant contact. Parents should inquire about this before birth.

Chlamydia (see p. 159) has replaced the gonococcus as the most common cause of eye infection in newborns in this country. Since silver nitrate is not effective against chlamydia and erythromycin is effective against both chlamydia and gonorrhea, an argument can be made for using erythromycin exclusively in treating the eyes of the newborn. Although tetracycline is also officially recommended, its effects have not yet been as well studied. Again, these choices should be discussed with the physician or midwife before birth.

PKU Test

The PKU (phenylketonuria) test is done soon after birth on several drops of blood obtained by pricking the baby's heel. It is usually done in the hospital without parental participation, but, since more babies are being discharged early or are born at home, it may be done either in the office or at home after the baby has had several feedings.

After the heel prick is made, the drops of blood are squeezed from the foot until the spaces provided for them on the test card are filled. This is obviously disturbing to the newborn. One resourceful mother in my (Richard Feinbloom's) practice, nursed her baby through this uncomfortable procedure and demonstrated that she could calm her infant most of the time. I subsequently recommended this approach, with success, to several other mothers. The bandaid on the heel can be removed the following day.

This test is done to identify the one baby in 10,000 with a biochemical disorder that can lead to mental retardation if left untreated. These babies are unable to process the amino acid (simple protein) *phenylalanine* found in human and cow's milk. As this chemical builds up in the blood, it damages the brain. Once identified, the condition is treated by restricting phenylalanine in the diet.

In a pregnant woman with PKU, the exposure of the fetus to high maternal blood levels of phenylalanine is likely to result in mental retardation and small head and brain size (microcephaly). Thus, a woman treated for PKU during childhood must resume the low phenylalanine diet before conception and during her pregnancy, to prevent damage to her baby. PKU in either mother or father increases the likelihood of an offspring with the disorder. So, not only should the baby be promptly tested, but the affected parents need to know about their disorder and should alert health professionals before pregnancy in order to take proper preventive measures.

Signs of Illness

Serious signs of illness in an infant are the following. A doctor or nurse should be contacted immediately.

- a fever above 100.5 degrees (see below)
- diarrhea (frequent watery, foul-smelling, loose stools)
- continuous vomiting at feedings, or vomiting that shoots out several feet from the baby (remember, however, that simple burping may sometimes be "projectile")
- weak or absent sucking
- blood in stools or in vomitus
- labored breathing
- persistent or unusual crying.

Use a *rectal thermometer* to take the baby's temperature. Shake the mercury column down to below 98.6 degrees and grease the bulb end with petroleum jelly taken from the jar on a tissue (to avoid contaminating the jar). Lay the baby across your lap face down and gently insert the thermometer about one inch into the rectum, holding the thermometer between index and middle fingers with palm down to grasp and hold the buttocks together. This allows you to move with the baby if he wiggles and to prevent the thermometer from breaking. Keep the thermometer in place for three minutes, then wipe it off with tissue to read it.

As for other worrisome symptoms, parents should trust their own instincts and consult the doctor or nurse if any unusual or sudden change in the baby's appearance or habits persists. See also Appendix D for books on child health.

Jaundice

During the first week, check the baby daily in natural light for jaundice, a yellow color of the skin and the whites of the eyes.

Any yellowness darker than "just visible" should be reported to the doctor or midwife. Yellowness as deep as the color of lemon peel or egg yolk, and jaundice of any kind during the first twenty-four hours, warrant *immediate attention.*

Jaundice is produced by the buildup of a chemical called *bilirubin.* Normally present in humans of all ages, bilirubin is a breakdown product of hemoglobin from red blood cells that have died. The bilirubin is carried by the blood to the liver where it is combined into the bile for elimination through the intestine. The newborn's liver normally takes a few days to reach peak efficiency in processing bilirubin. In addition, a newborn's red blood cells are undergoing a reduction in number, to accommodate the infant to life outside the uterus, thus liberating more hemoglobin, and, hence, bilirubin. For both these reasons, the newborn is apt to develop jaundice. If any other disorder that increases red cell destruction is present — such as maternal antibodies against fetal cells, as in Rh or ABO blood type incompatibility (see p. 56) — the likelihood of jaundice is even greater.

The problem with jaundice in a full-term newborn is that bilirubin in the blood above a certain level can injure the brain. Hence, jaundice needs to be assessed for degree and treated if excessive. While most full-term babies develop some jaundice, only a small percentage require therapy. Experienced midwives and doctors can estimate the degree of jaundice by simply looking. If the level seems high, an exact measurement of bilirubin can be made on several drops of blood obtained by pricking the heel.

The garden-variety jaundice in infants makes its appearance on the second or, more likely, on the third day, peaks on day four or five, and is pretty much gone by day seven. If jaundice occurs during the first twenty-four hours, contact your doctor right away, for the level is likely to move quickly into the dangerous range.

The mainstay of treatment of jaundice is light (phototherapy). Light activates a chemical in the baby's skin that breaks down bilirubin. The infant is placed naked with her eyes covered under one or two special fluorescent lights for as long as it takes to lower the bilirubin. Nursing can continue while "under the lights," but the rhythm of interaction may be disturbed because of the treatment. This interference, plus worry about the jaundice, can inhibit the mother's production of breast milk. The best approach is to stay calm, knowing that the disruption is only temporary. Pump the breasts if necessary to stimulate milk production. With the help of a doctor or midwife, phototherapy can be given in the home as well as in the hospital.

Borderline levels of jaundice can be treated by exposing the baby to natural sunlight near the window at home. In babies whose severe jaundice is not controllable by phototherapy, bilirubin is removed by withdrawing blood bit by bit and replacing it with donor blood having a normal level of bilirubin. This procedure is known as *exchange transfusion.*

A relatively common form of jaundice is related to breastfeeding, in particular to certain enzymes in the mother's milk. It comes on at the end of the first week and may persist for weeks — not, however, at levels high enough to threaten the baby. This type of jaundice can be reduced by replacing breast milk with formula for about two days. Pump the breasts to maintain milk production until nursing is resumed. Once nursing resumes, the jaundice may increase, but it will still remain less severe than before. One theory holds that the milk of mothers whose infants have "breast milk jaundice," as it is called, has, for reasons unknown, high concentrations of enzymes that digest the chemical compound of bilirubin, which is made in the liver and normally excreted in the bile to the intestine for elimination from the body. Instead, this digested bilirubin is reabsorbed from the intestine back into the baby's bloodstream.

Car Safety

Car safety is a critical issue for riders of all ages but especially for infants and children, since automobile accidents are a leading cause of death and disability in this age group. Even in the absence of a crash, infants and children are at risk from the swerving and stopping of a car. In many of these situations the child is thrown from the car. Until they are four years old and weigh forty pounds, children require *special safety devices.* (After this age the car's lap and shoulder belts can be used.)

In general, rearward facing devices are better for infants, and car seats that hook over seat backs are unsafe. Car seats must protect children from both front and rear crashes, cushioning them and keeping them from being thrown free. In addition, the seat must have a head restraint to protect against whiplash and have restraining belts at least 1.5 inches wide to restrain the upper parts of the child's body. Any seat constructed of easily bent, bare metal or flimsy strapping, or padded only with thin sponge rubber or sharp or pointed hardware, is unsafe and to be avoided.

In 1982 the U.S. government established guidelines for child and infant car restraints. Many states have passed laws requiring the use of restraints that meet the federal guidelines until children are large enough and old enough to use the belts that come with the car.

Whenever an infant is transported in a car, even on his first ride home from the hospital, a specially designed restraint should be used. It should be installed and used according to the manufacturer's instructions. The back seat is safer than the front, and the center of the car is safer than the sides. Everyone else in the car should use seatbelts, too (or inflatable airbags should be installed). In a crash, unrestrained passengers can literally crush others, as well as hurt themselves. A practice to be especially condemned is holding an infant in one's arms in a moving vehicle. In a crash, the baby will either be released or crushed by the person holding her. If you are driving or riding and need to remove the baby from the restraint, pull off the road and stop the car.

By insisting on seatbelt use in your car right from the start, you will find it much easier to enforce this policy later when your child is old enough to protest. He or she simply will never have known anything different.

A helpful pamphlet containing up-to-date information on approved crash-tested restraints and their proper use is available from Physicians for Automotive Safety, P. O. Box 798, Kent, Connecticut 06757. To receive a copy, send a stamped, self-addressed envelope and fifty cents in stamps or coin. (See also "Automobile Safety," p. 176.)

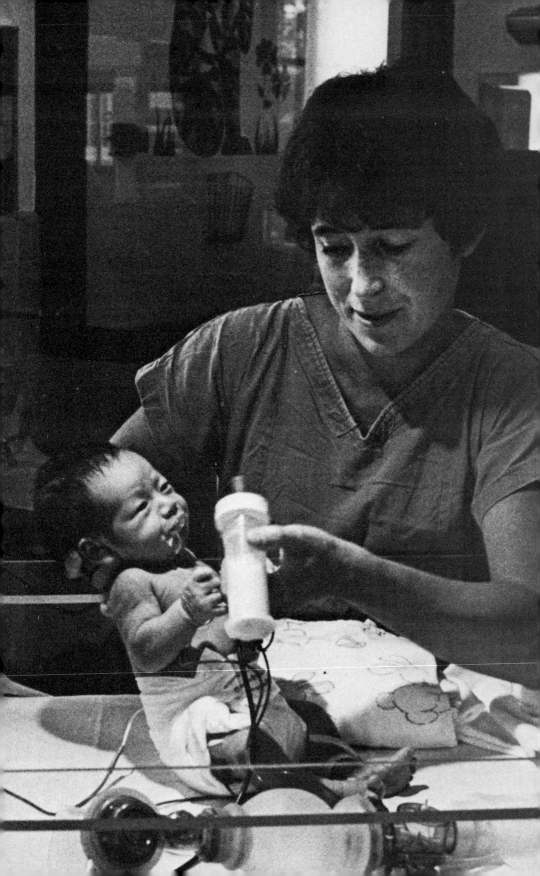

7

Complications of Pregnancy and Birth

Breech Presentation

Breech (buttocks first) birth has been feared for centuries because of increased risk to the baby during labor and delivery. Through modern obstetrical techniques, the risks have been greatly reduced. It is now reasonable to expect successful birth whether vaginally or by cesarean section.

About 3 percent of term pregnancies involve breech presentations. The more premature the baby, the greater the likelihood of a breech birth. In fact, it can be said that all babies are breech at least some of the time during the pregnancy. The explanation lies in the ratio of the size of the fetus to the volume of amniotic fluid. Early in pregnancy the fetus turns every which way. As the fetus grows, it occupies more of the intrauterine space, and there is less room for turning. After thirty-six or thirty-seven weeks it is unlikely that the fetus will flip over by itself. Without manipulation, a breech tends to stay a breech, and a vertex (head down) remains a vertex.

Prematurity is not the only factor associated with breech presentation. In mutiple pregnancies (p. 331) at least one twin is likely to be breech. Breeches are more common with various birth defects. For example, a baby with Down syndrome (p. 125) is twice as likely as a normal baby to be a breech. Breeches are also more common in hydramnios (p. 300) and in women who have carried many pregnancies. Sometimes more than one factor is operating; for example, when prematurity and a congenital defect are associated. In about 80 percent of breeches, however, there is no known cause.

There are three common types of breech presentations. In a *frank breech* (see Figure 21) the legs are flexed on the abdomen and the lower legs are straight or near straight at the knee. This position makes it very difficult for the baby to turn over on her own since the legs in effect splint the body. In this sense, frank breech can be said to maintain breech position and may explain why a majority of breeches at term are of the frank variety.

In a *complete breech* (see Figure 22) the thighs are flexed at the groin but the legs are bent at the knees. In an *incomplete breech* (see Figure 23) one or both hips are not flexed (that is, they are straight) and one or more of the feet or knees lies below the level

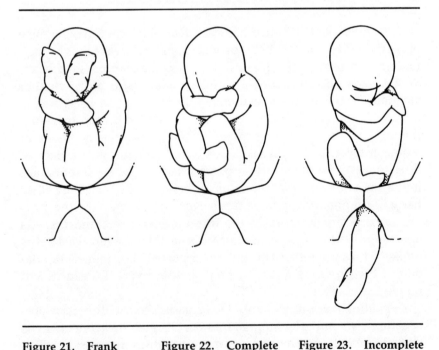

| Figure 21. Frank breech | Figure 22. Complete breech | Figure 23. Incomplete breech |

of the buttocks of the fetus. This type of breech is also called a "footling" breech because one of the feet is usually lying low.

The most common type of breech is the frank breech, accounting for 38 percent of all breeches weighing less than 2,500 grams (about 5 pounds) and 51 to 73 percent of those weighing over 2,500 grams. The corresponding figures for complete breeches are 12 percent and 11.5 percent respectively. For incompletes, the figures are 50 percent and 20 to 24 percent.

The frank breech is the only type in which the inlet to the pelvis is filled as well or nearly as well as in a normal head-first presentation during labor. When a foot or leg is adjacent to the buttocks, as in a complete or footling breech, the fit is not nearly as good. Because of this the umbilical cord is much more likely to prolapse (come out) around the buttocks and foot into the vagina (p. 325). The consequences of a prolapsed cord can be serious. At worst, the baby can die due to interruption of his blood supply which results from cord compression. At best, if the prolapse can be controlled temporarily by properly positioning the mother and pushing the baby back up into the uterus, an immediate cesarean section is usually done.

Compression of the umbilical cord by the baby's head as it passes through the birth canal during the end of labor is a risk in vaginal breech deliveries because it may lead to fetal asphyxia and even death. Mild compression may depress the baby at birth and result in the need for resuscitation. There is always the potential for some degree of brain injury, with possible long-term consequences for the baby.

In addition to the threat of cord compression during breech delivery, there is also an increased likelihood of physical damage if the head does not pass easily through the birth canal and force has to be applied.

There have been major shifts over the past fifty years in the approach to delivery of the breech baby. With improved techniques of surgery and anesthesia by the 1960s and 1970s, the overall results of cesarean section were found to be superior to vaginal delivery in terms of death and injury to breech babies, and cesarean section was widely practiced. Then, in the late 1970s, researchers found that frank breeches could, in most cases, be allowed a trial of labor and cesarean section done only if necessary, rather than routinely. The outcomes in the cesarean- and vaginally delivered infants were found to be essentially the same in the university hospital settings where the studies were performed. More recently some obstetricians have approached the non-frank breech with the point of view of sectioning only if necessary, with similar excellent results.

Aiding in the selection of breeches that can safely be allowed a trial of labor are X rays or CT scan (with much less radiation) to measure the dimensions of the pelvis, X rays (or CT scan) and ultrasound of the fetus to determine the relationship of the head to the body (babies whose heads are extended back are not considered safe candidates for vaginal delivery), a better understanding of the signs of fetal distress (whether through electronic or stethoscope monitoring of the fetal heart rate and pH testing — see p. 146 — of the baby believed to be in difficulty) and generally improved obstetrical techniques.

The best results achieved to date demonstrate that, in breeches for whom a trial of labor is considered appropriate, about 45 percent can safely deliver vaginally, while 55 percent will need cesarean section, a significant drop over the figures of a decade ago. (See also discussion of breech as a factor in the cesarean section rate, p. 284.)

Another interesting recent development is a growing recognition that the squatting position may offer significant advantages in the vaginal delivery of a breech baby. It is known, for example, that the area of the pelvic outlet increases as much as 28 percent when a woman squats. Efforts are under way to test this hypothesis.

Finally, it must be said that the medical malpractice crisis in the mid 1980's is strongly influencing obstetricians, even those increasingly few skilled in vaginal breech deliveries, to section breeches without exception. Problems in a breech baby delivered vaginally are hard to defend against the claim that a cesarean section could have avoided the problem. Faced with this legal reality, the majority of physicians have simply abandoned breech vaginal delivery.

Vaginal delivery of a breech presentation is carried out in most hospitals with the services of four physicians:

- the *obstetrician*
- an *assistant obstetrician*, who is especially needed if forceps are used to guide the birth of the head

- an *anesthesiologist* to supervise any anesthesia used in the delivery, and to be available to apply general anesthesia to increase relaxation of the uterus during the birth of the head, should the need arise
- a *pediatrician*, who can collaborate with the anesthesiologist in attending to the needs of the baby, especially if he is asphyxiated.

The birth of the head of a breech is the critical time. In the usual birth, the head, which is the largest part of the baby, leads the way and is born before the rest of the baby. Once the head has cleared, it is unusual for any other part of the baby to get stuck (see p. 325, "Shoulder Dystocia"). But, in a breech, the head is the last part to be born. Thus, passage of all but the head is no guarantee that all will be well. Not only can the head get stuck, but, at the same time, the cord will be compressed between the head and wall of the birth canal, an invariable characteristic of a breech vaginal delivery. So time is of the essence.

Forceps are often used in delivering the head to protect it and avoid undue traction on the neck. Four obstetrical hands are needed, two to apply the forceps and two to support the rest of the baby's body. With one hand, the obstetrician supports the baby's trunk and arms with a towel and pulls upward. The legs are supported and pulled upward with the other hand. The first obstetrician inserts the forceps into the vagina over the sides of the baby's head. The forceps bend downward at the perineum, and the handles lock below the baby. As the forceps exert traction on the head, the assistant pulls upward on the body until the head clears the perineum. As we said above, it appears likely that giving birth in the upright or squatting postion may help avoid the use of forceps and episiotomy as well.

In a cesarean section for a breech presentation, the ideal incision, in terms of avoiding cesarean sections in future pregnancies, is a *lower segment transverse incision* (see p. 278 on cesarean sections). This lower segment, particularly when the fetus is premature, may be underdeveloped, forcing the obstetrician to make a vertical incision, thereby destining the woman to repeat cesarean sections during subsequent pregnancies.

Because of the many serious issues surrounding the care of breeches, identifying these babies prior to labor is important, so that adequate plans can be made. At the physical examination of the uterus during the routine prenatal visit (p. 40), clues to a breech include feeling the head high in the abdomen and hearing the fetal heart tones *above* rather than below the mother's umbilicus. Ultrasound examination can then confirm the situation. (Ultrasound examination done for some other reason may also uncover an unsuspected breech.)

A safe way to convert a breech to vertex presentation before the onset of labor by turning the baby has been sought for some time. Two methods have been tried: positioning of the mother and manual rotation. In the *positioning method*, a woman lies on her back on a hard surface with her buttocks elevated on a pillow for ten to twenty minutes three to four times a day after the thirtieth week of pregnancy. She does this for up to four weeks or until turning has occurred, whichever is earlier. While the success rate of this maneuver has not been carefully studied, it appears to be effective in some cases.

In the *rotation method*, an attendant rotates the baby manually. One of the attendant's hands is placed on the mother's abdomen over the baby's head, the other over its buttocks. The hands are moved in opposite directions as the baby is gently stroked around. The maneuver takes a few minutes to perform. *External cephalic version*, as this maneuver is called, should be done by an experienced attendant. Some doctors first use ultrasound to locate the placenta and avoid the maneuver in cases where the placenta is near to or covering the opening to the cervix (see p. 312 on placental praevia). Some doctors recommend trying this method only in the hospital, using intravenous drugs to relax the uterus and thereby facilitate the maneuver. To avoid injuring the baby, the breech must not have settled into the pelvis.

The fetal heart rate is determined at the beginning and end of the procedure, and some doctors check it midway through as well. Marked increase, decrease, or irregularity of the rate are signs of fetal stress and are an indication for the immediate return of the baby to his or her original position. The fetus is turned through the shorter of the two possible arcs so that the head takes the shortest route to the pelvis. Following a successful turning, a woman is asked to stay in an upright position for the rest of the day. If necessary, the procedure may be repeated once. Usually, if the baby does not stay in the vertex position after two attempts following the thirty-seventh week, no further efforts are made to turn it. The expected success rate is about 70 percent at the thirty-seventh week and does not increase subsequently. Since there is a higher rate of reversion before the thirty-seventh week, thirty-seven weeks is considered the optimal time to do the procedure.

Reported complications of turning a breech manually include the death of the baby (presumably due to twisting and entanglement of the umbilical cord), placental abruption (p. 312), and rupture of the uterus. There are no good statistics on these complications, and they are considered rare. Nevertheless, many obstetricians do not subscribe to the notion of turning a breech and will refuse to perform the procedure. Not all obstetricians are experienced with the procedure, and it is done now less than in the past. If your obstetrician is not comfortable with it and you remain interested, ask for a consultation with a physician who has experience turning breech babies.

Carpal Tunnel Syndrome

Hand pain is quite common in pregnancy. Mainly occurring in the half of the hand that includes the thumb, and especially the middle finger, it is associated with "pins and needles" and numbness. It is caused by pressure on the nerve (the median nerve) that goes to these parts of the hand area as it passes through the wrist (carpal tunnel). This pressure seems to be related to the accumulation of fluid characteristic of pregnancy.

The symptoms vary widely in intensity, most commonly ranging from merely "annoying" and "interfering with sleep," to "intolerable" in a small minority of women. While the pain is focused in the hand, aching can be felt as high up the arm as the shoulder. In more severe cases, some degree of weakness may occur as well. Either one or both hands may be affected.

In most cases, complete improvement occurs after delivery. Symptoms may be relieved through the use of pain killers and by splinting the hand for part of the day or at night. If all else fails, the disorder can be corrected by a fairly simple operation done under local anesthesia.

Cesarean Section

Cesarean section ("C-section," for short) is the surgical procedure used to deliver a baby through an abdominal and uterine incision in cases when vaginal delivery is judged impossible or dangerous. While documented attempts at cesarean section date back to the seventeenth century, consistent success did not occur until well into the twentieth century. By the World War II era, cesarean section proved to offer dramatic benefits in dealing with such life-threatening problems as placenta praevia, placental abruption, eclampsia, and severe disproportion (all discussed in this section). During the 1960s and 1970s doctors increasingly recognized that cesarean section could benefit maternal and infant health even when life itself was not immediately at stake. For example, babies who had previously been delivered by forceps while still high in the birth canal (so-called mid-forceps delivery) were found to do much better in terms of neurological problems (fewer cases of cerebral palsy, learning problems, etc.) if they were instead delivered by cesarean section. Certain kinds of breeches were also found to do better after cesarean rather than vaginal birth.

Many factors have led to an increasing proportion of cesarean births. Improved ways of monitoring the well-being of the fetus have led to the interruption of pregnancy by cesarean section before and during labor when the fetus is found to be in jeopardy. When a woman has had a cesarean section, she is more likely to have one the next time she gives birth. The major rationale for this, the risk that the scar from the first operation will tear during a subsequent labor, is examined critically below. Another very important factor contributing to the rising cesarean section rate is physicians' fear of malpractice suits, especially in "grey areas" where information on the relative safety for the baby of vaginal versus cesarean delivery is inconclusive, as it often is. Under such circumstances, doctors tend to do a cesarean section rather than allowing what they perceive as a riskier, less controllable vaginal birth. Lawsuits are rarely initiated for *doing* an operation, other than for negligent technique. Doctors are more often sued for *failure* to operate.

While it is hard to deny the enormous contribution made by cesarean section, concern is now being expressed by doctors, midwives, and childbirth educators that too many of these operations are being performed, with the figures now reaching one-quarter to one-third of all births. A critical reappraisal of the reasons for cesarean delivery now under way has already led to some modest reductions, or at least leveling off, in the percentage of deliveries handled with surgery.

The childbirth education movement has responded to the increased frequency of cesarean section with help for the women involved and a constructive critique of the problem. Educators have urged that the term "cesarean birth" rather than "cesarean section" be used to emphasize that a birth, not merely an operation, is occurring. Fathers are being welcomed to the operating room, and early parent-infant interaction is encouraged despite the surrounding distractions. Discussion of cesarean birth is now included in prenatal classes, and organizations have been formed to meet the needs of women who have undergone or will undergo cesarean sections and of those who contemplate vaginal birth after a cesarean (VBAC). (See Appendices B and D for these resources.)

A TYPICAL CESAREAN BIRTH

In most hospitals, cesarean section is performed under spinal or epidural anesthesia (see p. 205). As a rule, general anesthesia is reserved for true emergencies, when time does not permit spinals or epidurals, or when these techniques have proved unsuccessful. Prior to surgery the lower abdomen is shaved from just below the navel to the pubic bone. A catheter is inserted in the bladder and left in place until after the operation. The skin is vigorously scrubbed with surgical soap and sterile drapes are placed over the abdomen to leave only the lower belly uncovered. The obstetrician and surgical nurse wear sterile garb — gowns, caps, masks, gloves. All others present, including the husband or partner and birth attendant, wear surgical scrub suits, masks, and caps in the operating room. Anesthesiologists and obstetricians usually reserve the right to ask nonprofessional participants to leave the room during an emergency. Policies on participation by husband or partners may vary from one hospital to another. Women are advised to clarify this issue ahead of time.

A vertical screen is usually placed above the woman's upper chest so that she cannot see the surgeons. However, she is able to hear them and can carry on a conversation with those around her. Ideally she should feel no pain, but, if she does, she should report it so that measures to stop it can be taken. She may feel some tugging and pressure, especially during the delivery of the baby. Once the amniotic sac is opened, she will hear the noise of the suction machine drawing the amniotic fluid from the uterus into a collecting bottle. Following the removal of the amniotic fluid, the obstetrician reaches into the uterus to take hold of the head, which is then worked through the incision. The assistant presses the top of the uterus to help push the head out. In a breech delivery, of course, the legs are delivered first.

After the head is born, the obstetrician clears the amniotic fluid from the baby's nose and mouth with a bulb syringe. If meconium (the baby's stools) has been passed into the amniotic fluid, this suctioning is more intense and is done with a plastic catheter. As the baby is delivered the obstetrician will usually ask the anesthesiologist to inject a dose of Pitocin into the mother's intravenous infusion to cause the uterus to contract. It is also common practice, following delivery of the baby, to give the mother a single dose of intravenous antibiotics to prevent uterine infection. Antibiotics are given the mother after the umbilical cord is clamped to prevent their passage into the baby. The cord is cut and the baby handed to the nurse or pediatrician who carries it to a nearby warming table. The baby is further suctioned and examined; when it is clearly doing well on its own, it is wrapped, capped, and handed to the father.

Meanwhile, the surgeons remove the placenta and sew up the incisions in the uterus and the abdominal wall. From beginning to end the surgery usually takes between thirty and forty-five minutes. After the operation the mother is wheeled to the recovery room. The baby should be able to remain with its parents, even though there may be a brief period during which it is taken to the nursery for weighing, measuring, and eye treatment.

During the postoperative period medications are administered to the mother to deal with the pain of the incision. Blood pressure, pulse, urine flow, amount of bleeding, and the tone of the uterus are checked every hour for four hours. Afterward, checks are carried out every four hours for the first day.

By the day after surgery, many women can drink fluids and the intravenous infusion can be slowed and pulled out after forty-eight hours. The urinary catheter is usually removed after twelve hours. On the second and third days, "gas pains" from ineffective bowel action are common, and a rectal suppository or enema is often helpful. Women can usually begin walking with assistance on the day after surgery. Early walking promotes quick recovery and prevents the formation of blood clots (thrombi) in the veins of the legs (thrombophlebitis). These clots can break off and travel through the bloodstream and heart into the lungs. By the third postdelivery day, the mother can usually bathe safely; on the fourth day her skin sutures or clips can be removed. As soon as she feels well enough, she can begin breast-feeding the baby. On the fifth postdelivery day, the mother and baby can usually go home.

RISKS OF CESAREAN SECTION

Since it is a major operation, cesarean section is not without risks. Although the overall maternal mortality rate in the United States is extremely low (9.9 deaths per 100,000 births in 1978), cesarean birth carries a two- to four-times greater risk of maternal death than vaginal delivery. Cesarean section also carries an increased risk for such complications as thrombophlebitis, uterine infection, urinary tract infection, and the complications of anesthesia. It carries all the economic costs of major surgery and, in comparison with vaginal delivery, causes a delay of at least one week before a woman can return to her normal activities.

Cesarean birth may actually be safer than these figures suggest. The excess mortality may be related more to preexisting conditions in the mother than to the operation itself. The deaths appear in statistics in the group of cesarean-related deaths, wrongly causing it to appear that the operation itself was the cause.

There is growing evidence that cesarean section can be done with very few maternal deaths, even in sick women. A recent report of 10,000 consecutive cesarean sections at the Boston Hospital for Women, which included some extremely sick women with disorders like eclampsia, diabetes, and heart disease, showed not a single death of a mother.

Improvements in the operation continue to be made. Increasingly, it is recognized that the traditional position of women who undergo cesarean sections (flat on the back) is related to some complications for the baby. The harmful effects of this position are now clear: the heavy uterus presses on the large artery and vein which run along the woman's spine, interfering with both the return of blood to the heart and the outflow of blood from the heart to the body in general, and to the uterus, placenta, and fetus. Various degrees of fetal distress can result. To avoid these problems, many surgeons tilt the woman to one side during the operation in order to roll the uterus off the major blood vessels. Other measures to reduce complications were described above: use of intravenous antibiotics at the end of the surgery; early walking to prevent phlebitis; and the use of spinal or epidural anesthesia instead of general anesthesia whenever possible.

Risks to the baby have also been reduced. The baby is more likely to have temporary breathing problems (known as *transient tachypnea* of the newborn). These problems are thought to be due to the absence of the squeezing out of fluid from the chest, which occurs normally in a vaginal delivery. Also, there is a risk of prematurity, with its associated problem of respiratory distress, because gestational age is sometimes not judged correctly. However, accurate tests to determine fetal maturity have minimized this problem.

WHEN ARE CESAREANS NECESSARY?

In statistical terms, the cesarean birthrate in the United States during the 1970s increased about threefold, from 5.5 percent of all births in 1970 to 15.2 percent in 1978. The rate is up to 23 to 25 percent in 1984. Similar trends obtain in most other industrialized societies. According to a 1980 National Institutes of Health (NIH) report that looked at ways to reduce the rate of cesarean sections, the diagnostic categories that had the largest effect on the increase in the rate between 1970 and 1978 were *repeat cesarean, breech presentation, dystocia,* and *fetal distress.*

Repeat cesarean section has been identified as the category most amenable to correction. In the past, doctors applied the dictum, "once a section, always a section," because they feared that the scarred uterus would rupture during a subsequent labor. This risk does exist with the "classical" vertical (up-and-down) uterine incision, which involves the body or middle portion of the uterus rather than its lower segment. The chances of tearing the scar are far less, however, with the transverse (side-to-side) lower uterine incision now in wide use. This incision cuts through part of the uterus that is less muscular and less full of blood vessels. Thus, if a tear should occur, bleeding, which can threaten the lives of both the mother and the fetus, is less likely. Although obstetricians now make every effort to use only this transverse lower uterine incision, it is unfortunately not always possible to do so.

A woman should be considered a good candidate for a vaginal birth after cesarean, or VBAC, if she had a lower segment transverse incision during her earlier cesarean and there are no predictable problems in moving the baby through the birth canal. In the trial, labor is allowed to progress as if it were normal. In one typical study of 634 women who had had only one previous cesarean section, 526 (or 83 percent) had a trial of labor; 313 (60 percent) delivered vaginally; the rest required a repeat cesarean section. Two uteri did rupture; one was repaired and the other had to be removed. In all, the risk of rupture was well under 1 percent. If labor is carefully watched, most uterine ruptures can be detected early enough to terminate the labor with another cesarean and a good outcome for both mother and baby.

Not only is vaginal delivery safe and largely achievable after one prior section, but even after two (and possibly more) as well. It also turns out that enhancement of labor with pitocin (see p. 198) and the use of epidural anesthesia can also be done safely. Despite the strong evidence supporting VBAC's and their official endorsement by the obstetrical society, many obstetricians have not yet changed their thinking on this topic. Fear of malpractice suits is a likely factor.

If a previous vertical incision was made into the body of the uterus, or into the lower uterine segment, the currently recommended course is to forego subsequent vaginal birth (the risk of rupture is 1 to 3 percent). In the case of a vertical lower uterine segment scar, there is a good likelihood that the incision actually extended into the upper uterine segment, with increased risk for tearing during subsequent labors. If, in making the lower transverse segment incision, tearing or deliberate cutting resulted in a "T" or "J" shaped incision (as opposed to a curved line incision), repeat cesarean section is also recommended. These recommendations regarding scars are presently being reevaluated.

This discussion of the intricacies of incisions and scars emphasizes the importance of obtaining records on the previous cesarean section. The doctor who deals with a subsequent pregnancy needs these to plan the course of labor and delivery.

In the case of a *breech birth*, the NIH panel recommended that vaginal delivery is an acceptable choice for full-term breech babies under the following circumstances:

- the expected weight of baby is less than eight pounds
- the woman has a normal pelvis
- the baby is in a frank breech; that is, with legs extended and head flexed
- the doctor and his or her assistants are experienced in vaginal breech delivery.

Because of the risks of a vaginal breech delivery, the woman and her family need to be fully informed and involved in the choices to be made. (For further discussion of breech presentation, see p. 271.)

Dystocia, or *failure to progress in labor,* is another reason for cesarean section. It was identified by the NIH panel as an explanation for much of the increased rate of cesarean section in the country. A reduction of the number of cesarean births done for this reason seems possible. For example, about 5 percent of all births in the United States are accomplished by cesarean section for dystocia; while, in a study done in Dublin, Ireland, only 0.7 percent of all births occurred by cesarean section for this reason. The difference may be due to various approaches to the care of the woman with ineffective uterine contractions. While oxytocin and other nonsurgical measures to stimulate labor are favored in Ireland, cesarean section is more quickly resorted to in the United States.

In considering *fetal distress* as reason for cesarean section, the NIH panel recommended further studies to improve the accuracy of the diagnosis of fetal distress, the development of new techniques for making the diagnosis, and improved nonsurgical ways of dealing with this problem.

The NIH report was issued four years before this book was written, and thus far the evidence is that the cesarean birth rate has continued to rise, although not as steeply as before. There are a number of troubling questions about this trend. Why, with what appear to be similar populations of patients, are there such differences in rates from one hospital to another with no apparent differences in the health and survival of babies? Granted that cesarean sections have played an important role in lowering infant mortality and illness, why is the section rate in a major teaching hospital in Dublin, Ireland, less than 5 percent while it approaches 30 percent in many of our university hospitals, with no apparent differences in the health of the babies? Why is there as much as a threefold difference between the lowest and the highest section rates in university hospitals in this country? Is the approach of the physicians or characteristics of the patients (such as inadequate prenatal care or level of education) accounting for some of these differences? What, then, should be our goals? Questions like these deserve answers.

We advise women to ask about the section rates of their physicians and hospitals (the rates for hospitals are now on public record in certain states). We would be concerned at this time if it were over 20 percent, if not 15 percent, unless the patients in the physician's practice or at that hospital were particularly high-risk.

Having presented this discussion of cesarean section, we thought it would be useful to look at what you yourself can do to minimize the need for an operation and to maximize your chances of having a vaginal delivery. One of the best summaries on this topic we have seen is contained in Table 5, distributed by the organization, C/SEC (see Appendix B). The cross references in the table are our additions. They refer to discussions in this book.

C/SEC provides mail and telephone counseling on questions concerning cesarean childbirth, cesarean prevention, and VBAC (vaginal birth after cesarean). C/SEC publications can be obtained individually or in quantity for parents, support groups, childbirth educators, and health care professionals.

The topic of cesarean section is a touchstone for many issues in contemporary obstetrical care. Once you understand this subject, you also understand a great deal about prenatal care and labor and the choices involved.

Table 5.   Avoiding Cesarean Section

Why Cesarean Section Is Performed	Avoidable Factors	Alternatives
I. Dystocia Failure to progress Prolonged labor Arrest of labor Uterine inertia Failed induction Failed forceps	1. *Lack of patience with normal labor process; misinterpretation of Friedman labor curve* (see p. 190). It's a mean, not a norm; there is a normal human variation in length and pattern of labor. 2. *Recumbent position; lack of mobility in 1st stage.* When woman is upright and ambulatory, 1st stage is shorter; contractions stronger and more efficient; gravity helps; baby enters pelvis at a better angle; mother is more comfortable and feels less pain. Supine position leads to maternal hypotension and reduced uterine blood flow (see p. 211). 3. *Exaggerated pushing with prolonged breath-holding in semi-reclining or reclining position.* Squatting increases pelvic diameters, can increase available area 20–30%; gravity helps; baby descends at better angle. Hard lengthy pushes result in ineffective pushing out of sync with uter-	1. Trust a woman's body unless clear clinical signs of fetal or maternal distress; stay at home until 5 cms., go home if arrive at hospital and less than 3–4 cms. 2. Stay out of bed and WALK! Avoid semi-reclining position; no I.V. unless specifically indicated, then on mobile stand; monitor by auscultation unless electronic fetal monitoring specifically indicated, then alternate EFM (electronic fetal monitoring) with periods of walking. 3. Avoid semi-reclining or reclining position for 2nd stage; squat, kneel, stand, or sit on toilet, especially if 2nd stage long or uncomfortable; use these or side-lying position to rotate posterior or transverse head. Push only with body's own rhythm; mother avoid holding legs

286

us's own bearing down efforts, as well as maternal exhaustion. Pushing with closed glottis, holding legs up, pushing with heels result in tense, tight legs, buttocks, pelvic floor, and vagina, delaying baby's descent and causing more stress on baby's head and mother's soft tissues.

4. *Too hasty use of Pitocin after premature rupture of membranes or post-dates* (see p. 314); *elective induction; artificial rupture of membranes early in labor.* If cervix unready for labor, induction will be ineffective or labor prolonged. Pitocin can result in contractions too strong, long, and close together, increasing likelihood of use of analgesics or anesthesia, and of fetal distress — see II below. Pitocin associated with excessive 3rd stage bleeding and neonatal jaundice. With precautions, risk of infection after ruptured membranes very small in healthy, well-nourished women. Induction solely on basis of dates runs risk of premature baby if dates wrong; there is normal human variation in length of gestation. Artificial rupture of membranes removes protection for baby's head; can lead to

up, pushing with heels, or closing glottis; mother's emphasis on opening up and tuning into body's signals, not technique.

4. No Pitocin after ruptured membranes unless signs of infection; wait at home for labor (risk of infection and anxiety both lower there); eat at will and drink lots (see p. 196). No induction post-date unless signs of placental deterioration. NO elective induction (banned by FDA). No artificial rupture of membranes except in late labor in a few selected cases (see p. 314).

Table 5. Avoiding Cesarean Section, *continued*

Why Cesarean Section Is Performed	Avoidable Factors	Alternatives
	excessive molding; increases likelihood of infection with internal exams; leads to concern over length of labor because of fear of infection.	
	5. *Fasting in labor.* Labor is hard physical work and requires lots of calories to burn. Digestion slows down in active labor, but continues slowly. A 5% glucose solution insufficient to supply energy needs. Times when inhalation anesthesia required are rare; fasting does not eliminate risk of acid aspiration; effects of prolonged fasting on maternal and fetal metabolism and uterine functioning not clearly known.	5. Eat at will in labor; drink lots (see p. 196).
	6. *Narcotics in 1st stage.* Central nervous system depressants can slow uterine functioning, especially if given in latent phase or if labor progressing slowly already (see p. 203). *Epidurals in 1st or 2nd stage.* Slow 1st stage by withdrawing blood from uterus and retarding uterine functioning; slow	6. No narcotics or epidurals. Walking or other positions, relaxation, massage, shower or bath, breathing patterns, loving support and encouragement instead (see p. 201).

2nd stage by eliminating urge to push, weakening abdominal muscles; higher incidence of failure of baby's head to rotate.

7. *Maternal anxiety and fear.* Cause release of catecholamines, which withdraw blood from internal organs and relax smooth muscle, thus slowing labor down. Release of oxytocin also inhibited by fear, anxiety, and tension.

7. Increase mother's self-confidence by emphasizing birth as NORMAL PHYSIOLOGICAL FUNCTION, not only in childbirth classes and during pregnancy, but from childhood; give extra support in labor; stay home in early labor; improve community options for safe out-of-hospital births and alternative in-hospital births.

II. Fetal distress

1. *Misinterpretation of electronic fetal monitoring (EFM) tracings.* Tracings are difficult to interpret, as some variations are normal; EFM produces many false positives (see p. 136). *Reliance on EFM for diagnosis.* According to NIH, EFM is a screening, not a diagnostic, tool.

1. Monitor by auscultation unless EFM specifically indicated. According to NIH [National Institute of Health], no benefit to EFM over auscultation demonstrated, except in high-risk cases. Confirm diagnosis with fetal scalp sampling before intervening (see p. 146).

2. *Reclining position.* Supine position can cause maternal hypotension; reduce blood flow to uterus; labor less efficient and prolonged. See 2 in I above. (See p. 211.)

2. Stay upright, out of bed, or on side. Also consider oxygen and tocolytics to decrease uterine contractions (see p. 150).

Table 5. Avoiding Cesarean Section, *continued*

Why Cesarean Section Is Performed	Avoidable Factors	Alternatives
	3. *Narcotics.* Central nervous system depressants, can depress maternal respiration; cross placenta quickly and depress fetus, especially if already stressed.) *Epidurals.* Can lead to maternal hypotension, withdraw blood from uterus, as well as prolong labor. See 6 in I above.	3. No narcotics or epidurals. See 6 in I above.
	4. *Pitocin.* Can cause contractions too long, strong, and close together for baby to recover oxygen supply in between, especially if already stressed. Increases maternal discomfort and anxiety, raises likelihood of use of narcotics or epidurals.	4. Use Pitocin rarely and sparingly; turn down or off once labor established. Stimulate labor by giving mother a rest; getting her up to walk; helping her relax; or stimulating nipples, instead of Pitocin (see p. 199).
	5. *Exaggerated pushing with prolonged breath-holding (Valsalva maneuver).* Can reduce oxygen to baby by retarding blood return through extreme intra-thoracic pressure; and by using up oxygen with mother's own efforts; supine position leads to maternal hypotension and reduced uterine blood flow.	5. Push physiologically with body's own rhythms, in upright or side-lying positions; hold breath no longer than 6–7 seconds.

		6. Help mother relax upper body; avoid rapid breathing.
		7. See 7 in I above.
	6. Hyperventilation. By several mechanisms, reduces oxygen available to baby.	
	7. Maternal anxiety. Reduces blood flow to uterus and oxygen available to baby. See 7 in I above.	
III. Breech presentation	*Automatic, blanket rules about how to deliver breech babies (see p. 271).*	Prenatal exercise to turn baby; external version; X ray at labor onset and trial of labor; skilled, confident midwife or obstetrician.
IV. Toxemia Hypertension Placental abruption Placental insufficiency Premature birth Low birth weight	*Inadequate nutrition, during intrauterine life, childhood, adolescence, and pregnancy.* *Use of drugs in pregnancy: prescription; over-the-counter; recreational, including alcohol and especially smoking (see p. 171 and p. 170).* *Restriction of blood volume and placental size by restricting salt intake or using diuretics.*	Education about nutrition and use of drugs in pregnancy — before pregnancy begins; in early pregnancy; and in childbirth classes. Avoid all drugs if possible (see p. 153). Avoid use of diuretics; salt to taste; increase protein intake; maintain fluid and salt intake, if fluid retention and high blood pressure become problems. Feed low-income pregnant women and growing girls. (Most low birth weight, premature births, perinatal and infant mortality in U.S. occur to poor and minority women.)

Table 5. Avoiding Cesarean Section, *continued*

Why Cesarean Section Is Performed	Avoidable Factors	Alternatives
V. Previous cesarean	*Automatic, once-a-C/S-always-a-C/S policies.* NIH and ACOG (American College of Obstetricians and Gynecologists) have both stated that vaginal birth is a safe option in most cases after a prior cesarean. 2–4 times greater risk of maternal mortality; increased risk of maternal morbidity and neonatal respiratory disease with elective repeat cesarean. Increased maternal-infant separation, stress on attachment process, decreased maternal self-esteem all may follow C/S. Risk of dehiscence (separation) of lower segment (horizontal) scar about 0.5%, with risk of serious rupture much less. Risk of maternal or fetal death little or no higher than without previous C/S.	Labor and vaginal birth unless: (1) classical uterine scar (skin incision doesn't matter)*; (2) new indication for C/S in this pregnancy. * Parents may choose to take 1–3% risk of serious rupture with classical scar. If so, may want to go to hospital as soon as labor begins; have I.V. in place, blood ready; Operating Room and anesthesia alerted; constant labor nursing supervision. With horizontal lower segment scar, same labor supervision and management as for any other labor.

Source: Reprinted from "Preventing Unnecessary Cesareans, A Guide to Labor Management and Detailed Bibliography," by Elizabeth Shearer, with permission of the author and C/SEC inc., 1982.

Disproportion

Cephalopelvic disproportion (CPD) refers to the inability of a particular fetus to fit through a particular pelvis. When the cervix fails to dilate as expected, and/or the baby does not descend in the birth canal after an adequate trial of labor, sometimes augmented with Pitocin stimulation, this condition is suspected.

As might be expected, labors complicated by CPD are long, hard, and frustrating. The lack of progress is discouraging to the woman, her partner, and all those attending the birth. One particular physical finding associated with CPD is caput or swelling of the baby's scalp. (See p. 238.)

Once CPD is diagnosed, the attempt at vaginal delivery is discontinued and a cesarean section (see p. 278) is carried out.

Ectopic Pregnancy

An ectopic pregnancy is one in which the fertilized egg implants somewhere outside the uterus. The word comes from the Greek, *ex*, "out of," and *topos*, "place." While most ectopic pregnancies by far are located in the Fallopian tubes, they can occur at other sites as well, including the ovary, the outside of the uterus, or within the abdominal cavity. Ectopic pregnancy is by no means rare. Various studies have shown a frequency ranging from one in sixty-four to one in 230 pregnancies. Apparently the rate is increasing. All sexually active women of childbearing age should know the commonly occurring symptoms of this disorder and, if necessary, be ready to act quickly to get help.

The greatest danger of an ectopic pregnancy to a woman is that the growing embryo can erode blood vessels in her Fallopian tube and cause internal hemorrhaging. A woman can go into shock and even die from such blood loss, a complication that is fortunately uncommon in this modern era. The symptoms and signs of such serious blood loss, which should be kept in mind, include *light-headedness, dizziness, pallor, and sweating along with rapid pulse and falling blood pressure* (seen initially when sitting or standing, later on when lying down).

A more common symptom of ectopic pregnancy is *lower abdominal pain*. Pain occurs as the embryo distends and erodes through the Fallopian tube, especially at the point when it actually breaks through the walls of the tube. Furthermore, the free blood in the abdominal cavity can irritate the diaphragm, producing *pain* in the shoulders when the woman breathes.

Because the growth and development of the ectopic embryo and placenta is eventually halted, hormonal support of the pregnancy is also halted and growth of the endometrium (inner lining of the uterus) affected. This endometrium is shed and is recognized as *vaginal bleeding*, another common sign of an ectopic pregnancy. The pattern of this bleeding is usually different from that of a normal period: it is later, lighter, and resembles spotting. However, it is easy to mistake this bleeding for a normal period. As will be discussed, bleeding due to an ectopic pregnancy can also resemble that seen in a miscarriage (p. 305), a condition with which an ectopic pregnancy can easily be confused.

There is usually little difficulty in diagnosis when a major rupture occurs in a woman who knows she is pregnant. Besides vaginal spotting, symptoms include: sudden sharp, stabbing, one-sided lower abdominal pain; shock; tenderness in the abdomen, and exquisite tenderness when the cervix is moved; a tender mass on one side of the uterus; and a soft swelling caused by pooled blood felt behind the cervix on rectal examination. A woman with these classical symptoms should be wheeled straight to the operating room without further delay.

However, most ectopic pregnancies are more subtle during the early phase of rupture. Over a period of days to weeks symptoms of mild lower abdominal pain, vaginal spotting, and tenderness on pelvic examination develop in a woman who may or may not know that she is pregnant. Any combination of these findings may be present in any degree of intensity. Women and their medical attendants must keep the possibility of an ectopic pregnancy foremost in their minds if a diagnosis is to be made early. It is often difficult to distinguish ectopic pregnancy from appendicitis, and other conditions.

Determining whether a woman is indeed pregnant is the first step in establishing whether her symptoms could be related to an ectopic pregnancy. Several tests can help, including an improved pregnancy test which measures human chorionic gonadotropin

(HCG) as early as five to nine days after conception in both intrauterine and ectopic pregnancy. (See p. 39, Pregnancy Tests.)

Since the level of HCG normally doubles every three days, if this increase fails to occur (taking the shape of a flat curve), or if there is an actual decline in the level (a falling curve), a pregnancy in trouble is indicated. And one possible reason for trouble is ectopic pregnancy. Thus, serial measurements are often made to determine the normalcy of a pregnancy when signs and symptoms such as spotting and pain raise doubt.

By five to six gestational weeks, ultrasound examination can detect a fetal sac in the uterus. In a pregnant woman its presence argues against an ectopic pregnancy, while its absence argues for it. But ultrasound cannot detect an intrauterine pregnancy younger than five to six weeks, so it is not useful as a diagnostic tool in ectopic pregnancies suspected before this stage. (In very rare cases — one in 5,000 — intrauterine and tubal pregnancies can coexist. Thus, while the presence of a fetal sac in the uterus argues against an ectopic pregnancy, it does not completely exclude it.) Ultrasound is also useful in detecting fluid behind the uterus, which is blood from a leaking ectopic pregnancy.

Direct visualization of a Fallopian tube with a laparoscope (passed into the abdomen through the umbilicus) can identify a Fallopian tube that is swollen and/or ruptured by an ectopic pregnancy. (The laparoscope is a kind of flexible telescope, pencil-thin in diameter, through which light beams are transmitted through bendable fiberoptic channels.)

Another diagnostic measure is the identification of blood in the pelvic cavity, through aspiration with a needle passed through the vaginal wall just behind the cervix. The finding of such blood is strong evidence for an ectopic pregnancy in a woman who is pregnant.

Even with these advanced diagnostic approaches, and our heightened awareness of the problem of ectopic pregnancy, this disorder can literally come as a bolt out of the blue. Ectopic pregnancies that occur in the part of the Fallopian tube contained within the wall of the uterus, so-called *interstitial pregnancies*, are particularly treacherous. About 2.5 percent of ectopic pregnancies in some series studied are of this variety. Because of the site of implantation in interstitial pregnancies, no mass is present in the tube, and the uterus enlarges much as it would in a normal intrauterine pregnancy. Because of the strength of the wall of the uterus in contrast with that of the tube, rupture of the pregnancy is likely to occur somewhat later, between the end of the second and the end of the fourth month. When rupture does occur, the bleeding is likely to be brisk and requires urgent attention.

In this country, the treatment for ectopic pregnancy is surgical, done as early as possible. During the operation every effort is made to preserve the tube, although its ability to transport a fertilized ovum successfully will be reduced, and its likelihood of again harboring an ectopic pregnancy is increased. However, in advanced tubal pregnancy it is often impossible for the surgeon to remove the products of conception without also removing the tube itself.

The site in the Fallopian tube where the pregnancy occurs determines the surgical procedure performed. Ectopic pregnancies near the open end of the tube grow under its surface and not in the central lumen or core and can often be removed without cutting through the tube, while those nearer to the uterus, which usually grow within the lumen of the tube, must be cut out; afterward, the surgically severed ends of the tube are reconnected. In an interstitial ectopic pregnancy, the uterus itself may have to be removed (hysterectomy) along with the tube and the products of conception. Depending on the location and size of the ectopic pregnancy and the associated blood clot, surgery is performed under visualization with a laparoscope, with its various mechanical attachments (pincers, etc.), or through a lower abdominal surgical incision. Recovery from the former procedure is usually easier and quicker.

Rh negative women should be given Rhogam at the time of treatment for an ectopic pregnancy, in order to prevent sensitization to the Rh factor and resulting risk to subsequent pregnancies (see p. 56).

While an ectopic pregnancy may have all the symptoms of a miscarriage, it is important to distinguish between the two conditions. Sometimes this is not possible, using presently available tests. Therefore, if a D. and C. is done because of a suspected incomplete abortion (miscarriage), or purposefully to interrupt a pregnancy, it is important to submit the curettings (scrapings) to a pathologist for examination. The absence of fetal tissue strongly suggests (but does not alone prove) an ectopic pregnancy and should prompt a search for this disorder. Some ectopic pregnancies are discovered in this way.

While the cause (or causes) of ectopic pregnancy is often not certain in an individual case, several factors are known to predispose a woman to this disorder. Each of these factors has to do with changes in the structure and function of the Fallopian tubes. Prior infection of the tubes (salpingitis) is perhaps the most common. Gonococcal infection (see p. 161) has been regarded as the most frequently responsible agent. Also there is growing recognition that infection with Chlamydia (see p. 159) plays a significant role.

In women who become pregnant with an intrauterine device (IUD) in place, the percentage of ectopic pregnancies is high. Since an IUD prevents implantation in the uterus but not elsewhere, ectopic pregnancies constitute a large percentage of all pregnancies that occur in IUD users. Since IUD's are no longer being distributed, complications related to their use can be expected to decrease.

The Fallopian tubes can be malformed in their development, with narrowing, blind pockets and misplaced openings. They can be scarred and stunted from prior inflammation within the abdominal cavity (such as caused by a ruptured appendix). Uterine tumors such as fibroids can block the entry of the tube into the uterus and predispose to tubal implantation. The failure of a previous operation on the tube to restore its ability to carry fertilized eggs, or sterilization procedures (especially those in which the tubes are tied rather than cut as well as tied) can also set the stage for an ectopic pregnancy. Finally, the woman who has had one ectopic pregnancy is at increased risk for another; her subsequent pregnancies have about a 10 percent chance of again being ectopic.

Women at increased risk for ectopic pregnancy should be monitored closely and should get in touch with their doctors when they intend to conceive. Monitoring includes early diagnosis of pregnancy through hormonal testing, serial measurements of the beta subunit, ultrasound, and increased awareness of the earliest signs of rupture, on the part of both the woman and those caring for her in pregnancy.

The earlier an ectopic pregnancy is recognized (ideally, even before symptoms occur), the better. Surgery done before rupture not only spares the woman a potentially life-threatening condition and much inconvenience, but also offers a better chance of leaving behind an intact and functioning Fallopian tube.

The issue of ectopic pregnancy is closely tied to that of infertility. Infertile women are at increased risk for ectopic pregnancies; and women who have had an ectopic pregnancy are at increased risk for infertility. Even with the best of today's care, only 50 percent of women who have had an ectopic pregnancy can expect to become pregnant. Of these, only 60 percent can expect to deliver a baby (30 percent of the original group), and 10 percent will go on to have a repeat ectopic pregnancy (5 percent of the original group).

Tubal problems that contribute both to infertility and to ectopic pregnancy can sometimes be repaired by microsurgery. When such measures fail or cannot be performed, the defective tubes can be bypassed altogether by using intrauterine fertilizations or embryo transfer. The dramatic successes of "test tube baby" research have so far dealt with these kinds of situations. In this latter, still somewhat experimental, but already successful technique, the egg is removed just prior to ovulation through use of a laparoscope and fertilized with the partner's sperm in a test tube. The resulting fertilized ovum is then implanted in the uterus, and the pregnancy proceeds normally.

The point needs to be made that, although the problem of ectopic pregnancy can be dealt with today much more effectively than in the past, its prevention is a major unresolved issue, which is growing in importance. Furthermore, from the point of view of achieving fertility, present-day treatment is far from ideal. And the loss of an ectopic pregnancy carries all the emotions associated with a pregnancy loss (see p. 305), even though the woman will also feel relieved to have survived a life-threatening situation.

It is of interest that, in the People's Republic of China, many ectopic pregnancies are treated nonsurgically. An antimetabolite drug commonly used in cancer treatment is used to destroy the developing fetal tissues; afterward, the woman's body absorbs the products of conception. The technique deserves to be studied in this country.

Gallstones

During and after pregnancy there may be an increased incidence of symptoms due to stones in the gallbladder. These symptoms include attacks of crampy upper abdominal pain, more often on the right side and sometimes radiating to the right shoulder, often accompanied by nausea and even vomiting. In addition to the obvious discomfort and inconvenience of such symptoms, there is a danger that a gallstone will actually block the bile duct and interfere with the flow of bile, a more serious problem. There is also some evidence that the gallbladder is less efficient in emptying itself of bile during pregnancy and that this might contribute to the formation of stones.

The standard recommendation is to remove stones (and the gallbladder that contains them) when they cause symptoms and preferably before they obstruct the bile duct, a development that significantly increases the mortality and morbidity of surgery. In pregnancy this approach needs to be balanced against the risk to the fetus, especially in the first trimester when miscarriage has been reported to occur with such surgery and general anesthesia. For this reason, surgery is postponed if possible until after delivery or, at least, until the second trimester.

Hydatidiform Mole

Hydatidiform mole is a rare tumor of the very early placenta. In the United States, it occurs in one out of 1,500 pregnancies. In this condition, there is no fetus present and the uterine cavity is filled with tissue which has the appearance of a cluster of small grapes.

The symptoms and signs of hydatidiform mole are marked nausea, elevated blood pressure, uterine enlargement out of proportion to the duration of the pregnancy, a markedly high level of chorionic gonadotropin (one of the pregnancy hormones); and, occasionally, the spontaneous passage of the hydatidiform "grapes." Ultrasound shows a characteristic picture, which includes absence of any evidence of a fetus, and naturally no fetal heart can be heard.

A hydatidiform mole that penetrates deep into the wall of the uterus is called an *invasive mole,* a form of nonspreading cancer. Another danger of hydatidiform mole is its potential transformation into a true cancer known as a *choriocarcinoma,* which can spread (metastasize) from the uterus throughout the body. Vaginal bleeding is a common symptom and, as in the case of hydatidiform mole, the chorionic gonadotropin level is very high. (Choriocarcinoma can also arise in the uterus after a pregnancy is terminated either by delivery or abortion.)

Treatment of hydatidiform mole consists of removal of the abnormal tissue through a dilation and suction curettage of the uterus. In some cases, the mole must be removed through an incision into the uterus reached through the abdomen (hysterotomy) or even by complete removal of the uterus itself (hysterectomy).

Following removal of a mole, it is important to follow the chorionic gonadotropin level until it falls to within normal range. Until it does, the possibility exists that cancerous changes in the mole have occurred and that not all of the abnormal tissue was removed.

If the hormonal levels do not fall, or if they rise, a finding that suggests cancer, the woman can be treated with drugs with an excellent outlook for cure. (Choriocarcinoma that does not arise from a mole is dealt with similarly.)

Hydramnios and Oligohydramnios

Hydramnios means excessive amniotic fluid, and oligohydramnios, a relative lack of it. When the size of the abdomen is, respectively, larger or smaller than predicted, these conditions are suspected. The diagnosis is confirmed by ultrasound. More often, too much or too little amniotic fluid is detected by an ultrasound exam done for some other purpose.

Each disorder is a symptom of some abnormality in the pregnancy which must be carefully checked. For example, congenital abnormalities of the fetus that interfere with swallowing, or with

production of urine, can result in hydramnios and oligohydramnios respectively. Oligohydramnios is also a risk factor when pregnancy exceeds forty-one weeks (see p. 314) and is taken into
account in deciding to induce labor. However, an explanation is
not always found, particularly when the increases or decreases in
fluid are small and detected only by ultrasound.

If excessive, hydramnios can, in itself, represent a problem for
the woman. If it interferes with breathing, it may need to be
treated by withdrawing amniotic fluid through amniocentesis (see
p. 130).

Intrauterine Growth Disturbance

The growth of a fetus becomes of concern if its birth weight is 10
percent less than that predicted for its gestational age. By this
definition, the growth of about 7 percent of all fetuses is too slow.
Prematurity alone does not mean that the growth of the infant is
disturbed, by this definition, since premature infants can be normal or subnormal in weight for their gestational ages.

One type of growth disturbance is called *asymmetric intrauterine
growth retardation*. While the lengths and weights of affected fetuses are abnormally low, their heads may or may not be small.
Their mothers are more likely than the mothers of infants of
normal weights to be ill in pregnancy, with high blood pressure,
chronic kidney disease, or advanced diabetes. In some of these
pregnancies growth failure appears related to impaired circulation
in the uterus and placenta, so that these fetuses are undernour-
ished. In many other cases the cause of the growth impairment
is still unknown.

A second type of growth disturbance is known as *symmetric
intrauterine growth retardation*. The overall growth of these fetuses,
including their heads, is stunted. This is usually due to an illness
of the fetus — irrespective of the health of the mother or the
placenta. The illness can be genetic or due to an infection or toxin.
Among the causes are: chromosomal abnormalities (see p. 123),
the congenital rubella syndrome (see p. 166); congenital cytomegalovirus infection (p. 160), and the fetal alcohol syndrome (see p.
171).

A third type of growth disturbance is known as *dysmaturity* or *postmaturity* (see p. 314) because this disorder occurs most commonly in fetuses whose gestations have exceeded forty-two weeks. These babies show signs of having regressed in nutritional status. Their length and head size may be normal while their weight may be reduced. After birth, they look as though they have lost weight: their skin is loose, dry, and wrinkled; and they have little of the fine long body hair (lanugo) of the normal newborn. Their nails are long and their skin may have a yellowish cast, suggesting staining from meconium passed in utero. (Meconium, the feces of the fetus, may be passed into the amniotic fluid when the fetus is subjected to stress.) Growth retardation of these infants seems related to problems in the placenta. As if, for reasons yet unknown, their placentas have "given out," after having reached a certain age, and are unable to supply the nutrients and oxygen needed by the fetus.

Growth disturbed fetuses run more risk for death before, during, and after labor. They are more likely to have difficulties as newborns and require special attention. Some of these difficulties include low blood sugar, low blood calcium, and temperature instability (hence the use of infant warmers).

The long-range outlook for growth-disturbed fetuses depends both on the cause and on the events surrounding birth and the immediate period following birth. For example, a baby with the congenital rubella syndrome is at great risk for permanent physical handicaps, and a postmature infant who has suffered lack of oxygen compounded by meconium in the lungs (which interferes with breathing at birth) is more likely to have resulting neurological handicapping. On the other hand, many babies who are small for gestational age but have normal head sizes do perfectly well. Head size seems important in predicting the outlook for these babies. For example, a study from the Queen Charlotte Maternity Hospital in London showed that children who were small for gestational age, and whose head growth began to slow before twenty-six weeks of gestation, demonstrated significantly lower scores in perceptual performance and motor ability at five years of age when compared to a matched control group of children who were normal for gestational age. Head size was of greater predictive value than weight or length, a logical relationship, given that head size corresponds to brain growth.

During every pregnancy the growth of the fetus should be monitored at each prenatal visit. In fact, the routine measuring of the height of the uterus is intended primarily to determine whether or not fetal growth is occurring. But the size of the uterus provides only indirect evidence, since it depends not only on the growth of the fetus, but on the amount of amniotic fluid present, as well as other factors.

At present, ultrasound is the most accurate means of assessing fetal growth (see p. 142). Examination by ultrasound allows measurement of the diameter of the head, the circumference of the abdomen, and other body parts. It makes possible a reasonably accurate prediction of fetal weight based on a combination of measurements of the fetal body. In addition to assessing the maturity of the fetus, ultrasound can also provide helpful information on the maturity and health of the placenta.

A series of ultrasound examinations of infants suspected of growth disturbance can show whether or not growth has occurred. Techniques for assessing fetal growth by ultrasound are undergoing constant improvement. A continuing problem, however, is that of identifying growth interference early enough to remove any treatable cause.

Because of increasing precision in determining fetal growth by ultrasound, many obstetricians advocate its routine use for this purpose (as well as for other reasons). But we do not yet know how often a growth-disturbed baby would be overlooked if ultrasound were used only in pregnancies that can be identified as being at high risk for this disorder. For this reason, prospective studies are needed. The potential risks of ultrasound must also be considered.

At the present time there is no effective intrauterine treatment for the fetus whose growth is impaired. Researchers are trying to find ways to increase blood flow to the placenta and to supply the fetus with nutrients by injecting them directly into the amniotic fluid. Research on how the placenta works and what can disturb this is also a high priority.

The preventable causes of growth disturbance are the responsibility of each individual. Pregnant women who smoke should stop, and rubella immunization should be routine before pregnancy. Deficient diets should be corrected. For the high-risk woman, bed rest, especially on the side (to prevent the uterus from pressing on the great blood vessels and impairing blood flow to the placenta), may be useful.

When growth disturbance is suspected, plans should be made for the delivery to take place in a maternity center equipped to care for high-risk newborns. Early delivery may be necessary to save the baby.

Late Childbearing

Advancing maternal age is a reason for extra caution during pregnancy. It is known to be associated with increased difficulty in becoming pregnant and an increase in such complications as: miscarriage (p. 305), babies with chromosomal abnormalities, especially Down syndrome (p. 125); premature labor (p. 318), breech presentations (p. 271), placenta praevia (p. 312), twins (p. 331), preeclampsia (p. 315), and hydatidiform mole (p. 299). The older a woman, the more likely she is to have developed uterine fibroids which may have a bearing on the pregnancy (p. 74). She is also more likely to have developed chronic diseases, such as diabetes (p. 167), which affect and are affected by pregnancy.

Older women must also make decisions early in pregnancy about amniocentesis (p. 130) and chorionic villous sampling (p. 132) for identifying a fetus with chromosomal abnormalities. After age thirty-five the risk of a fetus having Down syndrome roughly approaches the risk of losing a pregnancy as a complication of an amniocentesis done to obtain fetal cells for chromosomal analysis. For this reason, we recommend that all women thirty-five or older consider having an amniocentesis during the second trimester of pregnancy. It must be stressed, however, that, although the odds of having a baby with Down syndrome increase with the mother's age (and, it appears, with the father's as well), most babies with this disorder are actually born to younger women, because, in absolute terms, they have more babies. We also point out that, even for mothers at advanced maternal ages, the chance of any one child having Down syndrome is still relatively low (see p. 125).

Having presented this list of potential problems, we hasten to add that many of them can be dealt with effectively today. A woman who is old by once-usual childbearing standards has every reason today to be optimistic about bearing a healthy child. A study of Atlanta babies made by the Centers for Disease Control bears out this optimism. With *appropriate prenatal care,* the risk of women aged thirty-five to forty-four for bearing an infant with a severe birth defect was no greater than that of younger women (under thirty-five). For women over forty-five, however, the risk was twice that of women thirty-four or younger.

Miscarriage

A remarkably high percentage of pregnancies do not end in the birth of a live baby. While fetal death can occur at any gestational age, most deaths occur early in the first trimester, often even before the pregnancy is recognized. Such deaths are referred to as *spontaneous abortions* (or miscarriage), to distinguish them from induced or deliberate abortions.

The statistics on miscarriage are sobering. The chance in a first pregnancy is about 20 percent. After having a miscarriage in her first pregnancy, a woman runs a 28.2 percent risk of one in a second pregnancy. After two miscarriages, her risk rises to 37.9 percent; and after three, to 50 percent. Women who have had one miscarriage in a pregnancy that follows a normal pregnancy run a 16.1 percent risk in subsequent pregnancies. The more liveborn children a woman has, the less the risk, and the more miscarriages or stillborn births after liveborn births, the greater the risk of future miscarriage.

For any average figure, the percentages tend to be higher the older the woman. For example, a twenty-year-old runs a 15 percent chance of her first pregnancy ending in abortion; a twenty-five-year-old, 15 percent; a thirty-five-year-old, 25 percent; and a forty-year-old, 40 percent.

Genetic defects are at the root of most miscarriages. Of first trimester miscarriages of less than eight weeks' gestation, 70 to 75 percent are estimated to have chromosomal abnormalities. Between eight and twelve weeks 40 percent of abortions are chromosomally abnormal. In all, about 60 percent of first trimester abortions are estimated to have chromosomal abnormalities.

Another 20 percent of first trimester abortions result from the joining of two recessive lethal genes, one from each partner. (See p. 117.) Each of us carries between six and ten such genes. If partners each carry one or more of the same recessive lethal genes, their mating carries a 25 percent chance for two such genes to combine. Such combinations lead to the death of the fetus. Thus, chromosomal abnormalities and recessive lethal genes taken together account for about 80 percent of all first trimester abortions. Couples with a repeated history of miscarriage should read the genetic section of this book and seek genetic counseling.

Another 10 percent or more first trimester pregnancy losses appear to be related to immunological factors. Most of the work in this area centers on the blood and tissue types of the fetus and its parents. (Tissue types are important in determining which individuals can successfully donate organs to others with minimum rejection by the recipient.) While it is known that the rate of spontaneous abortion is significantly increased when mother and fetus have different blood types, a recent study showed that the rate is also increased when the mother and father are very similar in their tissue types. Common sense, of course, points to a different conclusion: the more alike the tissue types, the less likely a spontaneous abortion would seem to be. However, it appears that the initial immunological clash, which occurs when the sperm and ejaculate are of a tissue type different from that of the mother, leads to a maternal antibody and hormonal response that eventually *protects* the fetus from rejection, conferring on it a privileged immunological status.

When recurrent miscarriage is related to these tissue type similarities, the immunization of a woman with her husband's lymphocytes (a specific group of white blood cells) may overcome the problem of immunological compatibility by triggering the woman to produce antibodies against those tissue types that she does not share with her partner. It is likely that more will be learned about this intriguing topic in the future. It is possible that other problems in pregnancy, such as intrauterine growth disturbance, eclampsia, and perhaps even premature labor, may be based on similar immunological considerations.

Completing the list of causes of spontaneous abortion, including those in the second or third trimester, is a group usually designated as "environmental," meaning the environment of the fetus. Some of these factors are known, while others are as yet merely speculative. Among the known factors are anatomical abnormalities of the uterus and cervix. Instead of forming one chamber, the uterus may consist of two chambers with various degrees of separateness that range from partial to complete. This defect can be corrected surgically with a reasonable chance of success. Another well known but fortunately uncommon problem is *incompetent cervix*. This disorder is characterized by painless dilatation of the cervix in the second trimester or early in the third, followed by rupture of the membranes and the subsequent expulsion of a fetus that is usually too immature to survive. The same course of events tends to be repeated in subsequent pregnancies.

Surgical treatment of incompetent cervix involves sewing the cervix together early in pregnancy, tying it up with a suture like a purse string to close the cervical opening. The operation is done after the first trimester and before cervical dilation of 4 centimeters is reached. It is said to be 85 percent successful. The sutures are removed at once if uterine contractions begin or if the amniotic membranes rupture. Although some cases of cervical incompetence seem to be due to stretching of the cervix during an earlier dilation and curettage, the cause of this disorder is not well understood.

A history of two or more induced abortions has been implicated by some but not all studies as a factor in miscarriage. A recent study funded by the March of Dimes Birth Defects Foundation showed that women with prior induced abortions were two to three times as likely to abort spontaneously. The reasons for this presumed association are not well understood.

Pregnancies that occur while an intrauterine device (IUD) is still in place (representing a failure of that form of contraception) are more likely to abort either spontaneously or as a consequence of the removal of the IUD, which is usually done to prevent more serious complications.

Infection of the fetus with the mumps or rubella virus is a known cause of abortion, and infection is a major cause of abortion in cattle. Thus, it is quite plausible that as yet unidentified infections could also play a role in abortion in humans. Among the suspected microorganisms is *Mycoplasma*. Evidence is increasing that this germ is more likely to be found in the genital tracts of women with abortions than of those who do not abort. As far as is known, no symptoms (such as vaginal discharge) accompany these infections. There is also accumulating evidence that treatment of the woman from whom *Mycoplasma* can be cultured will reduce the incidence of miscarriage. It now appears to be worthwhile to culture women and their partners for *Mycoplasma* when recurrent (two or more) abortions have occurred. Whether *Mycoplasma* cultures will become a routine part of prenatal care is not yet clear. Another possible cause of abortion is infection with the organism *Listeria monocytogenes*, discussed on p. 165.

Some environmental factors may be hormonal. One that is uncommon is deficiency of chorionic gonadotropin (see p. 39) due to deficient function of the corpus luteum. Treatment with injections of chorionic gonadotropin through the first trimester into the second can be curative. Over- or underproduction of thyroid hormone can also contribute to spontaneous abortion.

Infection within the abdominal cavity (peritonitis) from a ruptured appendix can lead to spontaneous abortion; for this reason the early recognition of acute appendicitis in pregnancy before rupture of the appendix has occurred (p. 74), is very important.

Tobacco smoking (p. 170) is also known to lead to an increase in the frequency of abortion. Here, at least, is one clearly preventable cause.

Despite the fact that much is known about the actual causes of miscarriage, the human mind is rich in supplying imagined causes as well. Intense and unjustified feelings of guilt and self-blame for "causing" the abortion often result. Rare is the woman who does not search for some additional cause — what she did or didn't do, what she felt or didn't feel — even though there is no evidence that individual behavior or feelings play a role in spontaneous abortion.

Probably the greatest "non-cause" of miscarriage is sexual intercourse. So often one hears the lament: "If only we had not had intercourse, this would not have happened!" While it is true that intercourse may be the precipitating factor in the *timing* of spontaneous abortion, the pregnancy would have aborted anyway, perhaps several days later, if intercourse had not occurred. *Intercourse cannot be said to cause miscarriage*, which is primarily, as we have seen, a result of genetic abnormalities.

Other common examples of "non-causes" of miscarriage are horseback riding, skiing, and car accidents. A fall, like intercourse, could affect the timing of a miscarriage but not cause it. Mixed feelings about the pregnancy (what woman does not have them?) can also cause guilt, as can considering an induced abortion to terminate the pregnancy (few feelings are more guilt arousing). Women worry about morning sickness and not having eaten well as a result (presumably, so the fear goes, leading to malnutrition of the fetus), having had a cold or flu, having taken an alcoholic beverage either before or after knowing that one was pregnant, having taken acetaminophen (Tylenol) for a headache, and so forth. While feelings of guilt are understandable and the search for rational causes only human, the facts simply do not support any of the above factors as having anything to do with miscarriage. While drinking, smoking, and medications can affect the *health* of the fetus, they do not cause abortion.

The onset of a miscarriage is signified by vaginal bleeding. As long as the cervix has not dilated and fetal or placental tissue (sometimes euphemistically referred to as the "products of conception") has not been passed, the term used to describe the bleeding is *threatened abortion*. At this point there is no good way to predict whether the bleeding will stop and the pregnancy proceed normally, or whether an abortion will occur.

Traditionally, women who bleed are sent to bed and told to avoid intercourse and tub baths, to help prevent infection of the uterus should rupture of the membranes occur. As we have seen, it is also true that intercourse or orgasm may precipitate, or at least speed up, a miscarriage that is about to occur. Bed rest has never been convincingly demonstrated to prevent miscarriage, nor is there any reason to believe that it could or would. Given the causes discussed above, it is easy to see why it would not work. Nevertheless, going to bed and "taking it easy" seem to be ingrained responses to vaginal bleeding and are still widely recommended.

In cases of threatened abortion, it is important to review the steps to take if it progresses and tissue is passed before reaching the hospital or a doctor's office. Such tissue should be placed in a sterile (or, at least, clean) receptacle and brought promptly to the hospital for careful study by a pathologist. If the miscarriage occurs in the hospital or doctor's office, the doctor will follow the same procedure. The purpose of this recommendation is to determine whether or not the symptoms were results of a spontaneous intrauterine pregnancy, as opposed to an ectopic pregnancy (p. 293) or a hydatidiform mole (p. 299). If the bleeding stops and all is well, the condition is commonly referred to as the *cyclic bleeding of pregnancy*, a diagnosis that can be made only in retrospect.

If crampy uterine pain occurs in addition to the bleeding, the chances of a miscarriage increase. If there is a gush of amniotic fluid and dilation of the cervix, the miscarriage is inevitable. Once tissue is identified or the intact fetus in its sac is seen, a miscarriage has occurred (or is in the process of occurring). Continued bleeding and cramping lead to suspicion that parts of the pregnancy remain in the uterus, which will have to be removed by dilation and curettage (D. and C.), described below. Otherwise, cramping and bleeding will continue, with the possibility of significant loss of blood and the increased risk of infection.

Sometimes it is not clear whether or not a miscarriage has occurred, especially when no tissue is identified and no cervical dilation is observed. This uncertainty can occur either when the woman is examined after a complete miscarriage or when nothing has yet emerged. The latter condition is referred to as a *missed abortion*; it is the same as an intrauterine fetal death, which may or may not be associated with bleeding or cramping at the time the fetus dies.

When there is uncertainty about whether or not a miscarriage has occurred, ultrasound can be helpful; it can detect the presence or absence of the fetus and determine whether it is alive or not. Other signs of a lost pregnancy are the failure of the uterus to continue to grow, the loss of the associated signs of pregnancy (breast enlargement, and so forth), and a failure of the predicted increase in chorionic gonadotropin, the hormone commonly measured by the various tests of pregnancy. Instead of rising, the level may flatten out or actually decrease.

The D. and C. (dilation and curettage) is the technique used to complete an incomplete abortion. A D. and C. done to remove the contents of the uterus is more accurately referred to as a D. and E. (dilation and evacuation). If done during the first trimester, it may be performed in the doctor's office as well as in a hospital. It involves dilating the cervix to the point that a plastic cannula can be inserted into the uterus. The woman lies on her back, her legs spread and supported by straps or knee stirrups. A pelvic examination is performed to assess the size and position of the uterus. Next a clamp is used to grasp the rim of the cervix to stabilize it. The unanesthetized woman usually experiences this maneuver as a pinch which eases over the next few minutes. Then the vagina and cervix are cleansed with an antiseptic solution. If the woman chooses to be awake through the procedure, local anesthetic may be injected around the cervix to reduce the pain of stretching. The uterus is next measured by passing a metal or plastic measuring rod (sound) into its cavity and recording the depth of insertion. A series of small metal dilators of increasing diameter are inserted into the cervix to stretch the canal to the desired size. Next the plastic cannula is inserted. It is attached to a suction machine that draws the contents of the uterus out through the tube. The cannula is rotated and moved back and forth to have contact with the entire interior of the uterus. It is then removed and the size of the uterus rechecked with the sound (it should now be smaller); the clamp on the cervix is removed, and the procedure is completed.

If this procedure is done in a hospital, as is usually the case, general anesthesia (p. 209) is commonly used. The woman is asleep and unaware of what is happening, which can be an advantage for some and a disadvantage for others. When done without general anesthesia, a painkiller such as Demerol can be given prior to the procedure to take the edge off the pain, which women describe as similar to that of strong menstrual cramps. While anesthetizing the cervix with local anesthesia lessens the pain associated with cervical dilation, it does not affect the pain caused by intrauterine manipulation. Once the uterus has been entered, D. and E. takes about five minutes.

When the procedure is done in a doctor's office, some differences are noted. To minimize bleeding after the procedure, many doctors prescribe Ergotrate tablets (see p. 199), which cause the muscles of the uterus to clamp down. Sometimes antibiotics are prescribed as well to prevent infection. Such medications are taken every four to six hours for one or two days. The removed tissue is always sent to a pathologist for examination to make sure that fetal tissue is identifable, thereby excluding the possibility of an ectopic pregnancy or hydatidiform mole.

Many women like to have their partner or a friend with them during office D. and E.'s. While doctors vary in their receptivity to such requests, we have found that the participation of a partner is supportive to the woman during the procedure, as well as the doctor. Couples can use the D. and E. as an opportunity for the partner to demonstrate his support, as well as learn about the price women sometimes pay for being the members of our species who can conceive and bear children.

All losses of pregnancy, whether through miscarrage or induced abortion, will arouse strong emotions in the woman experiencing them. If she can acknowledge these feelings and give herself time to rest or be with close friends, she will recover more completely.

Placenta Praevia and Placental Abruption

Placenta praevia refers to a low-lying placenta which covers the inner opening to the cervix either partially or completely, or is close to the edge of the cervix. The problem with this location is that bleeding occurs as the cervix stretches before and during labor. Before the onset of labor, painless bleeding which stops of its own accord is the most common sign of placenta praevia. In the typical case, the woman awakens in a pool of blood. Usually the amount of the first bleeding is not sufficient to cause symptoms of blood loss.

When placenta praevia is suspected, the diagnosis is now made primarily by ultrasound, which is highly effective in locating the placenta. When the placenta covers the inside of the cervix entirely or in major part, there is no alternative to a cesarean section. However, it is often the case that the placenta is next to or near the cervix, in which case vaginal examination by the obstetrician is also needed to determine its exact location and whether a vaginal delivery can be tried without too much risk of bleeding. Such an examination is safely done only in the operating room with an intravenous infusion in place and running, and an anesthesiologist standing by so that an immediate cesarean section can be done should bleeding ensue. Such a "double set-up" is also used to diagnose placenta praevia when ultrasound in unavailable.

Once placenta praevia is diagnosed, the pregnancy is considered to be high risk, even when the bleeding has completely stopped. The woman should be admitted to the hospital and stay in bed up to the time of delivery. Because of the high risk of hemorrhaging in labor, delivery should be accomplished by cesarean section after the fetus reaches a mature thirty-seven weeks' gestation. If hemorrhage recurs before thirty-seven weeks or fails to stop after the first bleeding, cesarean section is performed immediately as an emergency procedure.

The cause of placenta praevia is not known. It affects about one-half of 1 percent of all pregnancies and is more common the more children a woman has had and the older she is. Previous induced abortions may also be a factor. It appears that placenta praevia may be involved in some first trimester miscarriages. Now that ultrasound is more commonly used during pregnancy, it has been found that in the second trimester a significant percentage of placentas are low lying, even though few of them become placentae praeviae at term. This observation suggests that the placenta is actually capable of migration during pregnancy. Why some placentas move and others do not is not understood.

Placental abruption refers to a peeling away of the placenta from the uterus with associated bleeding between the separated placenta and the uterus. It is the other major cause of bleeding late in pregnancy. The accumulated blood may be trapped within the uterus, or it may escape between the amniotic membranes, passing through the uterus and cervix into the vagina, where it is recognizable as vaginal bleeding. Other symptoms and signs are (1) spasm (increased muscle tone) of the uterus; (2) pain and tenderness over and in the uterus; (3) signs of shock due to blood loss (sweating, pallor, light-headedness on sitting, clammy skin, etc.); (4) changes in the pattern of the fetal heartbeat or complete loss of the fetal heart tones. Since there are various degrees of abruption, the signs and symptoms also vary. At one extreme the fetus may die and the mother be in profound shock from blood loss; at the other extreme, the mother may show no vaginal bleeding, the fetal heart rate may be normal, and only persistent uterine pain points to the problem. Sometimes partial abruption can be totally without symptoms and be discovered only after the placenta is examined following birth.

Once the diagnosis of placental abruption is made, delivery should be accomplished promptly by cesarean section after the woman's blood volume is brought back to a stable level.

Placental abruption occurs in less that 1 percent of pregnancies and its cause is not known. It is reported to be more common in women who have high blood pressure during pregnancy (see p. 315 on preeclampsia) and in the second born of twins. The risk for recurrence of placental abruption in a woman who has already experienced this complication is about ten times the normal rate.

Post-Term Pregnancies

Most pregnancies last between thirty-eight and forty-two weeks. About 3 percent last longer and are termed prolonged pregnancies. After forty-one full weeks a fetus is at increased (but still relatively small) risk (two to three times) for dying prior to or during birth. At forty-four weeks this risk is somewhat less than 5 percent. Thirty percent of overdue fetuses will also have various degrees of the postmaturity syndrome (see p. 302) which play a major role in their vulnerability.

Because of this increased risk to the fetus, labor is generally induced after the completion of forty-one weeks' gestation if the cervix is "ripe" and the fetal head is well fixed in the pelvis in contact with the cervix. If conditions for induction are not favorable, the well-being of the fetus is checked usually twice weekly (see p. 141 on the biophysical profile). If these tests are normal, the mother is reevaluated for induction one week later. If by the end of the forty-third week the cervix is still unready for induction, or if attempted induction has not been successful, a cesarean section is done.

If, on the other hand, any of the tests show that the fetus is in trouble, every attempt will be made to get the baby born quickly, either by induction or by cesarean section.

An alternative approach is to monitor the mother and fetus and wait until labor begins. An induction or cesarean section would be done only if the fetus were shown by testing to be in jeopardy or, according to some authorities, if labor had not occurred by the forty-fourth week. (Other authorities say that one can wait indefinitely.) There is no evidence at present that this alternative approach is any riskier than the mainstream one described.

The alternative approach, along with nipple stimulation to ripen the cervix and initiate labor, is favored by families and attendants planning out-of-hospital birth, since inductions are in general not carried out in such settings. The approach is also favored by families who wish to avoid, as a matter of preference, any interventions not absolutely required.

In identifying a truly prolonged pregnancy, accuracy of the dating (see p. 48, "Dating the Pregnancy") becomes critical. In fact, about three-fourths of "post-date" pregnancies are not actually prolonged, but errors in dating. It is also worth pointing out that gestational age, like other human characteristics such as height and longevity, shows a range of normal values along a bell-shaped curve. It is likely that some fetuses were "meant" to be in utero for forty-three weeks and others for thirty-eight weeks. The forty-one week figure for defining post-term pregnancies may be somewhat arbitrary. Nevertheless, on a statistical basis, the risk to the fetus does increase after this age. Therefore, many normal babies will be monitored and worried about in order to pick up the minority who are in actual trouble. Such are the limitations of our present-day understanding.

Preeclampsia and Eclampsia

Preeclampsia–Eclampsia, also known as pregnancy-induced hypertension, is a multifaceted disorder of pregnancy. Its cause is still unknown. It is characterized by high blood pressure, the presence of protein in the urine, and/or edema after the twenty-fourth week of pregnancy. Relatively common, it affects up to 6 or 7 percent of all pregnancies and can seriously threaten the well-being of both the fetus and the mother. Preeclampsia can also be superimposed on existing hypertension.

Blood pressure and urinary protein levels are routinely checked during prenatal visits (p. 47) in order to detect preeclampsia. When blood pressure rises above 140 (systolic) over 85 (diastolic), or if the systolic pressure increases 30 points over the pre-pregnancy level, or the diastolic pressure increases 15 or more points, preeclampsia is suspected. Urinary protein level of "two plus" or greater, as measured by the dip stick method and/or the excretion of more than 500 mg. of protein in the urine over a period of twenty-four hours, is considered significant.

The accumulation of fluid (edema) in the skin of a pregnant woman, especially in hands and face, can be a sign of preeclampsia. While edema, especially in the legs, is normal in pregnancy, rapid, sudden weight gain and development of edema point to the diagnosis of preeclampsia.

Preeclampsia can also cause symptoms such as upper abdominal pain, nausea, and vomiting, without elevated blood pressure, or protein in the urine. This is less common. Laboratory tests of liver function and blood count are then used in the diagnosis.

The possible effects on the fetus of preeclampsia include intrauterine growth disturbance (p. 301); premature labor (sometimes this must be induced), and prematurity (see p. 318); stillbirth (p. 326); and placental abruption (p. 312). Risks to the mother include death at the extreme, and convulsions, hemorrhage into the brain with possible permanent neurological deficits, loss of vision (usually temporary), hemorrhage into the liver, and kidney failure at the other. Whenever convulsions occur, *eclampsia* is said to exist.

While most of the symptoms of preeclampsia can be controlled, there is no real cure yet for preeclampsia other than ending the pregnancy through the birth of the baby. When measures to control preeclampsia fail, the baby is delivered as a last resort, either through induction or by cesarean section. Since convulsions can occur even after delivery, the mother is carefully monitored for the next seventy-two hours. In rare cases, convulsions can occur after delivery without any signs of preeclampsia having occurred prior to labor. In considering early delivery, the gestational age and well-being of the baby as determined by tests such as biophysical profile (see p. 141), are balanced against the risks to both mother and fetus if the pregnancy continues.

Short of delivery, the following measures have proved effective in controlling the symptoms of preeclampsia: bed rest, sometimes with sedation with phenobarbitol, and the use of drugs to control the elevated blood pressure. In mild cases, the mother can stay at home with arrangements for daily checks of blood pressure and protein in the urine. Preeclampsia is traditionally treated by increasing the intake of fluid and protein. These measures have not proven to be effective, however, and can be disregarded. Decreasing blood pressure with diuretics ("fluid pills"), to encourage the body to excrete fluid and salt, is risky in preeclampsia because, if the blood volume is decreased, the flow of blood to the placenta decreases, too.

If convulsions have occurred, or seem impending, the standard treatment is magnesium sulfate administered intravenously. Headache, confusion, an increase in blood pressure, abdominal pain, nausea, and vomiting can signal impending convulsions.

Despite much research, we do not yet know the cause of preeclampsia. It appears to be related to unexplained constriction of the blood vessels in the uterus, which in turn deprives the placenta and the fetus of much-needed blood. In about 20 percent of women with preeclampsia, the abnormality of the blood vessels of the uterus is related to preexisting kidney disease (with or without high blood pressure) which will persist after delivery, either along with high blood pressure or with the potential for developing it later. In the majority of women with preeclampsia, however, the changes in the kidneys follow the changes in the blood vessels of the uterus. In both types of cases the woman's blood volume decreases and her arteries constrict too much, thus leading to a rise in blood pressure.

Unless there is preexisting kidney disease, preeclampsia is primarily a disease of a woman's first pregnancy. The women most apt to develop preeclampsia are teenagers, women over thirty-five, and poorly nourished women. Women with blood relatives who have had preeclampsia are also more vulnerable, as are women who have been hypertensive before pregnancy. A woman who has not demonstrated preeclampsia during her first pregnancy is unlikely to develop the disorder in subsequent pregnancies unless the baby has a different father; this finding suggests that the man too contributes something to the disorder. Other predisposing factors are multiple (two or more) fetuses (p. 331), diabetes (p. 167), hydatidiform mole (p. 299), and fetuses whose red blood cells have undergone destruction by maternal antibodies (p. 56 on Rh incompatibility).

Prematurity

PREMATURE LABOR

Premature labor that results in the birth of premature babies is a major problem in maternity care, and is still largely unsolved. An estimated 10 to 15 percent of all live births are premature. Depending on the degree of immaturity, premature babies run a higher risk of disability and death, and face longer and often costlier hospitalizations.

Labor is called premature in the following situations:

- the fetus weighs less than 2,500 grams (roughly 5 pounds)
- the fetus is younger than thirty-seven weeks' gestational age
- the mother is experiencing regular uterine contractions, with the cervix thinning out and widening — the cardinal signs of labor (see p. 183).

The onset of premature labor is signified by menstrual-like cramps; tightening in the stomach; dull low backache, pressure in lower back, pelvis, abdomen or thighs, and intestinal cramping. Any of these symptoms should be promptly reported.

While we do not yet know the causes of most premature labors, contributing factors include: multiple birth (p. 331), abnormalities in the structure of the uterus; hydramnios (p. 300); smoking (p. 170); poor weight gain in an underweight woman (p. 82); bleeding prior to labor (p. 312 on placenta praevia and placental abruption); intrauterine growth disturbance (p. 301); intrauterine fetal death (p. 326); preeclampsia and eclampsia (p. 315); and infections (p. 159). Sometimes premature labor is purposely induced, as in the case of a fetus who has become infected because of premature rupture of the membranes (see p. 320).

Once premature labor has begun, the decision to allow it to continue or to try to stop it depends on the relative risks of continuing the pregnancy versus those of prematurity. In the case of preeclampsia, for example, the well-being of both mother and baby must be considered. If the life of the preeclamptic mother is in danger, the pregnancy may have to be terminated regardless of risk to the baby. But if the preeclampsia can be brought under control, the decision about delivery can focus on the well-being of the baby — weighing the risks of prematurity against those of remaining in a uterus where the circulation is not functioning properly.

There are at least two good reasons for stopping premature labor. The first and chief reason is to allow the fetus to mature in the most natural environment (assuming, of course, that this particular environment — uterus, placenta, and so on — is nourishing and supporting the fetus). The second reason, is to buy time during which the mother can be given cortisone-like steroid hormones to induce the lungs of the fetus to mature so that they will function adequately at birth. (See discussion of L/S ratio, p. 148.) Steroid injections are spaced twenty-four hours apart. If birth can be delayed for at least these twenty-four hours, the steroids lead to significantly less respiratory distress in infants born between twenty-eight and thirty-two weeks' gestation. The effect lasts for up to seven days after completion of the treatment. Beyond seven days, the protective action is reduced and retreatment is considered if premature labor still seems likely. (Recently, it was also shown that premature babies given steroids suffer less often from a severe and sometimes fatal inflammation of the intestines known as *necrotizing enterocolitis.*)

While a number of drugs have been used to stop labor, ritodrine, which inhibits contraction of the muscles of the uterus is, at this writing, the only drug approved by the U.S. Food and Drug Administration for use in the United States. It is administered intravenously at first, in small amounts which are gradually increased to the maximum safe dose. If labor stops, the drug is given intravenously for twelve more hours, and then orally in larger doses for twenty-four hours. If the uterus remains quiet, a lower dose is administered for as long as it is needed, then discontinued.

Ritodrine has been shown to reduce death rates in premature births by 24 percent, and to decrease the risk for respiratory distress syndrome by 29 percent. Because of its use, a significantly higher percentage of infants reach thirty-six weeks' gestation and a birth weight greater than 2,500 grams.

Side effects of ritodrine include tremors in 10 to 15 percent of the women who are given it, heart palpitations (33 percent), nervousness (5 to 10 percent), and restlessness (5 to 10 percent). No ill effects on the fetus have been observed. While ritodrine is the first FDA-approved drug for treatment of premature labor, it is far from perfect. Research is underway to identify safer and more effective drugs.

Research is now underway to see if monitoring of uterine contractions in high-risk women can detect the early signs of premature labor, thereby allowing prompt treatment. The monitor can be worn by the woman at home and the tracings transmitted to a medical center by phone.

If premature labor cannot or should not be arrested, every effort is made to arrange as safe a birth as possible. Because the premature baby faces increased risks during delivery due to cord compression (see p. 325 on prolapse of the umbilical cord) and other factors, the fetal heart rate is carefully monitored. An episiotomy is often done to minimize compression of the baby's head and soft skull bones. Some doctors also advocate the use of forceps, again to protect the baby's head, though not all doctors agree with this approach.

PREMATURE RUPTURE OF THE MEMBRANES

Premature rupture of the membranes is signified by leaking of amniotic fluid from the vagina prior to the onset of labor. Its cause is not well understood. Smoking (p. 170) and infection (see p. 159) may play a role. The risk of breaking the barrier formed by the amniotic membranes between the sterile intrauterine environment and the vagina where many bacteria reside is that bacteria can enter the uterus to infect both the fetus and the mother.

In most full-term infants, labor follows within hours of the "breaking of waters." Seventy percent of women will be in labor in twelve hours and over 90 percent by twenty-four hours with little to no risk to themselves or their babies. Until recently the general policy in obstetrical centers was to induce labor in those women at term with premature rupture of the membranes who had not gone into spontaneous labor by an arbitrary time, usually twenty-four hours. We have now learned through several studies that for women with unripe cervices, such inductions lead to increased rates of both fetal distress in labor and cesarean sections. They do better if left alone until labor begins on its own or until their cervices ripen to allow a safe induction.

Women with premature rupture of the membranes and ripe cervices can be induced successfully as one option, and most obstetricians recommend this approach. On the other hand, the watch and wait approach may be just as safe in this group as in women with unripe cervices, albeit with some as yet undefined risk of infection. Although this strategy has not been subjected to critical study, it seems reasonable to me that for a variety of reasons some women may choose not to be induced, to monitor themselves for the onset of infection, and to wait until labor begins. This is a choice they must negotiate with their obstetrician or midwife.

When premature rupture of the membranes occurs in a preterm fetus, one less than thirty-seven weeks' gestational age, an individualized decision must be made about whether it is safer to induce labor, attempt to stop labor if it has already begun, or simply to watch and wait. The major risks being weighed are those of infection of fetus and mother versus those of prematurity. Other concerns arise from the adverse effects of reduced amounts of amniotic fluid on the fetus: underdevelopment of the lungs, and deformities of the limbs secondary to prolonged restrictions in their movements.

Diagnostic tests which help to evaluate these risks include analysis of the amniotic fluid for evidence of infection and for the L/S ratio (see p. 148) to determine fetal lung maturity, and the fetal biophysical profile (see p. 141). The currently recommended policy is to induce labor when there is evidence of infection or fetal ill health and otherwise to support the continuation of the pregnancy to allow the fetus to mature (see the discussion of premature labor on p. 318).

If a woman falls into the watchful waiting category, she is followed and follows herself for early development of infection by regular checks of temperature and white blood cell count.

If no signs of infection develop and the leaking of fluid stops, suggesting that the tear has sealed over, women can return home and avoid tub baths and intercourse. If the leaking continues, the women remain in the hospital. If at any time signs of infection develop, labor is induced or a cesarean section is performed.

In caring for a woman with premature rupture of the membranes, vaginal examinations are kept to a minimum to avoid introducing bacteria through the cervix into the uterus. A vaginal speculum examination is performed to confirm the diagnosis of premature rupture, to diagnose infection, and to assess the ripeness of the cervix.

Women who have had premature rupture of the membranes in one pregnancy are at increased risk for a recurrence. Because sexual intercourse may be a factor contributing to premature rupture, it is probably prudent for women who have had such a history to refrain from intercourse after about the twentieth week.

PREMATURE BABIES

By definition, a premature baby is one born before thirty-seven weeks of pregnancy. Since babies less than twenty-four weeks old rarely live, *"preemies,"* as they are commonly called, are those babies born between twenty-four and thirty-seven weeks of gestation. Prematures vary enormously in how well they do and how much special care they require. The majority do very well.

The immediate problems of the sickest and usually smallest prematures include respiratory distress syndrome (difficulty in gas exchange because of fluid and protein accumulations within the small air sacs and collapse of the sacs themselves), difficulty in feeding due to weakness, increased incidence of jaundice and increased sensitivity to its effects (p. 266), increased susceptibility to infection; congenital defects, including those of the heart; danger of bleeding within the brain and the resulting development of hydrocephalus (dilatation of the fluid-filled cavities or ventricles in the brain). The care of these frail babies also can cause problems: the blowing out of a lung overinflated by a respirator (pneumothorax); blindness or impaired vision related at least in part to oxygen therapy, scarring of the lungs due to treatment with a respirator, errors in dosages of drugs and fluids, and so forth.

The smaller and more immature the infant the more long-range problems are encountered: cerebral palsy, mental retardation, learning disorders, and vision, hearing, and speech problems.

There is no question that the best treatment for prematurity is prevention. This is a goal, however, we still have not reached. Short of prevention, improved care for the sickest prematures in special intensive care units has made a major difference in rates of survival and the quality of the lives of the infants who survive.

During the days before neonatal (newborn) intensive care, fewer than 10 percent of babies weighing 1,000 grams (approximately 2 pounds) or less, and only about 50 percent of those weighing 1,000 to 1,500 grams (or 2 to 3 pounds), survived. Since the introduction of neonatal intensive care, reported survival rates have increased greatly. Survival rates of 45 percent or higher have been reported for babies weighing under 1,000 grams; for babies weighing 1,500 grams at birth, reported survival rates have been 80 percent or higher.

Recent data on survival from the Brigham and Women's Hospital in Boston gives an idea of how premature babies fare in the most up-to-date neonatal centers. Very few babies over 1,500 grams (3 pounds) have problems. Of babies between 1,000 and 1,500 grams, less than 10 percent have significant later problems, while 15 to 25 percent of those under 1,000 grams have problems, some of which undoubtedly improve with the passage of time.

One result of modern care is that many infants, who would not have survived in the past, now live on, but with various degrees of handicap. In the case of the smallest premature babies, parents and doctors face an ethical dilemma: whether to intervene and bring all of medicine's impressive technology to bear — with uncertain results, probable prolonged hospitalization, and the chance of saving a severely handicapped baby — or to "let nature take its course" and let the baby die. While there is no simple answer to this question, some neonatal care specialists who deal with the smallest babies encourage taking the cue from the baby, watching it for a short while to see "if it wants to go on or not."

The decision about how far to go in treating a tiny, sick premature is an exceedingly complicated one which unfortunately must often be made quickly under conditions of great stress. There are risks regardless of what is finally decided. If the baby does not do well, and particularly if he or she grows into a handicapped child, parents must live with the responsibility of having made the decision to intervene. If, on the other hand, life support measures are discontinued, the parents will have to accept responsibility for deciding to let the baby die.

The best advice we can give in these pressured situations is that parents request an estimate from the physicians about the probability of survival and the probability of survival with handicap. While each set of parents will deal with such probabilities in their own way, they will be in a better position to make decisions along with the physicians if they have full information on possibilities and actual odds. No decision can be a perfect one — it can only be the best decision that could be made under a particular set of uncertain circumstances. Ideally, parents-to-be should give some serious thought to these issues and how to deal with them before the possibility of confronting them arises. Recent efforts by the federal government may make this difficult problem even more complex. Legislation recently enacted into law prohibits (as "medical neglect") withdrawal of life support except when an infant is doomed to die regardless of medical treatment. This so-called "Baby Doe" legislation is directed to parents as well as to physicians. Just how rigidly this legislation will be implemented remains to be seen.

Present treatment of sick prematures includes a watchful nurse who is of critical importance; intravenous fluids delivered through finely controlled infusion pumps; respirators; monitors for breathing, blood pressure, pulse, and oxygen concentration; radiant heat warmers (or incubators); and feeding tubes. Amidst all of this paraphernalia it may be hard to find the tiny baby. The situation is a very stressful one for the parents, and the staffs of neonatal intensive care units usually try to be sensitive to their needs. They encourage parents to touch the baby, provide liberal visiting hours, support mothers in keeping a supply of milk going through the pumping of breasts and freezing of milk for later use, and make themselves available twenty-four hours a day by phone. They make every effort to include parents in making decisions. Nevertheless, the time that a premature must spend in an intensive care unit until he or she is out of danger and begins to progress is usually fraught with anxiety and concern.

If the baby does well and the tube feedings can be discontinued, mothers can start to nurse their infants. Many such mothers make several visits daily for this purpose and bring milk pumped at home to use when they cannot be present to nurse the baby themselves.

After discharge, the prematures who have been the smallest and sickest will need periodic evaluations by a team of specialists such as pediatricians, neonatologists, ophthalmologists, and psychologists, to monitor for handicaps and intervene as early as possible to arrest or minimize them.

Prolapse of the Umbilical Cord

Prolapse (or falling through) of the umbilical cord into the vagina is a true obstetrical emergency. The cord may be trapped and compressed between the baby and the cervix, cutting off blood flow to the placenta and the fetus. The fetus can be endangered and even die from such a catastrophe.

Prolapse of the cord is more likely when the fetus does not fit snugly into the lower part of the uterus. Circumstances in which this occurs include: breech presentation (p. 271), prematurity (p. 318), twins (p. 331), disproportion (p. 293), and situations in which the amniotic membranes rupture (or are ruptured) before the head or other presenting part has occupied the lower portion of the uterus near the entrance to the vagina.

Cord prolapse can be detected by actually feeling the loops of the cord protruding from the cervix into the vagina. The fetal heart rate is usually depressed. In emergency treatment for cord prolapse, the woman assumes a knees-to-chest position with her buttocks up, on her knees with her chest near or on the bed. This position takes advantage of gravity to shift the fetus higher into the uterus away from the cervix.

This may allow room for the cord to drop back into the uterus, or at the very least, take pressure off it. To achieve the same objectives, the attendant can place a hand in the vagina to push the fetus up higher and work the cord back into the uterus.

Depending upon the circumstances and the well-being of the fetus once a prolapsed cord is replaced, the woman may continue labor to delivery vaginally. In most situations, however, cesarean sections are performed because of the high likelihood of repeated prolapse.

Shoulder Dystocia

Shoulder dystocia refers to a baby's shoulders getting stuck during delivery. The upper shoulder can be trapped behind the symphysis pubis. The diagnosis is made if the contraction following the birth of the head fails to result in the birth of the rest of the baby. It is a very worrisome development, one which can be fatal in certain rare cases. The size of the baby in relation to the pelvic outlet is the major determining factor. Large babies such as those of diabetic or very overweight mothers are at increased risk. Recent studies suggest that ultrasound is useful in identifying the baby suspected of being very large so that a cesarean section can be performed and shoulder dystocia avoided entirely.

There are several turning maneuvers that can be performed to dislodge the shoulders and move them off dead center. These are usually done while applying pressure to the top of the uterus and to the uterus above the pubic bone to push the baby down. Drawing the woman's thighs up onto her abdomen may help increase the size of the outlet, as will squatting, which has the added advantage of bringing gravity into play as well, increasing the effectiveness of the woman's own pushing. An episiotomy is also necessary.

The asphyxia associated with prolonged cord compression during shoulder dystocia may lead the infant to begin breathing movements prior to actual birth, with the danger of sucking amniotic fluid and mucus from his mouth and upper airways into his lungs. For this reason, standard practice in cases of shoulder dystocia is to suction the baby's mouth as soon as this diagnosis is suspected.

Stillbirth

While most miscarriages occur during the first trimester, fetal death can occur at any time right up to and during labor itself. Causes include intrauterine growth retardation (see p. 301), accidents to the umbilical cord (p. 325), preeclampsia (p. 315), diabetes (p. 167), smoking (p. 170), or placental abruption (p. 312). These deaths may occur before or during labor. High-risk fetuses deserve careful testing before and during labor (see p. 130).

In a 1980 study from the Boston Hospital for Women, involving about 17,000 pregnancies of over thirty-seven weeks, there were sixty-four deaths. Lethal congenital birth defects accounted for fifteen, while thirty-two were normally formed infants who died from asphyxia. The remaining deaths were from other miscellaneous causes. The asphyxiated group is the focus of much attention, because these fetal deaths theoretically could have been prevented using presently available technology. Of this group, twenty-one died before labor, three in labor, and eight following labor. At least in theory, the largest group, that in which the deaths occurred prior to labor, could have been spotted before it was too late, but in practice many of the affected pregnancies showed no obvious signs of trouble. On the basis of findings like these, some obstetricians now argue that all pregnancies should be screened with non-stress or contraction stress tests in order to identify the approximately 1.6 per thousand fetuses in danger of dying before birth, as well as those likely to experience trouble in labor. While the cost of such screening would be great, the result could be fewer fetal deaths or handicaps due to asphyxia. However, given the limitations of our present methods of testing, it is also true that many more unnecessary cesarean sections would also be performed. More accurate tests are the answer. Death can also occur at the instant of birth, if, for example, the shoulders are trapped in the birth canal (p. 325) or the cord is compressed during the birth of the head of a breech baby (p. 271). Apart from occurring prior to birth, deaths can occur at various times after birth as well. The most common cause of such post-delivery deaths is prematurity.

Deaths before birth are called *intrauterine deaths* or *stillborns*. Fetal death after the eighteenth or twentieth week is usually suspected by the woman herself who no longer perceives fetal movement. The absence of growth of the uterus is another clue. Death is confirmed by a failure to detect the fetal heart tone either by fetoscope or by ultrasound; by a decrease, loss, or failure of increase of chorionic gonadotropin; and by lack of fetal growth as determined by ultrasound.

If a fetus has died and labor has not occurred, there are good reasons to bring about delivery promptly. Women commonly experience severe psychological problems in carrying a dead fetus. And, especially after several weeks have passed, absorption of the dissolved fetal tissue into the mother's blood can cause widespread and harmful clotting of her blood.

If a death has occurred in the third trimester, labor can often be induced with oxytocin. In the second trimester, when the uterus is relatively unresponsive to stimulation, several choices exist. A D. and E. (dilation and evacuation) may still be effective. Alternatively, contractions can be stimulated by injecting salt solution or the hormone prostaglandin with or without urea into the amniotic fluid. Prostaglandin can also be administered as a vaginal suppository or intravenously. The cervix can be "ripened" through the use of laminaria (a type of seaweed) which is inserted into it and allowed to swell, stretching the cervix open. Combinations of these approaches can also be used. They are the same techniques used when abortion is desired, because of a chromosomal defect, for example, or a serious nontreatable malformation.

The most common complications of the intrauterine injection of saline solution are retained placenta and blood loss. Less common complications include fever, uterine infection, and cervical tears. A D. and E. has few complications, but cannot always be used.

Complications of the use of prostaglandins include intrauterine infection, especially when the membranes have been prematurely ruptured; hemorrhage; and tears of the cervix. Almost all women who take prostaglandins, whether by injection into the uterus or by suppository, develop nausea, vomiting, and diarrhea, and some develop fever. Medication can be given to counteract these side effects.

When abortion is induced with prostaglandins or salt solution, about ten per 100,000 procedures result in death (1970s data) compared with 5.5 for D. and E.'s. Any woman who is to undergo these procedures should find out the outcome statistics of the doctor with whom she is dealing.

If the fetus cannot be delivered through the induction of labor because of some mechanical problem (such as a placenta praevia or cephalopelvic disproportion), a cesarean section (p. 278) may be necessary.

After the birth of a stillborn child, the risk of future stillbirths, postnatal death, and handicaps in surviving infants is more than doubled. In the case of two stillbirths, the combined risk increases fivefold and affects one-third of subsequent fetuses. The more that can be learned about a stillbirth, or early fetal death, from autopsy study and chromosomal analysis, the more information can be given to the parents to guide them in future pregnancies.

EMOTIONAL AFTEREFFECTS OF STILLBIRTH

The reaction of the parents to a stillbirth largely depends on the gestational age of the pregnancy and their own individual personalities. The closer to the predicted time of birth, the more likely they are to have identified with the fetus as a full-fledged human being.

In recent years investigators have paid great attention to how people cope with loss and death. They have identified some principles that can be helpful to those who mourn. They also can help attendants — physicians, nurses, midwives, labor coaches, and childbirth educators — to understand better how they can be most helpful to a grieving couple.

The guiding principles in coping with a death include dealing with the reality of the situation, fully communicating feelings, beliefs, and fantasies, and using others appropriately for support.

Parents are encouraged (but not required) to look at, talk to, and hold the dead baby, even one with deformities and even after autopsy if not before, and to be alone with him if they so wish. Photographs may be useful for later recall, to help make the unbelievable real again, as may retrieved locks of hair or pieces of clothing. Naming the child can also help concretize the reality of the baby's having been alive. Crying is healthy and should be fully accepted, not denigrated or suppressed.

The decision to obtain an autopsy and chromosomal studies must be made quickly. Both procedures are desirable, to provide information about the cause of death (and thereby remove fantasies about it) and to provide important information for future pregnancies. The medical examiner should be contacted when a death occurs out of hospital; he or she may request an autopsy as a matter of course. The parents should expect that the attendants will share the findings of the autopsy with them as soon as they are made available.

The parents should be encouraged to hold a simple funeral, memorial service, burial, or cremation, even if they would not otherwise be motivated to do so on religious or philosophical grounds. The funeral as rite of passage makes death real and allows the couple to experience the sympathy and support of friends and relatives. Funeral services for infants are generally not expensive.

Bereaved parents should be aware of the physical and psychological elements of normal grieving. These include unusual physical sensations such as headache and chest pain; the welling up of intensely sad feelings, especially during the first few weeks and for up to a year or more after the death; a recurrent bizarre experience of believing that the baby is still alive; and the fear of angry feelings that the parents may direct toward themselves, each other, the attendants, and others. In one typical study, over 50 percent of parents who had lost a baby experienced anger, guilt, irritability, loss of appetite, preoccupation with the death, difficulty in sleeping, and intense sadness.

Parents should talk with each other about their feelings, listening to each other at length. Most will need to discuss the events surrounding the death many, many times before resolving their grief. If one parent is reminded of the dead baby by any association (a toy, an anniversary, the birth of a friend's baby), it should be shared with the other parent as well.

Bereaved parents also need to pay careful attention to the needs of their own children. It does not help to hide sad feelings from children. Being honest about one's own feelings helps children express themselves and deal with their own conflicted feelings. Parents should listen carefully to a child's reactions, reaching for the deeper meaning underlying the words and behavior. Often, a young child will see herself as the cause of the death. Such self-blame in young children is not unlike that of the parents themselves. Parents commonly search their own actions and thoughts for a possible cause of the death, such as initial feelings of ambivalence toward the pregnancy, failure to stop smoking, or a cavalier approach to nutrition or other preventive issues. Parents need to accept the child's feelings fully while supplying the necessary corrective information: "It may feel that the baby died because you didn't want us to have him, but the way you felt had nothing to do with it." By helping a child in this way, the parent can clarify his or her own responses and also strengthen family relationships.

Ideally, the parents should meet with the attendants at the time of the death and several days later. Questions about procedures at the time of birth and their effects — what was or was not done — should be answered fully. Other family members who may want to join the second meeting should be welcomed. A third meeting to review the death and mourning should be planned for three to six months later. The results of the autopsy are shared with the parents when they are received, which is another opportunity to ask questions.

Support groups for bereaved parents now exist in many communities and can be a great help. Childbirth education organizations, such as the local affiliates of the ICEA, can direct parents to such groups. (See Appendix B for addresses and Appendix D for books that might help.)

In certain hospitals bereavement teams are being established. For example, at University Hospital in Stony Brook, New York, where one of the authors works, this team consists of a nurse, neonatologist, social worker, pathologist, and psychiatrist.

Parents are usually advised not to plan another baby until they complete their mourning, which means waiting, on the average, six months to a year after the death before conceiving another child. Women in particular may have an intense desire to have another baby immediately in the belief that their pain and feelings of emptiness will thereby be relieved. It may be preferable not to act on such impulses but to wait and then plan for a new baby who will have an identity of his or her own. However, individual differences in psychology and physical factors such as advancing age of the parents play a large role in these decisions. Parents, while respecting and considering the advice of others, should act on their own well-considered and heartfelt intentions.

Twins and Other Multiple Pregnancies

The thought of twins probably crosses the mind of every pregnant woman and her partner, and with good reason for twins are not uncommon. About one out of 250 births, regardless of ethnic background, will involve *identical* or *monozygotic* twins, those who originate from a single fertilized egg which later divides into two equal halves. The frequency of twins involving more than one egg fertilized during a single ovulation, the so-called *fraternal* or *dizygotic* twins, is more variable and depends on a number of factors. In Caucasians, the incidence of fraternal twins is about one in 100; in blacks, one in 79, in Japanese, one in 155. Being a twin oneself increases your chances of bearing or fathering twins.

The age of the mother also affects multiple births: the older the mother the greater her chances. A Swedish study showed that, in first pregnancies, multiple births occurred 1.27 percent of the time compared with 2.67 percent in fourth pregnancies.

A higher rate of twinning is reported in women who conceive within one month of stopping birth control pills, but this does not hold for subsequent months. The drugs and hormones used to promote ovulation in cases of infertility are notorious in producing multiple ovulations and conceptions. Following hormone treatment, multiple pregnancy may occur as often as 20 to 40 percent of the time. One study showed that, after administration of the drug clomiphene to induce ovulation, 6.9 percent of the resulting pregnancies were twins; 0.5 percent, triplets; 0.3 percent, quadruplets; and 0.13 percent, quintuplets. Another study of clomiphene effects showed the rate of occurrence of multiple fetuses to be 13 percent. For reasons we do not know, however, there seems to be an overall drop in recent years in the frequency of dizygotic twinning.

The figures quoted for twinning have to do with percentages of babies born. Now that ultrasound has been used to study the course of pregnancies, it is clear that the actual frequency of twin conceptions is much higher, with only one of the fetuses generally surviving to birth. In one study, twin fetuses were identified in thirty women in the first trimester, but only fourteen eventually gave birth to two infants. Eleven of the remaining sixteen gave birth to a single baby and an undeveloped one (blighted ovum), while four others had twin blighted ova and one had a blighted ovum and a miscarriage.

Determining whether twins are mono- or dizygotic (identical or fraternal) is more than a matter of mere curiosity. In this era of human organ transplantation, knowing who can donate to whom can be of critical importance. In all but the rarest instances, careful examination of the placenta or placentas helps to make this distinction. For this reason, great care should be exercised in delivering the placentas of twins intact with the membranes attached.

A common feature of the placentas of monozygotic twins is communication between the blood vessels of one placenta and the other, permitting an admixture of blood. A possible result is that one fetus can have too much of the combined blood while the other receives too little. Depending on degree, this imbalance can harm each of the babies in its own way. The baby with decreased blood volume can be runted (see p. 301 on intrauterine growth disturbance), hypotensive (have low blood pressure), and have an underdeveloped heart, while the twin with the excess blood volume can be larger, but subject to heart failure, abnormal clotting of its blood, and the increased likelihood for developing jaundice. The survival of both may be threatened at birth. If one baby has died in utero, the dissolving of the tissues of the dead fetus may liberate materials into the joined circulations, which can lead to clotting of the blood of the other twin, often with grave consequences. Because of the occurrence of these blood vessel connections in twins, it is very important that the cord of the first born be clamped immediately before the second is delivered. Otherwise the blood of the second can dangerously drain off through the cord of the first. Although the path to birth of twins is full of stumbling blocks, modern obstetrics is happily able to clear away many of the obstacles, or at least push them aside.

From the very outset, the twin fetuses are at increased risk. In one study, the average gestational age of twins at birth was thirty-five weeks compared to thirty-nine weeks for singletons. With triplets, the average age at birth was thirty-three weeks; with quadruplets, only twenty-nine weeks. Twins are more than twice as likely as singletons to be affected with major and minor birth defects. Despite these odds, however, let us emphasize that most twins do just fine, especially since our ability to deal with premature infants has undergone such steady improvement.

The mothers of twins are at increased risk for such complications of pregnancy as preeclampsia (p. 315), anemia, hemorrhage at delivery, and hydramnios (p. 300); and such complications of labor as premature labor (p. 318), prolonged labor, non-vertex fetal presentation, and prolapse of the umbilical cord (p. 325). Thus, pregnancies involving twins deserve special handling in all respects.

The mother of twins needs to eat for three people, not just two. Her caloric intake should increase by 300 calories per day and she should take 60 to 80 milligrams of supplemental iron. Folic acid needs are also increased. These can be met through either diet or supplementation.

There is some evidence that bed rest is beneficial in twin pregnancies, prolonging the pregnancy and reducing fetal growth impairment. In one Swedish study of low-income women, rest at home until the twenty-ninth week was prescribed when twins were identified through routine ultrasound examination during the second trimester. Hospitalization was encouraged at twenty-nine weeks. If undelivered at thirty-six weeks, and all else was normal, the women were discharged from the hospital. With few exceptions, the pregnancies were not allowed to go beyond thirty-eight weeks. The perinatal mortality rate of twins cared for this way was identical to that of single births, 0.6 percent, whereas for twin pregnancies not cared for in this way it was 17.5 times higher (10.5 percent). Other studies of bed rest show neither these dramatic differences nor, for that matter, any other significant differences. Given this uncertain data, we cannot recommend bed rest as a generally useful measure and suggest reviewing this issue with your doctor or midwife.

The problems surrounding twins do not end once labor has begun. As already discussed, complications of labor in multiple pregnancies are notorious. A decision will have to be made about vaginal versus cesarean delivery. There is general agreement that cesarean section is the preferred route if the presenting part of one or both fetuses is a part other than the head (for example, breech); especially if the first baby to be delivered is either unusually large or small or the umbilical cord prolapses. A particularly tricky period in vaginal delivery follows the birth of the first twin.

Ideally, twins should be identified prior to labor and delivery so that appropriate plans can be made. More help is needed at such a birth to deal with the unexpected, and more help is needed afterward to care for the babies.

Ultrasound is the most effective way of diagnosing twins early in pregnancy and can demonstrate the separate gestational sacs as early as the sixth to tenth weeks. The increasingly routine use of ultrasound in pregnancies has resulted in a higher percentage of twin pregnancies being identified early.

One dividend of testing for alpha fetoprotein in the second trimester (p. 59) is the identification of twins, for the presence of more than one fetus is one cause of persistent elevated maternal alpha fetoprotein levels.

In the complicated situation of twins suspected of having neural tube or other serious congenital defects, amniocentesis must be done on both sacs to determine whether one or both of the twins are affected. The same can be said of twins at high risk for chromosomal abnormalities, such as those carried by mothers who are thirty-five or older, or whose parents are known carriers of genetic diseases. Both twins need to be studied by amniocentesis and cell culture.

Twins are suspected, of course, when the size of the uterus is larger than would be expected on the basis of gestational age. This finding warrants an explanation that includes checking for twins with ultrasound. (Other explanations for a large uterus include an error in dating the pregnancy, hydramnios (p. 300), fibroid tumors of the uterus (p. 74), and, late in pregnancy, a large baby.)

Late in the second trimester, and throughout the third trimester, it is possible to identify twins by palpation of the uterus and to hear two distinct fetal heartbeats. There are two separate sites on the abdomen where the heart tones can be heard equally well. The rates are unequal, each beating at a different rate, as recorded by two observers listening and counting simultaneously.

Twins complicate the already difficult issue of therapeutic abortion. In conditions where abortion might be performed for an abnormal fetus, as in the case of Down syndrome (p. 125), the presence of a normal twin, along with the chromosomally abnormal one, creates a dilemma, because routine abortion procedures would lead to the loss of both. There is at least one report of selective termination of the life of an abnormal twin. In this ethically controversial procedure, the heart of the fetus was punctured with a needle guided through the uterus using ultrasound visualization, resulting in its death. The normal twin in the case went on to develop, be born, and survive without difficulties.

Women expecting twins should plan for more help at home in the early months. Not only will they want time to recover from the extra strain on their bodies, but twins take more time to feed, to bathe, and to enjoy. Once the adjustment has been made, and the hurdle of a more complicated birth is past, parents may be delighted and proud of producing two babies after only one pregnancy and labor.

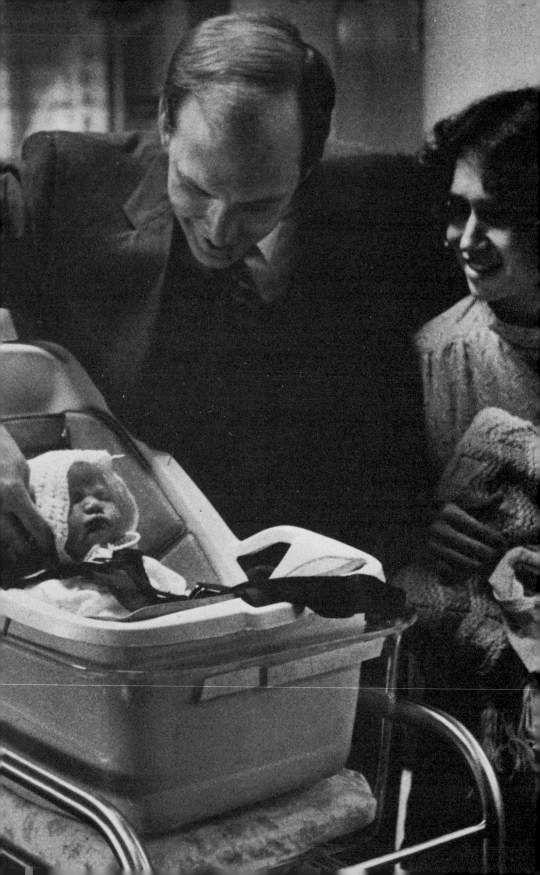

Statistics on Home, Birthing Center, and Hospital Birth

Great Britain saw a dramatic shift from predominantly home to predominantly hospital delivery after 1958. The benefits of hospital care are said to be reflected in the fact that the overall stillbirth rate for hospital delivery in England and Wales has fallen in recent years, while the stillbirth rate for home delivery infants has not. However, this may be due to the greater number of uncomplicated deliveries now taking place in the hospital, and to improved methods of treating the complicated conditions that occur among hospital births.

Other British studies cast considerable doubt on whether increased hospitalization has brought about improved outcomes. One study, surveying maternal and neonatal outcomes between 1965 and 1974, found, even after correcting for the higher concentration of risk factors in hospital births, no evidence that the move from home to hospital brought about a decrease in the perinatal mortality rate (deaths around the time of birth). In response to these data, and to consumer demand, there has been a small swing back to home birth in Great Britain.

The best natural laboratory for home birth outcome research is the Netherlands, where national health policy, a noninterventive philosophy of birth, and an excellent support system have enabled mid-

Portions of Appendix A are adapted from Sagov, Stanley E.; Feinbloom, Richard I.; Spindel, Peggy; and Brodsky, Archie. *Home Birth: A Practitioner's Guide to Birth Outside the Hospital*. Rockville, Md.: Aspen Systems Corporation, 1984.

wives and general practitioners to continue to attend almost half the nation's births at home. A study which analyzed data compiled by the Central Bureau of Statistics found no significant differences in outcomes between cities with almost 100 percent hospital births and cities of similar demography with only a 50 percent rate of hospital births.

Between 1960 and 1977 the proportion of deliveries in the Netherlands occurring in the home declined from 70 to 40 percent. Some observers attributed the decreasing perinatal mortality rate in Holland to this change. As in other Western industrialized countries, however, these improvements are attributable primarily to advances in public health, secondarily to improved prenatal and postnatal care, and only slightly to improved perinatal care.

Home birth in the Netherlands has a beneficial effect on that nation's entire system of obstetric care. Through the repeated experience and highly visible model of successful normal births in the home, as well as through the prominent role of midwives in hospitals as well as at home, a philosophy of nonintervention in maternity care (relative to other countries) is maintained even for hospital births. The incidence of cesarean section in the Netherlands was 2.0 percent in 1969, 3.0 percent in 1975, and 5.0 percent in 1980. In the United States the rate was 5.3 percent in 1969, 10.2 percent in 1975, and 15.2 percent in 1978. Although the rate of forceps delivery (see below) in the United States is declining as that of cesarean section rises, in 1975 it was still 33.5 percent compared with 4.9 percent in the Netherlands.

Cross-cultural comparisons between the Netherlands and other Western European countries such as Britain and West Germany also show no significant differences in outcomes, and strongly suggest that site is not a decisive factor in the outcome of birth. Studies comparing outcomes in America with those in countries like Norway and Sweden, which also have virtually 100 percent hospitalization for birth, yet have much lower perinatal mortality rates, have identified what does seem to be the most decisive factor — birth weight. The best hope for reducing perinatal mortality in the United States lies in reducing the proportion of low birth weight, high risk infants. This conclusion is echoed even in American studies of the beneficial effects of obstetric interventions. (Seen in this light, the current controversy about site may be a diversion from the real issue — prenatal prevention and the early identification of premature and other low birth weight deliveries.)

Data on out-of-hospital birth in the United States are available not only for home birth but also for freestanding birth centers such as that run by the Maternity Center Association of New York City. A report prepared for the U.S. Federal Trade Commission concluded that, during its first five years of operation (1975–1980), the Association's Childbearing Center had maintained a high standard of safety and offered low cost, high quality care, while exerting a positive influence on obstetric care in the New York area and the nation as a whole. In 1981 the Center had its 1,000th birth with overall results that could not be faulted in any serious way. A 1982 study of almost 2,000 labors in eleven such freestanding centers, each staffed by nurse–midwives with a noninterventive philosophy, yielded similar findings. Of the women who began labor at one of the centers, 5 percent had forceps deliveries and 5 percent had cesarean sections at a backup hospital. Apgar scores of 7–10 (see p. 229) were recorded for 93 percent of the infants at one minute and for 95 percent at five minutes. The neonatal death rate was 4.6 per thousand live births including transfers, and 3.0 per thousand excluding transfers. In a 1983 study, the neonatal death rate was 2.4 per thousand including transfers and 0.45 per thousand excluding transfers. Of a total of over 10,000 women in 97 centers, 13.8 percent were transferred.

A freestanding birth center is like a home birth service. Well-trained personnel follow strict screening and clinical procedures. Birth centers offer clients an established institutional reputation for safety, sparing them the necessity of evaluating the credentials of individual attendants or doctors. The birth center may also have marginal advantages. Procedures are routine and physical layout is set up for the convenience and familiarity of the attendants. But, since the center is not equipped for major obstetric emergencies, its procedures, including those pertaining to transfer to hospital, must be approximately the same as those observed in the home. It is reasonable to expect, then, that competently managed home birth services can duplicate the impressive safety record of the birth centers.

A highly successful and well-known example of a home birth service in America is the Frontier Nursing Service in Kentucky. The people it has served since 1925 have not been ideal candidates for home birth. They tend to be geographically isolated, inbred, impoverished, and under-educated. Yet the Service, whose nurse-midwives attended nearly all births at home until the late 1960s, has had fetal, infant, and maternal illness and mortality rates that compare favorably with those of middle-class Americans. Beginning in 1953, the Frontier Nursing Service has compiled a record of more than 10,000 births over a quarter of a century without a single maternal death. A recent increase in hospital deliveries by the Service (due in part to

Medicaid eligibility) has been associated with increased rates of intervention, but no significant improvement in outcome.

In a well-known matched comparison study by Dr. Louis Mehl and his colleagues (completed in 1976), 1,046 women who had planned a home birth (including 12 percent who transferred to hospitals during labor) were individually matched against an equal number of women who had planned to deliver in a hospital, for maternal age, number of previous pregnancies, educational level, socioeconomic status, length of pregnancy, and risk factor score prior to beginning of labor. This study is not the same as a randomized clinical trial, because the women chose where they would have their babies; and this choice may in and of itself represent a major difference between the groups or may be related to other major, hitherto unrecognized, differences. Other methodological problems make the study more suggestive than conclusive. There were no significant differences between the two groups in birth weight, perinatal mortality, neurological abnormalities, or other major complications. However, almost every type of obstetric intervention (including Pitocin, episiotomy, forceps delivery, cesarean section, and anesthesia) was employed more frequently in the planned hospital births. These hospital births also showed a significantly higher rate of complications, such as third- and fourth-degree perineal tears (despite more episiotomies), fetal distress, hypertension, and preeclampsia, shoulder dystocia, postpartum hemorrhage, respiratory distress syndrome, birth injuries, and neonatal sepsis. Overall, the planned hospital births showed a higher rate of need for resuscitation and more noncongenital neonatal complications than the planned home births. The home birth group showed more bleeding during delivery, more cases of posterior delivery (accepted as a normal variant by home birth attendants), and more second-stage dystocia (that is, delay of descent in the birth canal after full cervical dilatation). None of these home complications is associated with poor outcomes for mother or baby.

It should be pointed out that much has changed since 1976. A number of the practices that characterize the hospital group in this study have come under review. Many hospitals have become much more supportive of normal labor and more careful about intervention. Were the study repeated today, it is likely that the observed differences would be less pronounced.

Other studies (also by Dr. Mehl) have focused on the various types of home birth practitioners, particularly unlicensed lay midwives. A matched comparison of 421 home births attended by noncertified midwives, judged by the investigators to be experienced and knowledgeable, with an equal number of hospital births attended by physicians yielded better outcomes for the midwives. When only the less interventionist half of the physicians were compared with the midwives, however, few significant differences were found. An analysis of all out-of-hospital births recorded in Oregon in 1977 found that, while 19 percent of unlicensed attendants reported births with no prenatal care, a majority of these were fathers and fellow members of religious communities. All of the clients of lay midwives had prenatal care, 71 percent beginning in the first trimester. The neonatal and infant death rates for out-of-hospital births were lower than those for all births in Oregon and in the United States in the same year, while the incidence of full-term fetal deaths, although twice as high as that for all full-term births in Oregon, was still a relatively low 6.0 per thousand. Given that births attended by unlicensed, and in some cases unskilled, attendants were included, the outcomes for midwife-attended births are probably better.

In 1978 a news release by the American College of Obstetricians and Gynecologists (ACOG) (a leading and powerful opponent of home birth) claimed, on the basis of data from eleven state health departments, that the risk to a baby's life was two to five times greater in an out-of-hospital birth than a hospital birth. The media exposure given this announcement was, in our opinion, undeserved and unfortunate. Lumped together in the "out-of-hospital" category, along with elective home births, were many late miscarriages, premature and precipitous (i.e., unplanned) deliveries, and unattended home births. In California, for example, birth weight statistics indicate that two-thirds of the out-of-hospital deaths were premature deliveries.

As a corrective to such misuse of data, a major study of home births in North Carolina during 1974 through 1976, conducted by the U.S. Center for Disease Control in Atlanta, demonstrated the importance of eliminating confounding variables in comparisons between sites. This study concluded that "deliveries occurring at home ranged from lowest to highest risk of neonatal mortality depending on planning and the attendant present." Neonatal mortality rates were three per thousand live births for planned home births attended by a lay midwife, thirty per thousand for planned home births without a lay midwife, and 120 per thousand for unplanned home births. (Mortality figures for full-term infants born in a hospital can be as low as one per thousand, as discussed below.)

Pooled data from a family group practice in Cambridge, Massachusetts and the obstetrical practice of two physicians in Fresno, California, using similar screening procedures (including a requirement of twenty minutes or less driving time to backup hospitals), involved 875 women seeking home birth. Data on transfers and outcomes for this group are presented in Table A-1. The overall picture is encouraging, with no maternal deaths, modest rates of transfer and intervention, and few major complications. Birth weight clustered in the 6–8 pound range. Most of the infants born at home

Table A-1. Outcomes of Planned Home Births

	Number	Rate per 1,000 Labors Begun at Home
Total number of women seeking home birth	875	
Lost to follow-up (moved, transferred)	69	
Continued prenatal care	806	
Changed to planned hospital before labor	79	
Began labor at home	727	
Transfers during labor	56	
Postpartum transfers	17	
Maternal	10	
Neonatal	7	
Planned and completed without transfer	654	
Home births	671	
Stillbirths (see text)	6*	8.25
Before labor	4	5.50
During labor	2	2.75
Live home births	666	
Cesarean sections	22	30.26 (3.0%)
Maternal deaths	0	

*One stillbirth occurred in hospital.

Source: Family Practice Group, Cambridge, Mass., and David Dowis, M.D., and Janet Dowis, M.D., Fresno, Calif.

had Apgar scores (a less objective measure) of 8–10 at one minute (85.2 percent) and at five minutes (97.3 percent).

However, the stillbirth rate of 8.25 per thousand labors begun at home is higher than in other studies. Three of the six stillbirths were predelivery fetal deaths discovered in early labor (having occurred after the last prenatal examination from one day to one week earlier) and took place within one four-month period in the California practice. The stillbirth rate declined as more births were added. These three deaths, along with a similar fatality in the Massachusetts sample, had occurred by the time the birth attendant arrived — without delay — at the home and thus presumably before the woman would have chosen to go to the hospital had she planned to deliver there. In one case vasa praevia (a variant of placenta praevia; see p. 312) was identified as a probable cause, while no cause was established in the other three cases.

All four were judged not to have been site related or preventable. The fifth and sixth stillbirths might have been site related. The fifth occurred because of fetal-placental insufficiency (inadequate supply of oxygen to the fetus) after a prolonged pregnancy of 43.5 weeks (see p. 314). Post-term antenatal screening (urine estriol determination and non-stress tests) failed to predict the problem. Although this birth would have occurred in the hospital according to the subsequently revised protocol in this practice, clinical experience and a review of the literature do not support the contention that electronic fetal monitoring would have reliably prevented the stillbirth. Therefore, it cannot be said conclusively to have been site related. The other stillbirth occurred in a first pregnancy breech birth after extensive counseling in which attendants explained the risks and advised a hospital birth. When the couple announced their intention to deliver at home with or without professional assistance, the attendants agreed to attend the birth. In the presence of two doctors and two nurses, a stillborn infant who failed to respond to resuscitation measures was delivered. Since electronic fetal monitoring or elective cesarean section might have saved this baby, this death may be regarded as site related, as anticipated by the attendants when they strongly recommended hospital delivery. In all, only two of the six stillbirths in the Cambridge-Fresno series may have been site related.

Studies in two leading academic centers in Boston have shown that perinatal death rates for term infants can be reduced to very low levels — in one study one per thousand low-risk newborns; in the other study 0.43 per thousand during labor, along with 1.79 per thousand before labor and 1.3 per thousand deaths shortly after birth. In the second study the combined death rate during labor and after delivery for normally formed term infants was approximately one per thousand. These outcomes, achieved in two of the finest obstetric centers in the world, cannot be taken as representative of the hospital site generally, nor are they directly comparable with the home birth data reported here, since the study populations are not numerically equal and were not matched for comparison. It is, however, worth noting that, even with four of the six stillbirths in the Cambridge-Fresno sample classified as predelivery (since the fetal heart was not heard in labor despite the attendants' prompt response), the stillbirth rate during delivery for this home birth sample was 2.75 per thousand, low but still over twice that reported in Boston for hospital-delivered full-term infants.

The in-hospital population closest to a carefully screened home birth group is the one eligible to use the alternative birthing rooms in university hospitals. In this setting it is significant that about 25 percent of "low-risk" mothers have to be transferred out of the birthing room because of untoward developments in labor, according to the criteria used. This statistic further fuels the concern of obstetricians about the safety of home delivery. How to relate this in-hospital observation to the experience in the home is unclear, but it is a point worth noting and taking seriously.

MAKING AN INFORMED DECISION
ABOUT BIRTH SITE

In general, the studies surveyed yield reassuring findings about the safety of birth both in and out of hospitals. Nature has endowed human reproduction with good chances for success, and adequate prenatal care helps these prospects and allows for identifying most births that will require serious technical intervention. Competent attendants and appropriate use of technology at birth further improve the odds. Differences in safety between the out-of-hospital and hospital sites appear to be statistically very small. Nonetheless, any unnecessary loss of life is cause for deep concern and raises ethical issues for all those involved.

Support and Professional Organizations*

Aiding a Mother Experiencing Neonatal Death (AMEND)
c/o Mrs. Maureen Connelly, Coordinator
4325 Berrywick Terrace
St. Louis, Missouri 63128

American Academy of Family Physicians
1740 West 92nd Street
Kansas City, Missouri 64114

American Academy of Husband-Coached Childbirth (AAHCC)
Box 5224
Sherman Oaks, California 91413
(Information on the Bradley Method)

American Academy of Pediatrics
141 Northwest Point Road
P.O. Box 927
Elk Grove Village, Illinois 60007

American College of Nurse Midwives (ACNM)
1522 K Street, N.W., Suite 1120
Washington, D.C. 20005

American College of Obstetricians and Gynecologists (ACOG)
600 Maryland Avenue, S.W., No. 300
Washington, D.C. 20024

---

*Where aims and resources are not clear from the name of the organization, a few words of description are given.

American Foundation for Maternal and Child Health
300 Beekman Place
New York, New York 10022
(Clearinghouse for research on the perinatal period)

American Society for Psychoprophylaxis in Obstetrics (ASPO/LAMAZE)
1840 Wilson Blvd., No. 204
Arlington, Virginia 22201

Association for Childbirth at Home, International (ACHI)
P.O. Box 39498
Los Angeles, California 90039

Boston Women's Health Book Collective
465 Mt. Auburn Street
Watertown, Massachusetts 02172
(Publications include *Our Bodies, Ourselves*, the newly revised classic of the women's health movement)

Center for Science in the Public Interest
1757 S Street, N.W.
Washington, D.C. 20009
(Environmental and nutritional issues)

Center for the Study of Multiple Birth
333 East Superior Street, Suite 463–5
Chicago, Illinois 60611

Compassionate Friends
P.O. Box 1347
Oak Brook, Illinois 60521
(Self-help group for those experiencing the death of a baby)

COPE
(Coping with the Overall Pregnancy/Parenting Experience)
37 Clarendon Street
Boston, Massachusetts 02116

C/SEC inc. (CESAREANS/SUPPORT EDUCATION and CONCERN)
22 Forest Road
Framingham, Massachusetts 01701
(Emotional support and information on cesarean births and vaginal birth after cesarean (VBAC))

Environmental Defense Fund
475 Park Avenue, South
New York, New York 10016

Friends of the Earth
620 C Street, SE
Washington, D.C. 20003

HOME
(Home-Oriented Maternity Experience)
P.O. Box 450
Germantown, Maryland 20874

International Childbirth Education Association (ICEA)
P.O. Box 20048
Minneapolis, Minnesota 55420

La Leche League International, Inc.
9616 Minneapolis Avenue
Franklin Park, Illinois 60131
(Information, education, and support for breast-feeding)

The March of Dimes
P.O. Box 2000
White Plains, New York 10602
(Information and research on
genetics, genetic counseling,
and birth defects)

Maternity Center Association
48 East 92nd Street
New York, New York 10028
(A well-known freestanding
birth center with information
and advocacy functions)

**Midwives Alliance of North
America (MANA)**
c/o Concord Midwifery Service
30 South Main Street
Concord, New Hampshire
03301
(Nurse and lay midwives in
the United States and Canada)

**Mothers Against Drunk
Driving (MADD)**
669 Airport Freeway, Suite 310
Hurst, Texas 76053

NAPSAC, International
(National Association of Par-
ents and Professionals for
Safe Alternatives in Child-
birth)
P.O. Box 267
Marble Hill, Missouri 63764
(Umbrella group for the alter-
native birth movement in the
United States, provides infor-
mation and support)

**National Association for the
Advancement of Leboyer's
Birth Without Violence,
Inc.**
P.O. Box 248455
University of Miami Branch
Coral Gables, Florida 33124

**National Association of Child-
bearing Centers (NACC)**
Box 1, Route 1
Perkiomenville, Pennsylvania
18074
(Information and education
about freestanding birth centers)

National Genetics Foundation
555 West 57th Street
New York, New York 10019
(Information and referral for
genetic counseling)

**National Organization of
Mothers of Twins Clubs,
Inc.**
5402 Amberwood Lane
Rockville, Maryland 20853

**National Women's Health
Network**
224 7th Street, S.E.
Washington, D.C. 20003

Parenthood After Thirty
451 Vermont
Berkeley, California 94707

Parents of Prematures
13613 N.E. 26th Place
Bellevue, Washington 98005

Parents Without Partners, Inc. (PWP)
7910 Woodmont Avenue
Washington, D.C. 20014
(Resource for the single parent)

Physicians for Automotive Safety
P.O. Box 430
Armonk, New York 10504

Physicians for Social Responsibility
639 Massachusetts Ave.
Cambridge, Massachusetts 02139
(Information and activism around issues of the threat of nuclear weapons and wastes)

Planned Parenthood Federation of America
810 Seventh Avenue
New York, New York 10019

Remove Intoxicated Drivers (RID)
24 Elm Street
Schenectady, New York 12301

The Sierra Club
530 Bush Street
San Francisco, California 94108
(Activism and information on environmental issues)

APPENDIX C

Sources for Books and Supplies

Birth and Life Bookstore
P.O. Box 70625
Seattle, Washington 98107
Run by Lynn Moen, the store offers over 400 titles in all aspects of childbirth and child care, books for children, pamphlets, cassettes, and records. A useful catalogue, *Imprints*, which appears several times a year, offers listings and helpful reviews.

ICEA Bookcenter
P.O. Box 20048
Minneapolis, Minnesota 55420

The source for all ICEA publications and others, over 400 titles in all. The catalogue, *Bookmarks*, appears twice a year.

Cascade Birthing Supplies
Center
P.O. Box 1300
Philomath, Oregon 97370

Home birth kits and midwifery supplies.

Childbirth Education Supply
Center
10 Sol Drive
Carmel, New York 10512

Whole Birth Catalogue
20 London Road West
Guelph, Ontario
NIH 285, Canada

Books, supplies, and clothing. Issues a catalogue.

Moonflower Birthing Supply
8593 Highway 172
Ignacio, California 81137

Home birth information and supplies.

Suggested Reading

HISTORY AND CRITIQUE

Arms, Suzanne. *Immaculate Deception: A New Look at Women and Childbirth in America*. Boston: Houghton Mifflin, 1975.

Bursztajn, Harold; Feinbloom, Richard I.; Hamm, Robert M.; and Brodsky, Archie. *Medical Choices, Medical Chances: How Patients, Families and Physicians Can Cope with Uncertainty*. New York: A Merloyd Lawrence Book/Delacorte Press, 1981.

Rothman, Barbara Katz. *In Labor: Women and Power in the Birthplace*. New York: W. W. Norton, 1982.

Wertz, Richard, and Wertz, Dorothy C. *Lying-In: A History of Childbirth in America*. New York: The Free Press, 1977.

MYTHS AND TALES OF BIRTH

Franz, Marie von. *Creation Myths*. Zurich: Spring Publications, 1972.

Meltzer, David, ed. *Birth. An Anthology of Ancient Texts, Songs, Prayers, and Stories*. San Francisco: North Point Press, 1981.

WOMEN'S HEALTH

Boston Women's Health Book Collective. *Our Bodies, Ourselves: A Book by and for Women*. New York: Simon and Schuster, 1984.

OVERVIEWS OF PREGNANCY AND CHILDBIRTH

Brewer, Gail Sforza, and Presser, Janice. *Right from the Start: Meeting the Challenge of Mothering Your Unborn and Newborn Baby.* Emmaus, Pa.: Rodale Press, 1981.

Hotchner, Tracy. *Pregnancy and Childbirth: The Complete Guide for a New Life.* New York: Avon Books, 1979.

Kitzinger, Sheila. *The Complete Book of Pregnancy and Childbirth.* New York: Alfred A. Knopf, 1981.

———. *The Experience of Childbirth* (revised edition). New York: Penguin Books, 1978.

MacFarlane, Aidan. *The Psychology of Childbirth.* Cambridge, Mass.: Harvard University Press (The Developing Child Series), 1977.

McLaughlin, Clara, with Frisby, Donald; McLaughlin, Richard; and Williams, Melvin. *The Black Parents' Guide to Healthy Pregnancy, Birth and Child Care.* New York: Harcourt, Brace, Jovanovich, 1976.

Noble, Elizabeth. *Childbirth with Insight.* Boston: Houghton Mifflin, 1983.

Panuthos, Claudia. *Transformation through Birth. A Woman's Guide.* Massachusetts: Bergin and Garvey, Inc., 1984.

Pritchard, Jack A., and MacDonald, Paul C., *et al. Williams Obstetrics.* New York: Appleton-Century-Crofts, 1985.

Queenan, John T., ed. *A New Life: Pregnancy, Birth and Your Child's First Year.* New York: Van Nostrand Reinhold, 1979.

Shapiro, Howard I. *The Pregnancy Book for Today's Woman.* New York: Harper & Row, 1983.

Soman, Shirley Camper. *Preparing for Your New Baby.* New York: Dell/Delta Books, 1982.

Todd, Linda. *Labor and Birth: A Guide for You.* Minneapolis, Minn.: ICEA, 1981. [Simply written and intended for the pregnant teenager]

Wolfe, Maxine Gold, and Goldsmid, Margot. *Practical Pregnancy. All That's Different in Life Because You're Pregnant.* New York: Warner Books, 1980.

CHOICES AND ALTERNATIVES

Ashford, Janet Isaacs. *The Whole Birth Catalog.* Trumansburg, N.Y.: The Crossing Press, 1983.

Balaskas, Janet, and Balaskas, Arthur. *Active Birth*. New York: Mc-Graw-Hill, 1983.

Baldwin, Rahima. *Special Delivery: The Complete Guide to Informed Birth*. Millbrae, Calif.: Les Femmes, 1979.

Bean, Constance A. *Methods of Childbirth* (new revised edition). New York: Doubleday/Dolphin, 1982.

Berezin, Nancy. *The Gentle Birth Book: A Practical Guide to LeBoyer Family-Centered Delivery*. New York: Pocket Books, 1981.

Bing, Elisabeth. *Six Practical Lessons for an Easier Childbirth*. New York: Bantam Books, 1981. [Lamaze method]

Brackbill, Yvonne; Rice, June; and Young, Diony. *Birthtrap: The Legal Lowdown on High-tech Obstetrics*. St. Louis: C. V. Mosby Co., 1984.

Bradley, Robert A. *Husband-Coached Childbirth* (3rd edition). New York: Harper & Row, 1981.

Brennan, Barbara, and Heilman, Joan Rattner. *The Complete Book of Midwifery*. New York: E. P. Dutton, 1977.

Davis, Elizabeth. *A Guide to Midwifery: Hearts and Hands*. Santa Fe, N.M.: John Muir Publications, 1981 (New York: Bantam Books, 1983).

Dick-Read, Grantly. *Childbirth without Fear: The Principles and Practice of Natural Childbirth* (revised 4th edition). New York: Harper & Row, 1978.

Elkins, Valmai Howe. *The Rights of the Pregnant Parent* (revised). New York: Schocken Books, 1980.

Feldman, Silvia. *Choices in Childbirth*. New York: Grosset and Dunlap, 1979.

Fenlon, Arlene; Dorchak, Lovell; and Oakes, Ellen. *Getting Ready for Childbirth. A Guide for Expectant Parents*. Englewood Cliffs, N.J.: Prentice-Hall, 1979.

Gaskin, Ina May. *Spiritual Midwifery* (revised edition). Summerton, Tenn.: The Book Publishing Company, 1978.

Korte, Diana, and Scaer, Roberta. *A Good Birth, a Safe Birth*. New York: Bantam Books, 1984.

Lamaze, Fernand. *Painless Childbirth*. Chicago: Henry Regnery, 1970.

Leboyer, Frederick. *Birth Without Violence*. New York: Alfred A. Knopf, 1975.

Lesko, Wendy, and Lesko, Matthew. *The Maternity Sourcebook*. New York: Warner Books, 1984.

Long, Raven. *Birth Book*. Palo Alto, Calif.: Genesis Press, 1972.

McKay, Susan. *Assertive Childbirth. The Future Parent's Guide to a Positive Pregnancy*. Englewood Cliffs, N.J.: Prentice-Hall, 1983.

Odent, Michael. *Birth Reborn*. New York: Pantheon Books, 1984.

———. *Entering the World: The De-medicalization of Childbirth*. New York: Marion Boyars, 1984.

Parfitt, Rebecca Rowe. *The Birth Primer. A Source Book of Traditional and Alternative Methods in Labor and Delivery*. Philadelphia, Pa.: Running Press, 1977.

SEX DURING PREGNANCY

Bing, Elisabeth, and Coleman, Libby. *Making Love During Pregnancy*. New York: Bantam Books, 1977.

Kitzinger, Sheila. *Woman's Experience of Sex*. New York: Putnam, 1983.

THE SITE OF BIRTH

Kitzinger, Sheila. *Birth at Home*. New York: Penguin Books, 1981.

Sagov, Stanley E.; Feinbloom, Richard I.; Spindel, Peggy; and Brodsky, Archie. *Home Birth: A Practitioner's Guide to Birth Outside the Hospital*. Rockville, Md.: Aspen Systems Corporation, 1984.

Sumner, Philip E., and Phillips, Celeste R. *Shared Childbirth. A Guide to Family Birth Centers*. New York: New American Library/C. V. Mosby, 1982.

Young, Diony. *Changing Childbirth: Family Birth in the Hospital*. Rochester, N.Y.: Childbirth Graphics, Ltd., 1982.

LIFE BEFORE BIRTH

Annis, Linda Ferrill. *The Child Before Birth*. Ithaca, N.Y.: Cornell University Press, 1978.

Nilsson, Lennart. *A Child Is Born: The Drama of Life Before Birth*. New York: A Merloyd Lawrence Book/Delacorte Press, 1977.

PROTECTING THE UNBORN CHILD

Apgar, Virginia, and Beck, Joan. *Is My Baby All Right? A Guide to Birth Defects*. New York: Trident Press, 1972.

Freeman, Roger K., and Pescar, Susan. *Protecting Your Baby During High Risk Pregnancy*. New York: McGraw-Hill, 1983.

Hales, Dianne, and Creasy, Robert K. *New Hope for Problem Pregnancies. Helping Babies Before They're Born*. New York: Berkeley Books, 1984.

Henig, Robin Marantz. "Saving Babies Before Birth: The New Promise of Fetal Surgery," *New York Times Magazine*, February 28, 1982.

Milunsky, Aubrey. *Know Your Genes*. Boston: Houghton Mifflin, 1977.

Norwood, Christopher. *At Highest Risk: Protecting Children from Environmental Injury*. New York: Penguin Books, 1980.

Smith, David W. *Mothering Your Unborn Child*. Philadelphia, Pa.: W. B. Saunders, 1979.

EXERCISE AND COMFORT

Balaskas, Janet, and Balaskas, Arthur. *New Life. The Book of Exercises for Pregnancy and Childbirth* (revised). London: Sidgwick and Jackson, 1983.

Benson, Herbert. *The Relaxation Response*. New York: William Morrow, 1975.

Jimenez, Sherry Lynn. *The Pregnant Woman's Comfort Guide*. Englewood Cliffs, N.J.: Prentice-Hall, 1983.

Markowitz, Elysa, and Brainen, Howard. *Baby Dance: A Comprehensive Guide to Prenatal and Postpartum Exercise*. Englewood Cliffs, N.J.: Prentice-Hall, 1980.

Medvin, Jeannine O'Brien. *Prenatal Yoga and Natural Birth*. Monroe, Utah: Freestone Innerprizes, 1974.

Noble, Elizabeth. *Essential Exercises for the Childbearing Year* (2nd edition). Boston: Houghton Mifflin, 1982.

Olkin, Sylvia. *Positive Pregnancy Through Yoga*. Englewood Cliffs, N.J.: Prentice-Hall, 1981.

PRENATAL NUTRITION

Brewer, Gail Sforza, and Brewer, Thomas. *The Brewer Medical Diet for Normal and High-Risk Pregnancy*. New York: Simon and Schuster/ Fireside Books, 1983.

Brown, Judith E. *Nutrition for Your Pregnancy. The University of Minnesota Guide*. Minneapolis, Minn.: University of Minnesota Press, 1983.

Cronin, Isaac, and Brewer, Gail Sforza. *Eating for Two. The Complete Pregnancy Nutrition Cookbook*. New York: Bantam Books, 1983.

Klein, Diane, and Badalamenti, Rosalyn T. *Eating Right for Two. The Complete Nutrition Guide and Cookbook for a Healthy Pregnancy*. New York: Ballantine Books, 1983.

Lappé, Frances Moore. *Diet for a Small Planet* (revised and updated). New York: Ballantine Books, 1982.

BABY CARE

Bollinger, Taree, and Cramer, Patricia. *The Baby Gear Guide: How to Make Smart Choices in Essential Baby Equipment*. Reading, Mass.: Addison-Wesley, 1985.

Boston Children's Medical Center and Richard I. Feinbloom, M.D. *Child Health Encyclopedia*. New York: A Merloyd Lawrence Book/ Delacorte Press, 1975.

Jones, Sandy. *Crying Baby, Sleepless Nights (How to Overcome Baby's Sleep Problems and Get Some Sleep Yourself)*. New York: Warner Books, 1983.

Jones, Sandy. *To Love a Baby*. Boston: Houghton Mifflin, 1981.

Kelly, Paul, ed. *First-Year Baby Care. An Illustrated Guide for New Parents*. Deephaven, Minn.: Meadowbrook Press, 1983.

Leach, Penelope. *Babyhood* (2nd edition, revised). New York: Alfred A. Knopf, 1983.

————. *Your Baby and Child from Birth to Age Five*. New York: Alfred A. Knopf, 1981.

Rakowitz, Elly, and Rubin, Gloria. *Living with Your New Baby*. New York: Berkley Books, 1980.

Stoppard, Miriam. *Day-by-Day Baby Care*. New York: Villard Books, 1983.

NURSING

Eiger, Martin, and Olds, Sally Wendkos. *The Complete Book of Breast-feeding*. New York: Workman Publishing, 1972.

Kitzinger, Sheila. *The Experience of Breastfeeding*. New York: Penguin Books, 1980.

La Leche International. *The Womanly Art of Breastfeeding* (3rd edition, revised and enlarged). New York: New American Library, 1981.

Llewellyn-Jones, Derek. *Breast Feeding — How to Succeed. Questions and Answers for Mothers*. London: Faber and Faber, 1983.

Messinger, Maire. *The Breastfeeding Book*. New York: Van Nostrand Reinhold, 1982.

Presser, Janice, and Brewer, Gail Sforza. *Breastfeeding*. New York: Alfred A. Knopf, 1983.

Price, Ann, and Bamford, Nancy. *The Breastfeeding Guide for the Working Woman*. New York: Simon and Schuster/Wallaby, 1983.

Pryor, Karen. *Nursing Your Baby*. New York: Pocket Books, 1973.

Worth, Cecilia. *Breastfeeding Basics*. New York: McGraw-Hill/Sun Words Books, 1983.

THE NEWBORN BABY AND THE FAMILY

Bower, T. G. R. *The Perceptual World of the Child*. Cambridge, Mass.: Harvard University Press (The Developing Child Series), 1977.

Brazelton, T. Berry. *On Becoming a Family: The Growth of Attachment*. New York: Delacorte/Lawrence, 1981.

Galinsky, Ellen. *Between Generations: The Six Stages of Parenthood*. New York: Times Books, 1981.

Kaye, Kenneth. *The Mental and Social Life of Babies: How Parents Create Persons*. Chicago: University of Chicago Press, 1982.

Klaus, Marshall, and Kennell, John H. *Bonding: The Beginnings of Parent-Infant Attachment*. New York: New American Library/C. V. Mosby, 1983.

Tronick, Edward, and Adamson, Lauren. *Babies as People. New Findings on Our Social Beginnings*. New York: Macmillan/Collier Books, 1980.

Weiss, Joan Solomon. *Your Second Child. A Guide for Parents*. New York: Simon and Schuster/Summit, 1981.

BOOKS FOR MOTHERS

Brazelton, T. Berry. *Infants and Mothers: Differences in Development* (revised edition). New York: Delacorte/Lawrence, 1983.

Friedland, Ronnie, and Kort, Carol. *The Mother's Book: Shared Experiences*. Boston: Houghton Mifflin, 1981.

Schaffer, Rudolph. *Mothering*. Cambridge, Mass.: Harvard University Press (The Developing Child Series), 1982.

Stern, Daniel. *The First Relationship*. Cambridge, Mass.: Harvard University Press (The Developing Child Series), 1977.

BOOKS FOR FATHERS

Alliance for Perinatal Research. *The Father Book: Pregnancy and Beyond*. Washington, D.C.: Acropolis Books, Ltd., 1981.

Bittman, Sam, and Zalk, Sue Rosenberg. *Expectant Fathers*. New York: E. P. Dutton, 1979.

Coleman, Arthur, and Coleman, Libby. *Earth Father/Sky Father. The Changing Concept of Fathering*. Englewood Cliffs, N.J.: Prentice-Hall, 1981.

Parke, Ross. *Fathers*. Cambridge, Mass.: Harvard University Press (The Developing Child Series), 1981.

Phillips, Celeste, and Anzalone, Joseph. *Fathering: Participation in Labor and Delivery*. St. Louis, Mo.: C. V. Mosby, 1978.

CESAREAN BIRTH

Cohen, Nancy Wainer, and Estner, Lois J. *Silent Knife: Cesarean Prevention and Vaginal Birth After Cesarean (VBAC)*. South Hadley, Mass.: J. F. Bergin, 1983.

Hausknecht, Richard, and Heilman, Joan Rattner. *Having a Cesarean Baby* (revised edition). New York: E. P. Dutton, 1982.

Meyer, Linda D. *The Caesarean (R)evolution: A Handbook for Parents and Professionals* (revised edition). Edmonds, Wash.: Chas. Franklin Press, 1981.

Norwood, Christopher. *How to Avoid a Cesarean Section*. New York: Simon and Schuster, 1984.

Wilson, Christine Coleman, and Hovey, Wendy Roe. *Cesarean Childbirth: A Handbook for Parents*. New York: New American Library/ Signet, 1981.

PREMATURE BABIES

Avery, Mary Ellen, and Litwack, Georgia. *Born Early. The Story of a Premature Baby*. Boston: Little, Brown, 1983.

Nance, Sherri. *Premature Babies. A Handbook for Parents*. New York: Arbor House, 1982.

Pfister, Fred, and Grieseme, B. *The Littlest Baby: A Handbook for Parents of Premature Children*. Englewood Cliffs, N.J.: Prentice-Hall, 1983.

PREGNANCY LOSS

Berezin, Nancy. *After a Loss in Pregnancy*. New York: Simon and Schuster/Fireside, 1982.

Borg, Susan, and Lasker, Judith. *When Pregnancy Fails: Families Coping with Miscarriage, Stillbirth, and Infant Death*. Boston: Beacon Press, 1981.

Friedman, Rochelle, and Gradstein, Bonnie. *Surviving Pregnancy Loss*. Boston: Little, Brown, 1982.

Kubler-Ross, Elisabeth. *On Death and Dying*. New York: Macmillan, 1970.

Peppers, Larry, and Knapp, Ronald. *Motherhood and Mourning: Perinatal Death*. New York: Praeger, 1980.

LATE PARENTHOOD

Brewer, Gail Sforza. *The Pregnancy-After-30 Workbook*. Emmaus, Pa.: Rodale Press, 1978.

Daniels, Pamela, and Weingarten, Kathy. *Sooner or Later: The Timing of Parenthood in Adult Lives*. New York: W. W. Norton, 1982.

Price, Jane. *You're Not Too Old to Have a Baby*. New York: Penguin Books, 1978.

Rubin, Sylvia P. *It's Not Too Late for a Baby: For Women and Men Over 35*. Englewood Cliffs, N.J.: Prentice-Hall, 1980.

Index

Abdomen:
exercise for, 91–94
muscles in, 91
stretch marks on, 64–65
Abdominal pain, 38, 73–74
ABO disease, 58
Abortion:
spontaneous (see Miscarriage)
of twin, 150
Accutane, 156
Acetaminophen, 154, 158, 203, 247,
309
Acetylcholinesterase, 61
Acidosis, 195–196
Actifed, 155
Acquired Immune Deficiency Syn-
drome (AIDS), 159
Acupuncture, 210
Aerobic exercise, 99
AFP. See Alpha fetoprotein
Afterbirth. See Placenta
After-pains, 198, 199
Age:
gestational, 44, 48–50, 130, 147
maternal, 126–127, 128, 131, 304–
305
AIDS, 159
Alcohol, 38, 171–173
Allopurinol, 156
Alpha antitrypsin, 121
Alpha fetoprotein (AFP), 59–62,
122, 127, 130, 334

Alphaprodine, 204
Alternative birthing centers (ABCs),
20, 25, 34
AMEND, 345
American Academy of Family Phys-
icians, 35, 345
American Academy of Husband-
Coached Childbirth (AAHCC),
345
American Academy of Pediatrics,
345
American Board of Family Practice,
34
American College of Nurse Mid-
wives (ACNM), 34, 345
American College of Obstetrics and
Gynecology (ACOG), 34, 345
American Foundation for Maternal
and Child Health, 346
American Institute of Ultrasound in
Medicine, 145
American Society for Psychopro-
phylaxis in Obstetrics (ASPO/
LAMAZE), 346
Amikacin, 154
Amni-Hook, 5
Aminophylline, 155
Amniocentesis, 57, 126–127, 130–
132
Amniotic sac, 184
Amphotericin B, 154
Ampicillin, 154

359